BLACK&DECKER®

The Complete Guide to

BATHROOMS

Third Edition

Remodeling Projects on a Budget • Vanities & Cabinets
Plumbing & Fixtures • Showers, Sinks & Tubs

Creative Publishing international

MINNEAPOLIS, MINNESOTA
www.creativepub.com

Creative Publishing international

400 First Avenue North, Suite 300
Minneapolis, Minnesota 55401
1-800-328-0590
www.creativepub.com

Printed in China

10 9 8 7 6 5 4 3 2 1

Library of Congress Cataloging-in-Publication Data

The complete guide to bathrooms. -- 3rd ed.
p. cm.
At head of title: Branded by Black & Decker.
"Remodeling projects on a budget; vanities & cabinets; plumbing & fixtures; showers, sinks & tubs."
Summary: "Step-by-step photos and live DVD action demonstrate inexpensive projects that make a bathroom more pleasant and efficient"--Provided by publisher.
ISBN-13: 978-1-58923-562-5 (soft cover)
ISBN-10: 1-58923-562-2 (soft cover)
1. Bathrooms--Remodeling--Amateurs' manuals. I. Black & Decker Corporation (Towson, Md.) II. Title.

TH4816.3.B37C66 2010
643'.52--dc22

2010020979

President/CEO: Ken Fund

Home Improvement Group

Publisher: Bryan Trandem
Managing Editor: Tracy Stanley
Senior Editor: Mark Johanson

Creative Director: Michele Lanci-Altomare
Art Direction/Design: Jon Simpson, Brad Springer, James Kegley

Lead Photographer: Joel Schnell
Set Builder: James Parmeter
Production Managers: Laura Hokkanen, Linda Halls

Page Layout Artist: Parlato Design Studio
Edition Editor: Chris Peterson
Copy Editor: Karen Ruth
Shop Help: Charles Boldt
Proofreader: Drew Siqveland

The Complete Guide to Bathrooms
Created by: The Editors of Creative Publishing international, Inc., in cooperation with Black & Decker.

NOTICE TO READERS

For safety, use caution, care, and good judgment when following the procedures described in this book. The publisher and Black & Decker cannot assume responsibility for any damage to property or injury to persons as a result of misuse of the information provided.

The techniques shown in this book are general techniques for various applications. In some instances, additional techniques not shown in this book may be required. Always follow manufacturers' instructions included with products, since deviating from the directions may void warranties. The projects in this book vary widely as to skill levels required: some may not be appropriate for all do-it-yourselfers, and some may require professional help.

Consult your local building department for information on building permits, codes, and other laws as they apply to your project.

Contents

The Complete Guide to Bathrooms

Contents (Cont.)

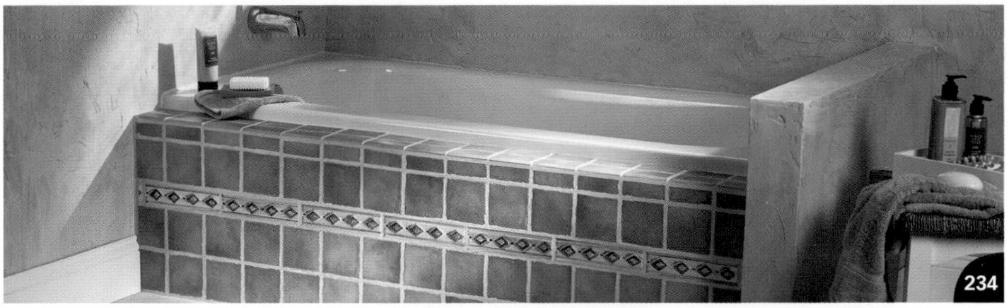
234

231

222

241

270

274

276

Introduction

A great bathroom means different things to different people. Some may need a bathroom that's designed to accommodate overlapping schedules by including double sinks, a separate shower enclosure, or even a partitioned privacy room for the toilet. Another homeowner might have always dreamed about enjoying a regular, rejuvenating soak, in which case her ideal bathroom might focus on a jetted tub or a deep soaking tub.

Creating a great bathroom (or bathrooms) in your home is important. Few rooms in the home affect our daily routine, relaxation, and health as much as the bathroom. It is the room where the essential functions of living intersect with our overwhelming need for comfort. The space must meet high standards of sanitation and moisture-resistance, provide adequate privacy, and maintain (or at least work with) the design style throughout the rest of the house. To ensure that your bathroom remodeling project results in a room that does all this and more, you need some guidance and some clear instructions.

The Complete Guide to Bathrooms is a comprehensive guide to remodeling bathrooms to precisely suit your individual needs and tastes. Including clear step-by-step instructions, full-color photos and illustrations, and the latest information about bathroom technology and style, this revised and updated edition provides all the information you need to create a bathroom that is perfect for you, your family, and your guests.

The book will guide you through the process of bringing your ideal bathroom to life, whether you're remodeling an existing space, building new, or adding on. We start with the Planning & Designing section, where you'll learn how to work out all the details that will go into your new bathroom, from putting your design on paper, to choosing and pricing the different materials that will define the space, to handling all the administrative details, such as working with contractors and building inspectors. We've also included a gallery of bathrooms, which provides a treasure trove of ideas for anyone looking to update or redesign a bathroom.

Of course, you can't talk about remodeling a bathroom without discussing how to strip out what's already there. That's why we've included the Removal & Demolition section, with helpful tips and techniques to make easy work of the dirtiest part of this process.

The Bathroom Projects section includes all the how-to information you'll need to implement your project designs in an actual bathroom space. You'll find step-by-step instructions on adding tubs and showers, vanities and faucets, and more. We've also included important information about installing lighting and ventilation, as well as do-it-yourself instructions for adding luxury touches like ceramic or stone tile.

Even if you choose to hire professionals to do the actual work, *The Complete Guide to Bathrooms* remains an incredibly useful tool. This book will give you an increased understanding of how to remodel a bathroom, work with contractors, and make the best use of your money.

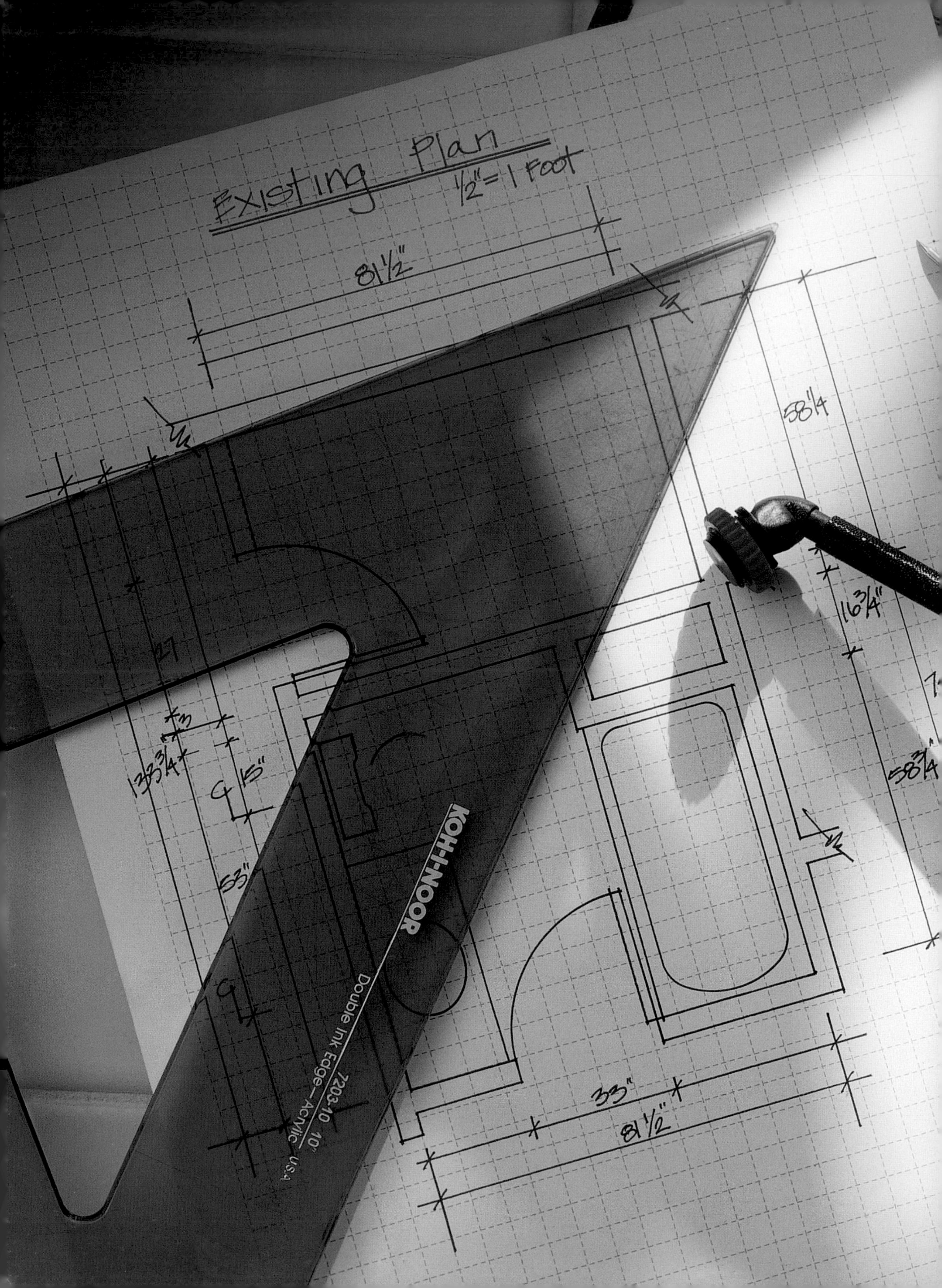
Existing Plan
1/2" = 1 Foot
81 1/2"
33"
81 1/2"
KOH-I-NOOR
Double Ink Edge—Acrylic
7203-10 10"
U.S.A.

PLANNING & DESIGNING YOUR BATHROOM

Gallery of Bathrooms

The bathroom fulfills many functions. First and foremost, it addresses the specific wishes of the homeowner—whether it's a standalone shower enclosure that's easier to walk into than a tub, or small luxuries like a towel warmer or an in-floor warming system. But the bathroom must be comfortable to use, with grab bars where necessary, vanities and cabinets that provide sensibly placed storage space, and surfaces that feel good to the touch.

The specific features of a well-designed bathroom also depend on what type of bathroom it is. A half bath for guests, or a powder room, may require only a quiet, highly efficient toilet and a focal-point vessel sink. The design of a family bath is more involved, with upgraded ventilation and multi-user features such as double sinks and a segregated toilet area. A master bathroom suite may include luxury touches such as sunken tub or a shower with multiple heads and a sound system.

Regardless of the type of bathroom you're looking to create, you'll find a wealth of design options in the following gallery pages. Even if the specific features shown in these pages aren't exactly what you want for your own project, they will inspire and help you to discover your perfect bathroom.

The polished stone tub deck and flooring lends a feeling of luxury to this bathroom. The hard surfaces have the added benefit of water and mold resistance. The wood floor adds warmth, but is kept away from the tub and toilet areas. The large window bathes the room with natural light.

Shelving can provide useful and attractive storage space in a bathroom. Here, the rolled towels stored in open shelves contrast with the angular, modern feel of this bathroom, adding a bit of softness. The natural color scheme provides a calm environment.

The poured concrete bathtub, with its low profile, simple lines, and soothing colors, sets the mood for a relaxing soak with a good novel. The ledge serves as a handy bookshelf in this dream bathroom and is just right for those who can't put a book down.

A stylish glass shower enclosure maintains an open, airy feel in this small bathroom. Multiple showerheads and in-wall shelves make for a luxurious shower experience.

An attic master suite blurs the lines between bathroom and bedroom. Although an unorthodox approach, the room design creates the perception of abundant and opulent space.

A wall-mounted countertop of glass and wood is right at home in this contemporary bathroom. The green glass adds brilliance to the otherwise neutral room, while the wood contributes warmth and texture.

The widespread bathroom faucet is mounted to the countertop and is paired with a stainless steel under-mount sink, adding to the high-tech look of the room. A striking backdrop of metal wall tiles reflects light and creates a bright atmosphere.

This wall-hung sink with its traditional two-handled faucet reflects the deco style of the floor tiles. The glass-and-steel base is mostly decorative.

This simple, square, wall-mounted sink blends well with the bright colors of the walls and distinctively mid-century-modern décor. The rich, dark wood floor warms up the room, while the flokati rug adds contrast and texture.

A towel warmer drawer built into a linen cabinet is a discreet yet extravagant addition to the bathroom.

Storage space is at a premium in bathrooms. Employing some kitchen-style cabinet organizing tricks helps boost efficiency.

Multiple showerheads are given a new twist with water tile body sprays. The spray face can be adjusted and the nozzles offer hydrotherapeutic benefits.

A lovely neutral color scheme gives this room a clean and calming appearance. A dark floor and accents ensure that the room isn't boring.

This modest guest bathroom is a perfect example of bringing a small space to life with bold colors and whimsical touches, such as the photos of water lilies used here.

Shutters, soft earth tones, and mood lighting give this bathroom a sense of dreamy seclusion, and create a comfortable private retreat.

Sleek his-and-her wall-mounted sinks are complemented by a low shelf underneath that provides a wealth of useful storage.

An oversized vanity mirror can make a small space seem much larger and lighter, as it does in this powder room.

A vibrant, bright orange brings this bathroom to life, serving as a wonderful counterpoint to the chunky, dark wall-mounted lavatory.

The large corner whirlpool tub adds big luxury to this sedate bathroom. Easily accommodating two bathers, the tub offers a spa indulgence at home.

Artfully arranged towel hooks and a whimsical toilet paper dispenser add touches of fun to an otherwise lovely but low-key bathroom.

Marble walls and floors, a high-tech toilet, and an oversized whirlpool tub with a multitude of adjustable jets all spell opulence in this European-style bathroom.

Bathroom Elements

Bathroom fixtures and materials have changed dramatically in recent years. Tubs can rival healthclub spas, toilets and showerheads are more water efficient, and sinks run the gamut from stainless steel to wood basins.

Before you jump into a bathroom remodeling project, decide what's most important to you. Budget determines how luxurious you can get, but maybe it's worthwhile to splurge on that one item that would make you feel most pampered.

This chapter covers the most common bathroom fixtures and materials, but several other good resources are also available, such as magazines and websites.

Home centers and kitchen and bath showrooms have a variety of bathroom setups you can browse through to see how the products look and feel. It's always a good idea to see a product in person before you buy.

In this chapter:

- Bathtubs & Jetted Tubs
- Showers
- Sinks
- Toilets, Bidets & Urinals
- Cabinets & Vanity Cabinets
- Lighting
- Heating & Ventilation
- Walls & Ceilings
- Flooring

Bathtubs & Jetted Tubs

Although you can find bathtubs in a wide variety of sizes and shapes, your existing bathroom floorplan usually dictates exactly what size you should buy. But if you don't mind moving some plumbing, or you are building an all-new bathroom, your options expand dramatically.

Tubs are categorized first by the method used to install them. The three basic installation styles are attached apron, deck-mounted, and freestanding.

Attached-apron tubs are the most common. They are often enclosed on three sides by alcove walls. One-piece tub-and-shower combination fixtures are also available to fit standard-size alcoves. Custom sizes can be made for odd-size alcoves.

Deck-mounted tubs and whirlpools, also called drop-in tubs, generally rest directly on the subfloor or in a thinset mortar base. They are surrounded by custom-built decks or platforms. Typically, these tubs have a larger capacity than attached-apron tubs. The cost of making the deck can cause tubs to be more expensive than other types, but the design possibilities are nearly limitless.

Freestanding tubs are available in modern styles and in the traditional claw-foot design. They're usually made of enameled cast iron, which retains heat well and is virtually indestructible. Although they are heavy and difficult to move, they are simple to install. The plumbing for making the supply and drain hookups is normally exposed and thus should have an attractive finish.

Rectangular tubs are the most common shape and are often combined with showers. They come in a wide range of widths, lengths, depths, and colors in addition to the traditional 30" × 60" × 14" white version.

Square and triangular tubs are very uncommon. They fit into corners to help visually open up small bathrooms, and they often are combined with a shower.

Oval, round, and hourglass shapes make a unique design statement but offer little by way of practical advantage.

This jetted tub with widespread faucet mounted on the deck lets bathers lean back and relax in a standard-size tub alcove.

Freestanding tubs are available in the traditional claw-foot design as well as up-to-date models.

A deck-mounted tub is often the focal point of the bathroom, providing both visual appeal and a luxurious bathing experience.

Compact tubs are available for small bathrooms. Often smaller tubs are deeper than standard tubs, which can allow for more comfortable bathing.

A claw-foot tub is an iconic bathroom fixture. The original models made of cast iron with an enameled porcelain finish can be found through architectural salvage companies, although the supply is dwindling and the prices are climbing. Reproductions of this style are made with lighter-weight composites and polymers.

(continued)

Tub Materials

Tubs are manufactured from many different materials, each with its own advantages and disadvantages.

Fiberglass is an inexpensive, lightweight material that can be finished in a variety of colors. It is easily molded, so fiberglass tubs can have seats, grab bars, soap dishes, and shampoo shelves molded into the sides. Though fiberglass has many benefits, its surface can scratch easily and its color will fade.

Acrylic, like fiberglass, can be molded into just about any size and shape required. Unlike fiberglass, however, the color runs through the entire substance rather than just on the surface coat, making it less likely to show scratches or to fade.

Enameled steel tubs are pressed from sheets of steel and coated with a baked-on enamel similar to that of cast-iron tubs. The enamel layer is usually thin, though, and is susceptible to chipping. In addition, enameled steel doesn't retain heat and tends to be noisy. When buying an enameled steel tub, check for a spray-on undercoating that helps muffle sound and retain heat.

Cast iron is the most durable material available for tubs. Iron is cast into a tub shape, then coated with a baked-on enamel that is relatively thick (1/16"), resulting in a richly colored finish. The enamel is strong, durable, and resistant to chips, scratches, and stains.

The cast iron itself is almost impervious to dents and cracks. Cast iron is just about indestructible, but it's also heavy—a standard tub weighs between 300 and 400 pounds. In some cases, the floor framing must be reinforced to support the additional weight. Cast iron is used most commonly for claw-foot and other stand-alone bathtubs. A rapidly increasing number of tubs, both freestanding and alcove type, are now being made from composite materials that are solid like cast iron but much lighter in weight.

The enamel finish of old, scratched, or marred cast-iron tubs can be reglazed, but the finish doesn't last as long as the original and is more susceptible to chips and scratches. Reglazing a cast-iron tub is not a do-it-yourself project, so hire a contractor who is familiar with the process, look for a two-year guarantee, and ask to see examples of previous work.

Specialty Tubs

Soaking tubs are deeper with higher sides than other styles. Traditional Japanese versions feature sides as high as 4 feet, but contemporary American soaking tubs usually have walls from 20 to 36 inches high. Traditional soaking tubs are tall enough that bathers may sit, rather than recline, although the shallowest modern models are soaking tubs only to the extent that they will allow an adult to be covered completely with water when reclined. The experience is luxurious and meditative.

Large deck-mounted tubs offer options when it comes to locating the spout and valve handles. In many cases this means you can position the spout near the tub center so you can lean back against either end of the tub without hitting any faucet parts.

Jetted tubs circulate water that's mixed with air through jets mounted in the body of the tub. The pumps move as much as 50 gallons of water per minute to create a massaging effect that relieves stress and muscle pain. Better quality jets can be adjusted to alter both the stream's direction and the proportion of air and water (more air means a more vigorous massage).

Jetted tubs are almost always made of acrylic, and sizes and shapes vary tremendously. Prices also vary—whirlpools can range from $700 to $10,000 and up before installation. Price is determined by the number of jets (from four to ten or more), size of the water pump, and options such as an in-line heater.

You can find a variety of accessories for jetted tubs. A multispeed motor allows you to choose various settings from a gentle, relaxing soak to a vigorous massage. An in-line heater maintains the water temperature. Grab bars, mood lights, pillows, timers, mirrors, and touch-pad controls are available for convenience and comfort.

Before you invest in a jetted tub, review the maintenance requirements. Some demand extensive upkeep of pumps, timers, and controls, and many roomy models require an extra large water heater.

A jetted tub can be installed by a skilled homeowner familiar with the basic techniques of carpentry, plumbing, and tile setting. Some are small enough to fit in the alcove used for standard bathtubs, though most models require the construction of a surrounding deck or platform. See pages 120 to 127 for installing an air-jet tub.

A tub platform can be tucked into a corner or even an alcove. If you add tile or another moisture-resistant wallcovering on the corner walls, you may consider adding a hand-held shower near the corner. Hand-held showers are not a good idea for island tubs.

An oversized tub can be installed in a bathroom with limited wallspace if you have sufficient floor area to accommodate an extra-wide tub.

Showers

Showers can stand alone or be combined with tubs, and they come in a number of styles and materials.

A tub/shower combination is more common than a standalone shower stall. It uses space efficiently, is cheap to install, and can easily be added to an alcove tub. One-piece molded fiberglass and acrylic tub-and-shower units are available, but they are often too large to fit through doors and are better suited for new construction.

Shower stalls are ideal for small bathrooms or as a supplement in master or luxury bathrooms. They can be purchased prefabricated or they can be custom-built.

One-piece alcove showers are a common option for do-it-yourself installation. The seamless stall is molded from a single piece of fiberglass or acrylic, making it easy to clean and maintain. A wide range of shower stall sizes and styles are available. Some feature seats, steam bath, or other added-value functions.

Neo-angle showers are designed to fit into a corner. They are usually made of acrylic or fiberglass, and have doors that open at an angle.

Shower surround panels are used to construct simple, inexpensive shower stalls. They are built above a preformed shower base made of PVC plastic, fiberglass, acrylic, solid-surface material, quartz, or natural stone. Three individual panels are bonded to the walls of the framed alcove, and the seams are sealed.

Freestanding showers are complete units that are not attached to walls. They range from inexpensive sheet metal or fiberglass units to elaborate glass block showers. The vast majority of showers, however, fit into corners or against one wall.

Custom shower stalls can be designed to fit into odd spaces (pages 86 to 91). The walls can be finished with ceramic tile, glass block, or a solid-surface material. Specialized options, such as seats, steam bath units, and soap dishes, can be incorporated into the design.

Barrier-free showers are designed for physically challenged users. The shower entrance has a low base curb or no curb at all, providing easy access to the shower. One-piece molded units are available, or

One-piece shower stalls are quick and easy to install, but the units are large and cumbersome—make sure you can get it through your house and into your bathroom before deciding to buy one.

Curved and neo-angle showers tuck efficiently into a corner and occupy only minimal floorspace. They are usually sold in a flat pack.

barrier-free showers can be custom-built. Most have built-in shower seats and grab bars. See pages 44 to 49 for more information on barrier-free showers.

Shower doors and curtains are usually purchased separately from the shower itself. Options range from simple plastic curtains costing a few dollars to custom-made tempered glass doors.

Multiple showerheads, shower towers, and steam showers can create a more luxurious shower. Steam showers require extra plumbing, wiring, and a shower stall with doors that seal tightly.

Shower Lights ▸

An overhead light ensures safety in the shower. Make sure that any light installed in a shower area is moisture-resistant. Some lights include a heating element.

A cast iron shower receptor is the ultimate in leak-free durability when building a custom shower stall.

A custom tile shower surround is a perfect choice for today's modern, multiport shower systems.

Glass block shower walls (many are actually clear acrylic) allow natural light into the showering area. They also have a distinctive visual appeal all their own.

Sinks

The variety of sinks available today practically guarantees that you can find a lavatory sink to match your space, budget, and taste. The most significant difference between the major sink types is the manner in which they are installed: wall mounted, pedestal or console, and countertop.

Wall-mounted sinks hang directly from the wall, taking up little space and offering easy access to plumbing hookups. Basic wall-mounted sinks are good options for utility bathrooms or half baths, where exposed plumbing and lack of storage space are not serious drawbacks. Designer wall-mounted styles feature attached bodies or aprons that hide plumbing and can even provide an extremely attractive focal point for a small bathroom.

Pedestal sinks and **console sinks** are wall-mounted styles that rest on a pedestal or legs that may or may not provide actual support to the sink bowl. A decorative pedestal may conceal plumbing and can be a smart choice for a small guest bathroom or powder room where floorspace is particularly scarce. Console sinks have legs supporting the front two corners and often feature an apron to mask plumbing connections. The advantage of a console sink over a pedestal model is that small baskets or a modest, simple shelving unit can be placed underneath for additional storage.

Self-rimming sinks drop into a cutout in the countertop, with its rim overlapping the cutout's edges.

Integral sinks, usually made of solid-surface material or cultured marble, are molded into countertops (page 140) and are easy to install and maintain.

Undermounted sinks are attached with clips beneath a cutout in a solid-surface, stone, or concrete countertop.

Vessel sinks sit on top of a countertop, with only a small cutout for the drain.

A pedestal sink has visual appeal and an efficient footprint, but lacks any storage function.

Wall-mounted sinks are sometimes installed in powder rooms and half-baths, where floor space is at a premium. A wall-mounted faucet creates dramatic design options.

Sinks can be made of a number of materials. **Cultured marble** is an inexpensive material often used to create integral sink-and-countertop combinations to fit standard vanity sizes. **Porcelain** (vitreous china) may be used for self-rimming sinks. It has a durable glossy surface that is nonporous and easy to clean. Porcelain sinks are readily available in white and almond, and you can special order other colors. For a truly unique addition to your bathroom decor, consider a hand-painted porcelain sink in a floral or other one-of-a-kind design.

Solid-surface material is long lasting and easy to clean; scratches can be buffed or sanded out. It is one of the more expensive choices for bathroom sinks, but its durability and ease of care help justify the price. Solid-surface sinks are available in self-rimming, undermounted, and integral models, with a variety of colors and patterns to choose from.

Stainless steel brings a high-tech look and durability to bathroom sinks. It is available in either a satin or mirror finish. Price varies according to thickness, or gauge—the lower the gauge number, the thicker the steel. Look for 18-gauge material with a noise-reducing undercoating. Because they are lightweight, stainless steel sinks are often used for undermounting.

Enameled cast iron is an extremely durable material. Made of thick, heavy iron with an enamel coating, these sinks are available in only a few shapes and sizes, and they are rather expensive. A low-cost alternative is enameled steel, but it is lightweight and not very durable—the enamel tends to chip easily.

Tempered glass is used to create stylish vessel sinks for bathrooms. Undermounted styles can be lit from underneath to create a mood-setting glow.

Other materials such as concrete, copper, carved stone, and wood can be used to create more stylized bathrooms. Before you select a sink made of an unusual material, consider the shipping time, installation procedures, maintenance, and cost.

Self-rimming sinks (also called drop-ins) fit into a cutout in a countertop and usually are secured with mounting clips from below.

Undermount sinks have a very contemporary appearance and offer some clean-up advantages, but they can only be installed in countertops that have a contiguous waterproof composition (such as solid surface or poured concrete).

Vessel sinks have a high impact visually, but because they are more prone to leaking and have greater exposure they aren't the best choice for a family bath.

Toilets, Bidets & Urinals

Toilets, bidets, and urinals don't usually boast fine design or a fancy finish, but these indispensable fixtures can have a significant impact on a bathroom's appearance if you let them. Or, they can recede into the background and let other less utilitarian features shine.

The bidet is a popular bathroom furnishing in much of Europe, but it just has never developed a significant following in the U.S., Mexico, or Canada. This may change yet, as those who have included a bidet in their bathroom design typically love them and would not consider ever going back to a single-purpose water closet. Urinals have even less presence in the residential area. In fact, you can pretty well bet that any home plumber you ask about urinals will confess to never having installed one. And yet, with water restrictions becoming more of an issue every year, these water-saving fixtures are showing up with some frequency on green project lists (flushing a urinal uses a small fraction of the amount of water consumed by the flush of a toilet).

So for most of us, the discussion of toilets, bidets, and urinals becomes mostly a look at toilets. Toilet flush technology has changed dramatically over the last couple of decades. Today, you can choose from a host of high-efficiency toilets with small, water-saving traps and optional flushing assistance mechanisms. You'll also find a vast range of designs and styles to choose from, including standard round or elongated toilets but venturing out to wall-mounted models, oversize toilets, or toilets made from materials other than standard enameled porcelain, such as stainless steel.

The toilet can be hidden in an alcove and kept as simple as can be, or it can exhibit a bit of design flourish. If you really want your toilet to make a design statement, combine it with a matching bidet for the ultimate in European-style luxury.

Fixture Types

Two-piece toilets have a separate tank and bowl, and they account for the vast majority of toilets in homes today. Their main advantage is low cost. They come with an elongated bowl (left) or a round bowl (right).

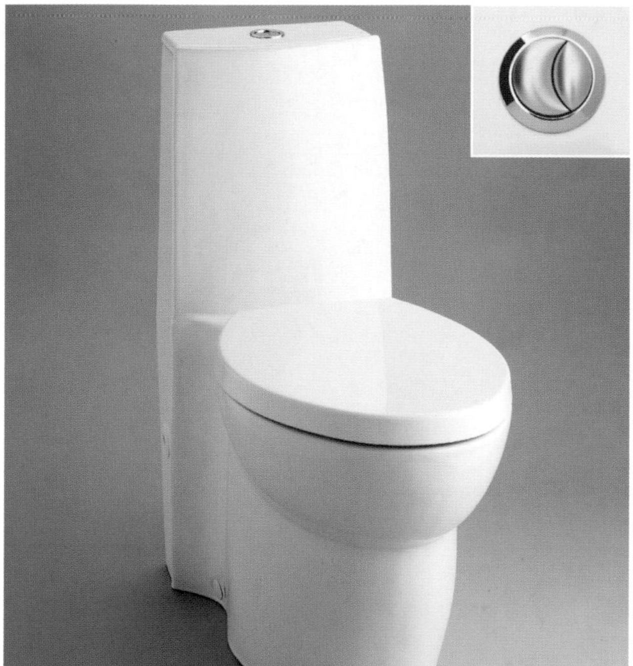

Flushing mechanisms are changing rapidly to keep pace with the demand for greater water economy. One new technology is the dual-flush design, which has a light flush option for liquid waste only that can save 20% on water usage over standard 1.6 gallon models.

Bidets are essentially wash basins with a very specific function.

Cabinets & Vanity Cabinets

The typical bathroom lacks storage space. In fact, creating better storage is one of the most common reasons people remodel their bathrooms. As you design your new bathroom, keep in mind three basic types of storage: cabinetry, open shelving, and linen closets.

Wall cabinets, because they are shallow, are versatile storage units for small spaces like bathrooms. They can be installed on any available wall space—the most popular spot is over the toilet. Some are freestanding units with legs that straddle the toilet tank. Wall cabinets can even be mounted low and topped with a counter. Or, they can be installed in banks.

Vanity cabinets hide plumbing, provide storage, and support the countertop and sink. A vanity is often a bathroom's visual focal point and can set the decorative tone for the whole room.

Cabinetry can be a dominating design element, as in the large, luxurious bathroom above. For floor-to-ceiling banks of cabinets you may use kitchen cabinetry, but choose a base cabinet that's specifically designed for bathrooms if you are including a sink or vanity. Vanity cabinets are 4" shorter than kitchen sink base cabinets.

Medicine cabinets offer quick access to toiletries and keep storage items beyond the reach of young children. Most are designed with a mirror on the door or doors and are installed above a sink. They can be either surface-mounted or recessed into walls between studs to exploit otherwise unused space (page 266). Many incorporate lighting.

Linen cabinets are tall and narrow, taking advantage of floor-to-ceiling space. They can add significant towel and bedding storage without taking much floor space.

Storage is one good reason to choose a vanity cabinet over other lavatory sink options, such as pedestal sinks or wall-hung sinks. Trends and styles change in relatively rapid fashion when it comes to cabinetry. Current styles favor cabinets that look like movable furnishings (see the bun feet on the vanity cabinet above) even though they are secured and plumbed the same way as traditional base cabinets with kickspaces.

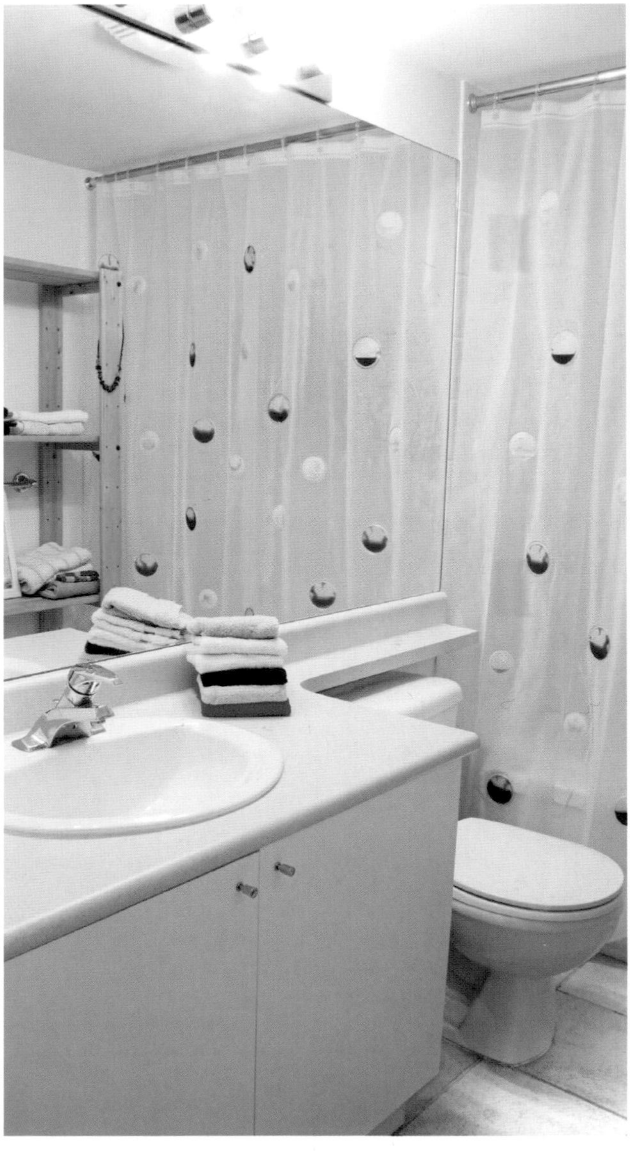

Cabinet countertops can be customized to add useful horizontal surfaces in otherwise unusable space. This banjo-style, cleat-supported countertop is extended to create a shelf directly above the toilet tank lid. Make sure to leave enough space to get the lid on and off easily.

(continued)

Whatever type of cabinet you're considering, you'll have the choice of stock or custom-made designs:

Stock cabinets are mass-produced in standard sizes and warehoused for quick delivery. They are less expensive than custom-made cabinets of comparable wood species, but a wide range of prices can be had within both categories.

Custom cabinets are built to order by a cabinetmaker or cabinet shop, so you get exactly the combination of size, style, material, and finish that you want. Start shopping for custom cabinets early and plan on at least six to eight weeks and probably longer from design to delivery.

Other storage options for bathrooms include shelves and closets:

Shelves are a useful addition to bathrooms that don't have room for elaborate cabinetry. They can be recessed or surface-mounted and are often combined with baskets and storage bins.

Linen closets are recessed in the wall and extend from floor to ceiling. Adding or relocating a closet requires significant structural modifications to your walls.

A medicine cabinet has mirrored doors that open to reveal shallow shelving. Often, they have an integral light above or to the sides of the mirror. Despite the name, avoid storing medicine in a medicine cabinet; instead, look for a locking or hard-to-reach cabinet with a cool, dry interior.

Slide-out storage racks are especially useful in base cabinets. Functioning basically as drawers, slide-out racks can be included at the time of purchase or added later.

A linen cabinet is a freestanding furnishing, but it can take on a built-in appearance if you integrate it with other cabinets and wall trim. Linen cabinets and linen closets can be made more efficient by customizing with features such as door-back shelves and pull-out laundry bins.

A full-length single door cabinet makes efficient use of space and can be matched stylistically to your medicine cabinet for extra impact.

Lighting

Lighting can set the mood of any room. Dim lights and lit candles are perfect for a leisurely soak in the tub. When it comes to shaving or applying makeup, though, bright lights are best.

As with the rest of the house, the bathroom is best served by a combination of general, task, and accent lighting, to ensure personal safety, provide ambience, and permit various uses of the space.

General lighting usually involves an overhead fixture or fixtures that illuminate the whole room. Natural lighting is considered part of your general lighting.

Task lighting provides directed light for specific activities, such as applying makeup or shaving.

Accent lighting can be used to highlight decorative points of interest, such as architectural details or artwork.

Recessed light fixtures provide nondirectional lighting and have a fairly neutral design impact.

A combination of general lighting, task lighting, and natural lighting ensures that all lighting needs are met.

Surface-mounted fixtures are easy to install and available in a variety of styles. Just be sure that all fixtures you choose are moisture-proof and meant for use in a bathroom environment.

Recessed ceiling fixtures are set into canisters and have trim kits that are mounted flush with the surface of the ceiling and some include adjustable heads that allow you to direct the light one way or another. This improves headroom in a small bath.

Wall-mount fixtures are common in bathrooms, and provide ideal lighting for personal grooming, especially when placed on both sides of a mirror, as well as above.

Ceiling mount fixtures are excellent overall light sources in the small spaces of most bathrooms.

Heating & Ventilation

Consider room size, the number of windows, and the type of heat in the rest of the house when making decisions about your bathroom heating system. Consult a professional before making final decisions. If your primary heat system is inadequate, you have three basic choices for auxiliary heat in bathrooms:

Electric heaters are mounted either by themselves or as part of light/vent/heating units.

Heat lamps use infrared lightbulbs to provide radiant heat.

Radiant floor-heating systems are installed beneath the flooring and circulate either hot water or electricity.

Good ventilation protects surfaces from moisture damage, deters mold and mildew, and keeps air fresh. Vents with electric fans (pages 200 to 203) are required by code in any bathroom without windows. The vent must exhaust moist air directly out doors, not into attics or wall cavities.

Purchase a vent fan that's rated at least 5 cfm higher than the square footage of your bathroom. Local building codes may have specific requirements, so check with your building inspector or HVAC contractor before selecting a ventilation unit.

DIY radiant heat floor systems are electric mats installed beneath floor coverings to warm your feet and heat your room.

Vent and light combinations serve the dual purpose of lighting the room and reducing moisture and odors. Some contain an infrared heating element for a third function (inset).

Walls & Ceilings

If you add, move, replace, or resurface walls in your bathroom, use the best materials for the job. Options include:

Drywall is adequate for most bathrooms, except for the area around tubs and showers.

Greenboard is a drywall with waterproof facing. It has fallen out of usage in recent years.

Cementboard is used primarily on an underlayment for ceramic tile.

Glass block is a decorative building block that has great visual appeal, but can't bear loads.

You'll want the wall and ceiling finishes to be easy to maintain. Wall finishes for tub and shower surrounds, and behind sinks and toilets should be waterproof.

Glass block allows light to penetrate the wall while serving as a partition.

Natural stone and ceramic tiles can be combined to create custom wall surfaces.

Paint finishes range from flat to glossy (enamel). Glossy finishes are best for areas that will be cleaned often. Latex (water-based) paints are more environmentally friendly than oil-based paints.

Wallpaper should be treated to withstand moisture. Choose smooth-textured, solid vinyl or vinyl-coated wallpaper.

Wall tiles are durable, easy to clean, and available in hundreds of styles, colors, and materials, including stone, ceramic, glass, and—if you want a really unusual look—metals.

Solid-surface material is often used to fashion walls in tub and shower surrounds.

Bathroom ceilings need moisture-resistant finishes. Avoid textured ceilings, which peel in humid conditions and are difficult to clean, repair, or paint.

Flooring

Bathroom floors should stand up to daily use, frequent cleaning, and moisture.

Resilient sheet vinyl flooring is inexpensive but is seldom the first choice of professional designers. It is simple to install, easy to clean, seamless, but available in a limited number of of colors, patterns, and styles.

Resilient tile and planks made of vinyl are easy to install. The latest versions are made to stand up to even the most demanding bathroom conditions.

Ceramic tile is available in three main types: glazed ceramic tile, quarry tile, and water-resistant porcelain tile. Although cleaning issues are created by the grout lines, mosaic sheets of ceramic tile are highly popular.

Natural stone tile is a premium flooring material. Granite, marble, and slate are the most common stone products for floors.

Hardwood floors are difficult to totally waterproof so they should be limited to half baths, where moisture is not a big problem.

Ceramic floor tile, a popular choice for bathrooms, is durable and water-resistant.

Vinyl flooring is popular with homeowners because it is relatively inexpensive, durable, and easy to clean.

Stone floor tile creates an inviting atmosphere with natural appeal.

Carpet typically doesn't have the water resistance required for bathroom floors, and it traps mold and mildew. Be sure to select a product that's designed especially for bathrooms.

The condition of your floor structure may affect the cost of installing new flooring. If the subfloor must be replaced or repaired, more time and money will be required. Consult a professional to assess the state of your subfloor.

HALL
BATH
SHELF & POLE
WARDROBE
TUB

Getting Started

A great bathroom provides a comfortable, attractive, and convenient setting. It is a private retreat, where you can tend to your needs in a relaxed and pleasant fashion.

When designing a new bathroom or renovating an existing one, style can be as big a consideration as function. From the choice of materials to the layout of fixtures, the space should reflect your individual sense of style through the use of particular colors, textures, and patterns.

And yet, a bathroom does have to be functional. Without a strong foundation on which to express your style, you may spend money and time creating your new bath, yet it may not turn out as you'd hoped. So the first step is to determine your needs and budget, and draw up some plans.

In this chapter:

- Determining Your Needs
- Designing for Accessibility
- Design Standards
- Drawing Plans

Determining Your Needs

A typical bathroom is divided into three activity areas: the toilet, the sink, and the shower/tub. To create a successful bath design, you need to consider the relationship of these areas, allowing for accessibility and safety. This relationship varies depending on the type of bathroom being renovated: half bath, family bath, or master bath.

Half baths, also called powder rooms or guest baths, are small rooms near common areas of the home. They are designed largely for visitors to use. They can be as small as 20 square feet and are often located near entrances or entertainment areas of a home. It's best to have their doors open into hallways.

Half baths typically feature a toilet and a vanity or pedestal sink finished with smaller fixtures and finer materials. When designed as a guest bath that includes a shower, these rooms require more space and are called three-quarter baths.

The family bath is usually located near the sleeping areas in a home. It is used by more than one family member, and it should provide storage for toiletries, towels, laundry, and cleaning supplies. It features at least one sink, one toilet, and a shower and tub or tub/shower combination.

The typical family bath can fit in a 5 × 7-foot area. A larger bathroom allows space for extra features, such as double sinks or separate shower and tub area. A small family bath may conserve space by combining the tub and shower, incorporating recessed shelving, and featuring space-efficient fixtures and storage cabinets. Finishes and fixtures should be low-maintenance and highly durable, such as ceramic tile and enameled fixtures.

Bathrooms for children must be safe for them to use unsupervised and should be easy to adapt as the children grow. Features that make daily hygiene easier and safer for children include single-handle faucets with antiscald guards, adjustable showerheads, safety plugs in receptacles, grab bars, smaller toilets, lowered sinks, and vanities with built-in step stools.

The master bath is usually connected to the master bedroom and is a sanctuary for the owners of the house. It is typically quite large and may have separate activity centers containing features such as a jetted tub, shower, toilet partition, and multiple sinks and vanities. It may even feature a sauna or steam room. The fixtures and finishing materials generally feature ceramic, stone, or marble tiles; custom cabinets; and upscale accessories.

The half-bath, sometimes called a powder room, consists of a toilet and sink, but no shower or tub. It is usually found near entertainment areas for guest convenience.

This master bath easily accommodates a busy couple's schedules with side-by-side sinks, separate tub and shower, and a roomy makeup table built into the vanity.

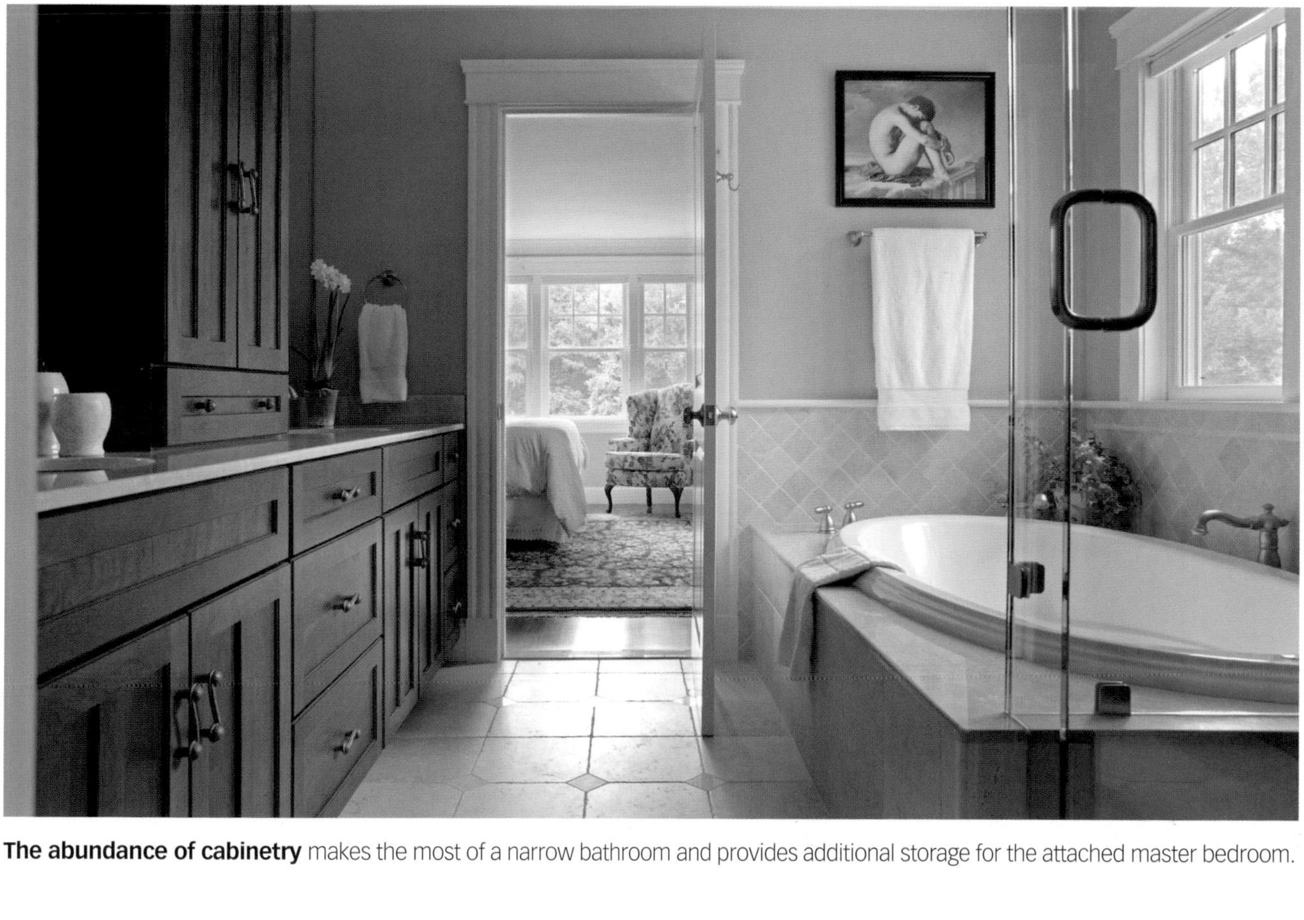

The abundance of cabinetry makes the most of a narrow bathroom and provides additional storage for the attached master bedroom.

Designing for Accessibility

The safety and accessibility of nearly all aspects of a bathroom can be improved.

For safer floors, add a slip-resistant glaze to ceramic tile, and add nonslip adhesive strips or decals to shower floors. If you're replacing your floor, look for mosaic tiles, vinyl, and cork materials. Matte finishes tend to be less slippery than polished surfaces and they reduce glare.

Toilets, faucets, sinks, cabinets, tubs, and showers can all be adapted or changed for increased usability by people who have experienced inflexibility or loss of strength.

Toilet height can be adjusted with the installation of a height adapter that raises a standard toilet seat 2 to 5 inches. You can also consider an adjustable-height toilet or a model with a power-lift seat.

A bathroom designed for accessibility is an increasingly important consideration as our population ages.

A personal hygiene system can be installed to help people with physical disabilities maintain independence. Here, the system is built into an after-market toilet seat that functions as a bidet, offering hands-free cleansing.

A touchless electronic faucet has a sensor that turns water flow on and off when hands are present.

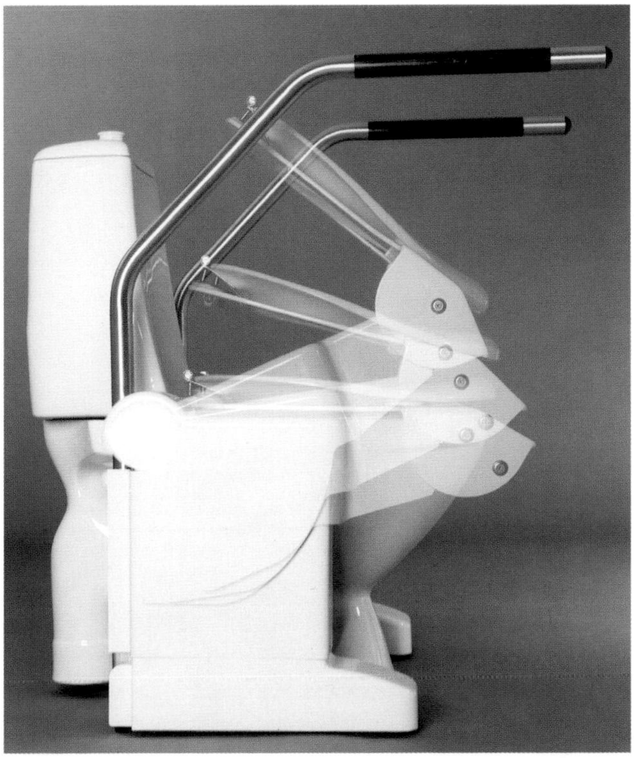

Power-lifts make toilet use easier for people with limited leg or joint strength.

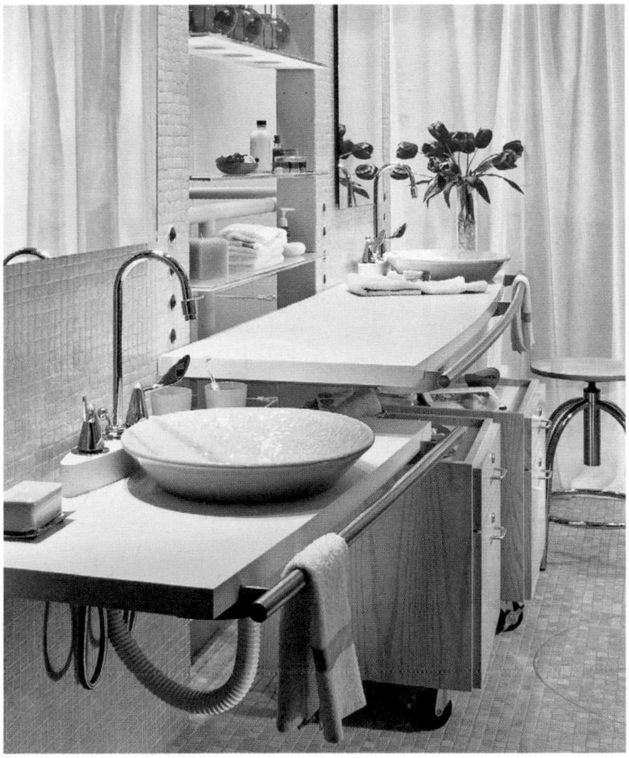

Roll-out base cabinets provide the option of seating space at the countertop.

(continued)

Consider replacing your toilet with a wall-hung style that can be installed at any height, providing additional clear space for maneuvering a wheelchair or walker. To help people with physical disabilities maintain independent personal hygiene, install either a bidet or a toilet with an integral personal hygiene system. Grab bars are a must on walls around the toilet.

Install antiscald guard and volume-control devices to faucets and showerheads. Replace double-handle faucets with single-lever models, which are easier to use. A faucet with motion-sensor operation for hands-free use is a plus.

Change a standard showerhead to an adjustable showerhead mounted on a vertical slide-bar to accommodate people of all heights. Look for handheld models for best control.

Vanities and cabinets with C-shaped pulls or magnetic touch latches are easy to use. Add pull-down hardware to cabinets to bring items within reach for seated people or those with limited mobility.

Install your countertops at varied heights to serve both seated and standing users. Also consider mounting the faucet controls at the side of the sink, rather than the back, for easier access.

If you are replacing your sink, choose a style that is shallower at the front and deeper at the drain. Or install a wall-mounted sink positioned at 30 to 32 inches. Providing a clear space under sinks and low sections of countertop allows seated users to comfortably reach the vanity. Use fold-away doors, remove face frames on base cabinets, or install roll-out base cabinets to gain clear space. Always finish the floor under fold-away or roll-out cabinets. Then insulate hot-water supply pipes or install a protective panel to prevent burns to seated users.

A side-mounted faucet is easier to reach on this accessible, wall-hung sink.

A tilted mirror allows seated or short users to easily see themselves.

Roll-in shower designs, roll-under sinks, grab bars, adjustable slide-bar showers, and open floor space make bathing easier for people with disabilities.

Install grab bars in and around the shower and tub. Adding a shower seat or installing a pull-down or permanent seat in the shower allows elderly or disabled family members to sit while bathing. Install a permanently mounted shower seat at 18 inches high, and be sure the seat is at least 15 inches deep.

Water controls and faucets on tubs repositioned toward the outside edge at a height of 38 to 48 inches allows the water to be turned on and adjusted before getting in to bathe. If you're buying a new bathtub, consider one with a side-access door.

Consider replacing a combination tub and shower with a stand-alone shower with a base that slopes gently toward the drain, rather than a curb to contain water. When fitted with a pull-down seat and an adjustable handheld showerhead, roll-in showers can accommodate people with a wide range of abilities.

Reverse door hinges so doors open out. That way, the door swing won't be blocked if someone falls.

If needed, widen doorways to 32 to 36 inches so wheelchair and walker users can enter the bathroom easily. Or, replace a swing door with a pocket door to gain clear space.

(continued)

A swing-in door makes bathtubs accessible to practically anyone. The door creates a tight seal when closed and cannot be opened if the tub is full.

Install a pocket door in your bathroom to gain more clearance room for wheelchairs and walkers. Pocket doors do not require door stop molding, allowing for some additional clearance.

Recommended Clearances ▸

A bathroom should be planned with enough approach space and clearance room to allow a wheelchair or walker user to enter and turn around easily. The guidelines for approach spaces (patterned areas) and clearances shown here include some ADA guidelines and recommendations from universal design specialists.

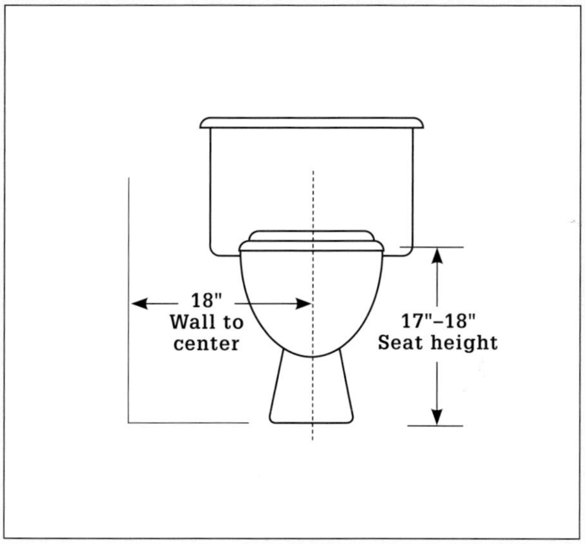

Toilet

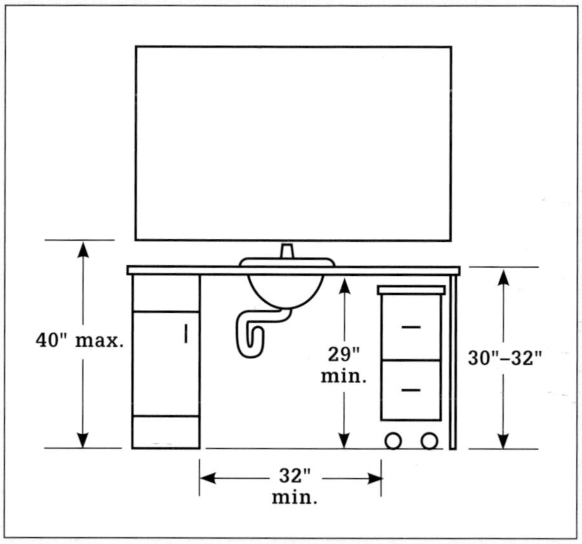

Sink & Vanity

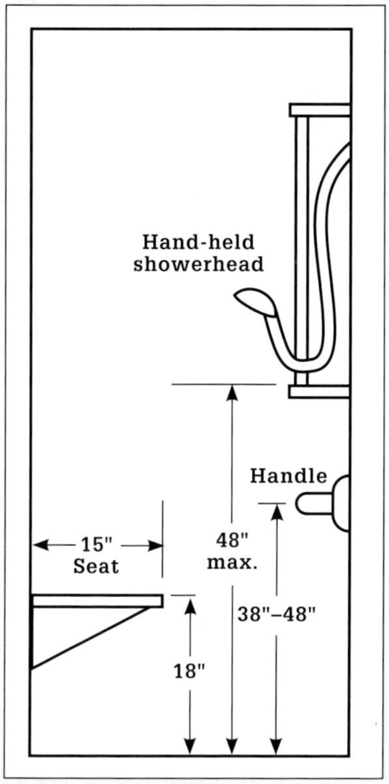

Shower

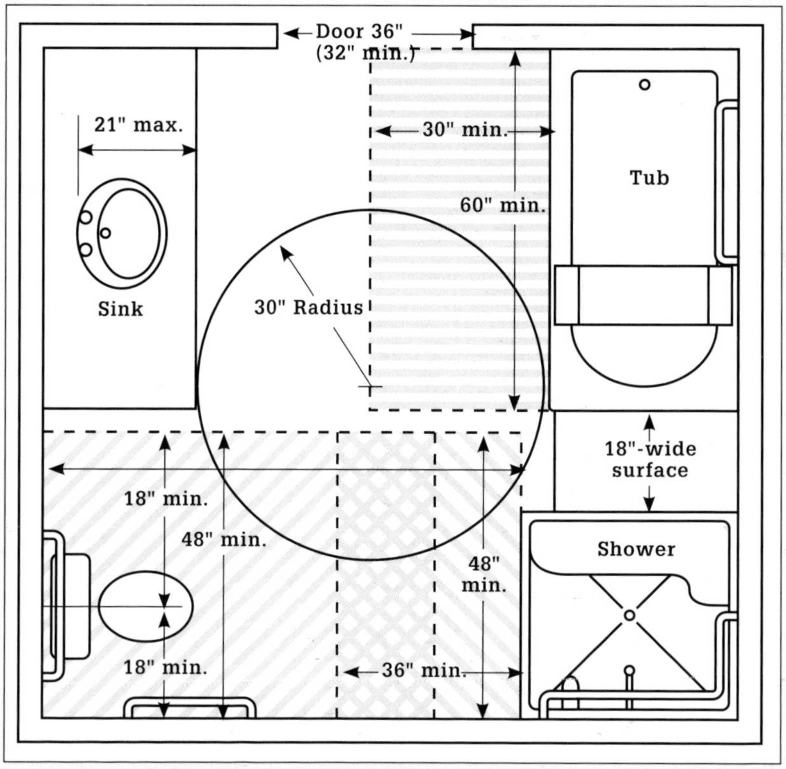

Floor Plan

Design Standards

Once you've drawn up your plan and created a materials list, you'll need to have them reviewed by your local building department. Getting approval early in the process can save you time and expense later. To help ensure success, here are some design standards for you to follow:

The National Kitchen and Bath (NKBA) publishes a list of bathroom design standards to help people plan rooms that are safe and accessible to all users (see Resources, page 283).

Your bathroom probably won't conform to all of the recommended standards, but they can help guide your overall plan. What your plan must include is everything prescribed by the local building codes, including plumbing and wiring codes (see pages 278 to 281).

Bathroom Design Standards ▸

Codes and permits are necessary to ensure safety in any remodel. They're not the most fun to focus on—not like choosing just the right floor covering or deciding between granite or marble countertops—but they are important.

- Plan doorways with a clear floor space equal to the door's width on the push side and greater than the door's width on the pull side. *Note: Clear floor spaces within the bathroom can overlap.*
- Design toilet enclosures with at least 36" × 66" of space; include a pocket door or a door that swings out toward the rest of the bathroom.
- Install toiletpaper holders approximately 26" above the floor, toward the front of the toilet bowl.
- Place fixtures so faucets are accessible from outside the tub or shower. Add antiscald devices to tub and sink faucets (they are required for shower faucets).
- Avoid steps around showers and tubs, if possible.
- Fit showers and tubs with safety rails and grab bars.
- Install shower doors so they swing open into the bathroom, not the shower.
- Use tempered glass or another type of safety glass for all glass doors and partitions.
- Include storage for soap, towels, and other items near the shower, located within 15 to 48" above the floor. These should be accessible to a person in the shower or tub.
- Provide natural light equal to at least 10% of the floor area in the room.
- Illuminate all activity centers in the bathroom with task and ambient lighting.
- Provide a minimum clearance of 15" from the centerline of sinks to any sidewalls. Double-bowl sinks should have 30" clearance between bowls from centerline to centerline.
- Provide access panels for all electrical, plumbing, and HVAC systems connections.
- Include a ventilation fan that exchanges air at a rate of 8 air changes per hour.
- Choose countertops and other surfaces with edges that are smoothed, clipped, or radiused.

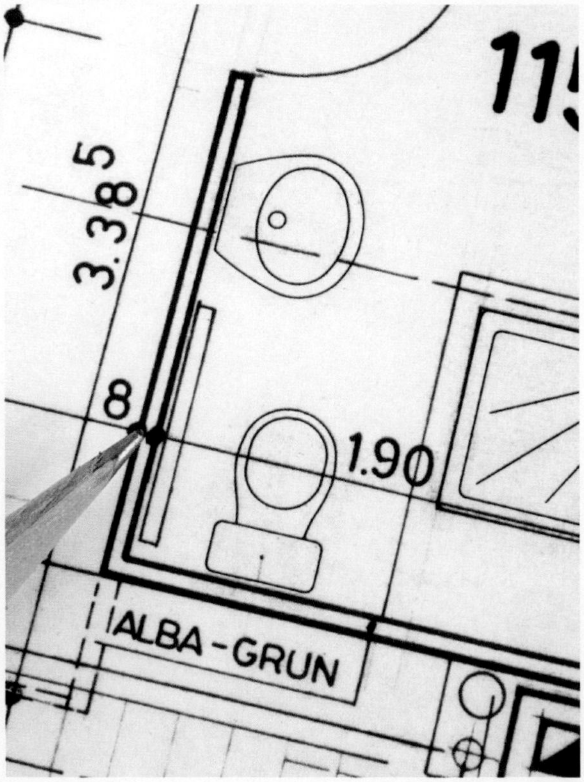

Building Codes for Bathrooms ▸

The following are some of the most common building codes for bathrooms. Contact your local building department for a list of all codes enforced in your area.

- The minimum ceiling height in bathrooms is 7 ft. (Minimum floor area is determined by clearances around fixtures.)
- Sinks must be at least 4" from side walls and have 21" of clearance in front.
- Sinks must be spaced 4" away from neighboring sinks and toilets, and 2" away from bathtubs.
- Toilets must be centered 15" from side walls and tubs, with 21" clearance in front.
- New and replacement toilets must be low-flow models (1.6 gal./flush).
- Shower stalls must be at least 30" × 30", with 24" of clearance in front of shower openings.
- Steps must be at least 10" deep and no higher than 7¼".
- Faucets for showers and combination tub/showers must be equipped with antiscald devices.
- Supply lines that are ½" in diameter can supply a single fixture, or one sink and one toilet.
- A ¾"-diameter supply line must be used to supply two or more fixtures.
- Waste and drain lines must slope ¼" per foot toward the main DWV stack to aid flow and prevent blockage.
- Each bathroom must be wired with at least one 20-amp circuit for GFCI-protected receptacles, and one 15-amp (minimum) circuit for light fixtures and vent fans without heating elements.
- All receptacles must be GFCI-protected.
- There must be at least one permanent light fixture controlled by a wall switch.
- Wall switches must be at least 60" away from bathtubs and showers.
- Toilet, shower, vanity, or other bathroom compartments must have adequate lighting.
- Light fixtures over bathtubs and showers must be vaporproof, with a UL rating for wet areas.
- Vanity light fixtures with built-in electrical receptacles are prohibited.
- Whirlpool motors must be powered by dedicated GFCI-protected circuits.
- Bathroom vent ducts must terminate no less than 10 ft. horizontally or 3 ft. vertically above skylights.

**Note: Codes for accessible bathrooms may differ (see page 53).*

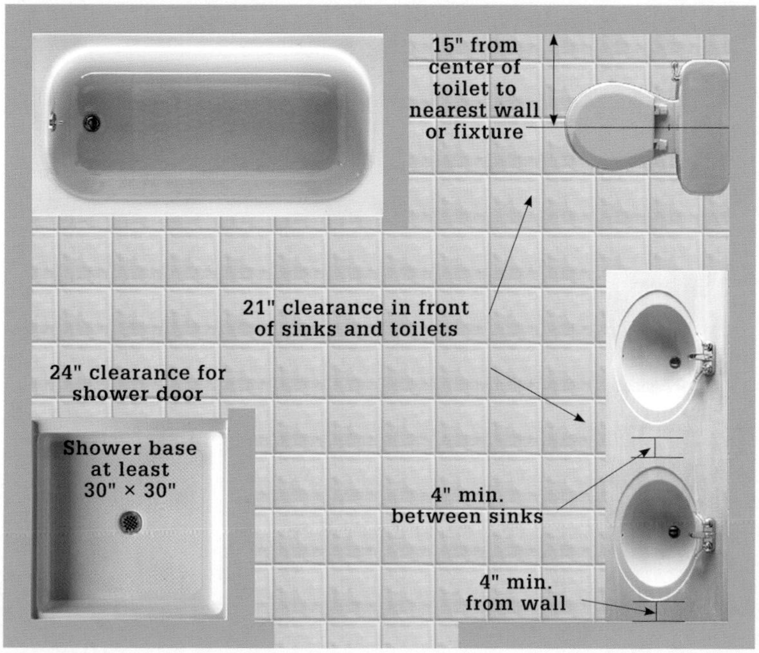

Follow minimum clearance and size guidelines when planning locations of bathroom fixtures. Easy access to fixtures is fundamental to creating a bathroom that is comfortable, safe, and easy to use.

Drawing Plans

If your new bathroom involves a layout change or expansion, you'll find it helpful to create floor plans and elevation drawings. A floor plan illustrates an overhead view, while an elevation drawing illustrates a face-on view. Your drawings will be the basis for obtaining permits, negotiating contracts with tradespeople, and ordering products.

To begin, make a rough sketch of the existing floor plan. Measure and record the size and location of all existing fixtures and mechanicals from a fixed point. Sketch an elevation of each wall.

Use these rough sketches to draft a precise scale drawing of your existing floor plan. You can now sketch variations of your new bathroom using the scale drawing of the floor plan as a guide.

Use the overall dimensions of your new floor plan to sketch elevation options. In the end, the elevations and floor plans must agree.

A scale drawing shows everything in accurate proportion. After measuring the dimensions of your existing bathroom, draft a floor plan, including any adjoining space that could be used for expansion of the layout (such as the storage closet shown below). The normal scale for bathroom plans is ½" = 1 ft.

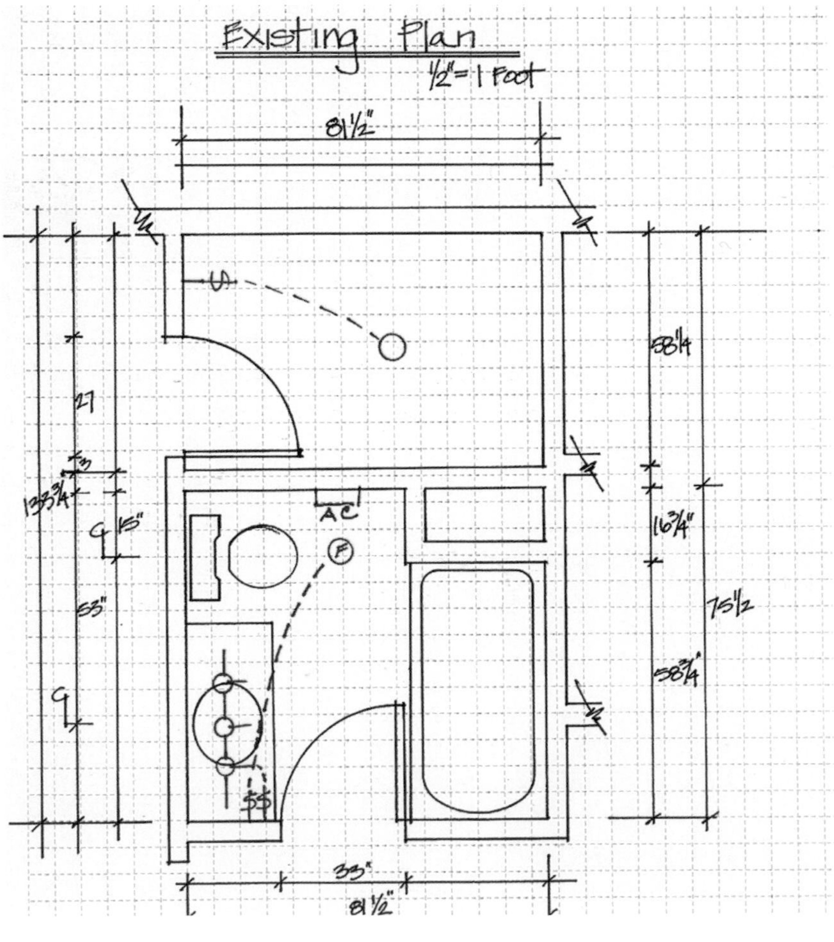

The existing floor plan draft should contain dimension lines noting the accurate measurements of the space, including the location of all existing fixtures. This draft also shows the location of electrical circuits. It is the starting point for your remodeled bathroom plan.

New Bathroom Floor Plan Samples ▸

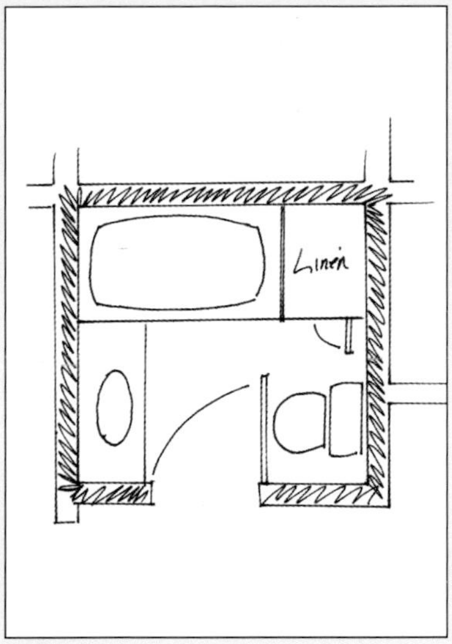

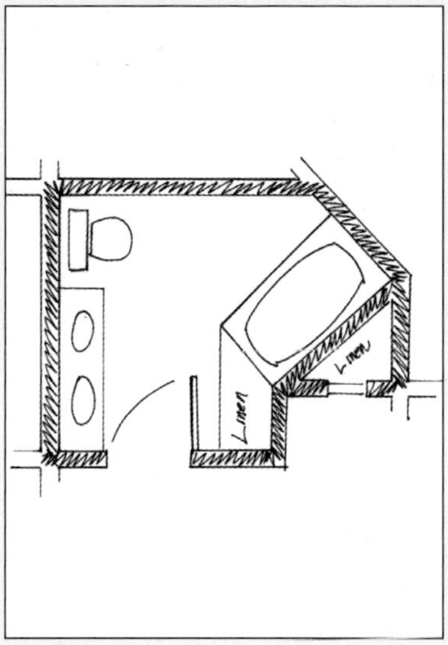

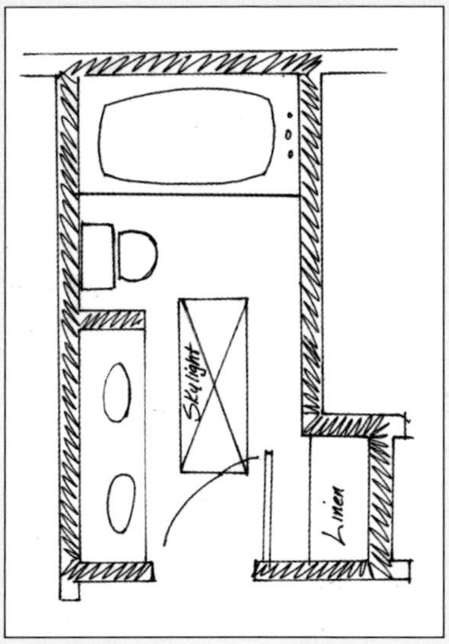

Option A: This floor plan option of the draft on the opposite page shows a layout change within the existing space. The sink and vanity stay in the same place, but the tub and toilet have been switched. There is room to add a linen cabinet, but the space is still very cramped.

Option B: This option explores expanding the room and experimenting with some interesting angles. There is now plenty of floor space for two people, plus room for a double vanity and a large linen cabinet for increased storage.

Option C: The existing room is expanded by annexing the adjacent closet. There's plenty of floor space, a double vanity, and a built-in linen cabinet. This plan has the practical benefits of Option B, but is less expensive to build.

Bathroom Elevation Options ▸

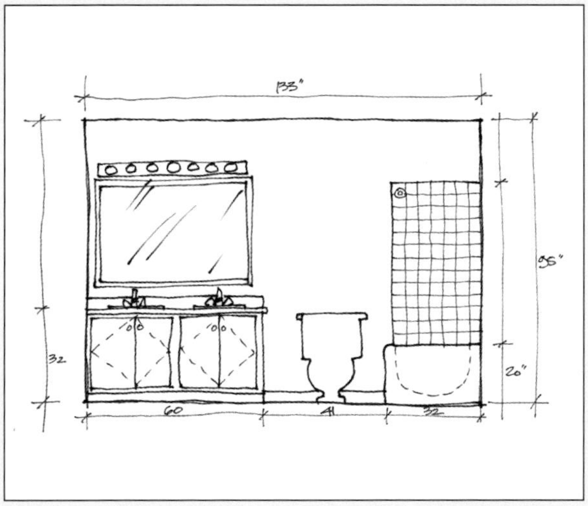

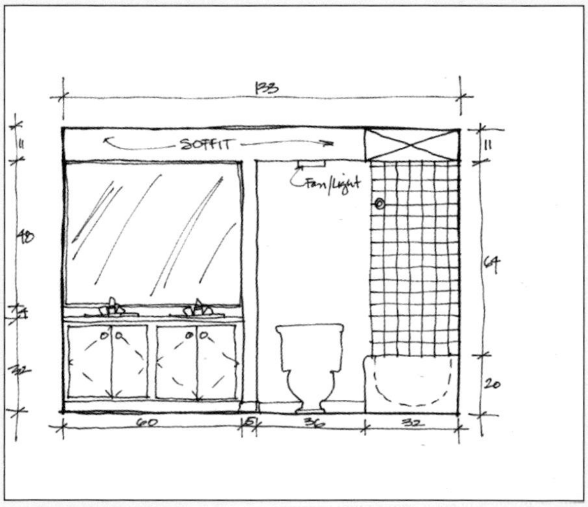

Option A: This elevation shows a simple arrangement with a standard mirror and light fixture. It also shows ceramic tile in the shower area, ending just above the shower curtain.

Option B: This variation shows a custom mirror framed in by a partition wall, and a soffit that runs above the vanity, toilet, and tub. Lights are recessed in the soffit.

Removal & Demolition

The teardown phase is one of the least glamorous aspects of a bathroom renovation. But without it, you can't get started on your bathroom remodeling project.

Begin this phase of the project by removing fixtures located near the door. Even if you plan on re-using these, get them out of the way so that they are not damaged, and to clear the way for removal of other bathroom elements. Then remove cabinets, vanities, electrical fixtures, and accessories.

Carefully remove old bathtubs and shower stalls only after you have created a clear path to get them out. Trim, wall, and floor surfaces may need to be removed first. Label all items you plan to reuse, then store them where they won't be damaged and won't be in the way. Get help when removing heavy fixtures such as a cast-iron bathtub.

Turn off water supply and electrical power to the bathroom before removing electrical and plumbing fixtures or cutting into walls or ceilings.

Work safely: wear eye protection, dust mask, and heavy gloves during any demolition and removal process. And protect the rest of the house by sealing off the bathroom under renovation with plastic sheeting or tarps placed over the doorway.

In this chapter:

Removing Toilets

The toilet is the first fixture to be removed in most remodeling projects. Loosening corroded or rusted nuts and bolts is the most difficult part of the process. See page 59 for tips on removing problem nuts.

Old toilets that will not be reinstalled may be broken up into small, easily managed pieces, using a sledgehammer. Disconnect the toilet and cover it with a heavy blanket before breaking it. Wear eye protection, long sleeves, and heavy gloves during the demolition.

Tools & Materials ▸

- Adjustable wrench
- Ratchet wrench and sockets
- Screwdriver
- Putty knife
- Basin wrench
- Sponge
- Rag
- Bucket
- Drop cloth

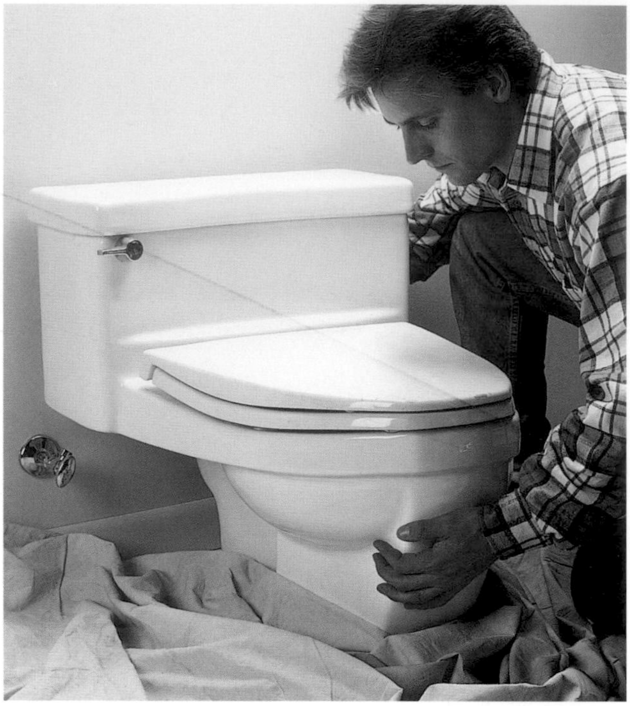

Most toilets are fragile and should be removed during full remodeling projects, even if you do not plan to replace them. Always use care when handling any fixture made of china or porcelain.

Tips for Removing Toilets ▸

Protect your floor with a drop cloth when removing the toilet, if you plan to keep the original floor covering. Residue from the wax ring seal between the bottom of the toilet and the toilet flange is very difficult to remove from floor coverings.

Disconnect any pipes between a wall-mounted toilet tank and the bowl, after turning off the water supply and emptying the tank. Older toilets often have a metal elbow that connects the tank to the bowl. Set 2 × 4 braces below the tank before detaching it from the wall.

How to Remove a Toilet & Wax Ring

Turn off the water, then flush the toilet to empty the tank. Use a sponge to remove the remaining water in the tank and bowl. Disconnect the supply tube with an adjustable wrench.

Remove the nuts from the tank bolts with a ratchet wrench. Carefully remove the tank and set it aside.

Pry off the floor bolt trim caps at the base of the toilet, then remove the floor nuts with an adjustable wrench. See page 59 for tips on removing corroded or rusted nuts.

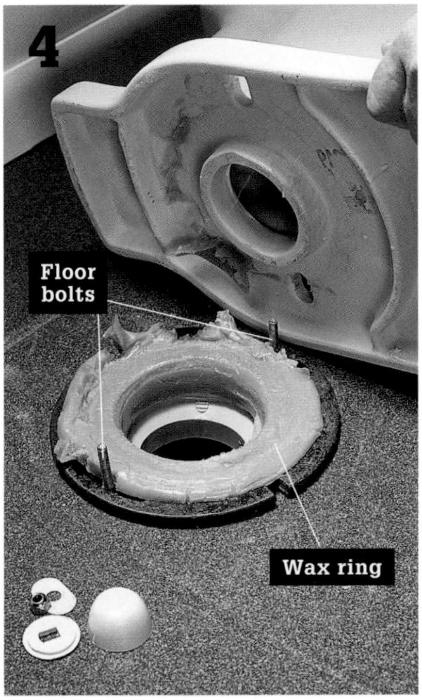

Straddle the toilet and rock the bowl from side to side until the seal breaks. Carefully lift the toilet off the floor bolts and set it on its side. A small amount of water may spill from the toilet trap.

Remove the old wax from the toilet flange in the floor. Plug the drain opening with a damp rag to prevent sewer gases from rising into the house.

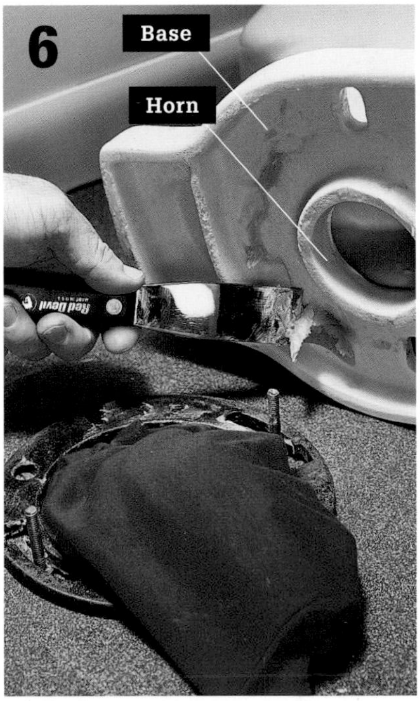

If the old toilet will be reused, clean the old wax and putty from the horn and the base of the toilet.

Removing Sinks & Cabinets

Replacing bathroom sinks, countertops, and cabinets are a quick and relatively inexpensive way to give your bathroom a fresh, new look.

First, disconnect the plumbing, then remove the sink basin or integral sink/countertop unit. Next, take out any remaining countertops. Finally, remove the cabinets and vanities.

Tools & Materials ▸

- Bucket
- Channel-type pliers
- Adjustable wrench
- Basin wrench
- Reciprocating saw
- Hacksaw or pipe cutter
- Screwdriver
- Utility knife
- Flat pry bar

Cut apart cabinets and vanities to simplify their removal and disposal. A reciprocating saw or jigsaw works well for this job. Wear eye protection.

How to Disconnect Sink Plumbing

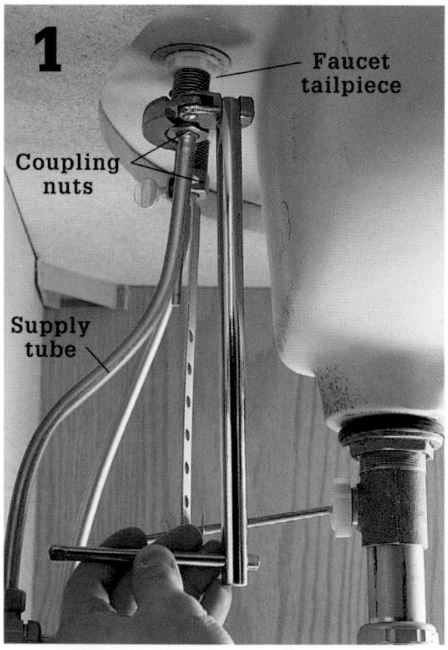

Turn off the shutoff valves, then remove the coupling nuts that connect the supply tube to the faucet tailpieces using a basin wrench. If the supply tubes are soldered, cut them above the shutoff valves.

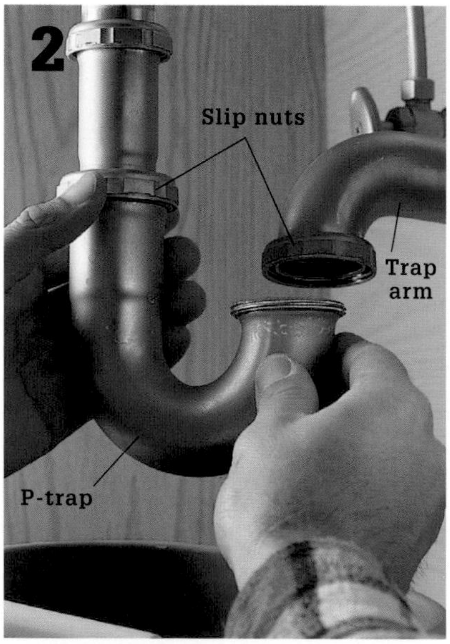

With a bucket beneath, remove the P-trap by loosening the slip nuts at both ends. If the nuts will not turn, cut out the drain trap with a hacksaw. When prying or cutting, take care to avoid damaging the trap arm that runs into the wall.

Disconnect the pop-up drain linkage from the tailpiece of the sink drain by unscrewing the retaining nut.

Tips for Removing Sinks ▸

Self-rimming sink: Disconnect the plumbing, then slice through any caulking or sealant between the sink rim and the countertop using a utility knife. Lift the sink off the countertop.

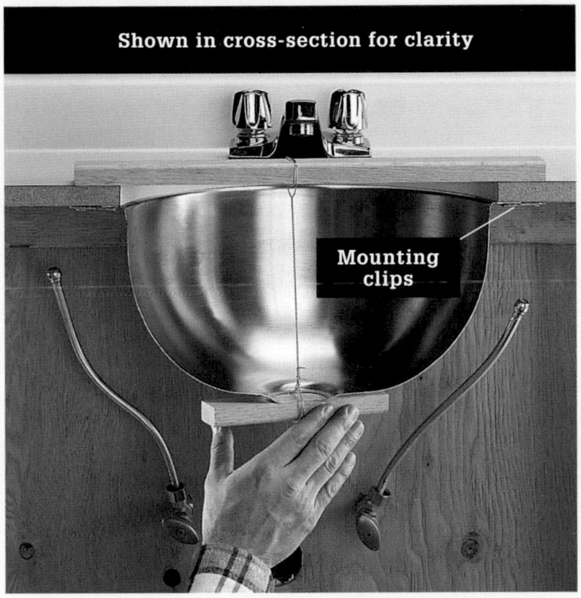

Rimless sink: Disconnect the plumbing, including the drain tailpiece. To support the sink, tie wire around a piece of scrap wood and set the wood across the sink opening. Thread the wire down through the drain hole and attach it to another scrap of wood. Twist the wire until taut, then detach the mounting clips. Slice through any caulking, slowly loosen the wire, then remove the sink.

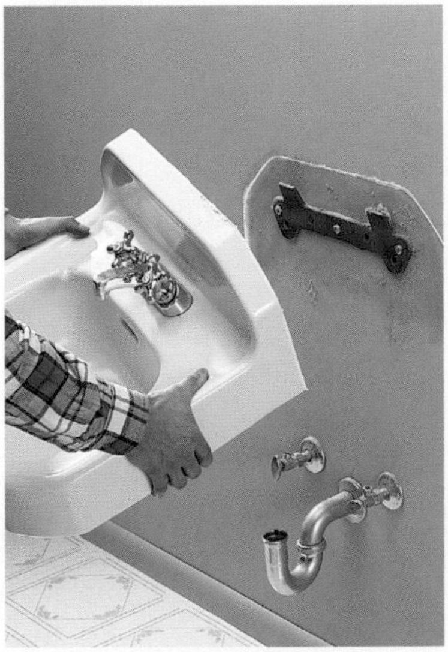

Wall-mounted sink: Disconnect the plumbing, slice through any caulk or sealant, then lift the sink off the wall brackets. For models attached with lag screws, wedge 2 × 4s between the sink and floor to support it while the screws are removed.

Pedestal sink: Disconnect the plumbing. If the sink and pedestal are bolted together, disconnect them. Remove the pedestal first, supporting the sink from below with 2 × 4s. Lift the sink off the wall brackets (photo, left).

Integral sink/countertop: Disconnect the plumbing, then detach the mounting hardware underneath the countertop. Slice through any caulk or sealant between the countertop and wall, and between the countertop and vanity. Lift the sink/countertop unit off the vanity.

How to Remove a Medicine Cabinet

Remove the cabinet doors and mirrors, if possible. If the cabinet has electrical features, see the variation shown below.

Remove screws or any other anchors that hold the sides of the cabinet to the wall studs.

Pull the cabinet out of the wall cavity. Pry the cabinet loose with a pry bar, or grip the face frame of the cabinet with pliers to pull it out.

Variations for Wall-Mounted Cabinets

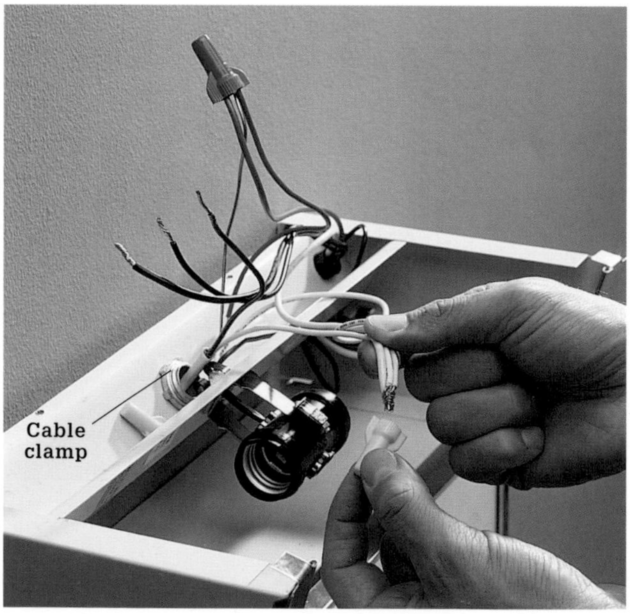

Cabinets with built-in electrical features: Shut off the power at the main circuit box, then disconnect the built-in lights or receptacles. Unscrew the cable clamp on the back of the connection box so the cable is loose when the cabinet is removed.

Surface-mounted cabinets: Support the cabinet body from below with 2 × 4 braces, then remove the mounting screws to free the cabinet from the wall. When removing a large cabinet, have a helper hold the cabinet while you work.

How to Remove a Countertop & Vanity

Disconnect the plumbing, then cut through any caulk or sealant between the backsplash and the wall.

Detach any mounting hardware, located underneath the countertop inside the vanity.

Remove the countertop from the vanity, using a pry bar if necessary.

Turn off the main water supply, then remove the shutoff valves, preserving as much of the supply pipe as possible. Cap the supply pipes or install new shutoff valves after the vanity is removed, then turn the water supply back on.

Remove the screws or nails (usually driven through the back rail of the cabinet) that anchor the vanity to the wall.

Cut through any caulk or sealant between the vanity and wall, using a utility knife, then pry the vanity away from the wall.

Removing Showers & Tubs

Bathtubs and showers are heavy and bulky fixtures, so they pose special problems for removal. Unless the tub or shower has unique salvage value, cut or break the unit into pieces for easy removal and disposal. This technique allows one person to handle most of the disposal chores. Always wear eye protection and heavy gloves when cutting or breaking apart fixtures.

For most tubs and showers, you need to remove at least 6" of wall surface around the tub or shower pan to gain access to fasteners holding it to the wall studs. Maneuvering a tub out of an alcove is also easier when the wall surfaces are removed. If you are replacing the entire wall surface, do all the demolition work before removing the tub.

Tools & Materials ▸

- Reciprocating saw
- Channel-type pliers
- Screwdriver
- Hacksaw
- Adjustable wrench
- Flat pry bar
- Wrecking bar
- Hammer
- Masonry chisel
- Wire cutter
- Eye protection
- Utility knife
- 2 × 4 or 1 × 4 lumber
- Rag

Disconnect the faucet through the access panel, usually located on the wall surface behind or next to the tub faucet and drain. (If the tub does not have an access panel, add one.) Turn off the shutoff valves, then cut the shower pipe above the faucet body. Disconnect or cut off the supply pipes above the shutoff valves.

How to Remove Handles & Spouts

Shut off the water supply, then remove the faucet handles by prying off the covers and unscrewing the mounting screws.

Remove the tub spout by inserting a screwdriver into the spout and twisting counterclockwise until it unscrews from the stub-out that extends from the wall plumbing.

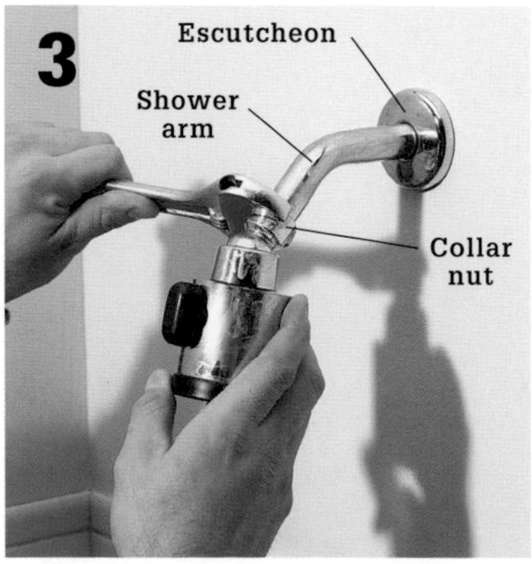

Unscrew the collar nut to remove the showerhead. Loosen the escutcheon, then twist the shower arm counterclockwise to unscrew it from the wall plumbing.

How to Disconnect Drain Plumbing

Remove the drain plug. Most bathtub plugs are connected to drain plug linkage that is lifted out along with the plug.

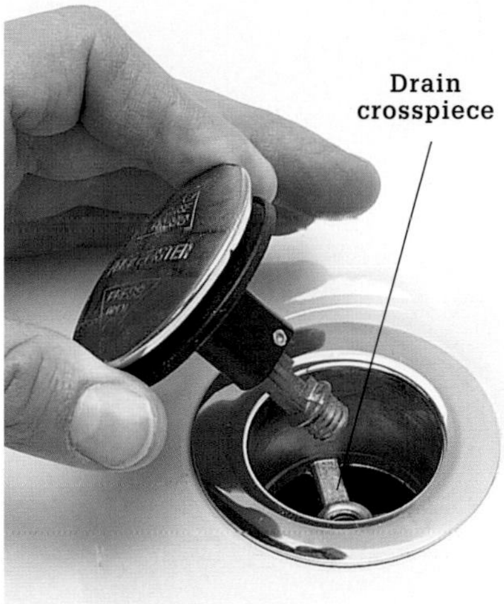

Spring-mounted drain plugs: Remove the plug by unscrewing it from the drain crosspiece.

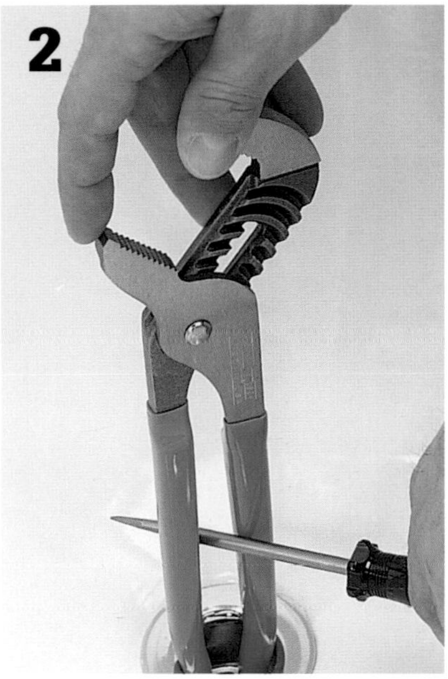

Disconnect the drain assembly from the tub by inserting a pair of pliers into the drain opening and turning the crosspiece counterclockwise. Insert a long screwdriver between the handles and use it to twist the pliers.

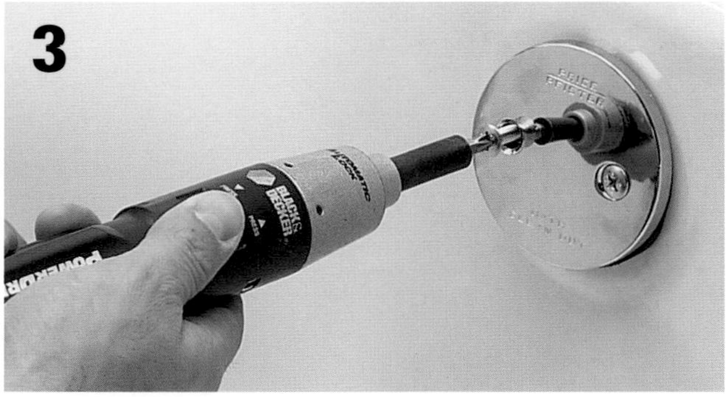

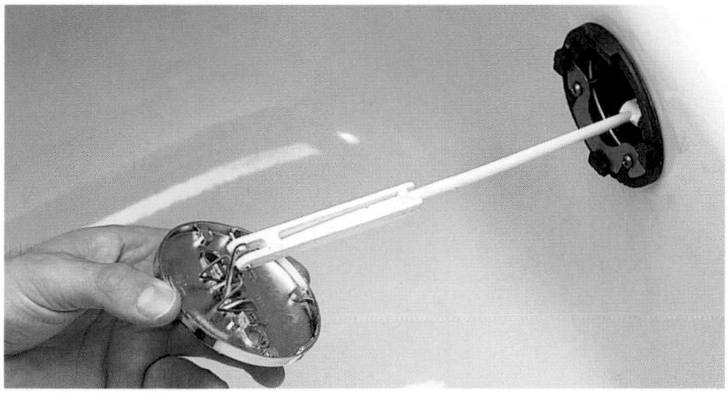

Remove the screws in the overflow coverplate (top photo). Remove the coverplate along with any attached drain plug (bottom photo).

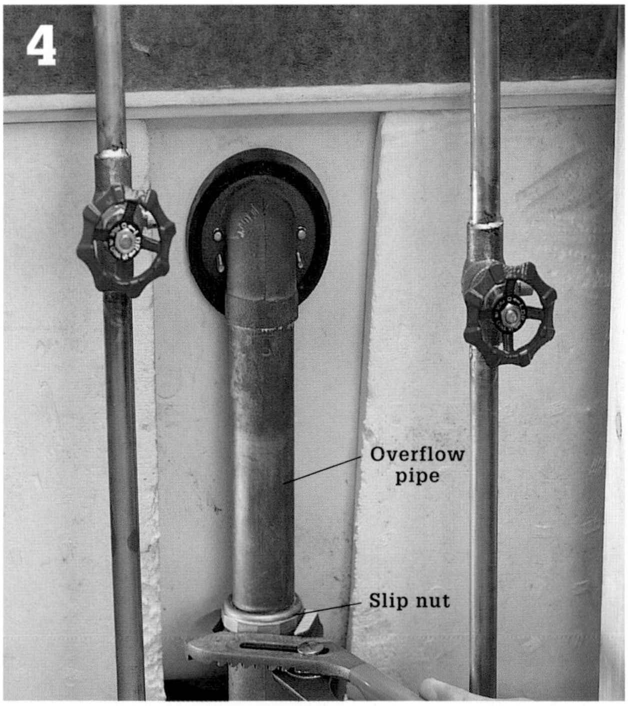

Remove the overflow pipe by unscrewing the slip nut that holds it to the rest of the drain assembly, then lift out the pipe. Stuff a rag into the waste pipe after the overflow pipe is removed to keep debris from entering the trap.

How to Remove a Shower Stall

After disconnecting the faucet handles, spout, and showerhead, remove the shower curtain rod or shower door, molding or trim, and any other accessories.

Slice the caulking around each shower panel using a utility knife. Remove any screws holding the panels together.

Pry shower panels away from the wall using a flat pry bar. If the panels are still intact, cut them into small pieces for easier disposal using a jigsaw or a sharp utility knife.

Fabricated shower bases (fiberglass or plastic): Slice the caulking between the base and the floor, then unscrew any fasteners holding the base to the wall studs. Pry the base from the floor with a wrecking bar.

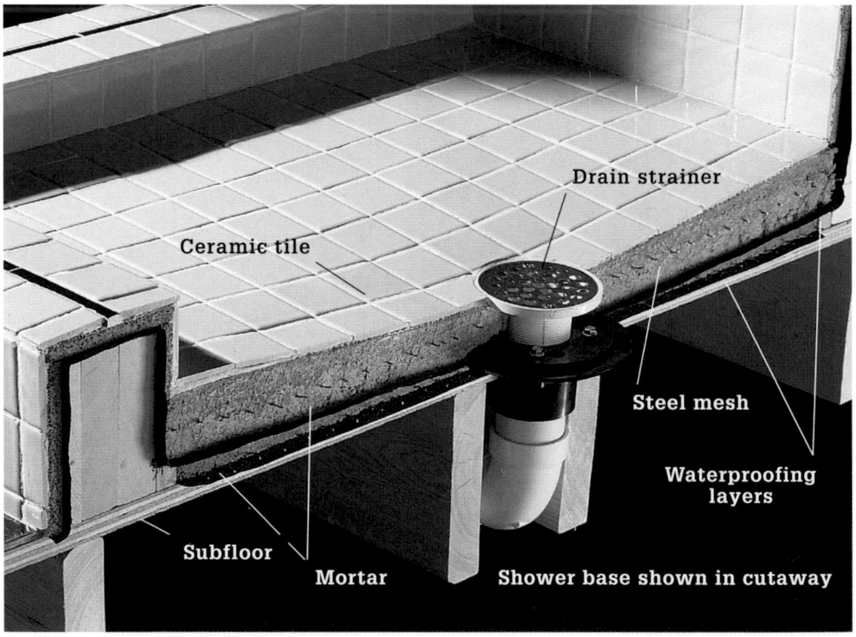

Ceramic-tile shower base: Remove the drain strainer, and then stuff a rag into the drain opening. Wearing protective equipment, break apart a section of tile with a hammer and masonry chisel. Cut through any steel mesh reinforcement using a wire cutter. Continue knocking tile and mortar loose until the waterproofing layers are exposed, then scrape off the layers with a long-handled floor scraper.

How to Remove a Bathtub

Use a reciprocating saw to cut away at least 6" of the wall surface above the tub on all sides. Before cutting into a wall, be sure faucet handles, spouts, and drains are all disconnected.

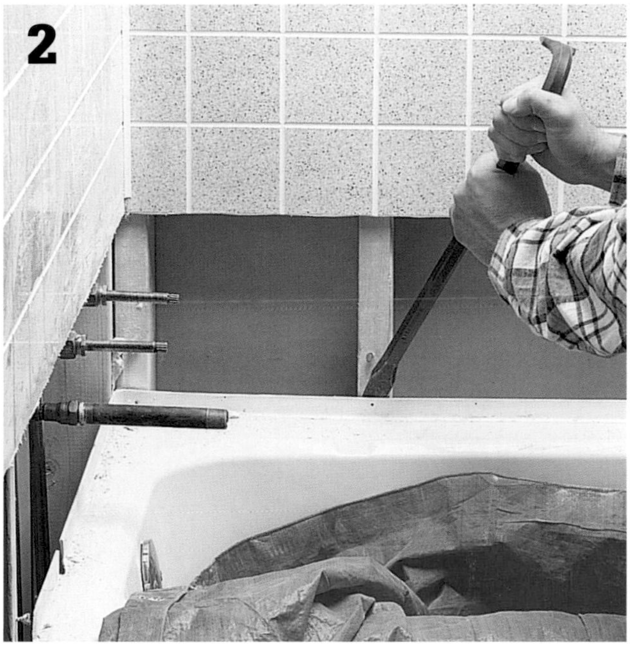

Remove the fasteners that hold the tub flanges to the wall studs, then use a wrecking bar or a piece of 2 × 4 to pry the bathtub loose.

Lift the edge of the bathtub and slip a pair of 1 × 4 runners beneath the tub apron. Pull the tub away from the wall using the runners as skids. Have helpers when removing steel and cast-iron tubs.

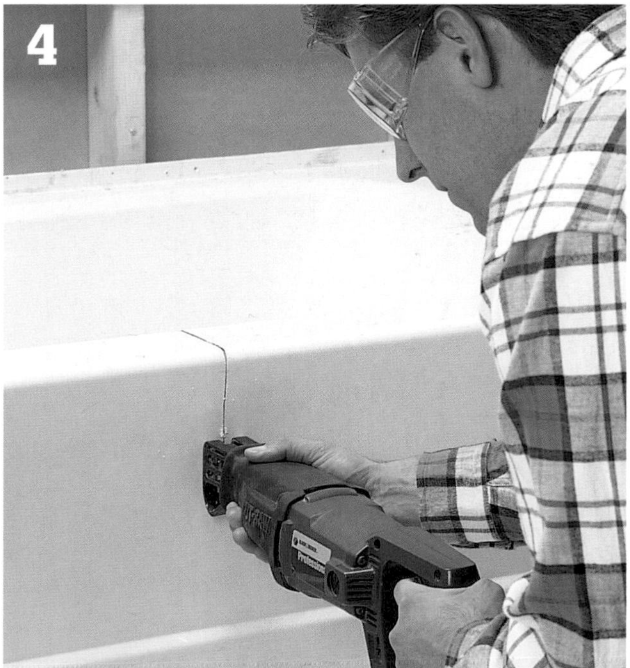

Cut or break the bathtub into small pieces for easy disposal. Fiberglass, reinforced polymer, or pressed steel tubs can be cut with a reciprocating saw. Cast-iron and steel tubs should be carried out.

BATHROOM REMODELING PROJECTS

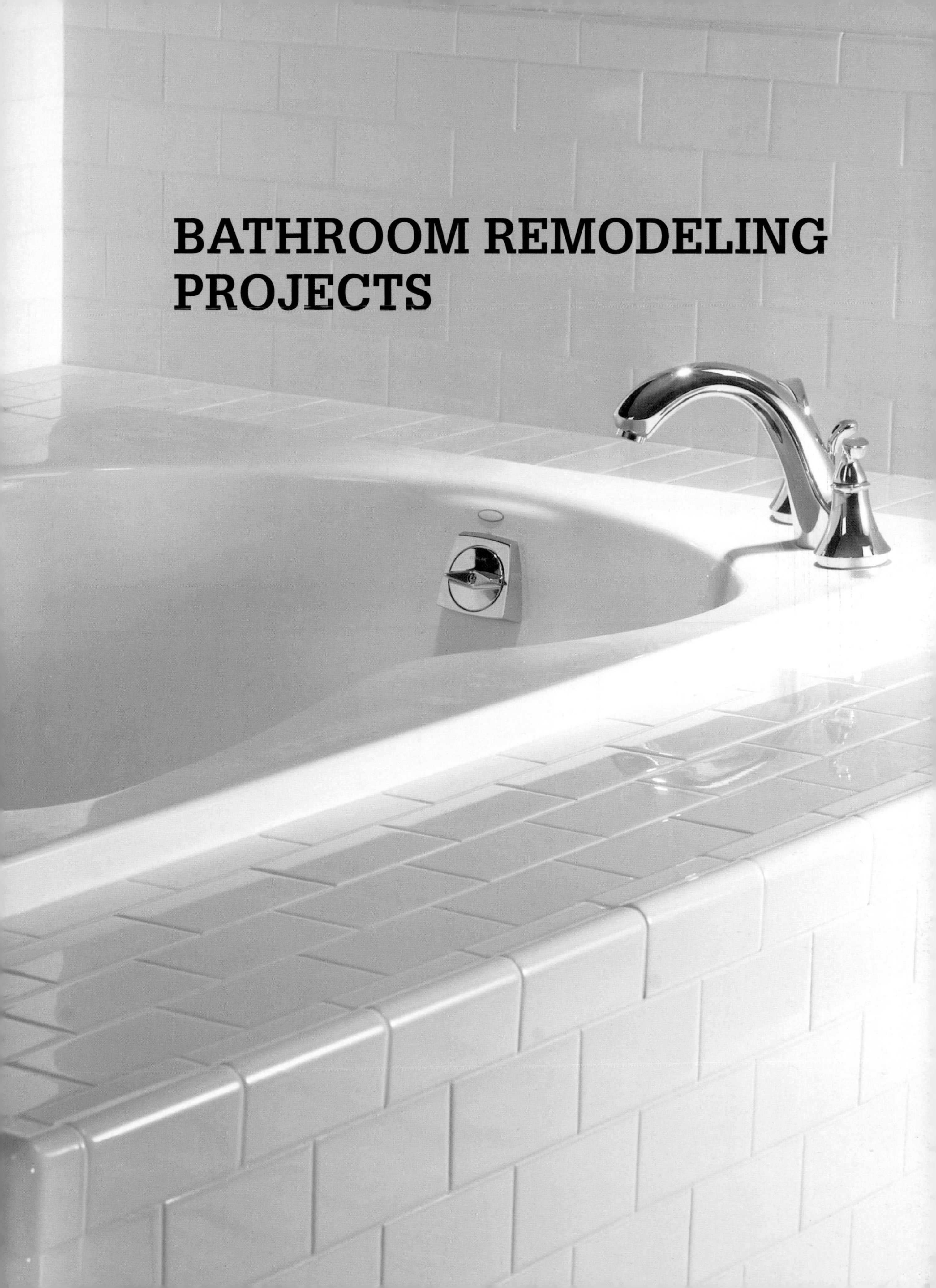

Showers, Tubs & Whirlpools

Installing and hooking up plumbing for bathtubs and showers is a fairly simple job. Jetted tubs are more complicated because they require electrical hookups, as well as structural frames.

The most difficult task you'll face when installing tubs, showers, and spas may be moving the bulky fixtures and materials up stairways and through narrow doorways. With a two-wheel dolly and a little help, the job is much easier. Be sure to measure doorways and hallways.

If you do not plan to remove and replace your wall surfaces, you should still cut away at least six inches of wall surface above a tub or whirlpool to allow easier access during installation.

In this chapter:

- Installing Showers
- Shower Enclosure Kits
- Neo-Angle Showers
- Custom Shower Bases
- Glass Block Showers
- Alcove Bathtubs
- 3-Piece Tub Surrounds
- Solid-Surface Surrounds
- Soaking Tubs
- Sliding Tub Doors
- Air-Jet Tubs
- Tub & Shower Fittings
- Adding a Shower to a Bathtub
- Dual Showerheads
- Slide-bar Showerheads

Installing Showers

Showers can be built in a number of ways, from a number of materials, as discussed on pages 26 to 27. One of the easiest ways to build a shower is to frame an alcove and line it with prefabricated panels. Though water-resistant drywall is the standard backer for prefab panels, always check the manufacturer's recommendations. Some building codes also require a waterproof membrane between the studs and the backer material.

The type of shower base you use will affect the installation sequence. Some bases are made to be installed after the backer; others should be installed first. If your base is going in after the wall surface, be sure to account for the thickness of the surface material when framing the alcove.

Ceramic tile for custom showers is installed the same way as in other applications. Ceramic shower accessories, such as a soap dish, are mortared in place during the tile installation.

Tools & Materials ▸

Circular saw	2 × 4 and 1 × 4 lumber
Drill	16d and 8d nails
Plumbing tools	Plumbing supplies
Hacksaw	Shower base
Channel-type pliers	Rag
Trowel	Dry-set mortar (optional)
Level	Soap

Antiscald Valves

Antiscald valves are safety devices that protect against sudden water temperature changes. They are required by most building codes for faucets in showers and combination tub/showers. Once installed, faucets with antiscald valves look like standard faucets.

Anatomy of a Shower

Shower stalls are available in many different sizes and styles, but the basic elements are the same. Most shower stalls have a shower alcove, a supply system, and a drain system.

Shower alcove: The alcove is the frame for the stall, with 2 × 4 walls built to fit around a shower base and blocking to secure the plumbing. The base sets into a mortar bed for support, and water-resistant drywall or cementboard covers the alcove walls.

The supply system: The shower arm extends from the wall, where an elbow fitting connects it to the shower pipe. The pipe runs up from the faucet, which is fed by the hot and cold water supplies.

The drain system: The drain cover attaches to the drain tailpiece. A rubber gasket on the tailpiece slips over the drainpipe, leading to the P-trap and the branch drain.

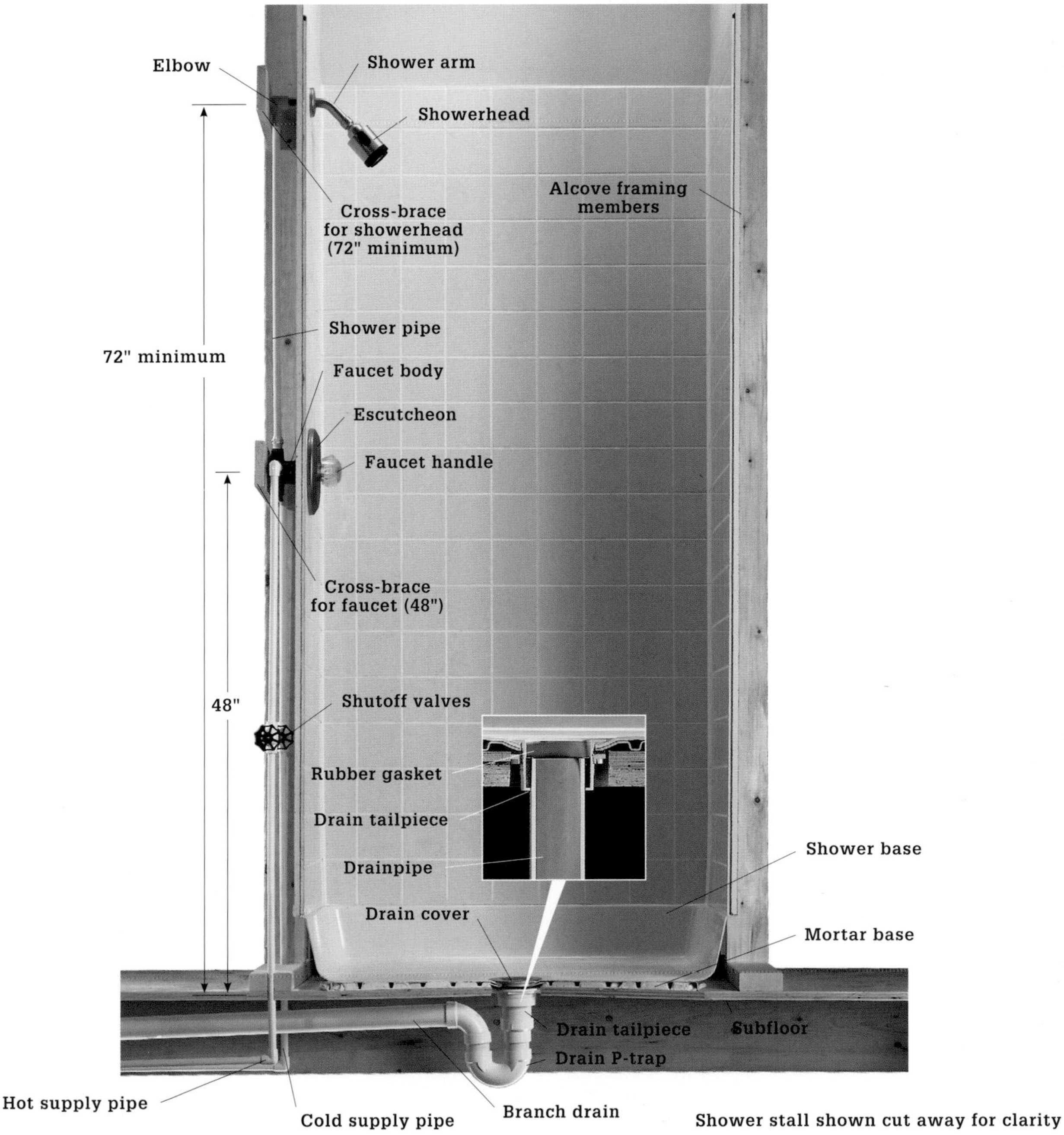

Shower stall shown cut away for clarity

Shower Enclosure Kits

The fastest and easiest way to create a new shower in your bathroom is to frame in the stall area with lumber and wallboard and then install a shower enclosure kit. Typically consisting of three fiberglass or plastic walls, these enclosure kits snap together at the corners and nestle inside the flanges of the shower pan to create nearly foolproof mechanical seals. Often the walls are formed with shelves, soap holders, and other conveniences.

If you are on a tight budget, you can find extremely inexpensive enclosure kits to keep costs down. You can even create your own custom enclosure using waterproof beadboard panels and snap-together connectors. Or, you can invest in a higher grade kit made from thicker material that will last much longer. Some kits are sold with the receptor (and perhaps even the door) included. The kit shown here is designed to be attached directly to wall studs, but others require a backer wall for support. The panels are attached to the backer with high-tack panel adhesive.

Tools & Materials ▸

- Tape measure
- Pencil
- Hammer
- Carpenter's square
- Screwdrivers
- Pipe wrench
- Level
- Strap wrench
- Adjustable wrench
- Pliers
- Drill/driver
- Center punch
- File
- Utility knife
- Hacksaw
- Masking tape
- Slicone caulk and caulk gun
- Shower enclosure kit
- Shower door
- Showerhead
- Faucet
- Plumbing supplies

A paneled shower surround is inexpensive and easy to install. Designed for alcove installations, they often are sold with matching shower pans (called receptors).

How to Install a Shower Enclosure

Mark out the location of the shower, including any new walls, on the floor and walls. Most kits can be installed over wallboard, but you can usually achieve a more professional looking wall finish if you remove the wall covering and floor covering in the installation area. Dispose of the materials immediately and thoroughly clean the area.

If you are adding a wall to create the alcove, lay out the locations for the studs and plumbing on the new wood sill plate. Also lay out the stud locations on the cap plate that will be attached to the ceiling. Refer to the enclosure kit instructions for exact locations and dimensions of studs. Attach the sill plate to the floor with deck screws and panel adhesive, making sure it is square to the back wall and the correct distance from the side wall.

Align a straight 2 × 4 right next to the sill plate and make a mark on the ceiling. Use a level to extend that line directly above the sill plate. Attach the cap plate at that point.

Install the 2 × 4 studs at the outlined locations. Check with a level to make sure each stud is plumb and then attach them by driving deck screws toenail style into the sill plate and cap plate.

(continued)

Cut an access hole in the floor for the drain, according to the installation manual instructions. Drill openings in the sill plate of the wet wall (the new wall in this project) for the supply pipes, also according to the instructions.

Install a drain pipe and branch line and then trim the drain pipe flush with the floor. If you are not experienced with plumbing, hire a plumber to install the new drain line.

Install new supply risers as directed in the instruction manual (again, have a plumber do this if necessary). Also install cross braces between the studs in the wet wall for mounting the faucet body and shower arm. *NOTE: Some local codes require that you use gate valve shutoffs, not ball valves.*

If the supply plumbing is located in a wall (old or new) that is accessible from the non-shower side, install framing for a removable access panel.

Attach the drain tailpiece that came with your receptor to the underside of the unit, following the manufacturer's instructions precisely. Here, an adjustable spud wrench is being used to tighten the tailpiece.

Option: To stabilize the receptor, especially if the floor is uneven, pour or trowel a layer of thinset mortar into the installation area, taking care to keep the mortar out of the drain access hole. Do not apply mortar in areas where the receptor has feet that are intended to make full contact with the floor.

Set the receptor in place, check to make sure it is level, and shim it if necessary. Secure the receptor with large-head roofing nails driven into the wall stud so the heads pin the flange against the stud. Do not overdrive the nails.

Lay out the locations for the valve hole or holes in the end wall panel that will be installed on the wet wall. Check your installation instructions. Some kits come with a template marked on the packaging carton. Cut the access hole with a hole saw and drill or with a jigsaw and fine-tooth blade. If using a jigsaw, orient the panel so the good surface is facing down.

(continued)

Position the back wall so there is a slight gap (about 1⁄32") between the bottom of the panel and the rim of the receptor—set a few small spacers on the rim if need be. Tack a pair of roofing nails above the top of the back panel to hold it in place (or use duct tape). Position both end walls and test the fits. Make clip connections between panels (inset) if your kit uses them.

Remove the end walls so you can prepare the installation area for them. If your kit recommends panel adhesive, apply it to the wall or studs. In the kit shown here, only a small bead of silicone sealant on the receptor flange is required.

Reinstall the end panels, permanently clipping them to the back panel according to the kit manufacturer's instructions. Make sure the front edges of the end panels are flush with the front of the receptor.

Once the panels are positioned correctly and snapped together, fasten them to the wall studs. If the panels have predrilled nail holes, drive roofing nails through them at each stud at the panel tops and every 4 to 6" along vertical surfaces.

Install wallcovering material above the enclosure panels and anywhere else it is needed. Use moisture-resistant materials, and maintain a gap of ¼" between the shoulders of the top panel flanges and the wallcovering.

Finish the walls and then caulk between the enclosure panels and the wallcoverings with silicone caulk.

Install the faucet handles and escutcheon and caulk around the escutcheon plate. Install the shower arm escutcheon and showerhead (see pages 128 to 137). Add a shower door (pages 78 to 79).

Make an access panel and attach it at the framed opening created in step 8. A piece of ¼" plywood framed with mitered case molding and painted to match the wall is one idea for access panel covers.

How to Install a Hinged Shower Door

Measure the width of the shower opening. If the walls of the shower slope inward slightly before meeting the base, take your measurement from a higher point at the full width of the opening so you don't cut the door base too short. Cut the base piece to fit using a hack saw and a miter box. File the cut ends if necessary to deburr them.

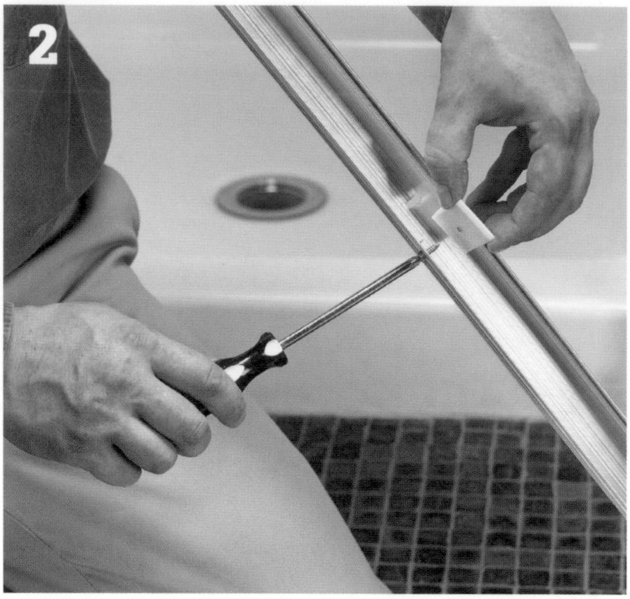

Identify which side jamb will be the hinge jamb and which will be the strike jamb according to the direction you want your hinged door to swing—an outward swing is preferred. Prepare the jambs for installation as directed in your instructions.

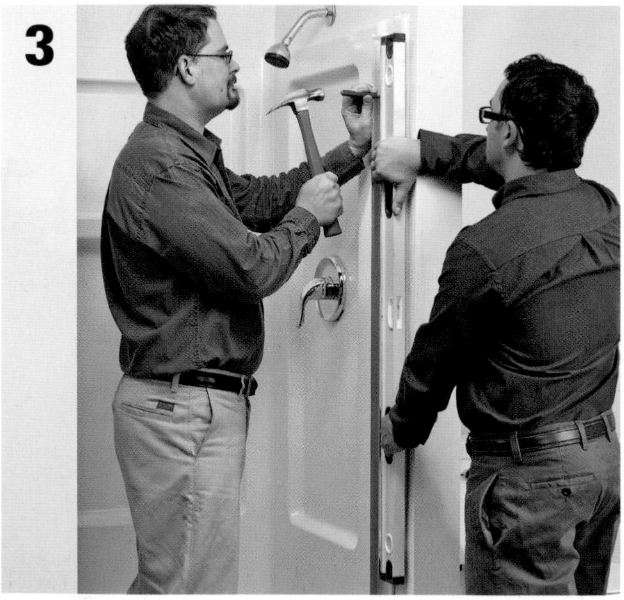

Place the base jamb on the curb of the shower base. If the joint where the wall meets the curb is sloped, you'll need to trim the corners of the base piece to follow the profile. Place a jamb carefully onto the base and plumb it with a level. Then, mark a drilling point by tapping a centerpunch in the middle of each nail hole in each jamb. Remove the jambs, drill pilot holes, and then attach the jambs with the provided screws.

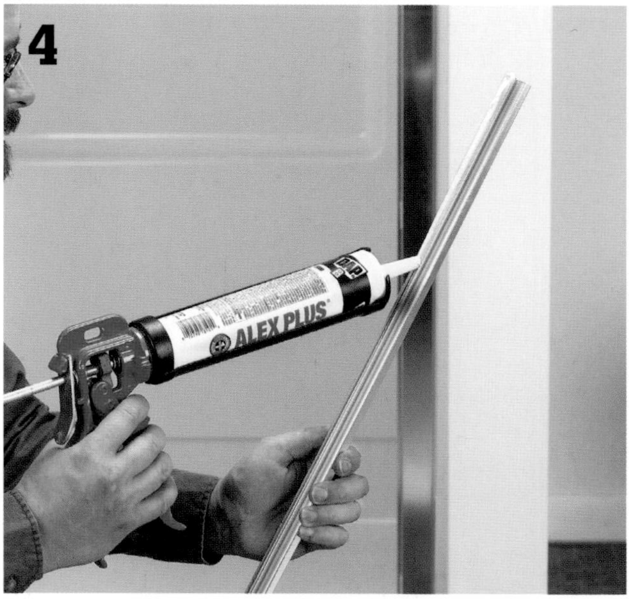

Remove the bottom track and prepare the shower base curb for installation of the base track, following the manufacturers directions. Permanently install the bottom track. Bottom tracks (not all doors have them) are usually attached to the side jambs or are held in place with adhesive. Never use fasteners to secure the tracks to the curb.

Working on the floor or another flat surface, attach the door hinge to the hinge jamb, if required. In most systems, the hinge is fitted over the hinge jamb after you attach it to the wall.

Attach the hinge to the door panel, according to the manufacturer's instructions. Attach any cap fitting that keeps water out of the jamb.

Fit the hinge jamb over the side jamb and adjust it as directed in your instruction manual. Once the clearances are correct, fasten the jambs to hang the door.

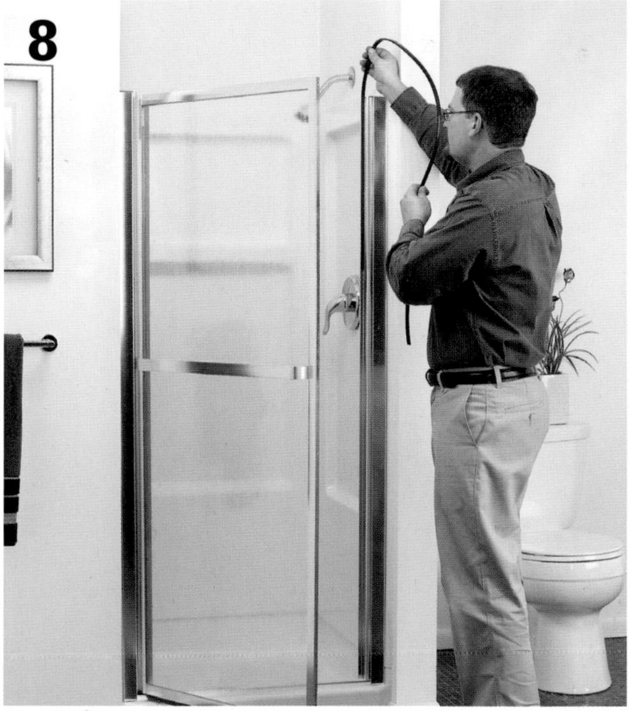

Install the magnetic strike plate and any remaining caps or accessories such as towel rods. Also attach the sweep that seals the passage, if provided.

Neo-Angle Showers

A neo-angle shower is the perfect choice when space is at a premium or when a corner is available. The shower surrounds are available as one-piece units or as two- or three-piece bases plus wall units. One-piece units are preferable because leakage is kept at a minimum, but they are so bulky that they are usually feasible only for new construction. The installation shown here features a neo-angle kit made by Kohler (see Resources, page 283). The specific steps for other models may slightly vary.

Tools & Materials ▸

Drill and bits	Basin wrench or large channel-type pliers	Roofing nails	Silicone sealant
Hole saw	Shims	Scissors	Moisture-resistant wallboard
Hammer	Lath strips	File	Shower base
Level	Open-end wrenches	Phillips screwdriver	Shower walls
Carpenter's square	Jigsaw	Drop cloth	Enclosure
Tape measure	Caulk gun	Center punch	Shower drain
C-clamps		Masking tape	

Neo-angle showers make efficient use of bathroom floorspace by fitting into a corner. The real reason for their popularity, however, may well be the appeal of the contemporary glass wall design. Many neo-angle showers have frameless glass panels and doors, which further intensifies the contemporary appearance.

How to Install a Neo-Angle Shower

Remove existing wall and floor surfaces in the shower location, or remove the existing corner shower. Add additional wall studs and cross braces according to the manufacturer's instructions. All studs must be plumb and stud faces even to create a flat surface. The corner must also be square. Cut and install spacers and shims to create plumb and even corners.

Mark the position and size of the drain according to manufacturer's specifications and cut the drain hole through the subfloor. Install the rough plumbing to the drain hole. Install the plumbing for the faucet and showerhead. If you are not experienced with home plumbing, hire a plumber for this portion of the job.

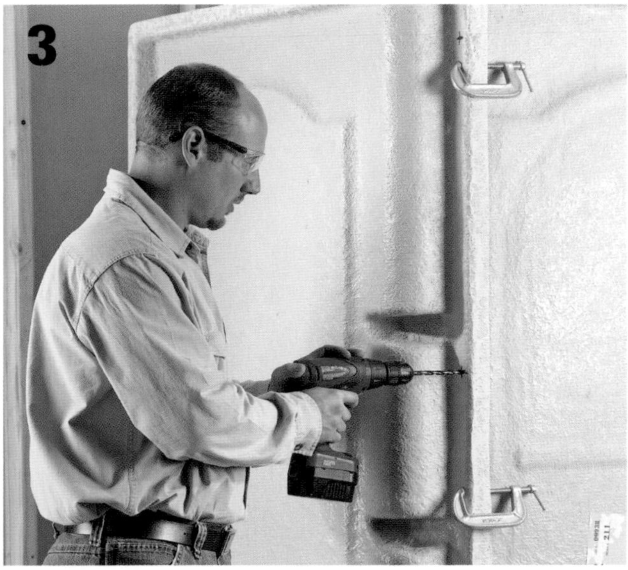

On a level surface, position the walls upright. Use C-clamps to join them at the top and bottom. Mark drilling points on the flanges with a marker according to the manufacturer's instructions. At the marks, drill through both flanges with a 5⁄16" bit. Remove the clamps and apply a minimum 1⁄4" bead of mildew-resistant clear silicone sealant to one mating surface. Reposition the walls and fasten them together with a bolt and washer on one side and a washer, lock washer, and nut on the other. Tighten with a wrench, but do not overtighten.

Hold the base on its side and apply a bead of plumber's putty around the underside of the strainer body flange. Position the strainer body through the shower drain hole. Fit the gasket and washer over the strainer body and secure it with the provided nut. Place the base over the drain hole. Check that the drain pipe extends 1¼" into the drain body.

(continued)

Place the base in the corner, tight up against the studs. The three front edges of the base should fit tightly to the floor. If not, you may need to use a leveling agent to level the floor. Check the base to make sure it's level along the two back sides and the angled front side. Shim along the back of the base to make the base level if needed. When level, drill holes through the base's nailing flanges at the stud locations, but do not nail it at this time.

Carefully cut the pipe entry holes in the shower walls. First, measure from the top ledge of the base to the valve stem of the faucet and the showerhead pipe. Be sure to measure carefully as misplaced holes cannot be repaired. Drill ¼" pilot holes, then use a hole saw to cut the outlets to the proper size. Refer to the faucet directions for sizing. Make all cuts from the inside of the shower walls.

Apply a minimum ¼" bead of silicone caulk around the back ledges of the base, where the walls will make contact with the base.

With a helper, carefully move and align the wall assembly onto the base. Check that walls are level and plumb and add shims if necessary. Drill pilot holes through the nailing flanges at the stud centers across the wall tops and every 8" down the nailing flanges on the sides.

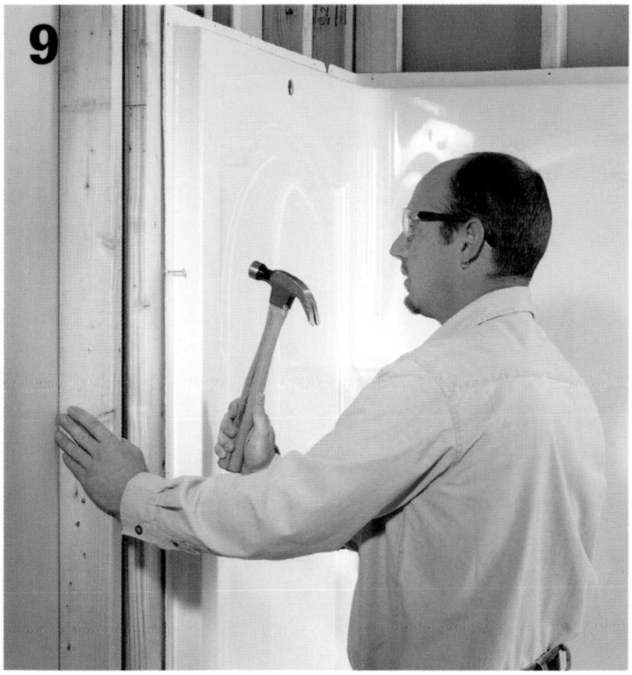

Check that the shower base is still level. Nail through the pilot holes in the nailing flange using galvanized roofing nails. The nails should penetrate the studs to at least 1". Use longer nails if necessary due to shimming. Drive a nail at each stud location and every 4 to 6" on vertical edges.

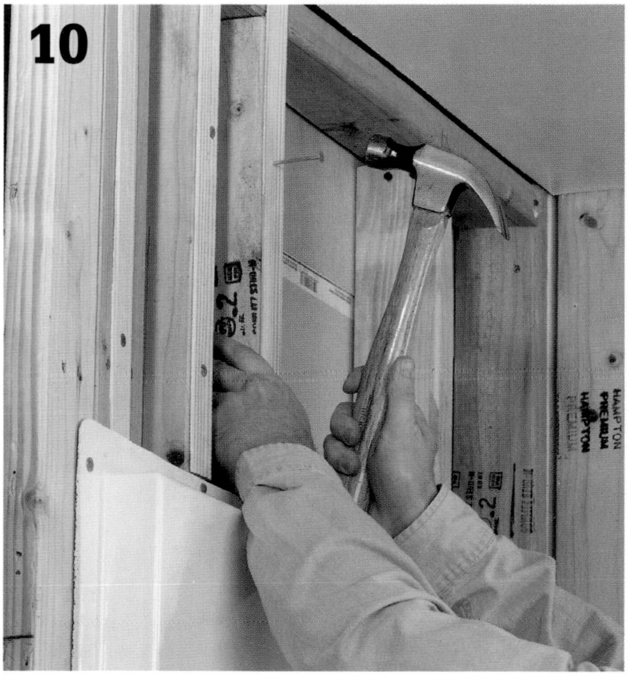

Nail lath strips the thickness of the shower's nailing flanges onto the studs so that the wallboard fits true. Apply silicone sealant to the nailing flanges before installing the wallboard.

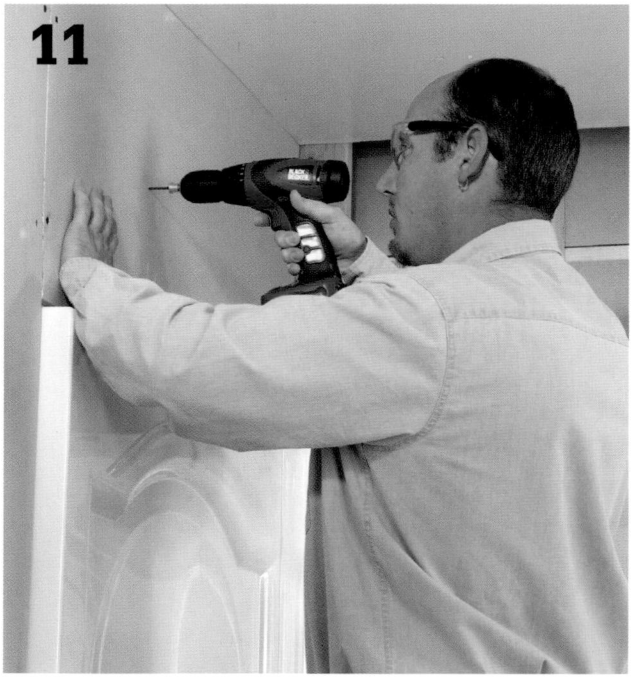

Install wallboard so the finished paper edge is a maximum of ¼" above the top of the shower walls. Use greenboard or a mold- and moisture-resistant wallboard such as Sheetrock brand Humitek gypsum panels. Finish the wallboard by mudding and taping. Do not use metal tools to scrape mud spills from the shower surface. Use wood or plastic if necessary.

Lubricate the drain gasket connector with soapy water. Push the connector down into the strainer body so it fits tightly. With a hammer and thin piece of wood, drive the connector as far into the drain body as possible. You can now attach the shower arm and faucet.

(continued)

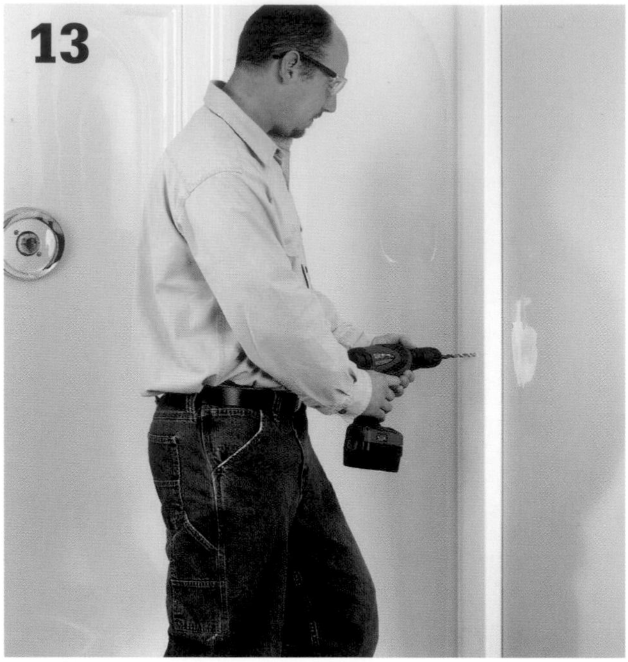

Mark the placement of the enclosure on the base ledge near the wall. Refer to the manufacturer's directions for the exact measurement. Align the outer edge of the wall jamb with the mark so that the sealing groove is on the outside edge. Use a level to check for plumb.

Mark the wall jamb screw locations onto the shower enclosure following the manufacturer's instructions. Then, predrill $\frac{5}{16}$" holes on the shower wall. Repeat for the second jamb.

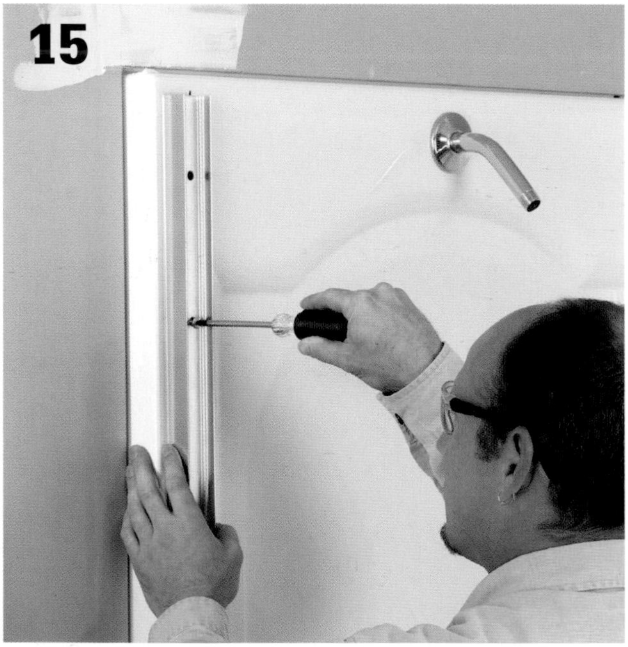

Align the jamb with the marks on the shower base and with the predrilled holes along the shower wall. Insert the wall anchors through the pilot holes in the shower walls. Slightly overfill the sealing groove with silicone sealant and reposition the jamb over the mounting holes. Drive three panhead screws through the holes that don't contain adjustment blocks. Drive screws by hand to avoid overtightening.

Carefully place the side panel expander jamb over the wall jamb. From inside the shower, use a phillips screwdriver to turn the adjustment blocks counterclockwise until they firmly contact the expander jamb. Repeat for the other side panel and check both panels for plumb.

Lay the shower door frame on a level surface with the beveled bridge members facing inward and the outside of the door frame facing up. Attach the flange and strike post to the bridge members with #8, 1" self-piloting screws. Place the doorframe between the side panels and align the flange lip and strike post lips with the column grooves. Push the lips into the grooves and secure with #8, ⅝" flat-head screws. Tighten by hand.

Decide whether the door will pivot to the left or to the right. Insert bushings into the holes on the pivot points and insert plugs into the opposite side. Insert the short end of the pivot pin into the bottom bushing and slide a nylon washer over the long end of the pivot pin. Push the door handle foam insert into the grooves of the door handle. Trim to fit.

Lift the door panel and place the pivot hole over the bottom pivot pin. Insert the long end of the second pivot pin through the top bushing and into the door. Open and close the door. If it rubs, make adjustments to the adjustment blocks as required. When adjustments are complete, drive a #8 × 3½" flat-head screw through the top and bottom adjustment holes to secure the side panels to the wall. Install column and post caps. Press the drain strainer plate into place.

Finish and seal the seams. Apply a bead of silicone sealant around the outside of the shower enclosure where it meets the base. Do not apply sealant to the inside of shower. Apply sealant on the top and outside of the bottom bridge member where it meets the door frame. Allow sealant to cure thoroughly before using the shower.

Custom Shower Bases

Building a custom-tiled shower base lets you choose the shape and size of your shower rather than having its dimensions dictated by available products. Building the base is quite simple, though it does require time and some knowledge of basic masonry techniques because the base is formed primarily using mortar. What you get for your time and trouble can be spectacular.

Before designing a shower base, contact your local building department regarding code restrictions and to secure the necessary permits. Most codes require water controls to be accessible from outside the shower and describe acceptable door positions and operation. Requirements like these influence the size and position of the base.

Choosing the tile before finalizing the design lets you size the base to require mostly or only full tiles. Consider using small tile and create a color graduation from top to bottom or in a sweep across the walls. Or, use trim tile and listellos on the walls to create an interesting focal point.

Whatever tile you choose, remember to seal the grout in your new shower and to maintain it carefully over the years. Water-resistant grout protects the structure of the shower and prolongs its useful life.

Tools & Materials ▸

- Tape measure
- Circular saw
- Hammer
- Utility knife
- Stapler
- 2-ft. level
- Mortar mixing box
- Trowel
- Wood float
- Felt-tip marker
- Ratchet wrench
- Expandable stopper
- Drill
- Tin snips
- Torpedo level
- Tools & materials for installing tile
- 2 × 4 and 2 × 10 framing lumber
- 16d galvanized common nails
- 15# building paper
- 3-piece shower drain
- PVC primer & cement
- Galvanized finish nails
- Galvanized metal lath
- Thick-bed floor mortar
- Latex mortar additive
- CPE waterproof membrane & preformed dam corners
- CPE membrane solvent glue
- CPE membrane sealant
- Cementboard & materials

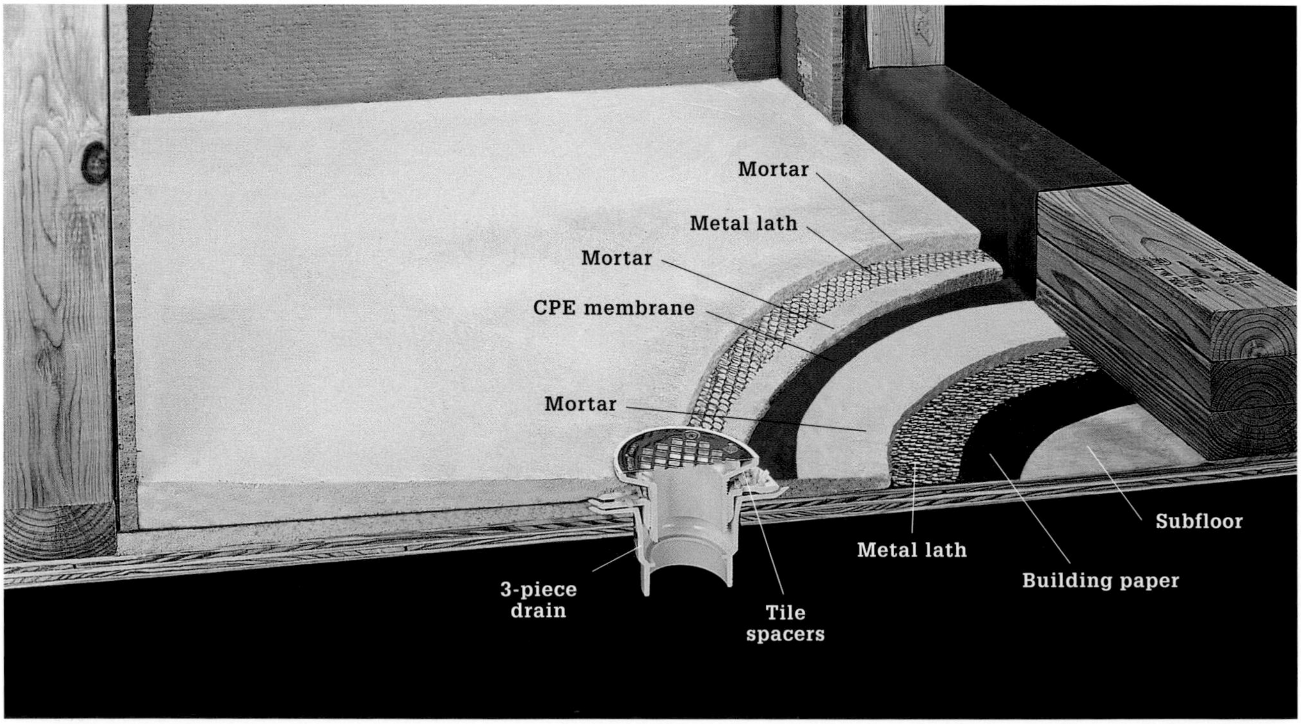

A custom shower base is built in three layers to ensure proper drainage: the underlayment, the shower pan, and the shower floor.

How to Build a Custom-tiled Shower Base

Remove building materials to expose subfloor and stud walls. Cut three 2 × 4s for the curb and fasten them to the floor joists and the studs at the shower threshold with 16d galvanized common nails. Also cut 2 × 10 lumber to size and install in the stud bays around the perimeter of the shower base. Install (or have installed) drain and supply plumbing.

Staple 15-pound building paper to the subfloor of the shower base. Disassemble the 3-piece shower drain and glue the bottom piece to the drain pipe with PVC cement. Partially screw the drain bolts into the drain piece, and stuff a rag into the drain pipe to prevent mortar from falling into the drain.

Mark the height of the bottom drain piece on the wall farthest from the center of the drain. Measure from the center of the drain straight across to that wall, then raise the height mark ¼" for every 12" of shower floor to slope the pre pan toward the drain. Trace a reference line at the height mark around the perimeter of the entire alcove, using a level.

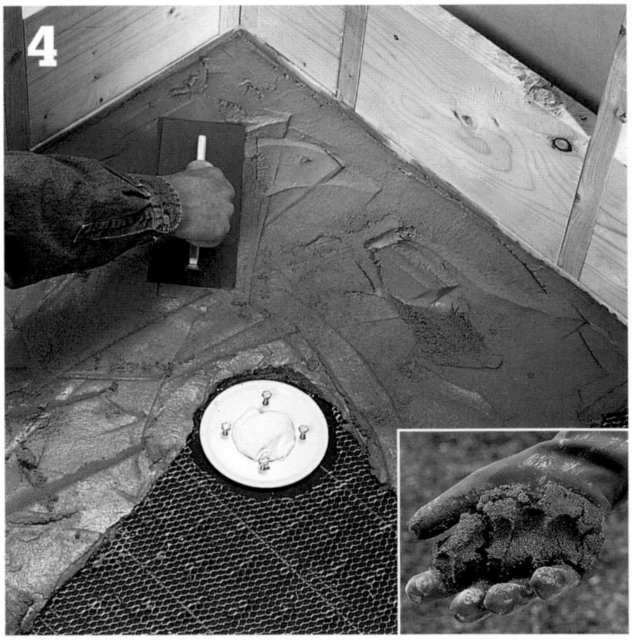

Staple galvanized metal lath over the building paper; cut a hole in the lath ½" from the drain. Mix thinset mortar to a fairly dry consistency, using a latex additive for strength; mortar should hold its shape when squeezed (inset). Trowel the mortar onto the subfloor, building the pre pan from the flange of the drain piece to the height line on the perimeter of the walls.

(continued)

Continue using the trowel to form the pre pan, checking the slope using a level and filling any low spots with mortar. Finish the surface of the pre pan with a wood float until it is even and smooth. Allow the mortar to cure overnight.

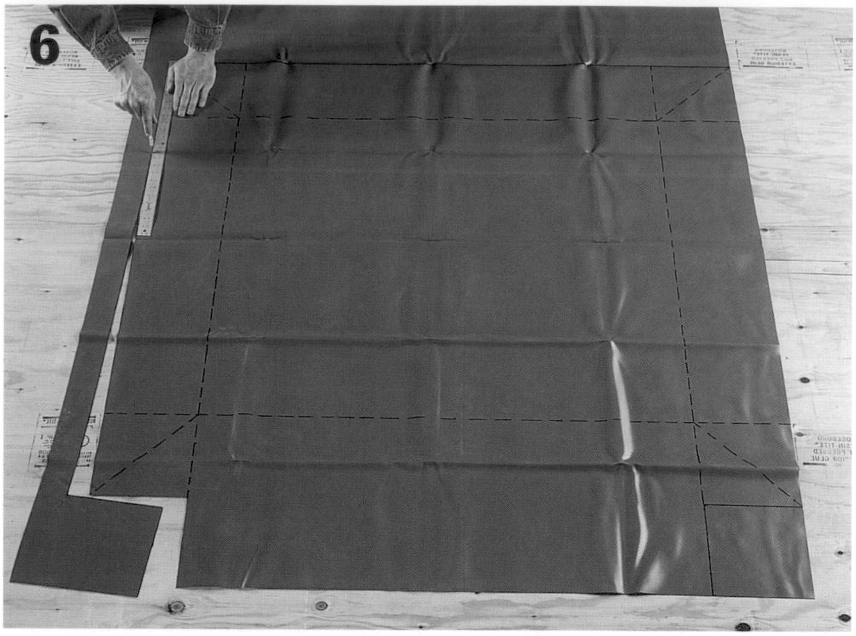

Measure the dimensions of the shower floor, and mark it out on a sheet of CPE waterproof membrane, using a felt-tipped marker. From the floor outline, measure out and mark an additional 8" for each wall and 16" for the curb end. Cut the membrane to size, using a utility knife and straightedge. Be careful to cut on a clean, smooth surface to prevent puncturing the membrane. Lay the membrane onto the shower pan.

Measure to find the exact location of the drain and mark it on the membrane, outlining the outer diameter of the drain flange. Cut a circular piece of CPE membrane roughly 2" larger than the drain flange, then use CPE membrane solvent glue to weld it into place and reinforce the seal at the drain.

Apply CPE sealant around the drain. Fold the membrane along the floor outline. Set the membrane over the pre pan so the reinforced drain seal is centered over the drain bolts. Working from the drain to the walls, carefully tuck the membrane tight into each corner, folding the extra material into triangular flaps.

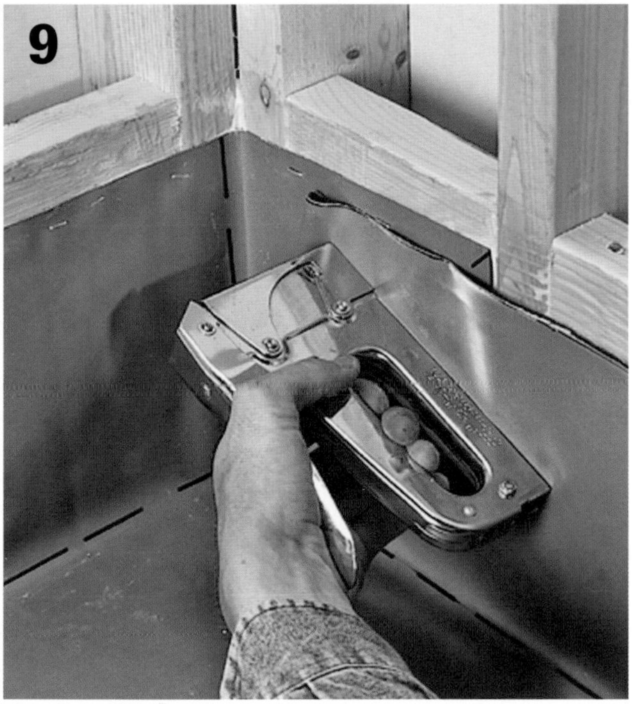

Apply CPE solvent glue to one side, press the flap flat, then staple it in place. Staple only the top edge of the membrane to the blocking; do not staple below the top of the curb, or on the curb itself.

At the shower curb, cut the membrane along the studs so it can be folded over the curb. Solvent glue a dam corner at each inside corner of the curb. Do not fasten the dam corners with staples.

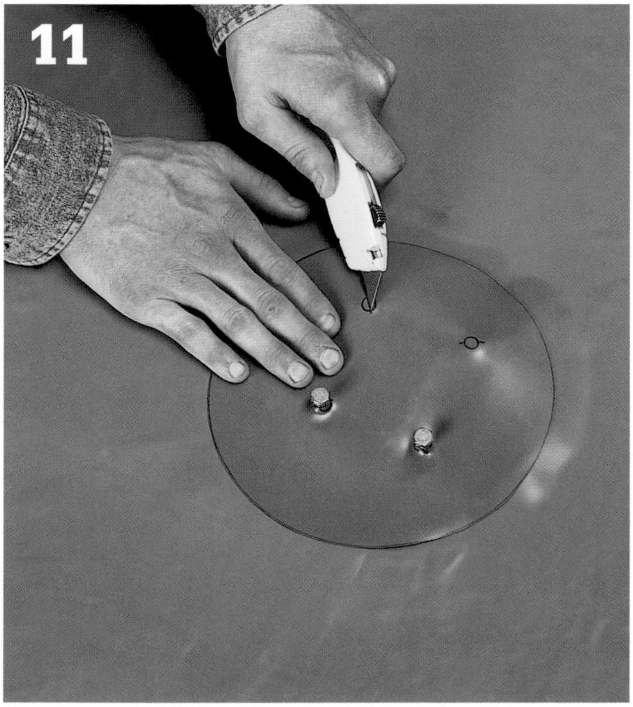

At the reinforced drain seal on the membrane, locate and mark the drain bolts. Press the membrane down around the bolts, then use a utility knife to carefully cut a slit just large enough for the bolts to poke through. Push the membrane down over the bolts.

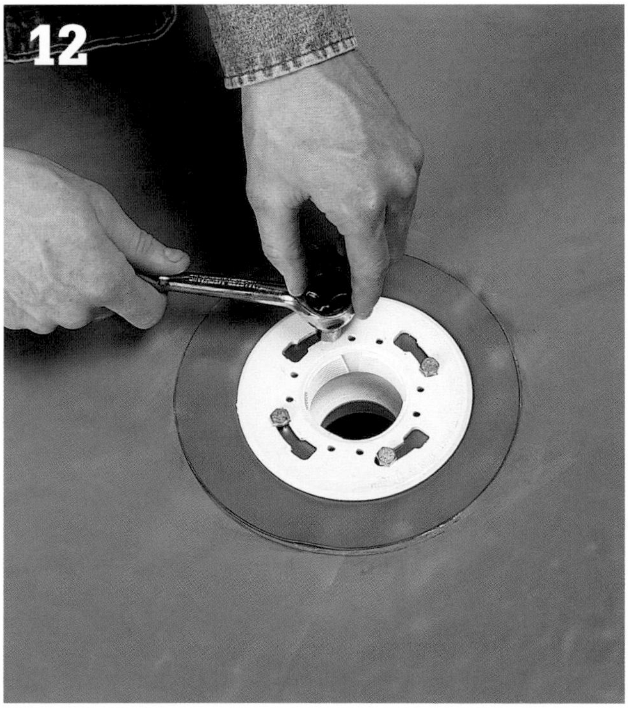

Use a utility knife to carefully cut away only enough of the membrane to expose the drain and allow the middle drain piece to fit in place. Remove the drain bolts, then position the middle drain piece over the bolt holes. Reinstall the bolts, tightening them evenly and firmly to create a watertight seal.

(continued)

Test the shower pan for leaks overnight. Fill the shower pan with water, to 1" below the top of the curb. Mark the water level and let the water sit overnight. If the water level remains the same, the pan holds water. If the level is lower, locate and fix leaks in the pan using patches of membrane and CPE solvent.

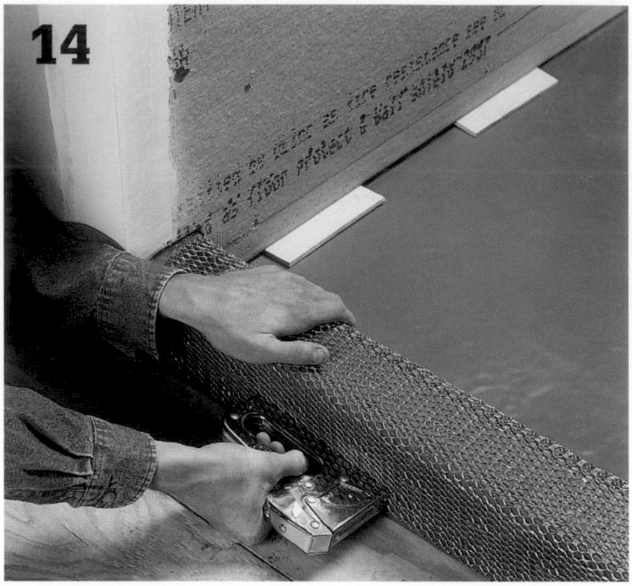

Install cementboard on the alcove walls, using ¼" wood shims to lift the bottom edge off the CPE membrane. To prevent puncturing the membrane, do not use fasteners in the lower 8" of the cementboard. Cut a piece of metal lath to fit around the three sides of the curb. Bend the lath so it tightly conforms to the curb. Pressing the lath against the top of the curb, staple it to the outside face of the curb. Mix enough mortar for the two sides of the curb.

Overhang the front edge of the curb with a straight 1× board so it is flush with the outer wall material. Apply mortar to the mesh with a trowel, building to the edge of the board. Clear away excess mortar; then use a torpedo level to check for plumb, making adjustments as needed. Repeat for the inside face of the curb. *Note: The top of the curb will be finished after tile is installed (Step 19). Allow the mortar to cure overnight.*

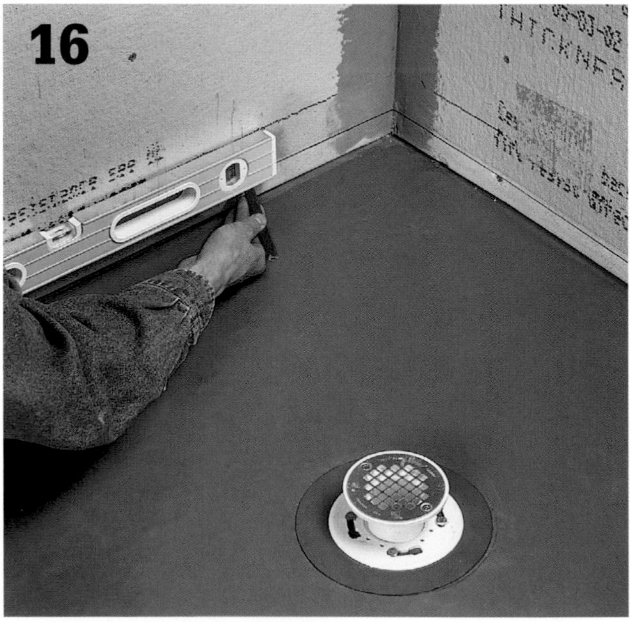

Attach the drain strainer piece to the drain, adjusting it to a minimum of 1½" above the shower pan. On one wall, mark 1½" up from the shower pan, then use a level to draw a reference line around the perimeter of the shower base. Because the pre pan establishes the ¼" per foot slope, this measurement will maintain that slope.

Spread tile spacers over the weep holes of the drain to prevent mortar from plugging the holes. Mix the floor mortar, then build up the shower floor to roughly half the planned thickness of this layer. Cut metal lath to cover the mortar bed, keeping it ½" from the drain (see photo in Step 18).

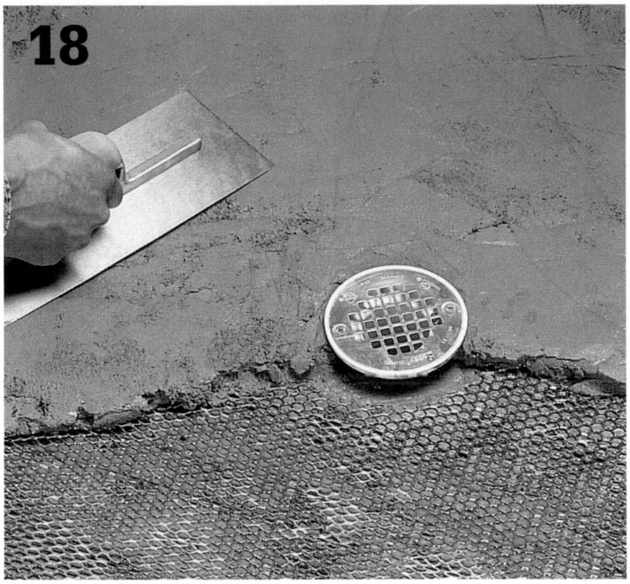

Continue to add mortar, building the floor to the reference line on the walls. Use a level to check the slope, and pack mortar into low spots with a trowel. Leave space around the drain flange for the thickness of the tile. Float the surface using a wood float until it is smooth and slopes evenly to the drain. When finished, allow the mortar to cure overnight before installing the tiles.

Install the tile. At the curb, cut the tiles for the inside to protrude ½" above the unfinished top of the curb, and the tiles for the outside to protrude ⅝" above the top, establishing a ⅛" slope so water drains back into the shower. Use a level to check the tops of the tiles for level as you work.

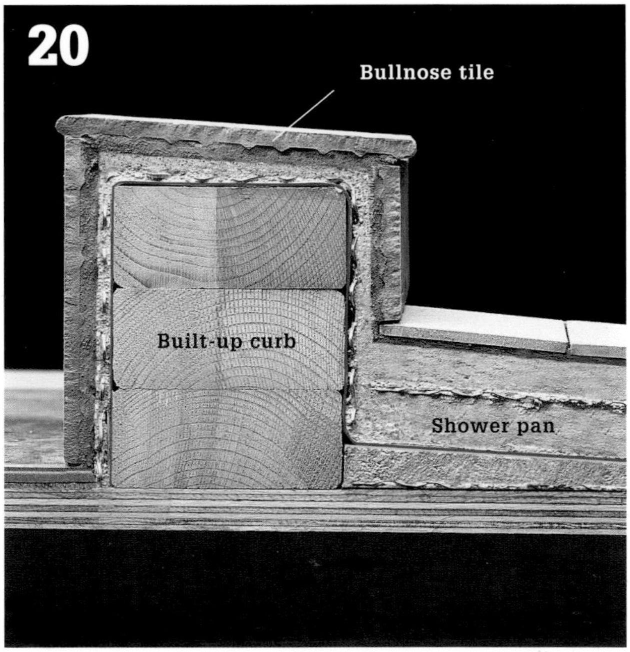

Mix enough mortar to cover the unfinished top of the curb, then pack it in place between the tiles, using a trowel. Screed off the excess mortar flush with the tops of the side tiles. Allow the mortar to cure, then install bullnose cap tile. Install the wall tile, then grout, clean, and seal all the tile. After the grout has cured fully, run a bead of silicone caulk around all inside corners to create control joints.

Glass Block Showers

Glass block has been a popular building material for nearly a century. Its unique combination of strength, transparency, and beauty make it the perfect solution for brightening a space without giving up privacy or security. And those same characteristics make glass block ideal for shower enclosures: it creates a washable, waterproof barrier that lets plenty of light into the shower while obscuring bathers from view.

Glass blocks come in several sizes, including 8" and 12" square blocks and 6 × 8" rectangular units. The standard thickness of blocks is about 4". As with brick and other masonry units, the nominal size of glass block includes an allowance for the mortar joints. An 8" square block actually measures 7¾" square, allowing for ¼"-thick mortar joints in the finished wall. Unlike standard masonry, glass block cannot be cut, so be sure to lay out your walls carefully, and do a dry run with the actual blocks (and using spacers to represent mortar joints) to make sure everything fits. Specialty blocks are available to let you turn corners, create curves, or finish the exposed ends or tops of walls.

Tools & Materials ▸

- 4-ft. level
- 2-ft. level
- Drill
- Mixing box or bucket
- Pointed (brick) trowel
- Rubber mallet
- Jointing tool
- Sponge
- Caulking gun
- Glass blocks
- Shower base
- Wall ties
- Track
- Plastic glass block spacers
- Glass block mortar
- Foam expansion strips
- Flat 1× board
- ⅜" and ¼" scrap wood
- Glass block panel anchors and reinforcing wire
- 2" corrosion-resistant screws and washers
- Nonsag polyurethane sealant

Adding Color ▸

To give your glass block wall a colorful accent, spray paint the edges of the block prior to setting the blocks in place.

Real glass block creates a beautiful, light-filled shower with low-maintenance walls that are far more elegant than a shower curtain or a flimsy glass-paned enclosure. Blocks are available with various patterns and textures for special light effects and different levels of privacy (inset).

Planning a Glass Block Shower ▸

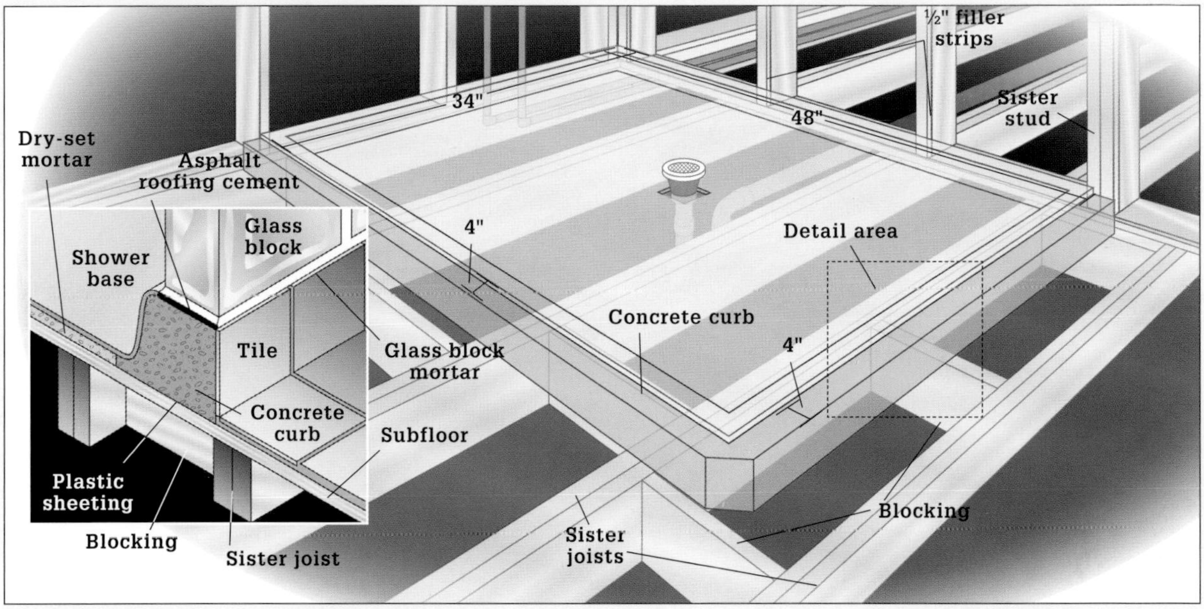

Install water supply and drain pipes before you begin the construction of the glass block shower. If you have to adjust the position of your base to fit the block wall, take this into account as you mark the location for the shower drain.

Reinforcement ▸

Reinforcement

A glass block installation must be anchored to a supporting wall stud on at least one end by means of panel anchors.

The block is mortared to its supporting base (see right) but not to the adjoining walls or ceiling—at these locations, foam expansion strips allow for movement between the adjoining structures.

Ladder-like reinforcement wire set into the mortar between alternating courses strengthens the block wall internally.

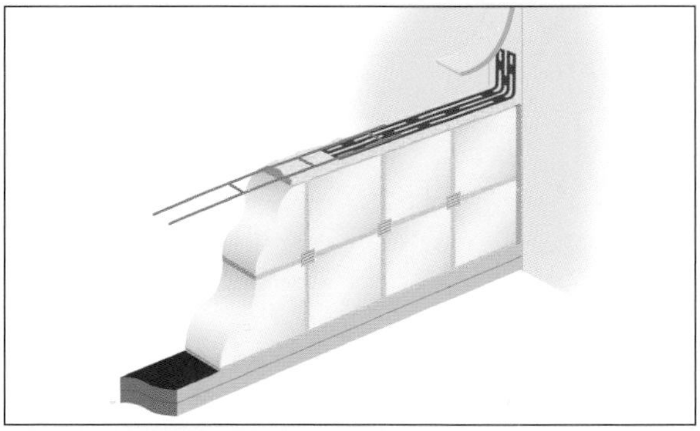

Glass Block Mortar Mix Calculator ▸

NUMBER OF BLOCKS	6" BLOCK # OF BAGS REQUIRED*	8" BLOCK # OF BAGS REQUIRED*	12" # OF BAGS REQUIRED*
40	1	2	2
100	3	4	5
200	5	7	10
500	13	16	25

*50-lb bags

How to Build a Glass Block Shower Wall

Build the shower base with curb (see illustration, previous page) or install a custom-order manufactured shower base with integral glass block curb following the manufacturer's directions. Here, a custom concrete curb and lined shower receptor have been installed.

Lay out the project area. Using a 4-ft. level, draw a plumb line onto the wall to represent the inside (or outside) face of the glass block wall.

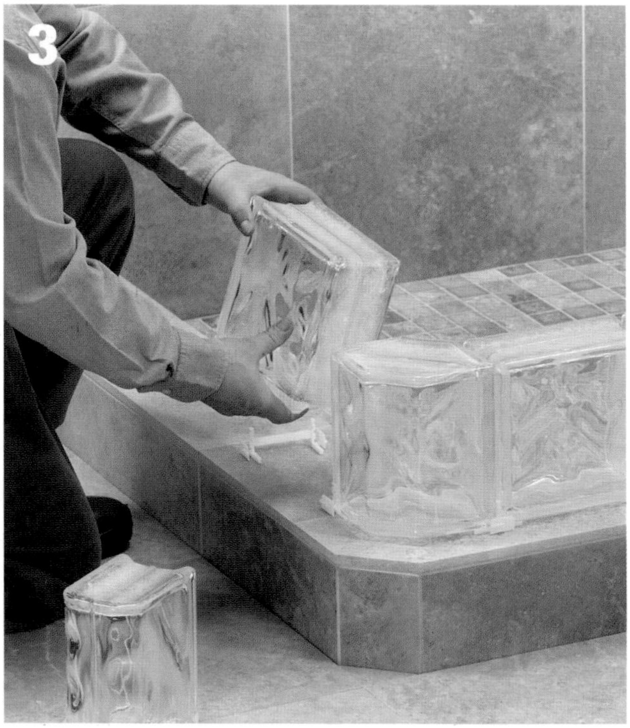

Dry-lay the first course of glass blocks to establish a layout and so you can mark the height of the first course on the wall or walls you'll be fastening the glass block wall to.

Install wall ties to the walls after every other course. Use wall anchors to secure the ties, and make sure the ties will reach past at least two glass block units in the layout.

Add $\frac{3}{8}$"-thick foam expansion strips between the panel anchors on the supporting wall, cutting them to fit if necessary. You can use daubs of caulk or sealant behind the strips to keep them in place.

Mix a batch of glass-block mortar following the product directions. A stiff mix is easiest to work with, so add water carefully to achieve the driest recommended consistency. (As you work, mix only enough mortar as you can use in about 30 minutes.)

Spread a $\frac{3}{8}$"-thick full mortar bed along the curb for the first few blocks using a pointed trowel. Do not furrow the mortar. Set the first block into the mortar using spacers at the wall and curb. Tap the block with a rubber mallet or trowel handle to set it into the mortar.

Butter one edge of the next block with a $\frac{3}{8}$"- to $\frac{1}{2}$"-thick layer of mortar. Install the block using a T-spacer, and push it against the first block to create a $\frac{1}{4}$" mortar joint. Install the third block in the same manner.

(continued)

Check the blocks with a level as you work to make sure each one is plumb, level, and aligned with the other blocks. Tap the blocks with the mallet or trowel handle to adjust them. You can set a flat board across several blocks to check for level and make adjustments.

When the first course is complete, fill any low spots at the tops of the joints with mortar. Set the spacers for the next course, then lay a full ⅜"-thick mortar bed. Install the second course of block, checking your work with a level.

Using Glass Block Spacers ▸

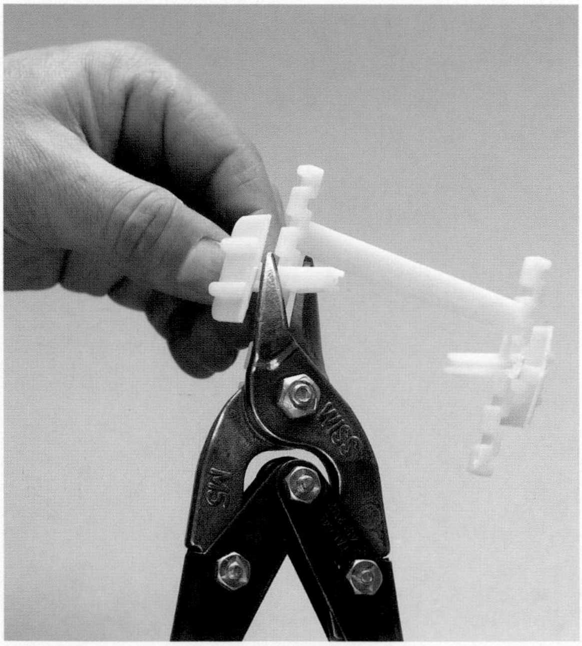

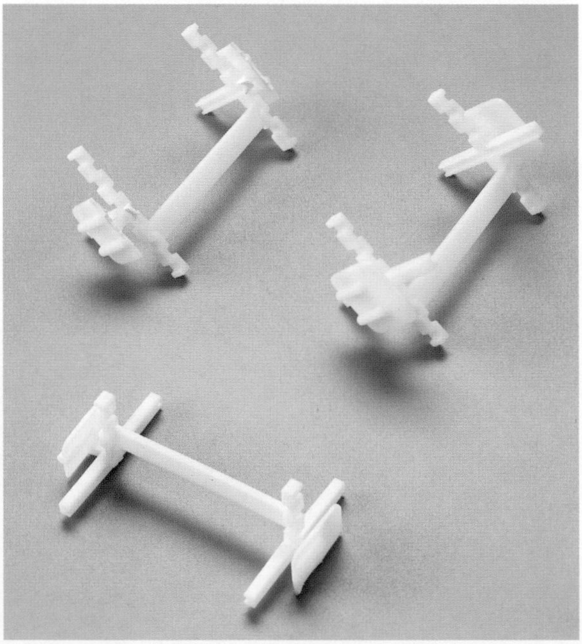

Full spacers help maintain joint spacing where four glass blocks meet. To use spacers where blocks adjoin a wall, ceiling, or curb, break off the side tabs, then trim off two of the spacer legs to create T-spacers. For the outside corners of a wall, trim off four legs to create L-spacers.

Lay down a half-thickness mortar bed for the third course, and then set the first panel anchor into the mortar. Cut a length of glass block reinforcement track to span the wall, and set it into the mortar, overlapping the anchor by 6". Add the other half of the mortar over the wire and anchors, and install the next course of block.

Clean up the joints. When the mortar in the lower courses is hard enough to resist light finger pressure (typically within 30 minutes), twist off the T-spacer tabs and pack mortar into the voids. Smooth the joints with a glass block jointing tool. Fill in low spots with mortar and remove excess and spilled mortar with a soft brush or damp sponge, rinsing frequently.

Clean as you go. As you complete each row (about 30 minutes after tooling the joints), clean and smooth the joints with a wet tile setter's sponge, rinsing frequently. After the wall is complete, remove the cloudy residue from the blocks using a clean, dry cloth, and then buff with a piece of scrap carpeting.

Let the mortar cure for at least 24 hours, and then seal around the glass block wall(s) with silicone sealant or non-sag polyurethane sealant. Apply a sealant to the mortar joints, if desired, following the manufacturer's directions.

Alcove Bathtubs

Most of our homes are equipped with an alcove tub that includes a tub surround and shower function. By combining the tub and the shower in one fixture, you conserve precious bathroom floorspace and simplify the initial installation. Plus, you only have one bathing fixture that needs cleaning.

But because tub/showers are so efficient, they do get a lot of use and tend to have fairly limited lifespans. The fact that the most inexpensive tubs on the market are designed for alcove use also reduces the average tub/shower lifespan. Pressed steel tubs have enamel finishes that crack and craze; plastic and fiberglass tubs get grimy and stained; even acrylic and composite tubs show wear eventually (and as with other fixtures, styles and colors change too).

Plumbing an alcove tub is a relatively difficult job because getting access to the drain lines attached to the tub and into the floor is often very awkward. Although an access panel is required by most codes, the truth is that many tubs were installed without them or with panels that are too small or hard to reach to be of much use. If you are contemplating replacing your tub, the first step in the decision process should be to find the access panel and determine if it is sufficient. If it is not (or there is no panel at all), consider how you might enlarge it. Often, this means cutting a hole in the wall on the adjoining room and also in the ceiling below. This creates more work, of course, but compared to the damage caused by a leaky drain from a subpar installation, making an access opening is little inconvenience.

Tools & Materials ▸

- Channel-type pliers
- Hacksaw
- Carpenter's level
- Pencil
- Tape measure
- Saw
- Screwdriver
- Drill
- Adjustable wrench
- Trowel
- Shims
- Galvanized deck screws
- Drain-waste-overflow kit
- 1 × 3, 1 × 4, 2 × 4 lumber
- Galvanized roofing nails
- Galvanized roof flashing
- Thinset mortar
- Tub & tile caulk
- Propane torch

A tub alcove is sized to accept a standard bathtub, usually 5 ft. long in most of North America. A tub with an apron is typical, but you can build out the front instead if you choose.

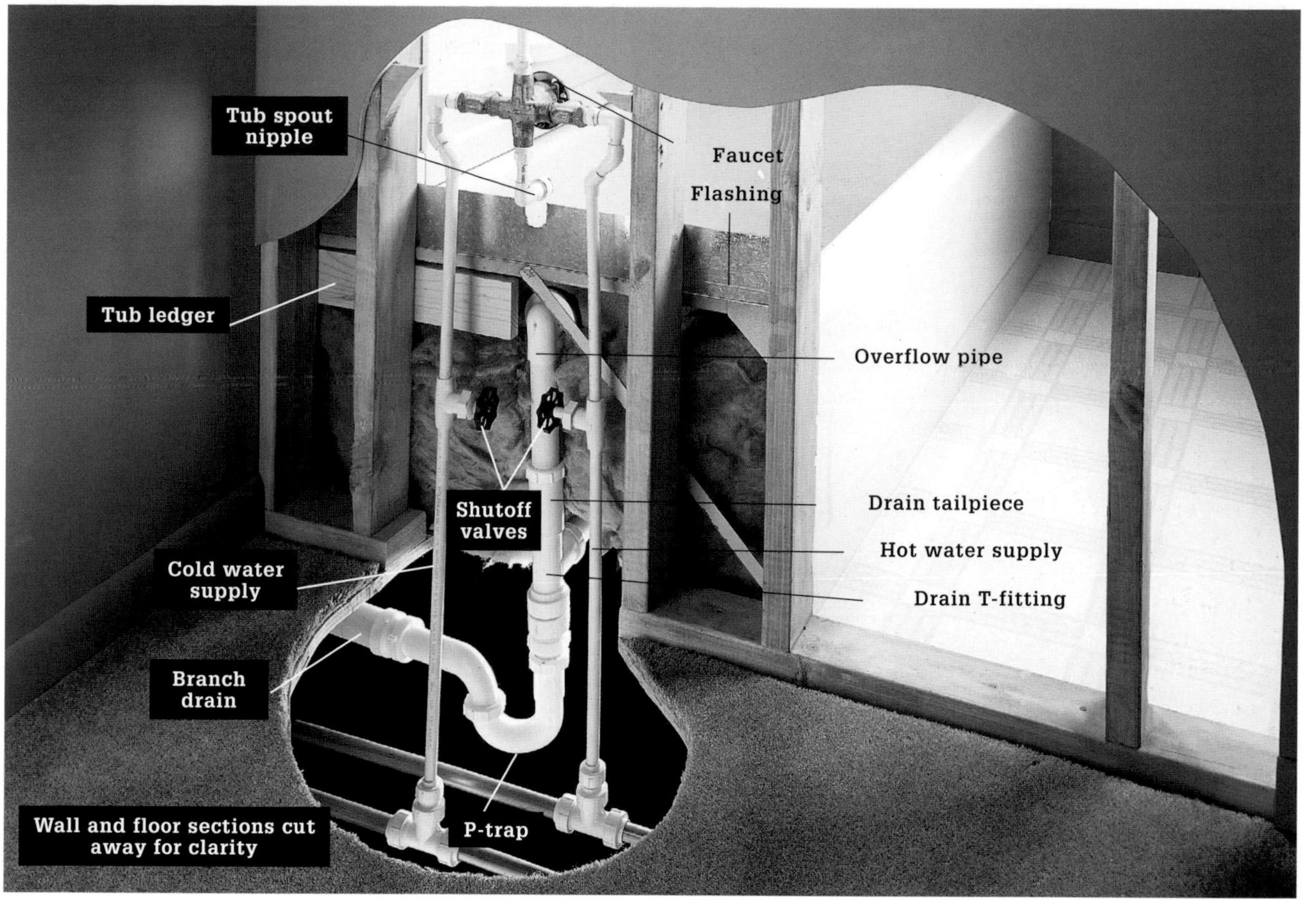

The plumbing for a bathtub includes hot and cold supply pipes, shutoff valves, faucet, and a spout. Supply connections can be made before or after the tub is installed. The drain-waste-overflow system for a bathtub includes the overflow pipe, drain T-fitting, P-trap, and branch drain. The overflow pipe assembly is attached to the tub before installation.

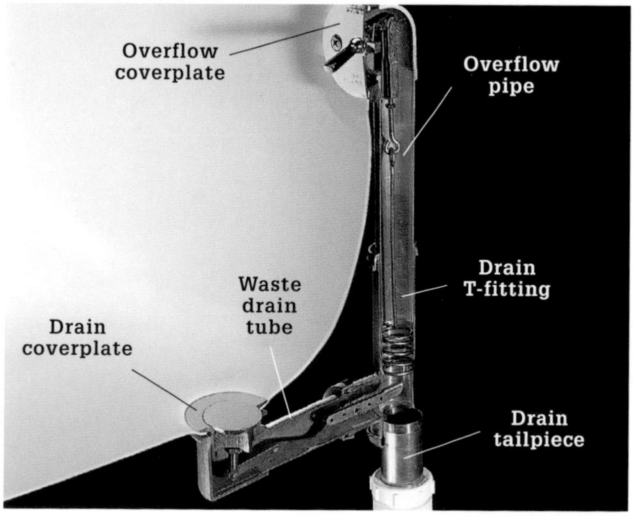

A drain-waste-overflow kit with a stopper mechanism must be attached to the tub before it is installed. Available in both brass and plastic types, most kits include an overflow coverplate, a height-adjustable overflow pipe, a drain T-fitting and tailpiece, a waste drain tube, and a drain coverplate that screws into the drain tube.

Add fiberglass insulation around the body of a steel bathtub to reduce noise and conserve heat. Before setting the tub in position, wrap unfaced batting around the tub, and secure it with string or twine. For showers, deck-mounted whirlpools, and saunas, insulate between the framing members.

How to Install a New Alcove Tub

Prepare for the new tub. Inspect and remove old or deteriorated wall surfaces or framing members in the tub area. With today's mold-resistant wallboard products, it makes extra sense to go ahead and strip off the old alcove wallcoverings and ceiling down to the studs so you can replace them. This also allows you to inspect for hidden damage in the wall and ceiling cavities.

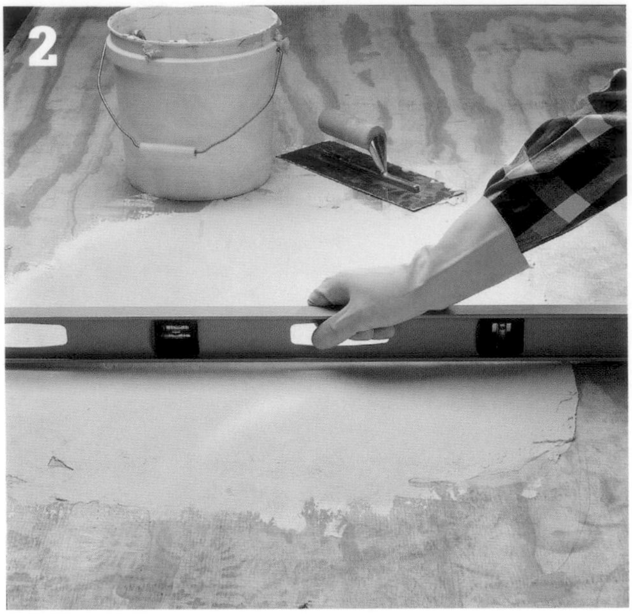

Check the subfloor for level—if it is not level, use pour-on floor leveler compound to correct it (ask at your local flooring store). Make sure the supply and drain pipes and the shutoff valves are in good repair and correct any problems you encounter. If you have no bath fan in the alcove, now is the perfect time to add one.

Check the height of the crossbraces for the faucet body and the showerhead. If your family members needed to stoop to use the old shower, consider raising the brace for the showerhead. Read the instructions for your new faucet/diverter and check to see that the brace for the faucet body will conform to the requirements (this includes distance from the surround wall as well as height). Adjust the brace locations as needed.

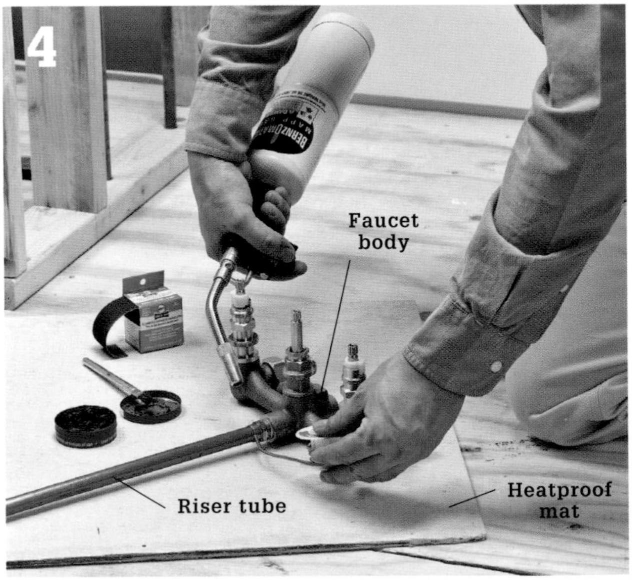

Begin by installing the new water supply plumbing. Measure to determine the required height of your shower riser tube and cut it to length. Attach the bottom of the riser to the faucet body and the top to the shower elbow.

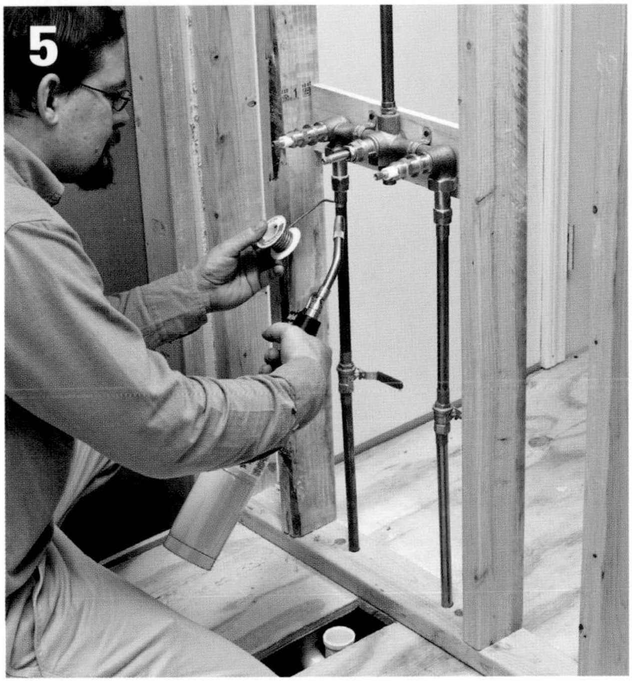

Attach the faucet body to the cross brace with pipe hanger straps. Then, attach supply tubing from the stop valves to the faucet body, making sure to attach the hot water to the left port and cold to the right port. Also secure the shower elbow to its cross brace with a pipe strap. Do not attach the shower arm yet.

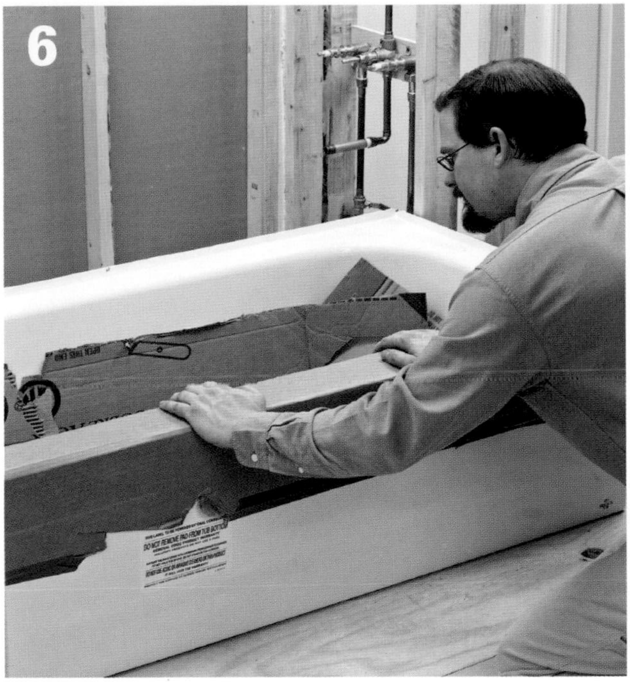

Slide the bathtub into the alcove. Make sure tub is flat on the floor and pressed flush against the back wall. If your tub did not come with a tub protector, cut a piece of cardboard to line the tub bottom, and tape pieces of cardboard around the rim to protect the finish from shoes and dropped tools.

Mark locations for ledger boards. To do this, trace the height of the top of the tub's nailing flange onto the wall studs in the alcove. Then remove the tub and measure the height of the nailing flange. Measure down this same amount from your flange lines and mark new ledger board location.

Install 1 × 4 ledger boards. Drive two or three 3"-galvanized deck screws through the ledger board at each stud. All three walls should receive a ledger. Leave an open space in the wet wall to allow clearance for the DWO kit.

(continued)

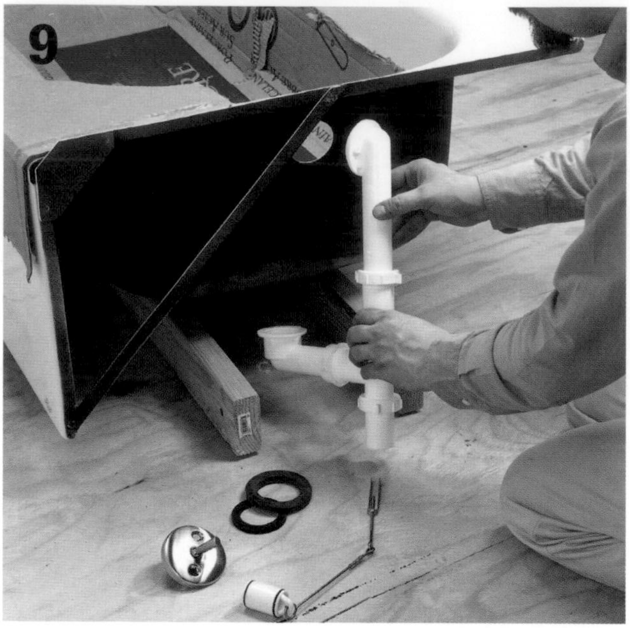

Install the drain-waste-overflow (DWO) pipes before you install the tub. Make sure to get a good seal on the slip nuts at the pipe joints. Follow the manufacturer's instructions to make sure the pop-up drain linkage is connected properly. Make sure rubber gaskets are positioned correctly at the openings on the outside of the tub.

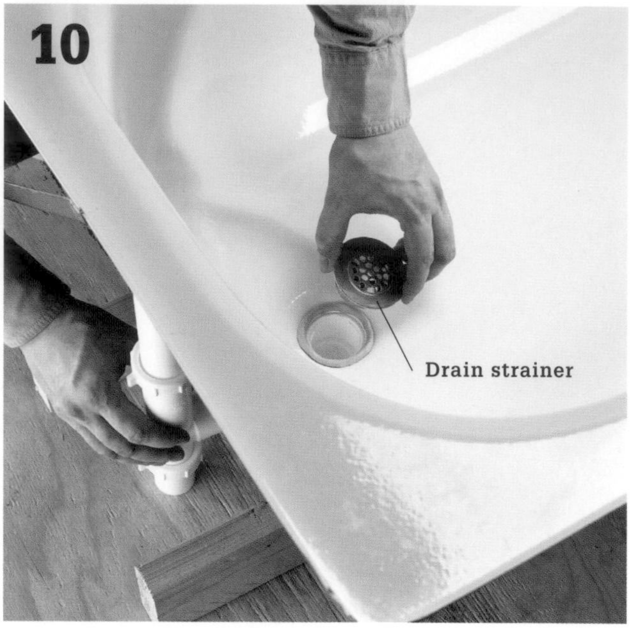

Thread the male-threaded drain strainer into the female-threaded drain waste elbow. Wrap a coil of plumber's putty around the drain outlet underneath the plug rim first. Hand tighten only.

Attach the overflow coverplate, making sure the pop-up drain controls are in the correct position. Tighten the mounting screws that connect to the mounting plate to sandwich the rubber gasket snugly between the overflow pipe flange and the tub wall. Then, finish tightening the drain strainer against the waste elbow by inserting the handle of a pair of pliers into the strainer body and turning.

Place the tub back into the alcove, taking care not to bump the DWO assembly and disturb the connections. You definitely will want a helper for this job. If the drain outlet of the DWO assembly is not directly over the drain pipe when the tub is in position, you'll need to remove it and adjust the drain line location.

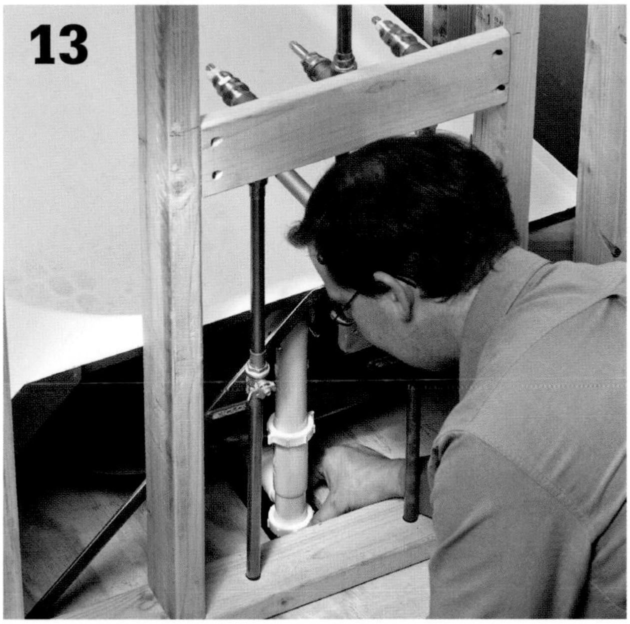

Attach the drain outlet from the DWO assembly to the drain P-trap. If your alcove walls are covered, you will appreciate that you spent the time to create a roomy access panel for the tub plumbing. Test the drain and overflow to make sure they don't leak. Also test the water supply plumbing, temporarily attaching the handles, spout, and shower arm so you can operate the faucet and the diverter.

Drive a $1\frac{1}{2}$" galvanized roofing nail at each stud location, just over the top of the tub's nailing flange (inset). The nail head should pin the flange to the stud. For extra protection against moisture penetration, nail strips of metal flashing to the studs so they cover the tub flange.

Install the wallcoverings and tub surround (see pages 104 to 107 for a 3-piece surround installation). You can also make a custom surround from tileboard or cementboard and tile.

Install fittings. First, thread the shower arm into the shower elbow and attach the spout nipple to the valve assembly. Also attach the shower head and escutcheon, the faucet handle/diverter with escutcheon, and the tub spout. Use thread lubricant on all parts.

3-Piece Tub Surrounds

No one wants bathroom fixtures that are aging or yellowed from years of use. A shiny new tub surround can add sparkle and freshness to your dream bath.

Tub surrounds come in many different styles, materials, and price ranges. Choose the features you want and measure your existing bathtub surround for sizing. Surrounds typically come in three or five pieces. A three-panel surround is being installed here, but the process is similar for five-panel systems.

Surface preparation is important for good glue adhesion. Plastic tiles and wallpaper must be removed and textured plaster must be sanded smooth. Surrounds can be installed over ceramic tile that is well attached and in good condition, but it must be sanded and primed. All surfaces must be primed with a water-based primer.

Tools & Materials ▸

- Jigsaw
- Hole saw
- Drill
- Measuring tape
- Level
- Caulking gun
- Adhesive
- Screwdriver
- Adjustable wrench
- Pry bar
- Hammer
- 3-piece tub surround

Three-piece tub surrounds are inexpensive and come in many colors and styles. The typical unit has two end panels and a back panel that overlap in the corners to form a watertight seal. They are formed from fiberglass, PVC, acrylic, or proprietary resin-based polymers. Five-piece versions are also available and typically have more features such as integral soap shelves and even cabinets.

How to Install a 3-Piece Tub Surround

Remove the old plumbing fixtures and wallcoverings in the tub area. In some cases you can attach surround panels to old tileboard or even tile, but it is generally best to remove the wallcoverings down to the studs if you can, so you may inspect for leaks or damage.

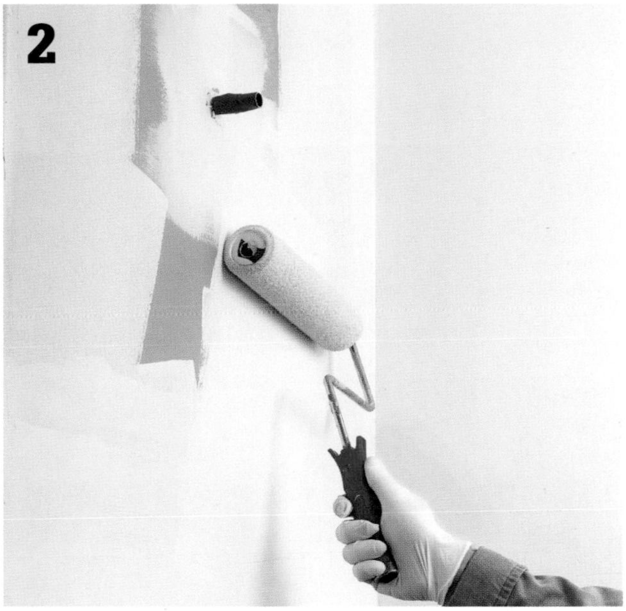

Replace the wallcoverings with appropriate materials, such as water and mold resistant wallboard or cementboard (for ceramic tile installations). Make sure the new wall surfaces are smooth and flat. Some surround kit manufacturers recommend that you apply a coat of primer to sheet goods such as greenboard to create a better bonding surface for the panel adhesive.

Test-fit the panels before you start; the tub may have settled unevenly or the walls may be out of plumb. Check the manufacturer's directions for distinguishing right and left panels. Place a panel in position on the tub ledge. Use a level across the top of the panel to determine if it is level. Create a vertical reference line to mark the edge of the panel on the plumbing end.

Test-fitting ▸

Ensure a perfect fit by taping the surround panels to the walls in the tub area. Make sure the tops are level when the overlap seams are aligned and that you have a consistent gap between the panel bottoms and the tub flange. Mark the panels for cutting if necessary and, once the panels have been removed, make any adjustments to the walls that are needed.

(continued)

After performing the testfit, check the fitting instructions to see if you need to trim any of the pieces. Follow the manufacturer's instructions for cutting. Here, we had to cut the corner panels because the instructions advise not to overlap the back or side panel over the corner panels by more than 3". Cut panels using a jigsaw and a fine-tooth blade that is appropriate for cutting fiberglass or acrylic tileboard.

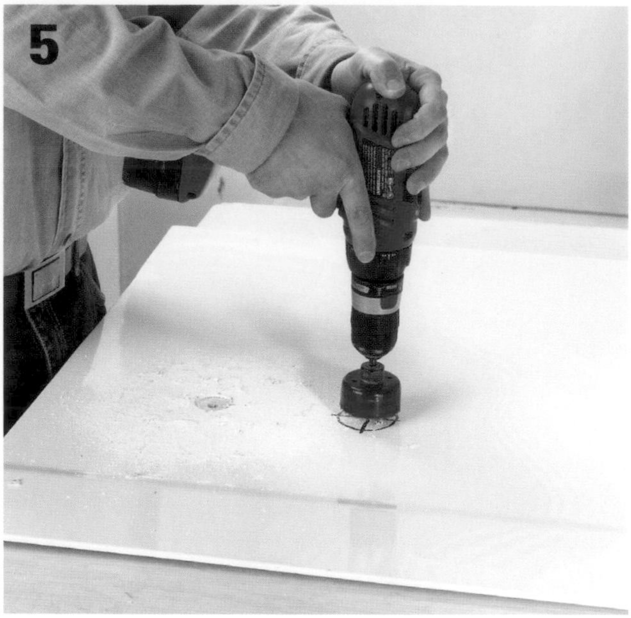

Lay out the locations of the faucets, spout, and shower arm. Measure in from the vertical reference line (made in Step 3) and up from the top of the tub ledge. Re-measure for accuracy, as any cuts to the surround are final. Place the panel face-up on a sheet of plywood. Mark the location of the holes. Cut the holes ½" larger than the pipe diameter. If your faucet has a recessed trim plate, cut the hole to fit the recess. Using a hole saw or a jigsaw, cut out the plumbing access holes.

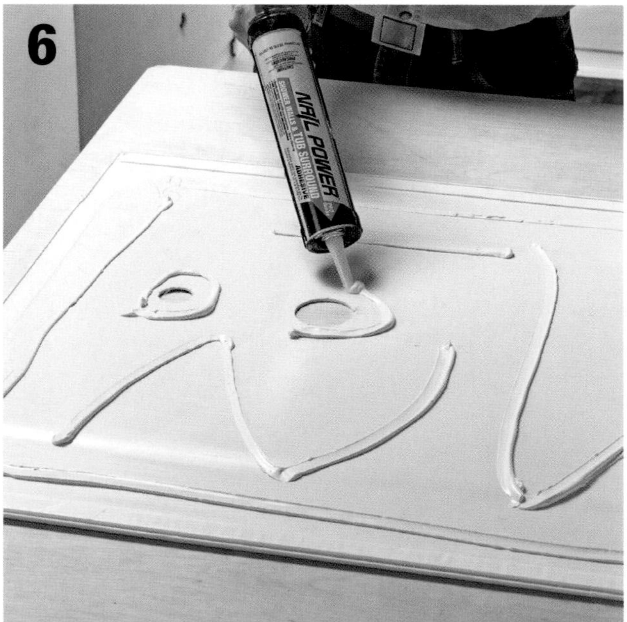

Apply the panel adhesive to the back of an end plumbing panel. Circle the plumbing outlet holes 1" from the edge. Follow the manufacturer's application pattern. Do not apply adhesive closer than 1" to the double-sided tape or the bottom edge of the panel.

Remove the protective backing from the tape. Carefully lift the panel by the edges and place against the corner and top of the tub ledge. Press firmly from top to bottom in the corner, then throughout the panel.

Test-fit the opposite end panel and make any necessary adjustments. Apply the adhesive, remove the protective backing from the tape, and put in place. Apply pressure to the corner first from top to bottom, and then apply pressure throughout.

Apply adhesive to the back panel following the manufacturer's instructions. Maintain a 1" space between adhesive tape and the bottom of the panel. Remove protective backing from the tape. Lift the panel by the edges and carefully center between the two end panels. When positioned, firmly press in place from top to bottom.

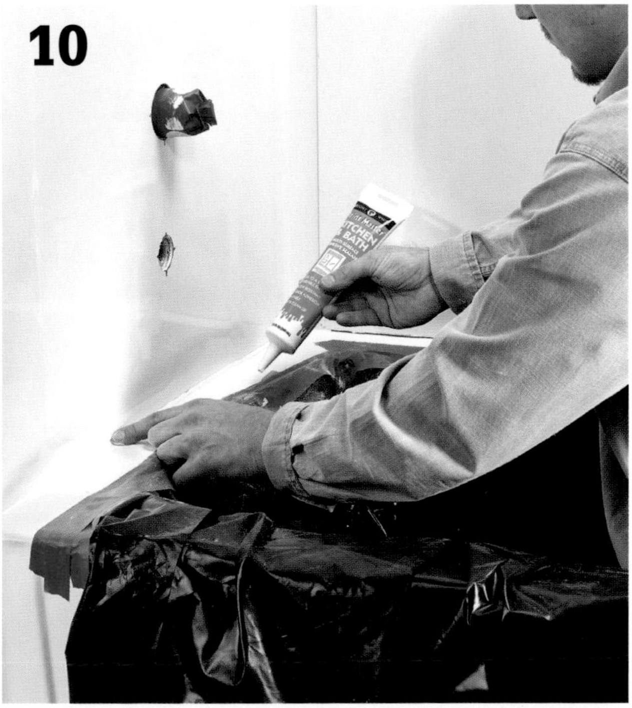

Apply caulk to the bottom and top edges of the panels and at panel joints. Dip your fingertip in water and use it to smooth the caulk to a uniform bead.

Apply silicone caulk to escutcheons or trim plates and reinstall them. Allow a minimum of 24 hours for caulk and adhesive to cure thoroughly before using the shower or tub.

Solid-Surface Surrounds

Bathtub surrounds are designed and installed in the same way as shower surrounds. Though fiberglass and plastic fabricated enclosures, as well as custom ceramic tile, are traditional materials for surrounds, the use of solid-surface materials—materials common to sinks and countertops—are growing in popularity.

Solid-surface surrounds are available in kits with ¼" panels that are installed much the same way as fiberglass enclosures. The panels can be fastened to any wall material—cementboard and greenboard are the most common in new construction. Walls must be free of debris and sealed with two coats of primer. Solid-surface panels can be installed over old tile, though you must chisel out any loose tiles and install filler strips the same thickness as the tiles (usually ¼") to fill any gaps between the walls and panels.

Tools & Materials ▸

- Tape measure
- 4-ft. level
- Jigsaw
- Drill with a hole saw or spade bits
- Caulk gun
- Solid-surface surround kit
- Sandpaper
- Pressure-sensitive tape
- Panel adhesive
- Tub & tile caulk
- Masking tape
- 1× and 2× lumber

Solid-surface bathtub surrounds are becoming ever-more popular and are available as kits.

How to Install a Solid-Surface Bathtub Surround

Begin panel installation with the back wall. Measure and mark the dimensions on the back side of the panel, then cut using a jigsaw (left photo). Remove rough edges with fine or medium sandpaper. Test-fit the panel to ensure a proper fit. On the back side of the panel, apply pressure-sensitive tape 1" from each edge, then apply panel adhesive in the field (right photo). Keep the adhesive 1" from the tape edges.

Remove the backing of the pressure-sensitive tape. Lift the panel into position, tight into one corner, then firmly press the panel to the wall. Using your hands, smooth across the entire panel while applying pressure to ensure firm contact with the wall. Follow the same procedures to install the panel on the side wall, opposite the plumbing outlets.

For the wall with the plumbing outlets, measure and trim the panel to size. Measure the location of the plumbing outlets on the wall, then transfer the dimensions to the finished side of the panel. Drill holes ½" larger than the plumbing outlets, using a drill and a hole saw or spade bits. Place a scrap board beneath the cutout area to ensure a clean cut.

Test-fit the panel and make any necessary adjustments, then install, following the same procedures as with the first two panels. After all the panels are installed, seal each joint, seam, and edge with a bead of caulk.

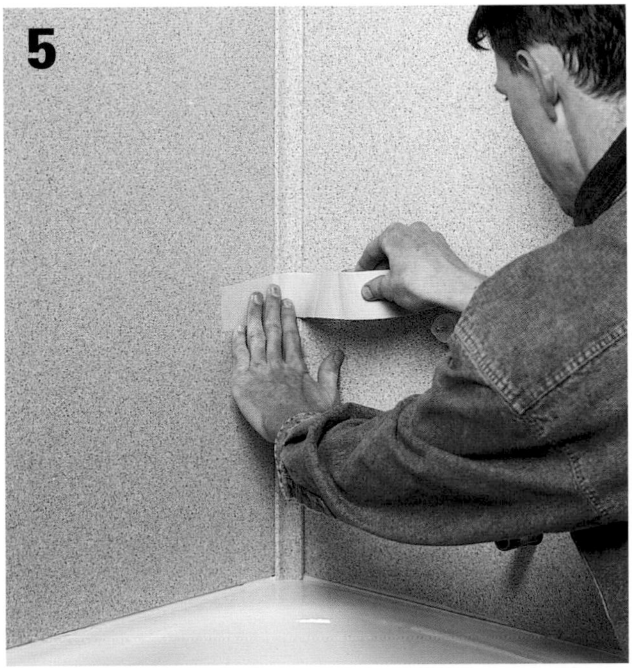

Follow the manufacturer's instructions to install any trim. For corner molding, test-fit each piece and trim to size, then apply a bead of panel adhesive down the corner joints and firmly press the moldings into position. Temporarily secure the molding with tape.

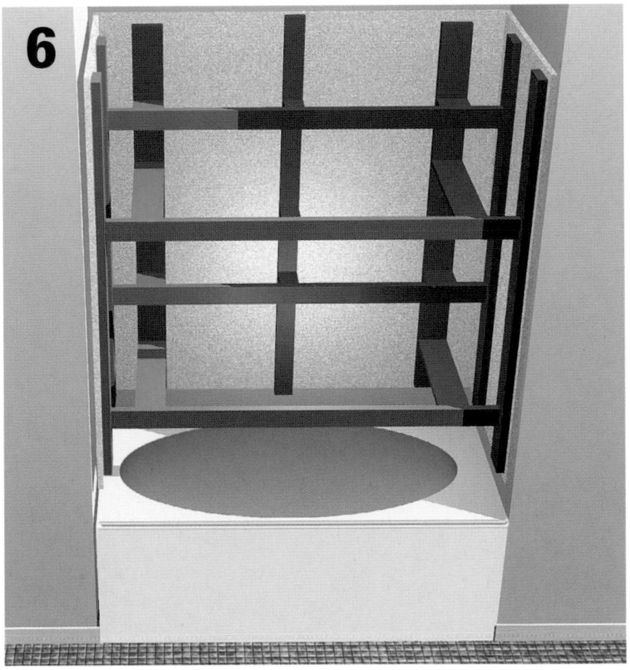

Use 1× and 2× lumber to construct temporary bracing to ensure a strong adhesive bond. Use soft cloth or carpet scraps to prevent the bracing from scratching the surround. Allow the adhesive to cure overnight, then remove the bracing. Wipe the surround clean with a damp cloth.

Soaking Tubs

Long a favorite in the Japanese culture, soaking tubs continue to gain fans in America. Although you can soak in any tub, an actual soaking tub is designed so that the bather sits—rather than reclines—immersed in water up to the chin. It usually only takes one long soak for a person to become a devotee of the soaking tub's relaxing benefits.

The key difference between a soaking tub and other styles is the wall height, which allows for true immersion. Traditional soaking tubs are manufactured with sides that can rise 36" high or higher; but today's soaking tubs for home use are available in a range of sizes, many with sides around 24" deep. (It's crucial for proper soaking that the overflow drain is positioned 20" or more from the bottom to allow the tub to be almost completely filled.)

Getting in and out of these types of tubs can be a challenge, which is why they are often installed into a platform built especially for the tub. The platform allows you to sit and then ease into the tub, and it offers a surface to just relax as the tub fills with water. A wide and impressive platform such as the one discussed here leaves plenty of space for abundant candles, bath salts, plants, or other decor- and mood-enhancing additions.

The platform described in the instructions that follow is 22" high with a 14" wide ledge—comfortably accommodating seating around the tub. The tub itself is 24" high, with a 2" lip. You can build a platform so that the tub rim fits flush, but a lip is a good idea to keep towels and other items from accidentally sliding off the platform and into the bathwater.

As with other types of tubs, soaking tubs come in a range of styles, shapes, and colors. We've used a deck-mounted fiberglass tub with a keyhole basin shape, courtesy of Kohler Cos. (see Resources, page 283).

Tools & Materials ▸

- Plumbing tools & supplies
- Tape measure
- Drill
- Hammer
- 4-ft. level
- Utility knife
- 2 × 4 lumber
- 2" screws
- 1¼" cementboard screws
- Notched trowel
- Grout sponge
- CDX plywood
- Cementboard
- Hacksaw
- Circular saw
- Torpedo level
- Thin-set mortar
- Silicone caulk
- Deck mount faucet set
- Soaking tub
- Tile mortar
- Tile grout
- Grout float
- Ceramic tile (field and bullnose)

Access Panels ▸

Making the supply and drain hook-ups on a bathtub usually requires access from below or behind the installation area. When installing a drop-in tub in a framed deck platform, you can gain access through the platform apron area, too. If you are hooking up the drain with a slip connection, the Universal Plumbing Code requires that you install a permanent access panel (see page 77) in the wall behind the tub or in the floor and ceiling below. But regardless of codes, you should make a point of creating permanent access to the plumbing hook-ups whenever possible—you need only have one leaky drain or supply connection to appreciate this. In the tub installation seen here, a removable access panel on the opposite side of the wet wall provides access to both the drain and supply hookups. This allows the platform deck and apron to be tiled in a contiguous manner. Because the faucet plumbing is readily accessible, each supply tube is connected to a shutoff valve next to the fixture and supply risers are used to bring water to the faucet valve.

How to Install a Soaking Tub with Platform

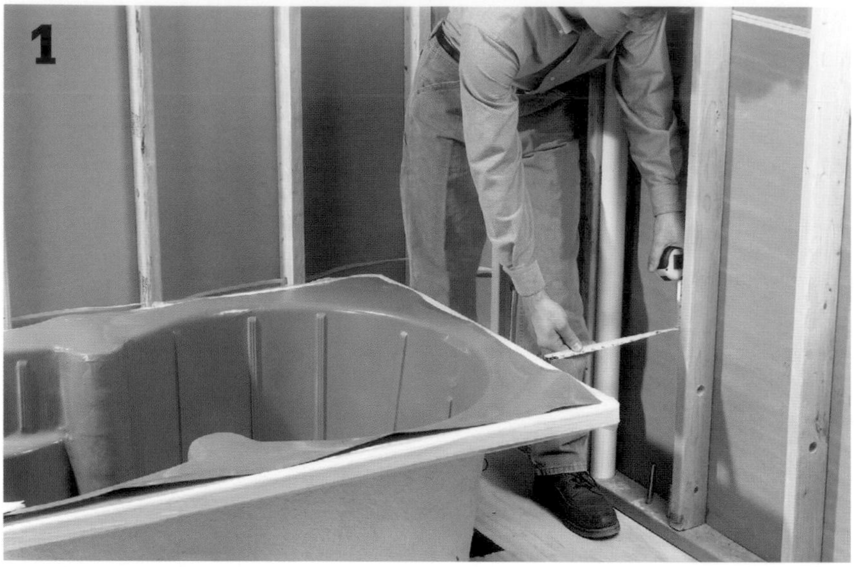

Place the tub in position on the subfloor. The tub should be 14½" from the two corner walls, measured from the underside of the tub lip—where the inside edge of the platform deck will run—to wall studs. This allows for ½"-thick wall surface. Shim as necessary to level the tub both ways, or adjust self-leveling feet if tub has them. Hang plumb bob from the underside of the lip at each corner of tub and mark the subfloor. Check that marks on adjacent corners are the same distance from the wall.

Measure from under lip edge to subfloor. This will be the height of the platform wall framing, minus the CDX plywood decking, ½" cementboard, and tile.

Remove the tub and hammer a nail in at each corner point. Snap chalk lines to represent the inside lines of the inner platform wall. Measure, cut, and align the 2 × 4 sole plates with the chalk lines. Screw all four sole plates for the inside platform wall into position. Check diagonal measurements or use a framing square to ensure the sole plates are square.

Measure and mark 13½" from the inside edge of the open side sole plates, at several points along the plates. These marks will serve as guide points for placing the sole plates of the outside platform walls. Line up the outside edge of the two outer wall sole plates and screw them in place to the subfloor. Measure again to ensure sole plates are positioned correctly.

Measure and cut studs to create the proper platform height. Install studs for both inside and outside platform walls, spacing them every 16". Use L configurations at corners so that the top plates intersect opposite the sole plates. Cut cross braces and screw them in place, staggering with the stud placement.

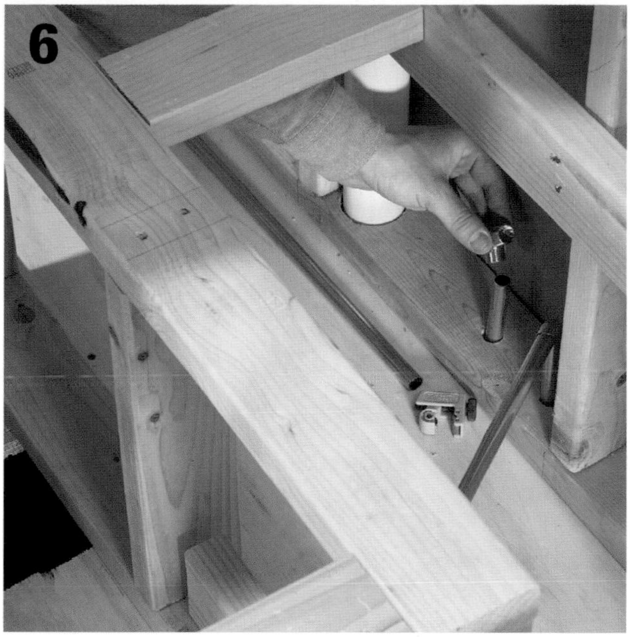

Route supply lines from the wet wall to the location of the deck-mount faucet. The connections will depend on what type of deck mount faucet you've chosen. Follow the manufacturer's instructions for securing the hot and cold connections for the faucet. If you're unsure of how to plumb the faucet, hire a plumber.

Measure and cut CDX plywood for the platform deck (plywood deck for the two open sides should overhang outside wall edge by ½" to cover the cementboard that will be used on the walls). Screw plywood decking into position. If you will be mounting the faucet on the deck, cut holes for the valve handles and spout before screwing down that portion of the deck.

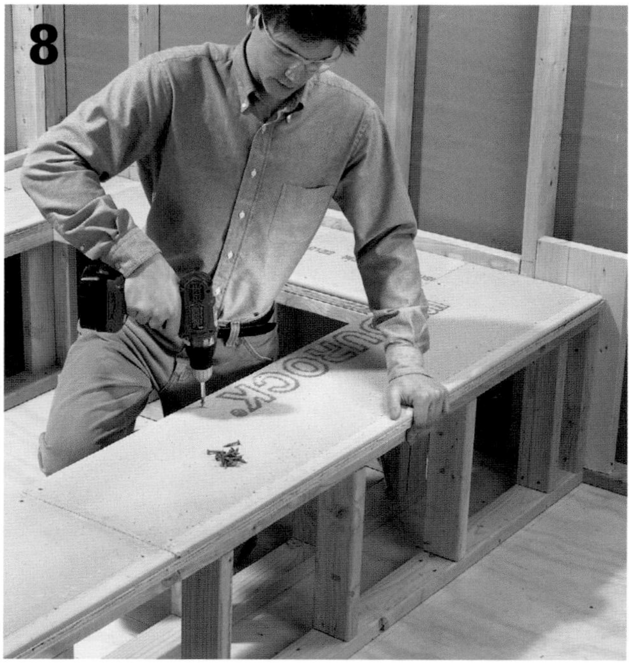

Measure and cut the deck cementboard to cover the plywood. Cut to the same overhang as the plywood and drill holes for faucet if it will be deck-mounted (the one seen here is mounted to the tub deck). Screw cementboard to the plywood deck over top rail and cross braces. Also attach cementboard to the platform aprons.

(continued)

Attach wallcoverings in the installation area. Here, six courses of wall tile will be installed on the walls above the tub deck. A strip of cementboard the same width as the total tile height is attached to the wall as a backer for the tile. Then, water-resistant drywall is installed to span from the cementboard to the ceiling to create a smooth, paintable wall surface.

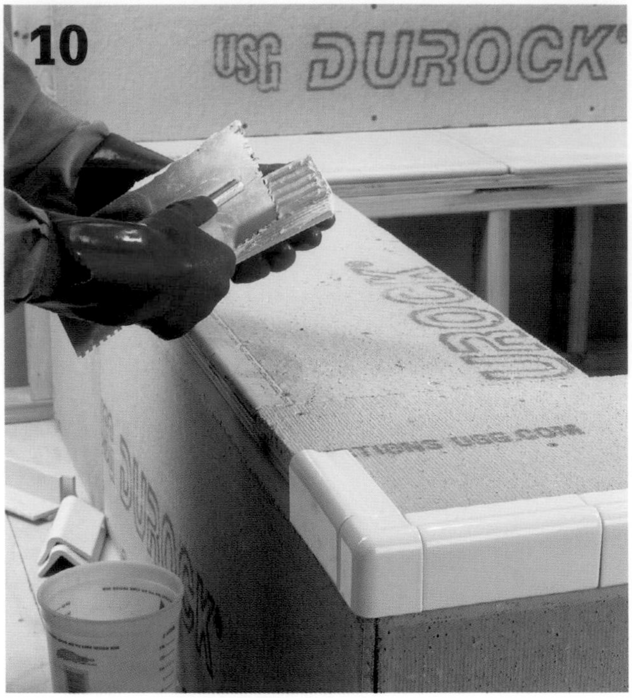

Lay tile over the deck surface and the platform aprons using bullnose tile around the two outside edges. Tile on the inside edge of the platform does not need to be finished—it will be covered by the tub lip. See pages 234 to 239 for more information on tiling a tub apron. Also install wall tiles.

Grout the platform and walls with sanded grout. Buff off excess grout with a coarse rag. Apply a grout sealing product after the grout has dried for several days (this may be done after the tub is installed if you do not want to wait).

Install the tub. Attach the drain-waste-overflow connection to the tub. Trowel a ½" bed of mortar on the subfloor where the tub bottom will sit (unless manufacturer's directions state otherwise). Set the tub in place in the platform opening, press down into the mortar, and check for level. There should be a very slight gap between tub lip bottom edge and top of tile.

Let the mortar bed dry and, working through the open walls and under the platform deck, connect the drain tailpiece to the trap. A large access panel lets you get at both the supply and drain hook ups. See page 99.

Apply a bead of tab and tile caulk around the edges of the tub deck.

Sliding Tub Doors

Tools & Materials ▸

- Measuring tape
- Pencil & marker
- Hacksaw
- Miter box
- Level
- Drill
- Center punch
- Masonry bit for tile wall
- Phillips screwdriver
- Caulk gun
- Masking tape
- Silicone sealant
- Tub door kit

Curtains on your bathtub shower are a hassle. If you forget to tuck them inside the tub, water flows freely onto your bathroom floor. If you forget to slide them closed, mildew sets up shop in the folds. And every time you brush against them they stick to your skin. Shower curtains certainly don't add much elegance or charm to a dream bath. Neither does a deteriorated door. Clean up the look of your bathroom, and even give it an extra touch of elegance, with a new sliding tub door.

When shopping for a sliding tub door, you have a choice of framed or frameless. A framed door is edged in metal. The metal framing is typically aluminum but is available in many finishes, including those that resemble gold, brass, or chrome. Glass options are also plentiful. You can choose between frosted or pebbled glass, clear, mirrored, tinted, or patterned glass. Doors can be installed on ceramic tile walls or through a fiberglass tub surround.

A sliding tub door in a metal frame gives the room a sleek, clean look and is just one of the available options.

How to Install Sliding Tub Doors

Remove the existing door and inspect the walls. Use a razor blade to cut sealant from tile and metal surfaces. Do not use a razor blade on fiberglass surfaces. Remove remaining sealant by scraping or pulling. Use a silicone sealant remover to remove all residue. Remove shower curtain rods, if present. Check the walls and tub ledge for plumb and level.

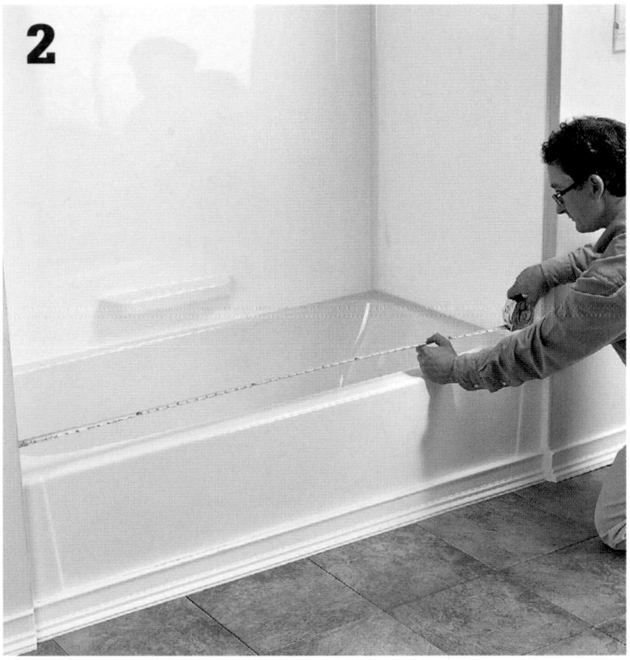

Measure the distance between the finished walls along the top of the tub ledge. Refer to the manufacturer's instructions for figuring the track dimensions. For the product seen here, 3⁄16" is subtracted from the measurement to calculate the track dimensions.

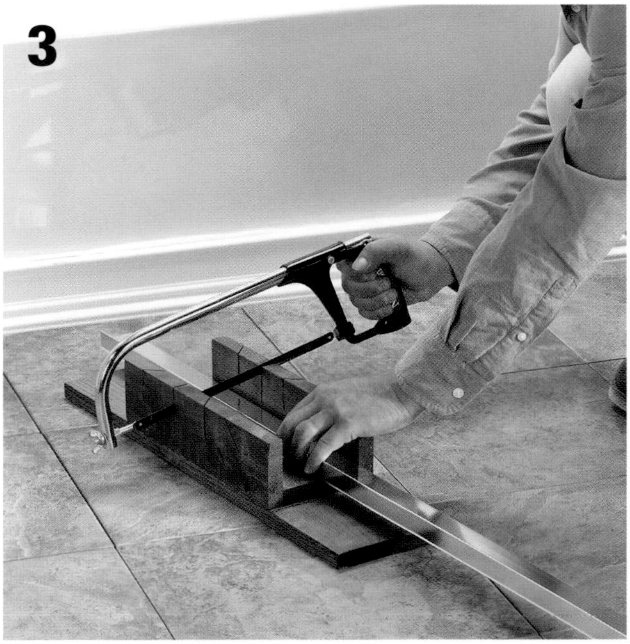

Using a hacksaw and a miter box, carefully cut the track to the proper dimension. Center the track on the bathtub ledge with the taller side out and so the gaps are even at each end. Tape into position with masking tape.

Place a wall channel against the wall with the longer side out and slide into place over the track so they overlap. Use a level to check the channel for plumb, and then mark the locations of the mounting holes on the wall with a marker. Repeat for the other wall channel. Remove the track.

(continued)

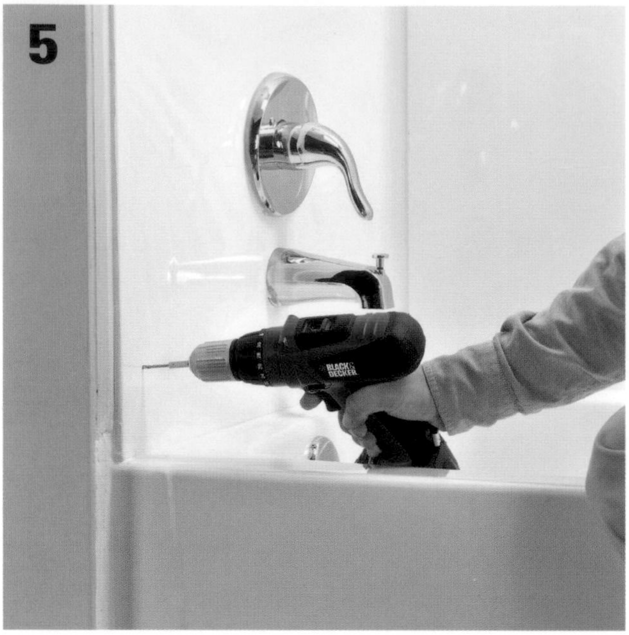

Drill mounting holes for the wall channel at the marked locations. In ceramic tile, nick the surface of the tile with a center punch, use a ¼" masonry bit to drill the hole, and then insert the included wall anchors. For fiberglass surrounds, use a ⅛" drill bit; wall anchors are not necessary.

Apply a bead of silicone sealant along the joint between the tub and the wall at the ends of the track. Apply a minimum ¼" bead of sealant along the outside leg of the track underside.

Position the track on the tub ledge and against the wall. Attach the wall channels using the provided screws. Do not use caulk on the wall channels at this time.

At a location above the tops of the wall channels, measure the distance between the walls. Refer to the manufacturer's instructions for calculating the header dimensions. For the doors seen here, the header dimension is the distance between the walls minus 1⁄16". Measure the header and carefully cut it to length using a hacksaw and a miter box. Slide the header down on top of the wall channels until seated.

Mount the rollers in the roller mounting holes. To begin, use the second from the top roller mounting holes. Follow the manufacturer's instructions for spacer or washer placement and direction.

Carefully lift the inner panel by the sides and place the rollers on the inner roller track. Roll the door toward the shower end of the tub. The edge of the panel should touch both rubber bumpers. If it doesn't, remove the door and move the rollers to different holes. Drive the screws by hand to prevent overtightening.

Lift the outer panel by the sides with the towel bar facing out from the tub. Place the outer rollers over the outer roller track. Slide the door to the end opposite the shower end of the tub. If the door does not contact both bumpers, remove the door and move the rollers to different mounting holes.

Apply a bead of silicone sealant to the inside seam of the wall and wall channel at both ends and to the U-shaped joint of the track and wall channels. Smooth the sealant with a fingertip dipped in water.

Air-Jet Tubs

A jetted spa is basically a bathtub that recirculates water, air, or a combination of the two to create an effect known as hydromassage. Hydromassage increases blood flow, relieves pressure on joints and muscles, and relieves tension. Indoor hydromassage tubs usually have a water pump that blows a mixture of air and water through jets located in the tub body. Many include an integral water heater.

The product you'll see installed on these pages is a bit different. It is an air-jet tub: a relatively new entry in the jetted spa market that circulates only warm air, not water. This technology makes it safe to use bath oils, bubble bath, and bath salts in the spa. A model with no heater requires only a single 120-volt dedicated circuit. Models with heaters normally require either multiple dedicated 120-volt circuits or a 240-volt circuit.

Like normal bathtubs, jetted tubs can be installed in a variety of ways. Here, we install a drop-in tub (no nailing flange) in a 3-wall alcove. This may require the construction of a new stub wall, like the short wall we plumbed as the wet wall for this installation. Unless you have a lot of wiring and plumbing experience, consider hiring professionals for all or parts of the project.

Tools & Materials ▸

- Plumbing tools & supplies
- Utility knife
- 4-foot level
- Square-edge trowel
- Drill or power driver
- Channel-type pliers
- Hacksaw
- Level
- Circular saw
- Screwdriver
- Adjustable wrench
- Drain-waste-overflow assembly
- Shims
- 1 × 4 lumber
- Deck screws
- Roofing nails
- Plumber's putty
- Dry-set mortar
- Trowel
- Silicone caulk
- Jetted tub
- Faucet set

Air-jet tubs create massaging action, stirring the water with warm air. Air-jets eliminate concerns about stagnant water and bacteria that can remain in the pipes of whirlpool tubs.

Whirlpools ▸

Installing a whirlpool is very similar to installing a bathtub, once the rough-in is completed. Completing a rough-in for a whirlpool requires that you install a separate GFCI-protected electrical circuit for the pump motor. Some building codes specify that a licensed electrician be hired to wire whirlpools; check with your local building inspector.

Select your whirlpool before you do rough-in work, because exact requirements will differ from model to model. Select your faucet to match the trim kit that comes with your whirlpool. When selecting a faucet, make sure the spout is large enough to reach over the tub rim. Most whirlpools use "widespread" faucets because the handles and spout are separate, and can be positioned however you like, even on opposite sides of the tub. Most building centers carry flex tube in a variety of lengths for connecting the faucet handles and spout.

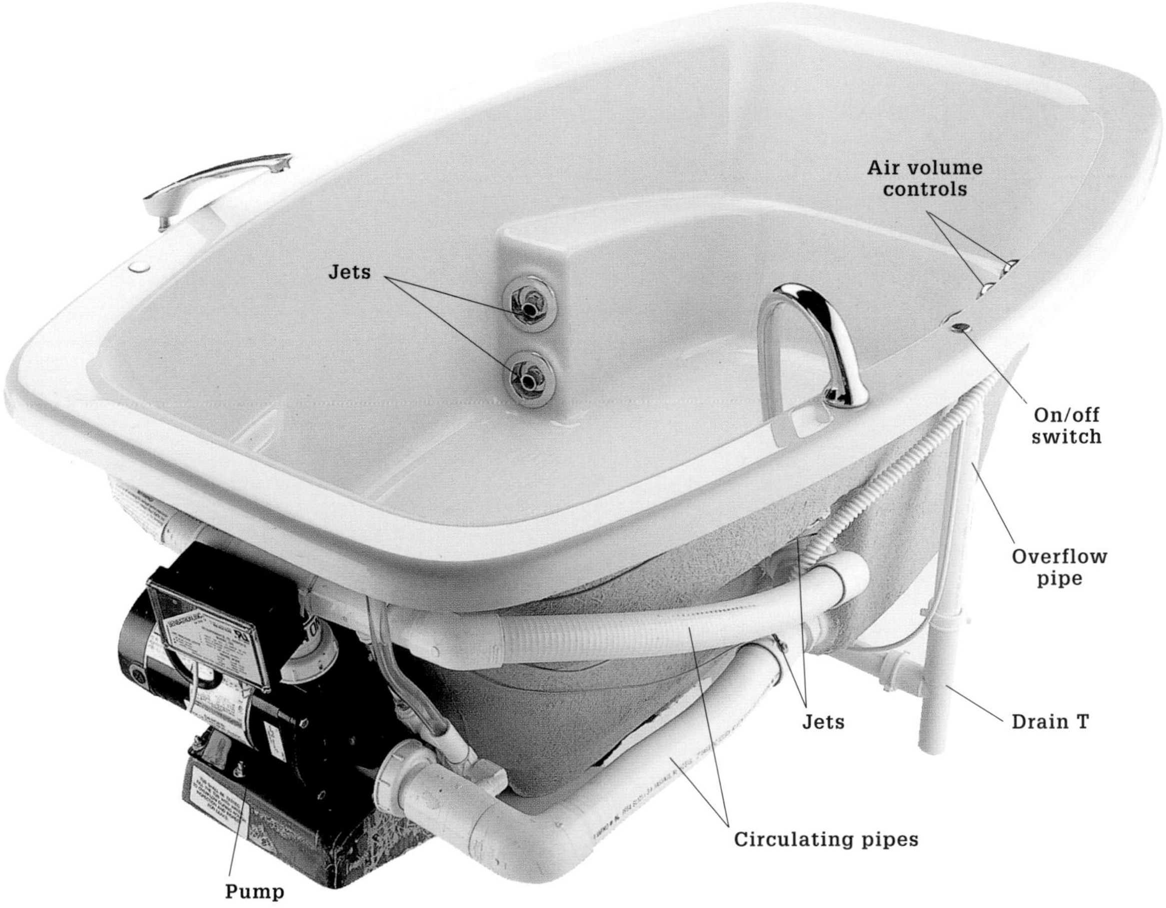

A whirlpool circulates aerated water through jets mounted in the body of the tub. Whirlpool pumps move as much as 50 gallons of water per minute to create a relaxing hydromassage effect. The pump, pipes, jets, and most of the controls are installed at the factory, making the actual hookup in your home quite simple.

How to Install a Jetted Tub

Prepare the site for the installation. Remove wall coverings in the installation area to expose bare studs. Provide a dedicated electrical circuit or circuits to the tub area according to the specifications in your installation manual (hire an electrician if you are not comfortable with wiring). This model plugs into a GFCI-protected receptacle on a dedicated 120-volt, 20-amp circuit.

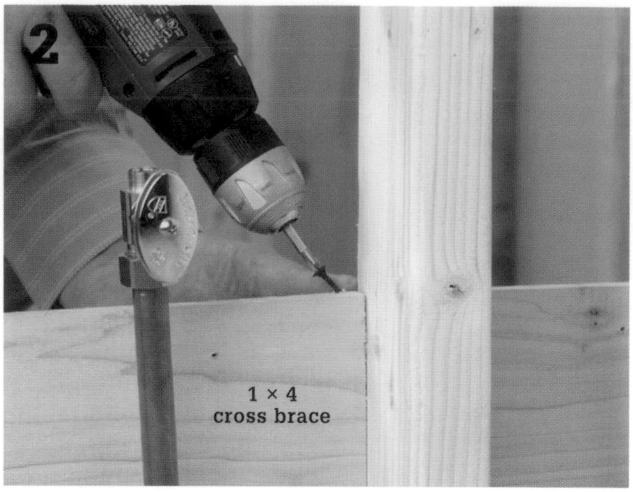

Make framing improvements such as adding 1 × 4 bracing at supply risers and the faucet body location. For drop-in tubs that do not have nailing flanges, you may need to add short stub walls to provide a stable resting point. Here, a short stub wall was installed at one end to serve as the tub wet wall.

Requirements for Making Electrical Hookups ▸

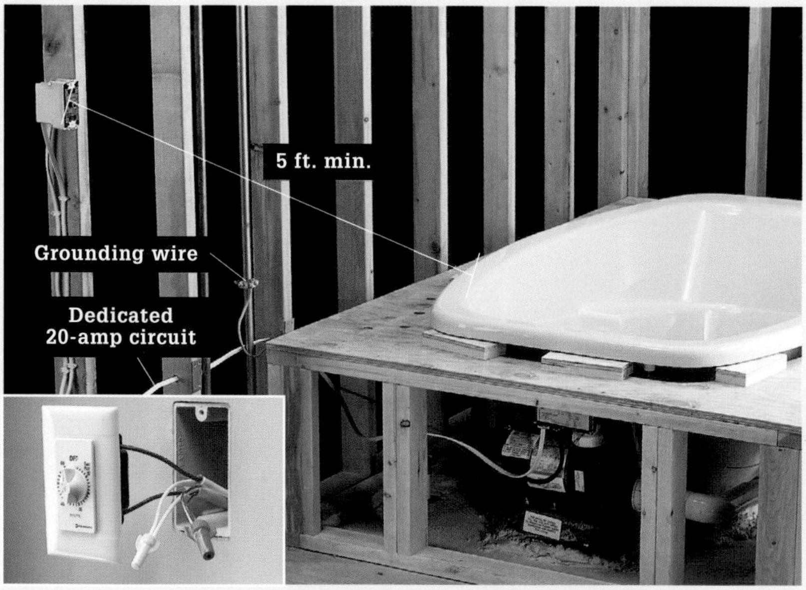

The electrical service for a whirlpool should be a dedicated 115- to 120-volt, 20-amp circuit. The pump motor should be grounded separately, normally to a metal cold water supply pipe. Most whirlpool motors are wired with 12/2 NM cable, but some local codes require the use of conduit. Remote timer switches (inset), located at least 5 ft. from the tub, are required by some codes, even for a tub with a built-in timer.

A GFCI circuit breaker at the main service panel is required with whirlpool installations. Hire an electrician to connect new circuits at your service panel if you are uncomfortable installing circuit cables on your own.

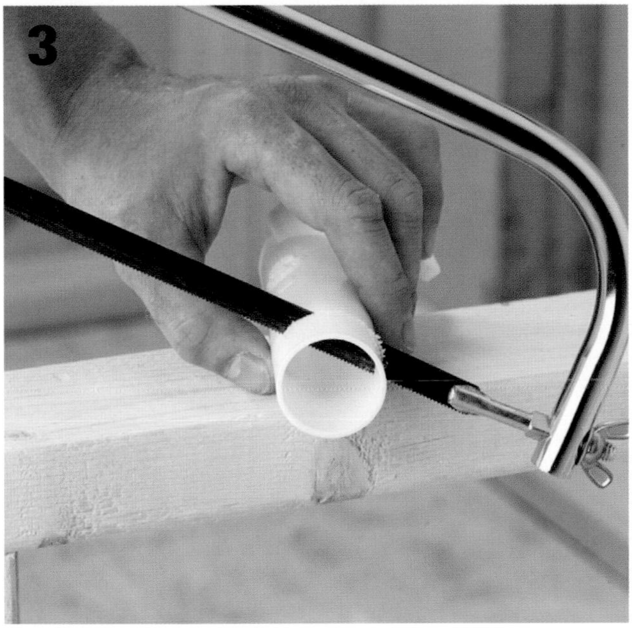

Cut the drain tailpiece to length depending on the distance you'll need to span to the trap. Use a hacksaw or tubing cutter to make the cut.

Prepare the floor or subfloor. Check with a level and fill any dips with floor leveling compound or mortar. If there is a joint in the subfloor in the installation area, make sure the sides are level. (The floor has to be level in order to support the weight of the tub, the water, and bathers.) Also make sure there is no rot or weakness in the structural elements.

Test the tub fit. First, cut a piece of the shipping carton to fit inside the tub and protect its surface. Have someone help you slide the tub into the installation area, flush against the wall studs, so you can check the fit. *Tip: Lay a pair of 1 × 4s perpendicular to the tub opening and use them as skids to make it easier to slide the tub in. Remove the skids and lower the tub on the floor.*

Set a 4-ft. level across the rim of the tub and check it for level. If it is not level, place shims under the tub until it is.

(continued)

Mark the top of the tub's rim or nailing flange at each stud as a reference for installing additional supports or ledgers. Remove the tub from the alcove.

Add support frames or ledgers as directed by the manufacturer and secure them in the installation area so the top of the tub or nailing flange will be at the height you scribed in Step 7.

Assemble the drain-waste-overflow kit to fit the drain and overflow openings, following the tub manufacturer's directions. Install the DWO kit (it is virtually impossible to attach it once the tub is in place).

Fasten the threaded parts of the drain assembly. A ring of plumber's putty between the drain coverplate and the tub will help create a good seal. If you will be installing a pop-up drain, install it now as well.

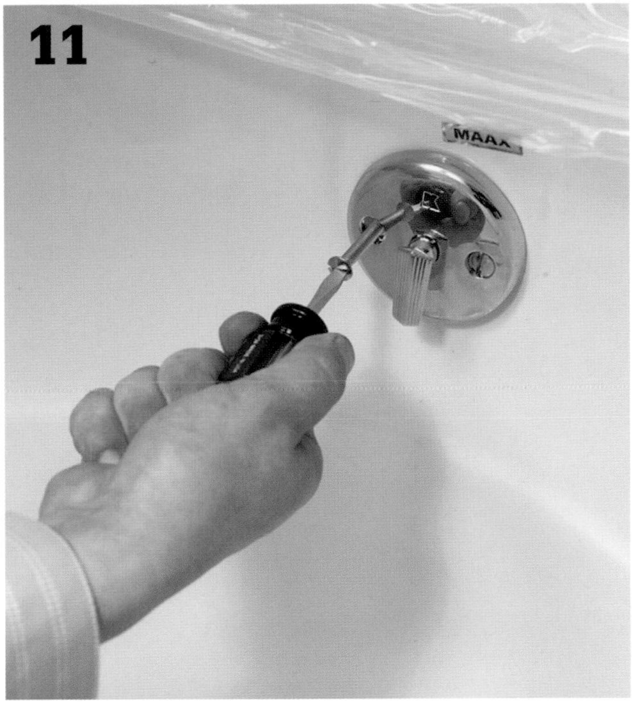

Attach the overflow coverplate so it conceals the overflow opening. Adjust the pop-up drain plug linkage as directed by the manufacturer.

Begin the actual installation. For some tubs, it is recommended that you trowel a layer of thinset mortar in the installation area. But read your instructions carefully. Many tubs feature integral feet that are meant to rest directly on the floor.

Slide the tub back into the opening. Remove the skids, if you are using them. Press down evenly on the tub rims until they make solid contact with the ledgers or frames.

Provide support for the tub on the open side if it does not have a structural skirt. Here, a 2 × 4 stub wall is built to the exact height of the underside of the rim and then attached in place. Screw it to both end walls and to the floor.

(continued)

Drain Hookups ▸

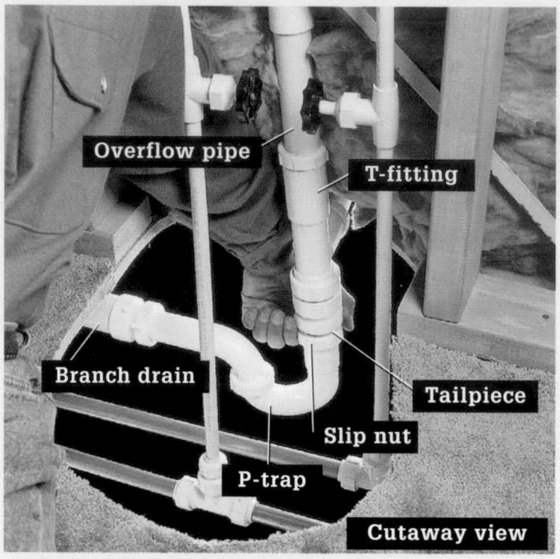

Make the plumbing drain connections before you proceed further. To connect the drain tailpiece to the trap you will need access either from below or from an access panel. The photo above shows a typical tub drain configuration seen cutaway through the floor.

Cover the gaps in the wallcoverings around the tub. Here, cementboard is installed in preparation for a tile backsplash. If your tub has nailing flanges, attach strips of metal flashing to the wall so they extend down to within about ¼" of the tub rim. If your tub has a removable apron, install it.

Make wiring connections according to the tub manufacturer's instructions. The requirements vary greatly among jetted spas. Some municipalities may require that a licensed professional do this work. Here, the airflow regulator is being wired. Note that most codes have a safety requirement that the on/off switch must be located so it cannot be reached by a bather in the tub.

Test the operation of the jetted spa before you finish the walls or deck in case there is a hidden problem. Fill it with a hose if you have not installed the faucet (the faucet normally is installed after the wall surfaces, unless you are deck-mounting the faucet on the tub rim). Run the spa. If it works, go ahead and drain the water.

Finish the wall surfaces. Here, a tile surround and backsplash is being installed over the cementboard backer. The wallcovering at the front of the wet wall is installed so it is easy to remove for plumbing access.

Hook up the faucet to the water supply plumbing according to the manufacturer's directions (or have your plumber do the job). Remove the aerator from the tip of the spout and run water through it to clear out any debris. Attach the aerator, fill the tub, and have yourself a nice, relaxing soak.

Optional Accessories ▸

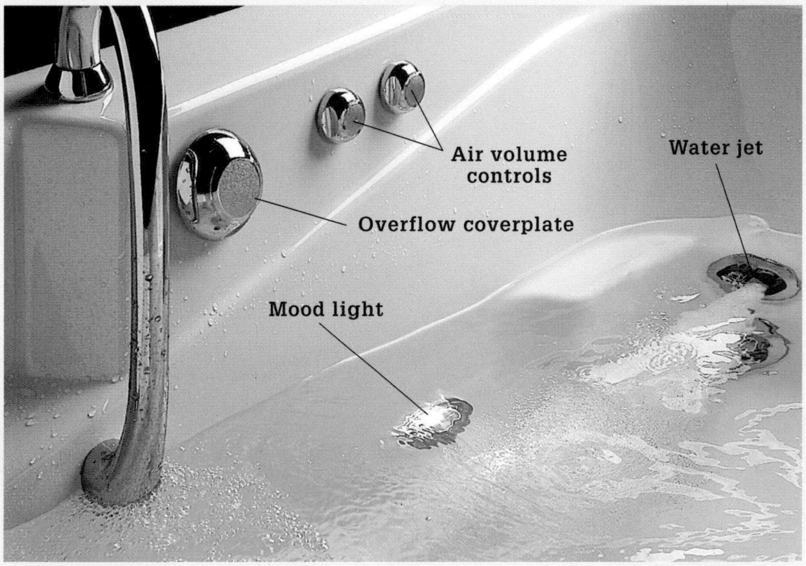

Mood lights are sold as factory-installed accessories by many manufacturers. Most are available with several filters to let you adjust the color to suit your mood. Mood lights are low-voltage fixtures wired through 12-volt transformers. Do not wire mood lights or other accessories into the electrical circuit that supplies the pump motor.

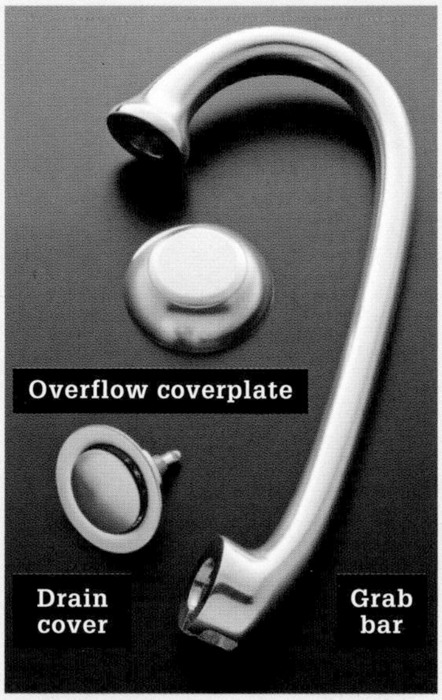

Trim kits for whirlpools are ordered at the time of purchase. Available in a variety of finishes, all of the trim pieces except the grab bar and overflow coverplate are normally installed at the factory.

Tub & Shower Fittings

In many situations, replacing a bathtub spout can be almost as easy as hooking up a garden hose to an outdoor spigot. There are some situations where it is a bit more difficult, but still pretty simple. The only time it's a real problem is when the spout is attached to a plain copper supply nipple, rather than a threaded nipple. You'll know this is the case if the spout has a setscrew on the underside where it meets the wall. Many bathtub spouts are sold in kits with a matching showerhead and handle or handles. But for a simple one-for-one replacement, spouts are sold separately. You just need to make sure the new spout is compatible with the existing nipple (see page 121).

Tub spouts can be relatively complicated plumbing fittings, often performing three or four important functions. The spout itself is simple enough, since its only function is to deliver bathwater to the tub. But the diverter network and pop-up drain contain multiple moving parts that require precise adjustment and occasional repair or replacement (see photo, next page). The diverter is basically a stop valve that's activated by a lever or knob to block flow of water from the spout, forcing it up to a showerhead or out through a handheld showerhead, as seen here.

In many bathtub/shower plumbing systems, the spout has the important job of housing the diverter—a gate inside the spout that is operated by a lever with a knob. An open gate allows water to come out of the spout when the faucet is turned on. When the diverter is pulled shut, the water is redirected up a riser pipe and to the showerhead. Failure of the diverter is one of the most common reasons for replacing a spout.

Tub & Shower Combination Faucets

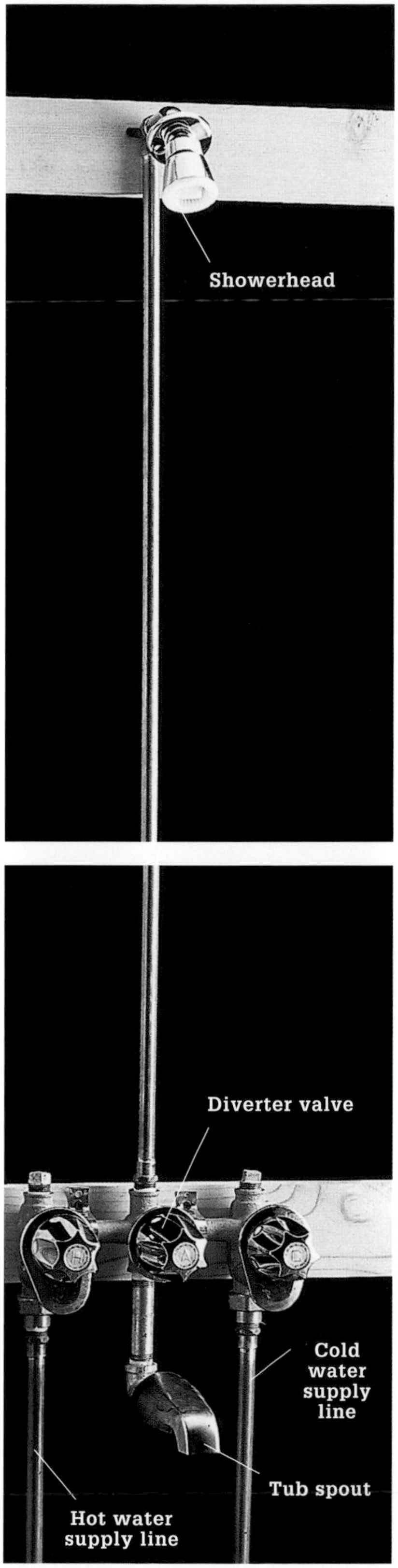

Three-handle faucet has valves that are either compression or cartridge design.

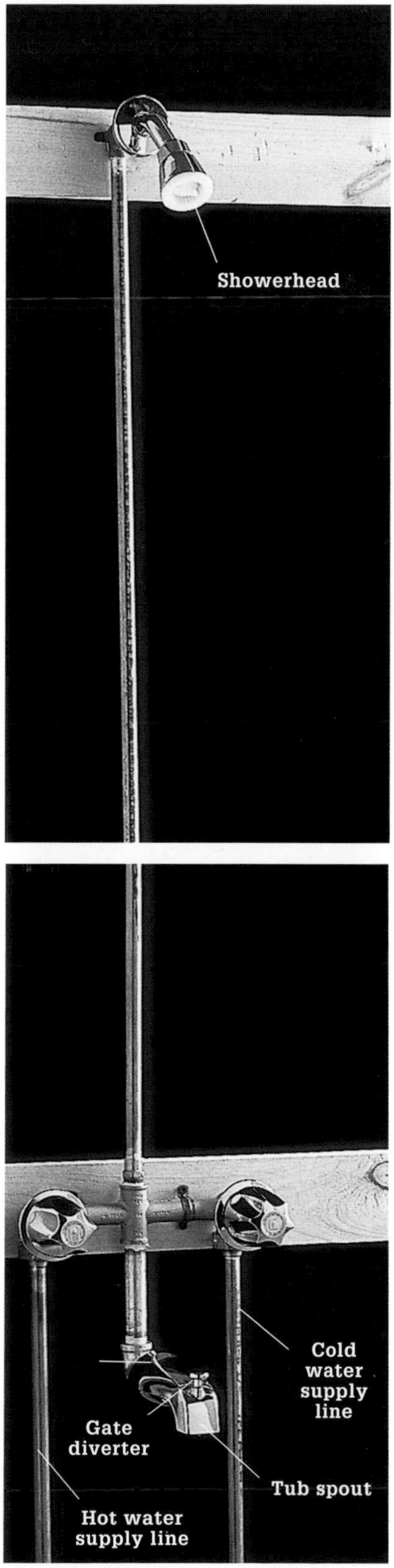

Two-handle faucet has valves that are either compression or cartridge design.

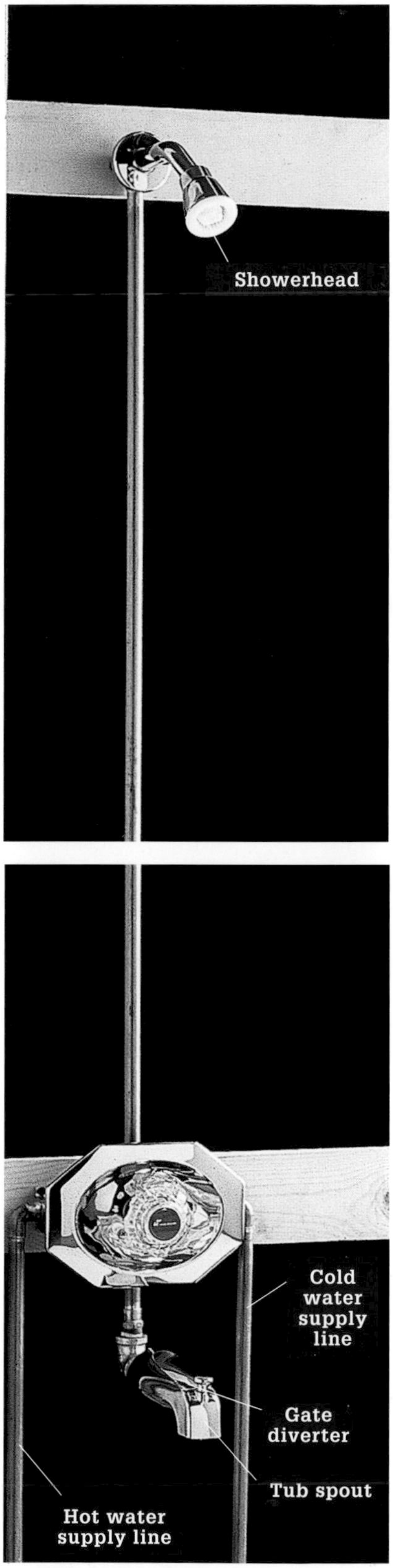

Single-handle faucet has valves that are cartridge, ball-type, or disc design.

How to Install a Slip-Fit Spout

Slip fitting: Check underneath the tub spout to look for an access slot or cutout, which indicates the spout is a slip-fit style that is held in place with a setscrew and mounted on a copper supply nipple. Loosen the screw with a hex (Allen) wrench. Pull off the spout.

Clean the copper nipple with steel wool. If you find any sharp edges where the nipple was cut, smooth them out with emery paper. Then, insert the O-ring that comes with the spout onto the nipple (see the manufacturer's instructions) and slide the spout body over the nipple in an upside-down position.

With the spout upside down for ease of access, tighten the setscrews on the clamp, working through the access slot or cutout, until you feel resistance.

Spin the spout so it's right-side-up, then tighten the setscrew from below, making sure the wall end of the spout is flush against the wall. Do not overtighten the setscrew.

How to Install a Threaded Spout

If you see no setscrew or slot on the underside of the spout, it is attached to a threaded nipple. Unscrew the tub spout by inserting a heavy-duty flat screwdriver into the spout opening and spinning it counterclockwise.

Option: Grip the spout with a padded pipe wrench or channel-type pliers. Buy a compatible replacement spout at a home center or hardware store.

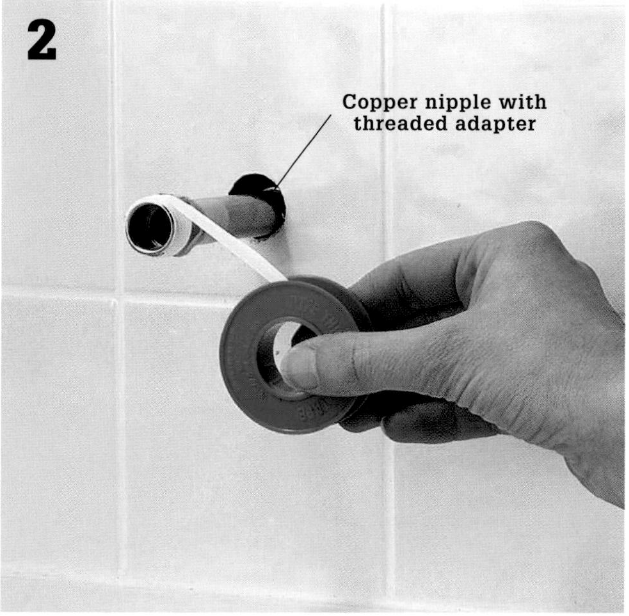

Wrap several courses of Teflon tape clockwise onto the pipe threads of the nipple. Using extra Teflon tape on the threads creates resistance if the spout tip points past six o'clock when tight.

Twist the new spout onto the nipple until it is flush against the wall and the spout is oriented properly. If the spout falls short of six o'clock, you may protect the finish of the spout with tape and twist it a little beyond hand tight with your channel-type pliers—but don't overdo it; the fitting can crack.

Adding a Shower to a Bathtub

Your dream bath remodel may include adding a shower to your old built-in bathtub—finally you will be able to enjoy the ease of waking up and hopping into a steamy shower. All you need to do is remove the spout and replace it with one equipped with an adapter hose outlet to which you can screw a flexible shower hose. Then you need to install a mounting bracket so you can hang the showerhead and free your hands. Add a telescoping shower curtain rod and a shower curtain and your new shower stall is ready for duty.

A

¾" × 3"

B

½" × 3"

C

¾" × 1½"

The appearance of the spout gives good clues as to which kind of nipple it is connected to. A) A spout with no diverter is probably connected to a 3"-long threaded nipple. To install a diverter spout you'll need to replace the 3" threaded nipple with a shorter threaded nipple that sticks out no more than ½" from the wall—not too big of a job. B) If the spout has a small setscrew in a slot on the underside, it is probably attached with a slip fitting to a ½" copper supply nipple. Unless you are able to solder a new transition fitting onto the old pipe after cutting it, call a plumber to install the new spout here. C) Spouts with outlets for shower adapters require a short threaded nipple (or comparable union) that sticks out from the wall no more than ¾".

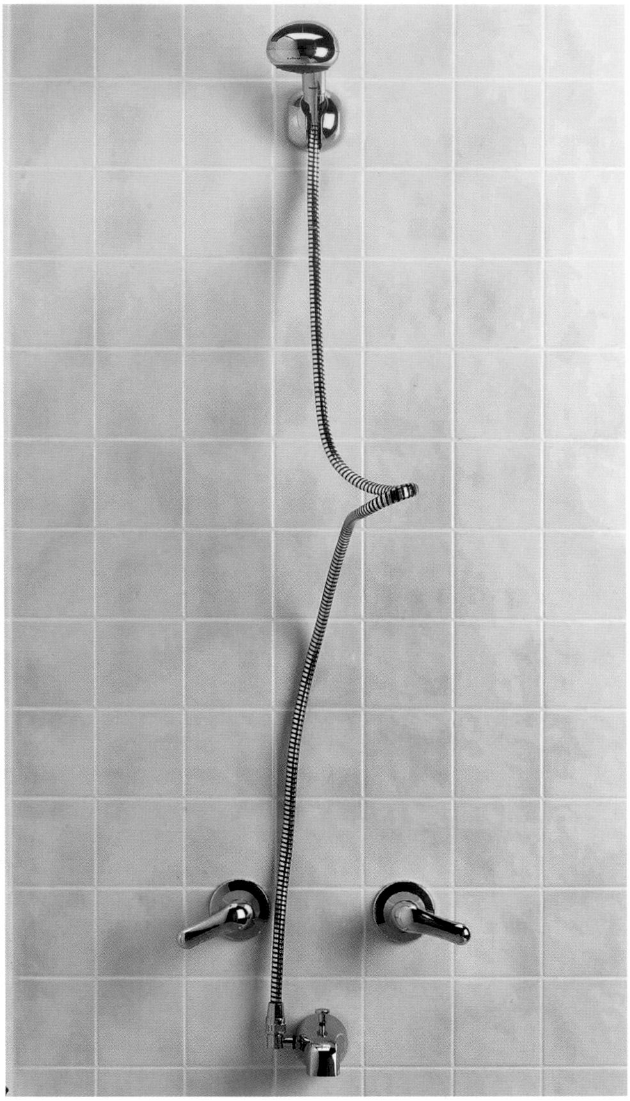

Converting a plain bathtub into a tub/shower is a relatively easy task when you use a flexible shower adapter that fits onto a special replacement tub spout.

Tools & Materials ▸

Pipe wrench
Drill
Glass and tile drill bit
Measuring tape
Screwdriver
Marker
Teflon tape
Brass nipple
Spout with diverter outlet
Hand-held mountable showerhead with flexible hose
Mounting hardware

Make sure the old spout is not held in place with a setscrew (see previous page) and then remove it by wrapping it with a cloth and turning the spout with channel-type pliers or a pipe wrench.

If you have a long iron or brass nipple like this, you need to replace it with a short one. Threaded nipples have threads at each end, so you can usually unscrew the old ones. Mark the nipple at the face of the wall and write "front" on your side. Unscrew it counterclockwise with a pipe wrench. Get a threaded brass nipple of the same diameter that is about half an inch longer than the distance from the back of your old nipple to your line.

Wrap six layers of Teflon tape clockwise on the nipple and thread into the wall. Thread the reducing bushing onto the nipple. Thread the adapter spout on. Tighten farther with a screwdriver or dowel to orient the spout correctly.

Attach a flexible shower hose to the adapter hose outlet. Tighten with an adjustable wrench.

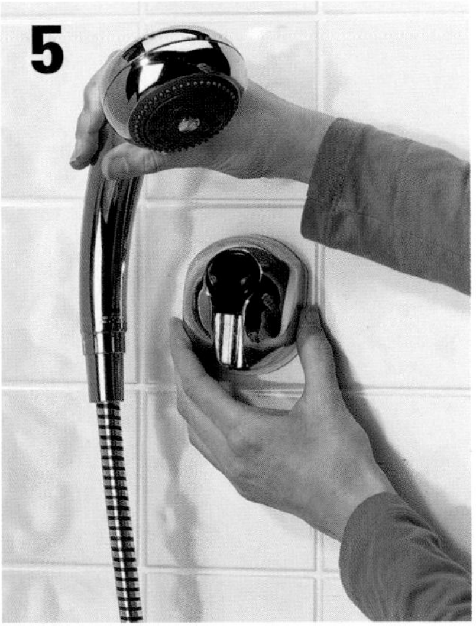

Determine the location of the showerhead bracket. Use the hose length as a guide, and make sure the showerhead can be lifted off the bracket with ease.

Mark hole locations. Use a glass-and-tile drill bit for your electric drill in the size recommended by the shower bracket manufacturer. Put on eye protection and drill holes in the ceramic tile on your marks. Insert anchors into the holes and tap in place with a wooden or rubber mallet. Fasten the showerhead holder to the wall using a Phillips screwdriver and the mounting screws.

Dual Showerheads

What's more luxurious than a hot shower? Two hot showers at one time. That's what you get with a dual-head, multifunction shower such as the one shown in this project. Multiple showerheads let you aim the pulsing action at your neck and shoulders, your chest and legs, your hair and torso—you decide where you need it most.

Although some multifunction showerheads require elaborate and painstaking installation, others, such as the one shown here, take less than an hour, start to finish. This showerhead produces a lot of enjoyment in return for a reasonable investment of time and money.

At a flow of 2.5 gallons per minute, this showerhead won't overwhelm a water heater, either. Unless you and your family members take longer showers to extend your enjoyment of its pleasures, it shouldn't radically increase your water usage or your utility bills.

Gentle streams, invigorating massage, soothing pulses—they're all available at the touch of a finger after you replace a standard showerhead with a two-head model.

Tools & Materials ▸

- Pipe wrench
- Dual-head multifunction showerhead
- Stiff bristle brush
- Teflon tape
- Soft rag or cloth
- Electrical tape

How to Replace a Showerhead with a Multi-head fitting

Place electrical tape on the jaws of a pipe wrench to protect the metal showerhead parts from the teeth of the pipe wrench.

Grasp the end of the existing showerhead. Using a pipe wrench, turn the collar nut counterclockwise to remove the showerhead. Leave the shower arm and flange in place.

Carefully clean the threads at the end of the shower arm with a stiff bristle metal brush. Be careful not to damage the threads. Run the water for a few seconds to flush debris from the arm.

Make sure the pre-installed rubber washers are in place inside each showerhead as well as the shower arm's swivel nut.

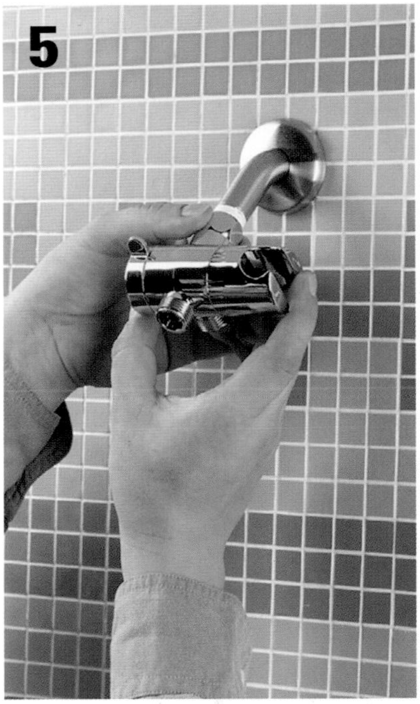

Wrap Teflon tape clockwise around the shower arm threads, making three or four loops of tape. Thread the shower arm extension from the new, dual-head showerhead onto the shower arm, turning clockwise. Hand-tighten firmly.

Wrap three or four loops of Teflon tape clockwise around the threads at each end of the shower arm extension.

Install one showerhead on each end of the arm, hand tightening them by turning clockwise. Wrap several courses of electrician's tape around the pipe wrench jaws and gently tighten the showerhead nut. Do not overtighten.

Adjust and rotate the showerheads as desired. Turn on the water and check for leaks. Gently tighten if necessary.

Slide-bar Showerheads

The slide-bar showerhead is an attractive and practical shower addition for any bathroom. It combines the flexibility of a handheld sprayer with a sliding mounted showerhead. This convenient height adjustability makes it perfect for all family members, including children or disabled users who must sit to shower. The model shown uses a slide-lock mechanism that allows you to easily set the sprayer height anywhere along the 2-foot span of the bar.

Slide-bar showerheads are generally sold as a kit that includes the bar, sprayer, hose, and mounting hardware. Many basic kits contain only a simple coupling that attaches the hose to the end of the shower arm. For a cleaner look, purchase a matching supply elbow that attaches to the pipe stub at the wall via a galvanized nipple connector, as shown in this project.

Tools & Materials ▸

- Pipe wrench
- 3⁄16" masonry drill bit
- ½" masonry drill bit
- Screwdriver
- Level
- Nailset
- Hammer
- Drill
- Caulk gun
- Slide-bar showerhead kit
- ½"-diameter × 1½"-long galvanized nipple
- Teflon tape
- Chrome supply elbow
- Wall anchors or toggle bolts
- ¼"-20 stainless steel machine bolt
- Silicone caulk

A slide-bar showerhead allows you to set the spray at varying heights, which makes it a perfect choice for the family bathroom.

How to Install a Slide-bar Showerhead

Remove the existing showerhead. Wrap the threads of a galvanized nipple with Teflon tape and thread it into the stub-out, leaving about $\frac{9}{16}$" of the nipple protruding from the wall. Thread the supply elbow onto the nipple. Cover the elbow with a soft cloth and tighten it with a pipe wrench.

Attach a mounting bracket to each end of the slide-bar. Place the bar 4" to 6" to the side of the wall supply elbow to avoid the water pipes. Locate the lower end of the bar about 48" from the bottom of the tub or shower. Use a level to make sure the bar is plumb, then mark the location of the mounting holes.

Drill holes in the tile using a masonry bit. If you hit a stud, attach the slide-bar to the wall, using the screws and wall anchors provided with the kit.

Anchoring to the Wall ▸

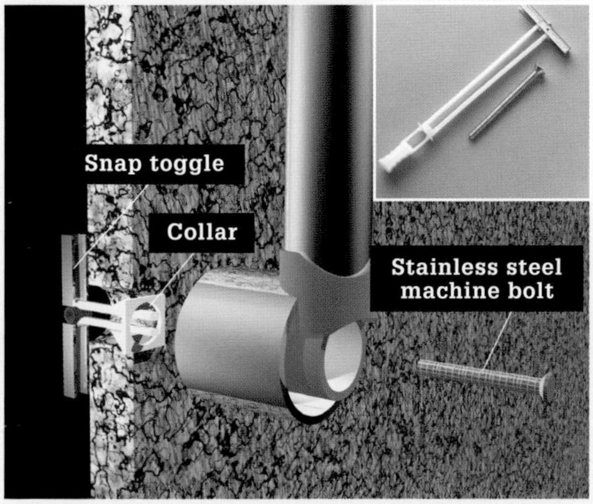

If you don't hit a stud, enlarge the hole, using a ½" masonry bit, then insert a toggle anchor (inset) into the hole. Slide the collar forward to hold the toggle against the back of the wall, then snap off the plastic straps. Attach the slide-bar to the wall with ¼"-20 stainless steel machine bolts.

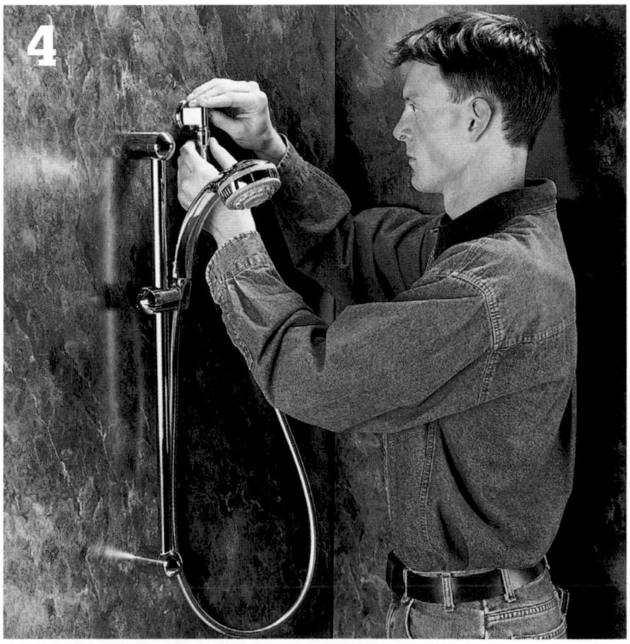

Slide the decorative end caps onto the mounting brackets. Thread the shower hose onto the wall supply elbow. Clip the showerhead into the slide-lock mechanism. Apply silicone caulk around the supply elbow and mounting brackets.

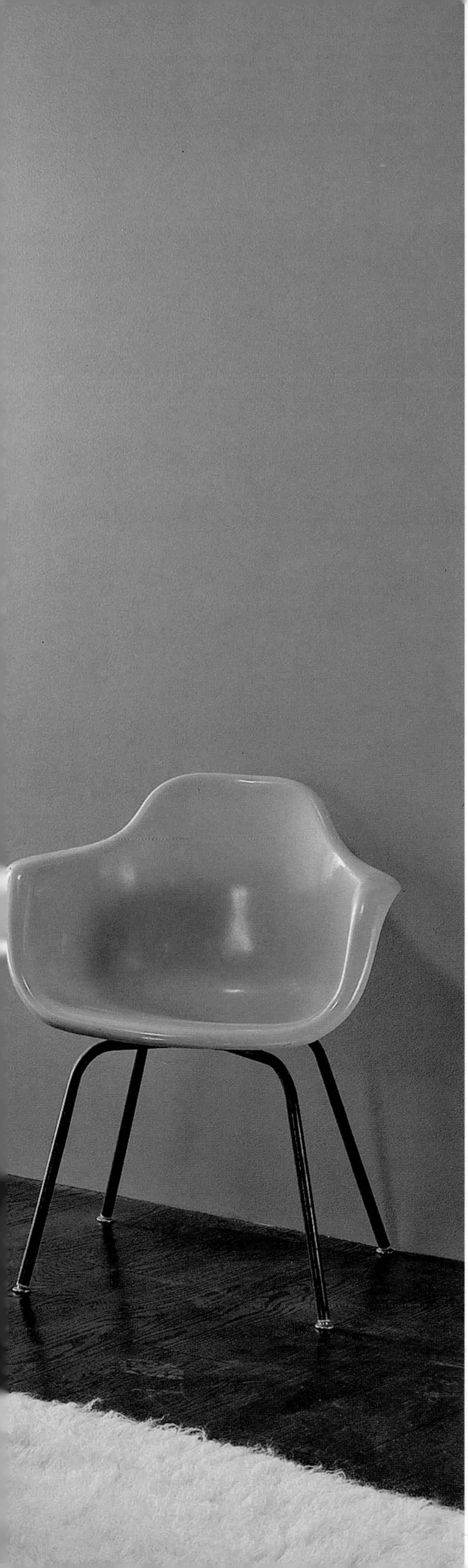

Sinks & Vanities

When discussing bathroom sinks (lavatories) and vanities, it is sometimes difficult to decide if the conversation is about cabinetry or plumbing. In some cases, such as installing a traditional vanity cabinet, you'll definitely need to do work in both areas. But for other sink types, such as a wall-hung lavatory, the job is mostly about plumbing.

Wood vanity cabinets with integral sinks have been established as the standard in residential bathrooms, but changing design standards have given rise to newer, more modern-looking options. Wall-hung vanities are one new choice. And instead of an integral cultured marble top, they are often fitted with gleaming glass countertops and intriguing vessel sinks—sometimes with a high-end wall-mounted faucet and spout. Drop-in sinks and pedestal sinks are familiar options that continue to enjoy popularity.

If you have some experience with carpentry, consider building your own custom vanity cabinet. In this chapter we've included plans for a contemporary cabinet that's designed to support a very modern double-bowl bathroom countertop.

In this chapter:

Pedestal & Console Sinks

Pedestal and console sinks move in and out of popularity more frequently than other types, but even during the times that they aren't particularly trendy they still find a place in many remodels because of their classic and adaptable styling. You'll find them most frequently in small half baths or powder rooms, where their modest footprints make them space-efficient options. Designers are also increasingly using these styles as his-and-her sinks for bathrooms in which the sinks are meant to visually dominate the design.

The primary drawback to pedestal sinks is that they don't offer any storage. Their chief practical benefit is that they conceal plumbing some homeowners would prefer to keep out of sight. Console sinks (see page 142), with their two front legs and modest apron, offer some space underneath for rolling shelf units or a towel basket.

Pedestal sinks are mounted in one of two ways. Most inexpensive models are hung in much the same way as wall-mounted sinks. The pedestal is actually installed after the sink is hung and its purpose is purely decorative. But other, higher-end pedestal sinks have structural pedestals that bear the weight of the sink. All console sinks are mounted to the wall, although the front legs offer additional support and resistance to users leaning on the front of the sink.

Tools & Materials ▸

- Pedestal sink
- 2 × 4 lumber
- Water-resistant drywall
- Ratchet wrench
- Basin wrench
- Silicone caulk
- Lag screws
- Studfinder

A console bathroom sink is a wall-mounted lavatory with two front legs that provide back-up support. Many have a narrow apron to conceal the drain trap.

A pedestal sink typically is hung on the wall. The primary function of the pedestal is to conceal plumbing and provide visual appeal.

How to Install a Pedestal Sink

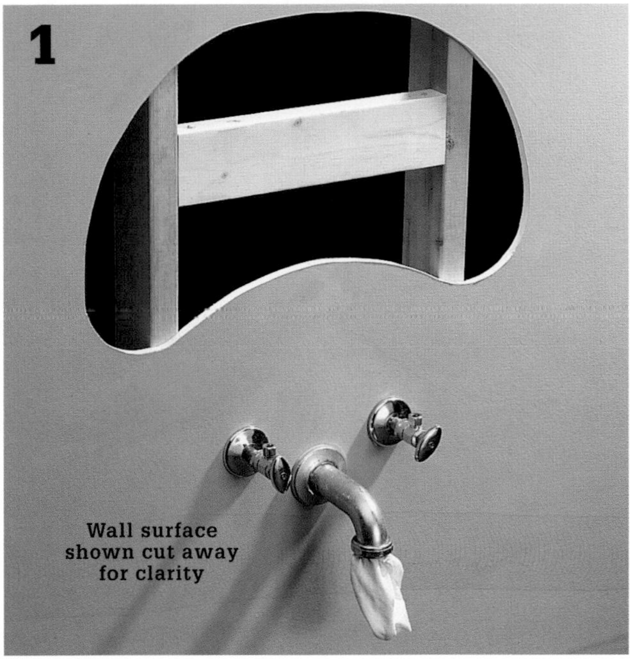

Install 2 × 4 blocking between the wall studs, behind the planned sink location. Cover the wall with water-resistant drywall.

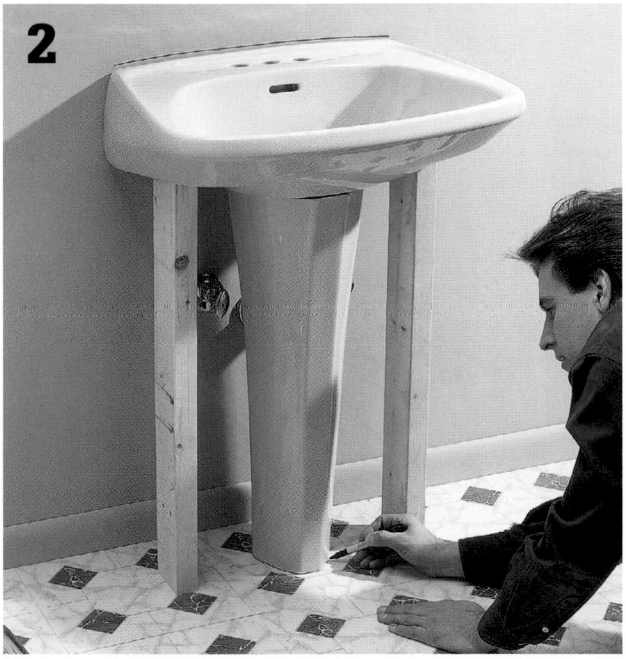

Set the basin and pedestal in position and brace it with 2 × 4s. Outline the top of the basin on the wall, and mark the base of the pedestal on the floor. Mark reference points on the wall and floor through the mounting holes found on the back of the sink and the bottom of the pedestal.

Set aside the basin and pedestal. Drill pilot holes in the wall and floor at the reference points, then reposition the pedestal. Anchor the pedestal to the floor with lag screws.

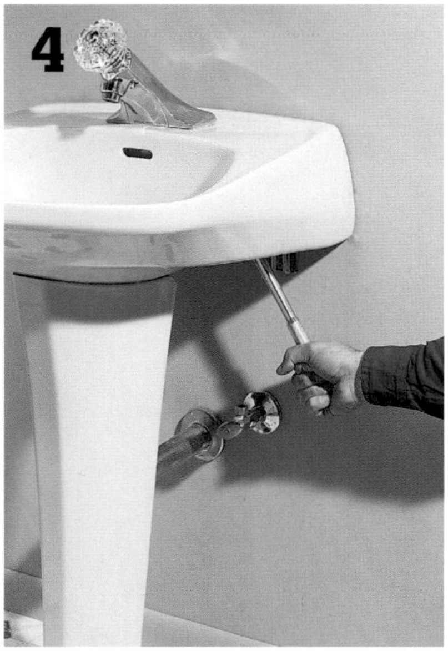

Attach the faucet, then set the sink on the pedestal. Align the holes in the back of the sink with the pilot holes drilled in the wall, then drive lag screws and washers into the wall brace using a ratchet wrench. Do not overtighten the screws.

Hook up the drain and supply fittings. Caulk between the back of the sink and the wall when installation is finished.

Wall-Hung Vanities

Think of a wall-mounted sink or vanity cabinet and you're likely to conjure up images of public restrooms, where these conveniences are installed to improve access for floor cleaning. However, wall-hung sinks and vanities made for home use are very different from the commercial installations. Often boasting high design, beautiful modern vanities and sinks come in a variety of styles and materials, including wood, metal, and glass. Some attach with decorative wall brackets that are part of the presentation; others look like standard vanities, just without legs. Install wall-hung sinks and vanities by attaching them securely to studs or wood blocking.

Tools & Materials ▸

- Studfinder
- Drill
- Level
- Pencil
- Vanity

Today's wall-hung sinks are stylish and attractive, but they require mounting into studs or added blocking to keep them secure.

How to Install a Wall-hung Vanity Base

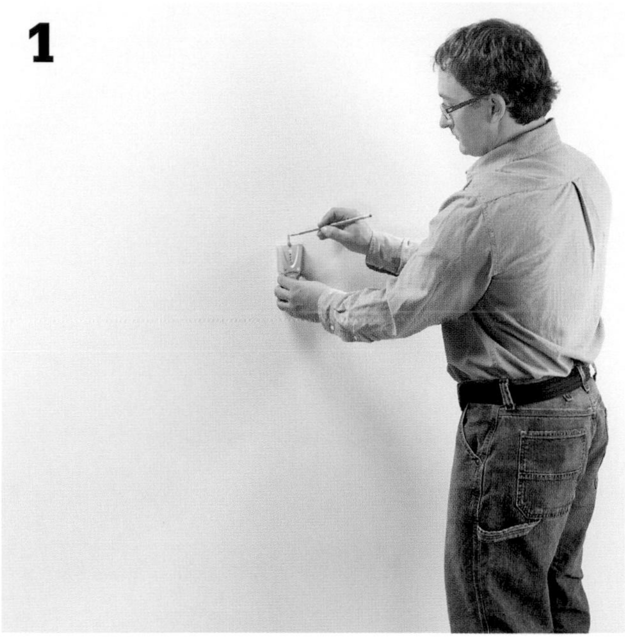

Remove the existing sink or fixture (pages 58 to 61) and inspect the wall framing. Also determine if plumbing supply and waste lines will need to be moved to accommodate the dimensions of the new fixture. Locate the studs in the sink location with a stud finder.

Hold the sink or cabinet in the installation area and check to see if the studs align with the sink or sink bracket mounting holes. If they do, skip to Step 3. If the studs do not align, remove the wallboard behind the mounting area. Install 2 × 6 blocking between studs at the locations of the mounting screws. Replace and repair wallboard.

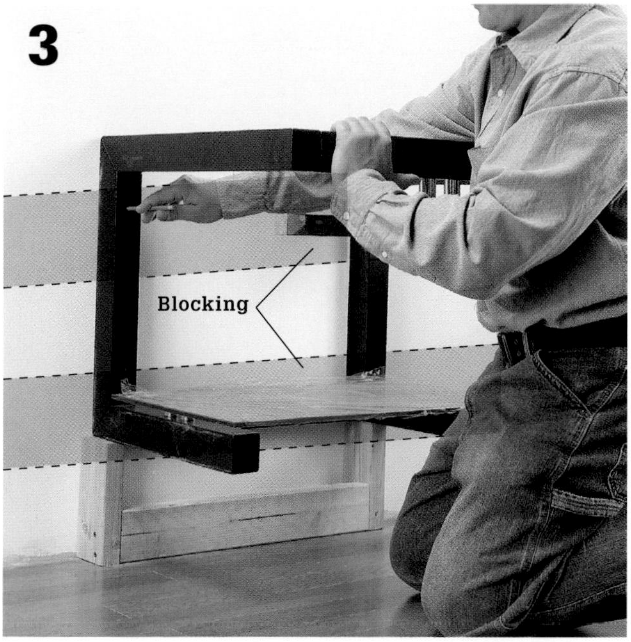

Mark the locations of the mounting holes on the wall using a template or by supporting the sink or vanity against the wall with a temporary brace (here, made from scrap 2 × 4s) and marking through the mounting holes.

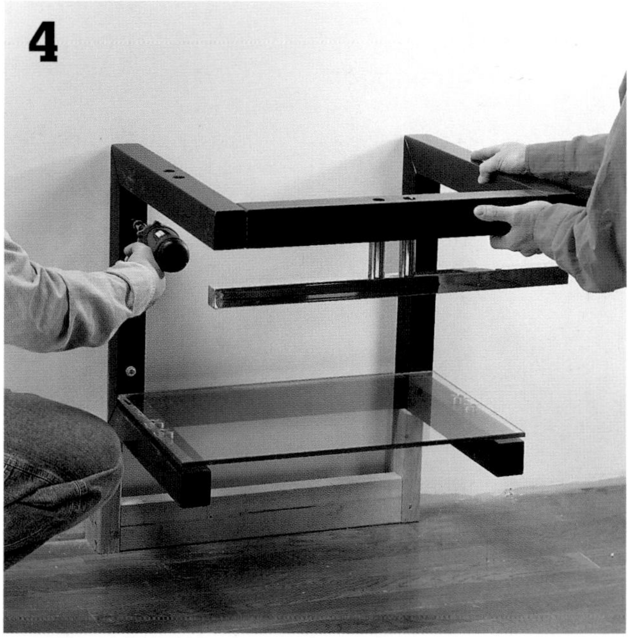

Drill pilot holes at the marks. Have a helper hold the vanity in place while you drive the mounting screws. Hook up the plumbing.

Vessel Sinks

The vessel sink harkens back to the days of washstands and washbowls. Whether it's round, square, or oval, shallow or deep, the vessel sink offers great opportunity for creativity and proudly displays its style. Vessel sinks are a perfect choice for a powder room, where they will have high visibility.

Most vessel sinks can be installed on any flat surface—from a granite countertop to a wall-mounted vanity to an antique dresser. Some sinks are designed to contact the mounting surface only at the drain flange. Others are made to be partially embedded in the surface. Take care to follow the manufacturer's instructions for cutting holes for sinks and faucets.

A beautiful vessel sink demands an equally attractive faucet. Select a tall spout mounted on the countertop or vanity top or a wall-mounted spout to accommodate the height of the vessel. To minimize splashing, spouts should direct flow to the center of the vessel, not down the side. Make sure your faucet is compatible with your vessel choice. Look for a centerset or single-handle model if you'll be custom drilling the countertop—you only need to drill one faucet hole.

Tools & Materials ▸

Pliers
Wrench
Vanity or countertop
Vessel sink
Pop-up drain
P-trap and drain kit
Faucet

Vessel sinks are available in countless styles and materials, shapes and sizes. Their one commonality is that they all need to be installed on a flat surface.

Vessel Sink Options

This glass vessel sink embedded in a "floating" glass countertop is a stunning contrast to the strong and attractive wood frame anchoring it to the wall.

The natural stone vessel sink blends elegantly into the stone countertop and is enhanced by the sleek faucet and round mirror.

The stone vessel sink is complemented by the wall-hung faucet. The rich wood vanity on which it's perched adds warmth to the room.

Vitreous china with a glazed enamel finish is an economical and durable choice for a vessel sink (although it is less durable than stone). Because of the flexibility of both the material and the glaze, the design options are virtually unlimited with vitreous china.

How to Install a Vessel Sink

Secure the vanity cabinet or other countertop that you'll be using to mount the vessel sink.

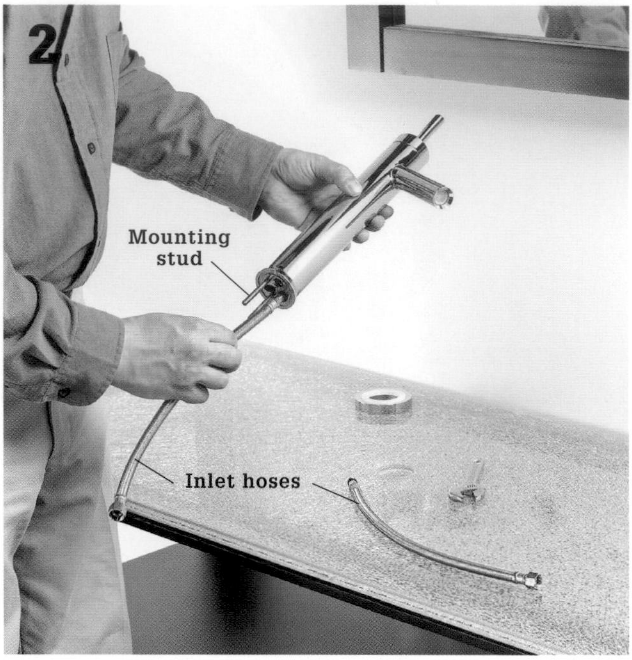

Begin hooking up the faucet. Insert the brass mounting stud into the threaded hole in the faucet base with the slotted end facing out. Hand tighten, and then use a slotted screwdriver to tighten another half turn. Insert the inlet hoses into the faucet body and hand tighten. Use an adjustable wrench to tighten another half turn. Do not overtighten.

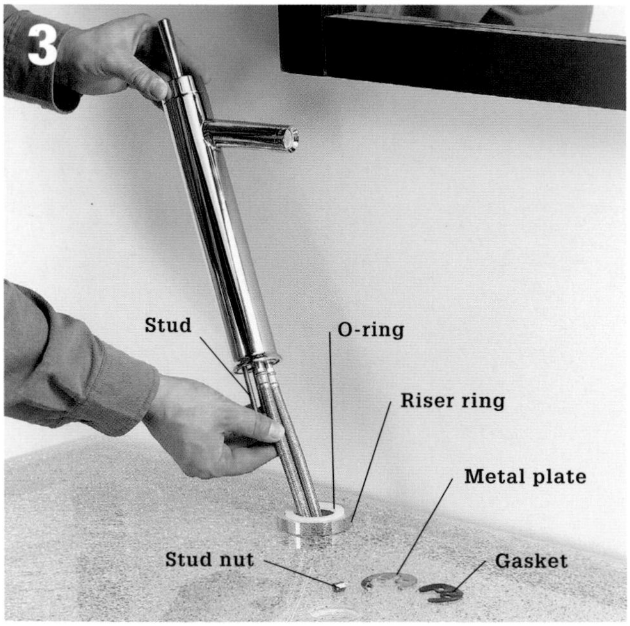

Place the riser ring on top of the O-ring over the faucet cutout in the countertop. From underneath, slide the rubber gasket and the metal plate over the mounting stud. Thread the mounting stud nut onto the mounting stud and hand tighten. Use an adjustable wrench to tighten another half turn.

To install the sink and pop-up drain, first place the small metal ring between two O-rings and place over the drain cutout.

Place the vessel bowl on top of the O-rings. In this installation, the vessel is not bonded to the countertop.

Put the small rubber gasket over the drain hole in the vessel. From the top, push the pop-up assembly through the drain hole.

From underneath, push the large rubber gasket onto the threaded portion of the pop-up assembly. Thread the nut onto the pop-up assembly and tighten. Use an adjustable wrench or basin wrench to tighten an additional half turn. Thread the tailpiece onto the pop-up assembly.

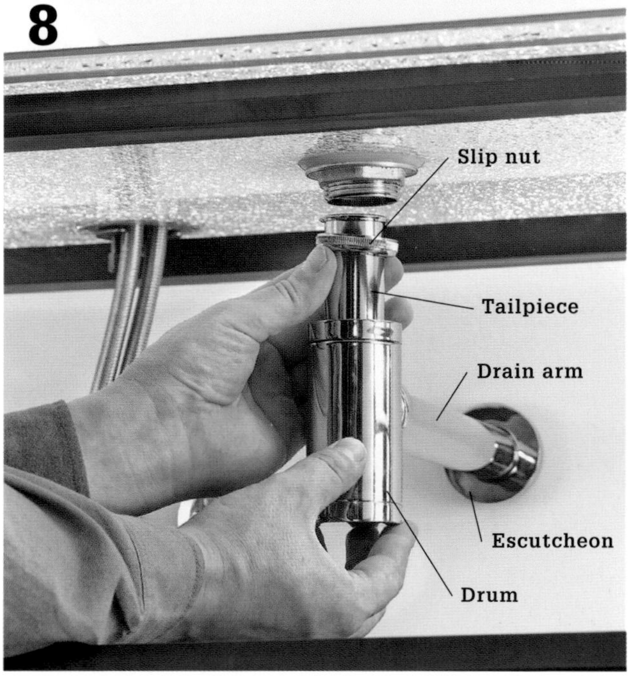

Install the drum trap. Loosen the rings on the top and outlet of the drum trap. Slide the drum trap top hole over the tailpiece. Slide the drain arm into the side outlet, with the flat side of the rubber gasket facing away from the trap. Insert the drain arm into the wall outlet. Hand tighten the rings.

Traditional Vanity

Most bathroom countertops installed today are integral (one-piece) sink/countertop units made from cultured marble or other solid materials, like solid surfacing. Integral sink/countertops are convenient, and many are inexpensive, but style and color options are limited.

Some remodelers and designers still prefer the distinctive look of a custom-built countertop with a self-rimming sink basin, which gives you a much greater selection of styles and colors. Installing a self-rimming sink is very simple.

Tools & Materials ▸

Pencil	Lag screws
Carpenter's level	Tub & tile caulk
Screwdriver	Studfinder
Basin wrench	4-ft. level
Cardboard	Shims
Masking tape	3" drywall screws
Plumber's putty	Drill

Integral sink/countertops are made in standard sizes to fit common vanity widths. Because the sink and countertop are cast from the same material, integral sink/countertops do not leak, and do not require extensive caulking and sealing.

How to Install a Vanity Cabinet

Measure and mark the top edge of the vanity cabinet on the wall, then use a 4-ft. level to mark a level line at the cabinet height mark. Use an electronic stud finder to locate the framing members, then mark the stud locations along the line.

Slide the vanity into position so that the back rail of the cabinet can later be fastened to studs at both corners and in the center. The back of the cabinet should also be flush against the wall. (If the wall surface is uneven, position the vanity so it contacts the wall in at least one spot, and the back cabinet rail is parallel with the wall.)

Using a 4-ft. level as a guide, shim below the vanity cabinet until the unit is level.

Variation: To install two or more cabinets, set the cabinets in position against the wall, and align the cabinet fronts. If one cabinet is higher than the other, shim under the lower cabinet until the two are even. Clamp the cabinet faces together, then drill countersunk pilot holes spaced 12" apart through the face frames so they go at least halfway into the face frame of the second cabinet. Drive wood screws through the pilot holes to join the cabinets together.

At the stud locations marked on the wall, drive 3" drywall screws through the rail on the cabinet back and into the framing members. The screws should be driven at both corners and in the center of the back rail.

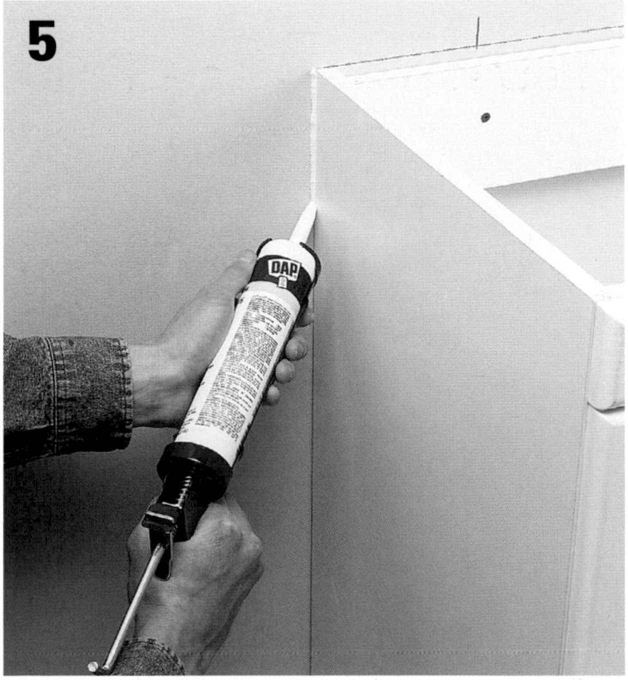

Run a bead of caulk along small gaps between the vanity and wall, and between the vanity and floor. For larger gaps, use quarter-round molding between the vanity and wall. Between the vanity and floor, install the same baseboard material used to cover the gap between the wall and floor.

How to Install an Integral Vanity Countertop

Set the sink/countertop unit onto sawhorses. Attach the faucet and slip the drain lever through the faucet body. Place a ring of plumber's putty around the drain flange, then insert the flange in the drain opening.

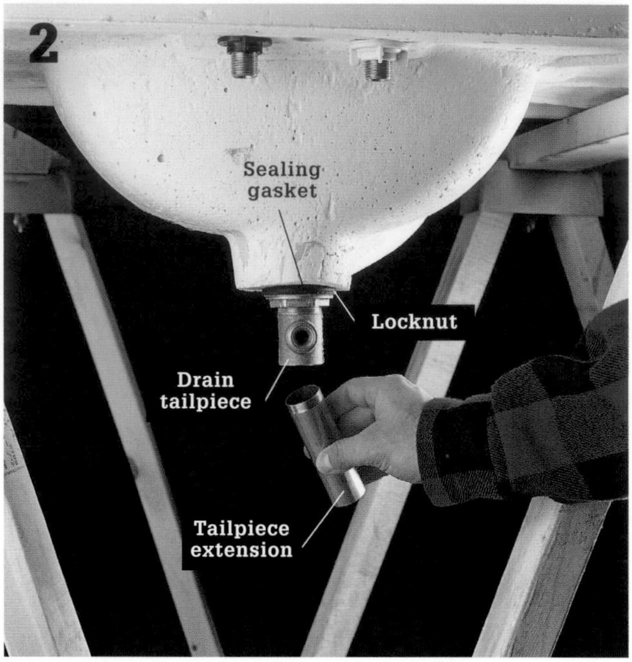

Thread the locknut and sealing gasket onto the drain tailpiece, then insert the tailpiece into the drain opening and screw it onto the drain flange. Tighten the locknut securely. Attach the tailpiece extension. Insert the pop-up stopper linkage.

Apply a layer of tub & tile caulk (or adhesive, if specified by the countertop manufacturer) to the top edges of the cabinet vanity, and to any corner braces.

Center the sink/countertop unit over the vanity, so the overhang is equal on both sides and the backsplash of the countertop is flush with the wall. Press the countertop evenly into the caulk.

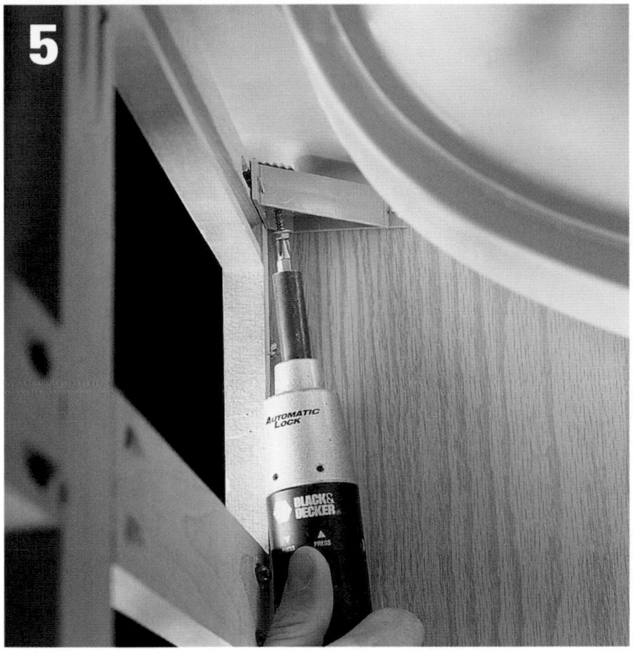

Cabinets with corner braces: Secure the countertop to the cabinet by driving a mounting screw through each corner brace and up into the countertop. *Note: Cultured marble and other hard countertops require predrilling and a plastic screw sleeve.*

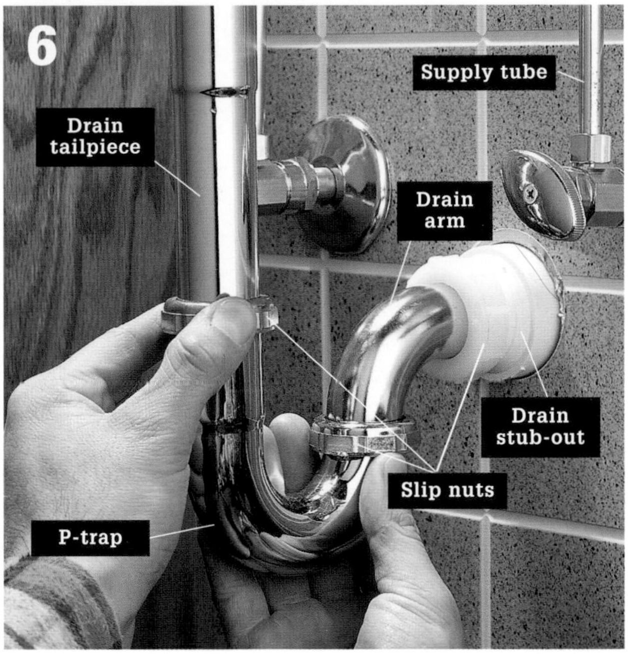

Attach the drain arm to the drain stub-out in the wall using a slip nut. Attach one end of the P-trap to the drain arm, and the other to the tailpiece of the sink drain, using slip nuts. Connect supply tubes to the faucet tailpieces. Seal the gap between the backsplash and the wall with tub and tile caulk.

Variation: Drop-In Sinks

An inexpensive alternative to an integral vanity countertop is to build your own countertop from postform laminate or another kitchen-style countertop material. Be sure to add buildup strips and caps to the exposed ends. Position the countertop on your vanity cabinet and trace a cutout for the drop-in lavatory.

Install the drop-in sink. Some sinks rely mostly on their own weight to stay put, requiring only a bead of plumbers putty for setting the sink flange. Lighter sinks are held in place with clips from below. It's usually recommended that you attach your faucet to the sink before installing it, and then make your hookups.

Custom Double Vanity Cabinet

You can purchase vanity tops with a matching stock vanity cabinet, or you can put your own design stamp on the bathroom by building a custom vanity cabinet. Crafting a your own vanity cabinet is a great way to seamlessly integrate the unit into the overall bathroom design, especially when you haven't been able to find the cabinet of dreams at retail.

The custom double vanity cabinet in this project was designed to support the double-bowl vanity shown on page 158. The cabinet is built with ½", 9-ply Baltic birch plywood and solid birch framing. This particular plywood is a favorite of cabinetmakers because of its beautiful grain structure and appealing edge appearance. The look of the finished cabinet is contemporary and clean, making it suitable to a wide range of bathroom decors. The unit is wall mounted, but two legs at the front of the cabinet provide stability and create the appearance of a standalone piece of furniture.

All panels are cut with the grain running horizontally. The doors offer easy access to the abundant storage space inside the cabinet, and the bottom drawer is operable while the top is a false front. The project requires moderate woodworking skills and an precise measurements. But with a little effort, you'll wind up with gorgeous vanity cabinetry that is uniquely your own.

This custom-made cabinet is built using Baltic Birch plywood for a clean, contemporary feel. Because it is wall-hung it feels open and light, but the front legs guarantee that it is stable.

Tools & Materials & Cutting List ▸

Circular saw
Router
Drill
Door pulls
Pocket jig
Door pulls
2" flathead wood screws
⅜" × 3½" lag screws with washers
½" Baltic birch plywood
½" plywood
Self-closing cup hinges
2 self-leveling 10" furniture legs
Bottom-mount drawer slide
2 × 4
1½" finish nails
No. 8 × ¾" panhead screws

KEY	NO.	PART	SIZE	MATERIAL
A	2	Door	½ × 23¾ × 19"	Baltic birch
B	2	Drawer fronts	½ × 12 × 9¾"	Baltic birch
C	2	End Panels	½ × 12 × 20"	Baltic birch
D	1	Bottom panel	½ × 19 × 59"	Baltic birch
E	2	Top frame rail	¾ × 1½ × 59"	Birch
F	3	Top frame stile	¾ × 1½ × 18"	Birch
G	2	Cabinet divider	¾ × 1½ × 18¾"	Birch
H	1	Back spreader	¾ × 1½ × 58½"	Birch
I	1	Wall cleat	1½ × 3½ × 59"	2 × 4
J	1	Drawer bottom	½ × 11 × 18"	Plywood
K	2	Drawer end	½ × 11 × 6"	Plywood
L	2	Drawer side	½ × 17 × 6"	Plywood

HARDWARE
4 Self closing cup hinges for ½" stock
Bottom mount drawer slide (16")
2 10" × 2" dia. brushed steel adjustable legs (item CM250 at www.tablelegsonline.com)
4 Brushed steel door pulls

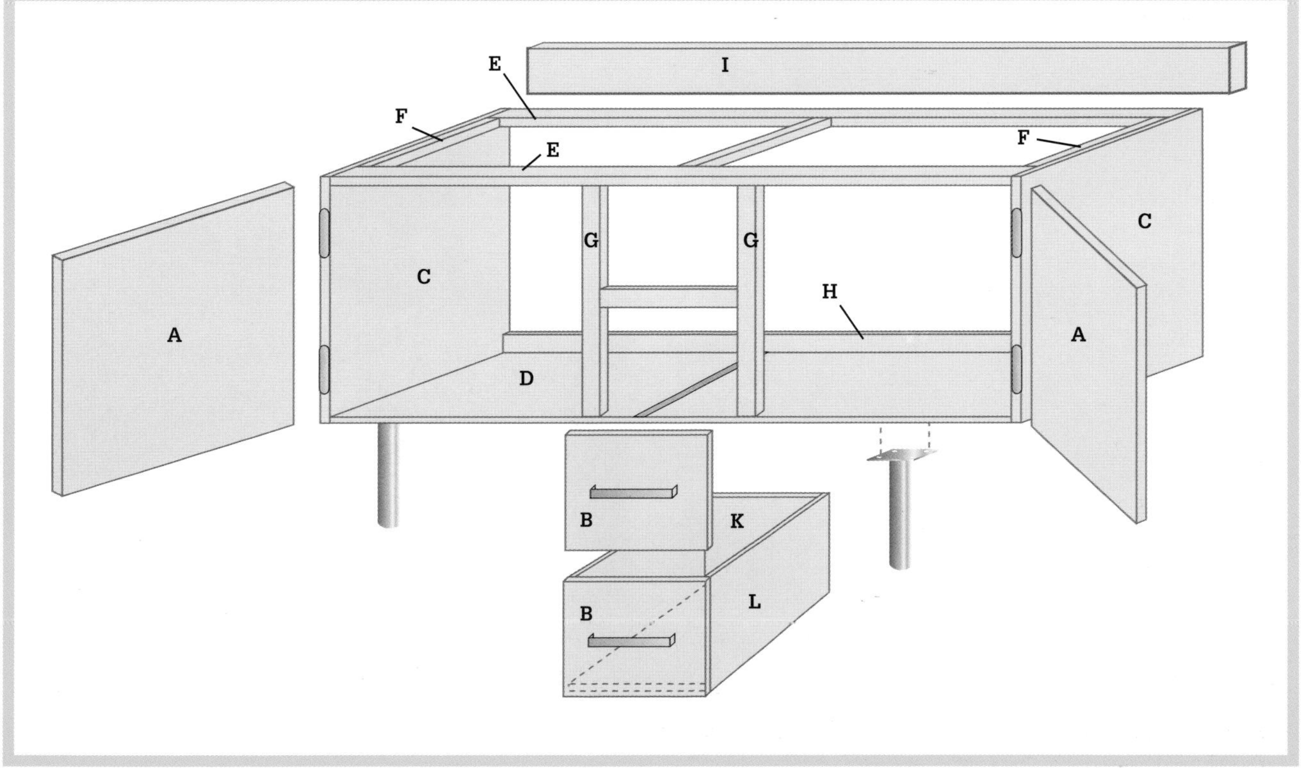

Baltic Birch ▸

Baltic birch is considered the premier cabinetry plywood because of its extremely attractive and consistent surface patterns, and its uniform edge appearance that can eliminate the need for additional edge treatments such as wood veneer tape. This type of plywood features voidless plies, so the layers have no visual gaps along the edges. The facing takes stain well, but most people choose to use a clear finish such as polyurethane to allow the beauty of the wood to come through. If you're determining the measurements for your own vanity cabinet, be aware that Baltic birch plywood comes in 5 × 5' sheets, as opposed to the standard 4 × 8' sheets.

How to Build a Custom Vanity Cabinet

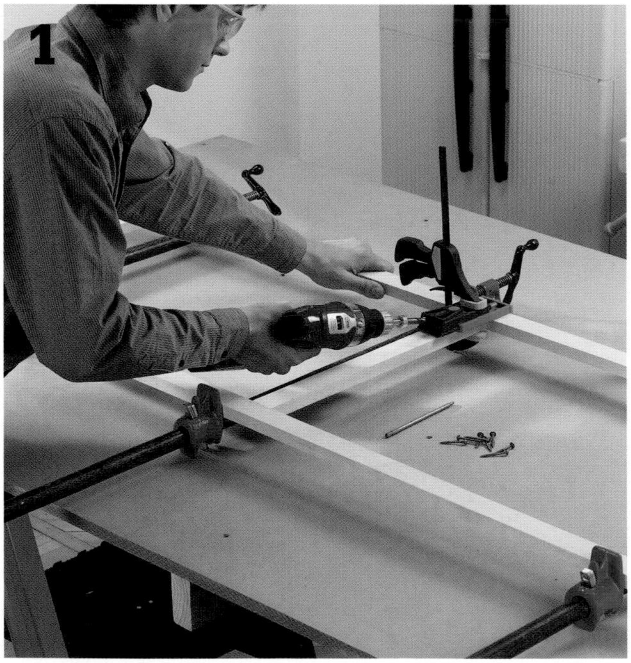

Cut the pieces for the top frame from solid ½" birch—two 59" rails and three 18" stiles. Use a pocket jig to drill two pocket holes at each end of the stiles, and then glue and screw them to the rails with pocket screws.

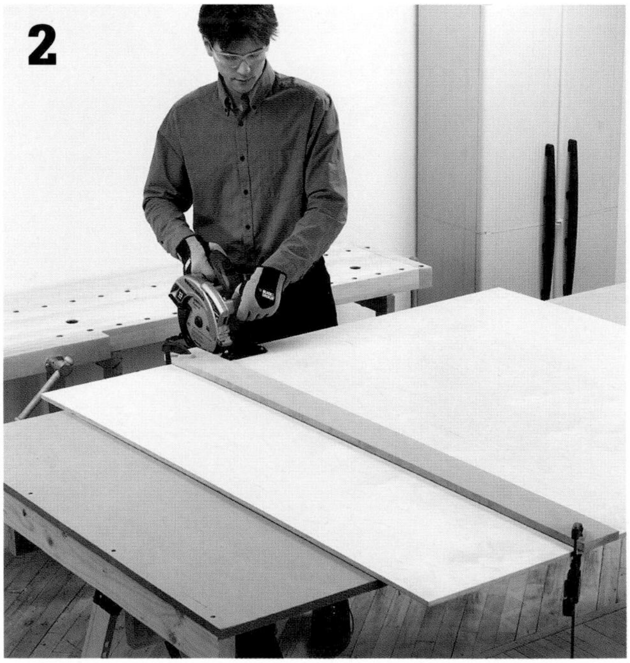

Cut the side and bottom panels, and door and drawer fronts, from a single sheet of Baltic birch plywood. Use a circular saw equipped with a sharp, thin-kerf ripping blade. Use a straightedge guide and saw the panels with the good side facing down.

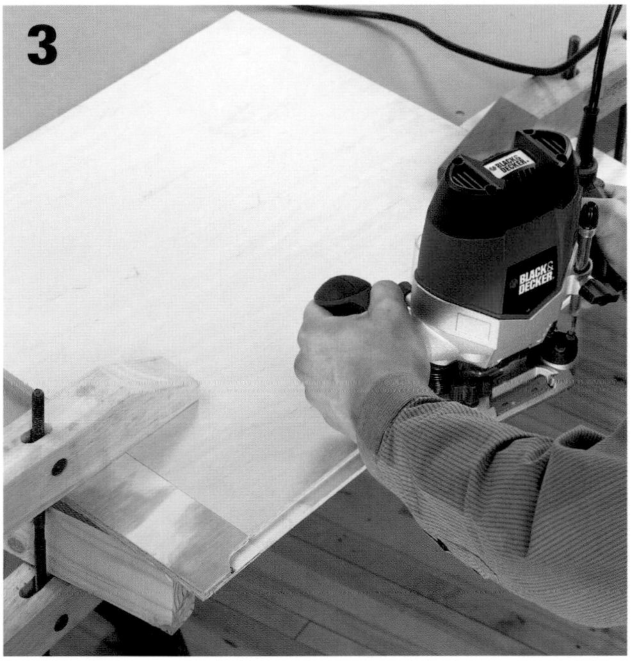

Cut rabbets for the bottom panel in the bottom inside edges of the both side panels. Use a router fitted with a ½" piloted rabbeting bit, set to ¼" depth. Sand as necessary to clean and smooth the rabbets.

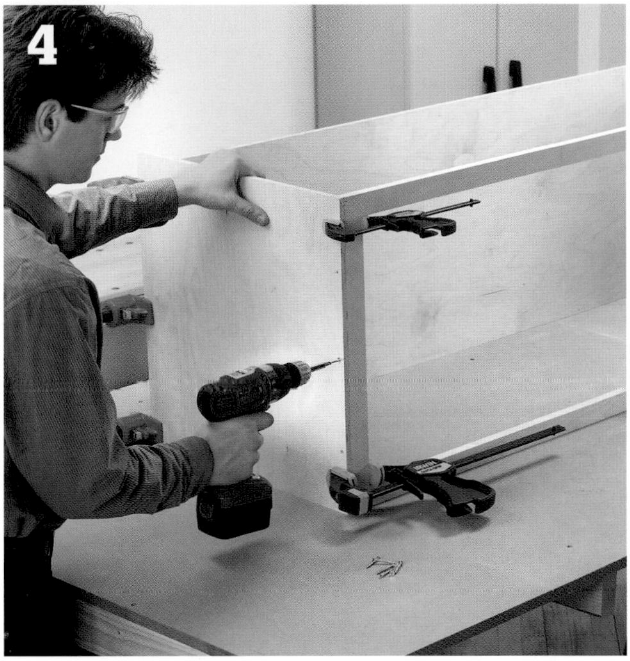

Assemble the cabinet case by gluing and clamping the end panels to the bottom panel. Glue and clamp the top frame into position between the tops of the end panels. Screw the end panels into the top frame with two 2" woodscrews on either side. Secure the bottom panel in place with finishing nails through end panels into the bottom panel.

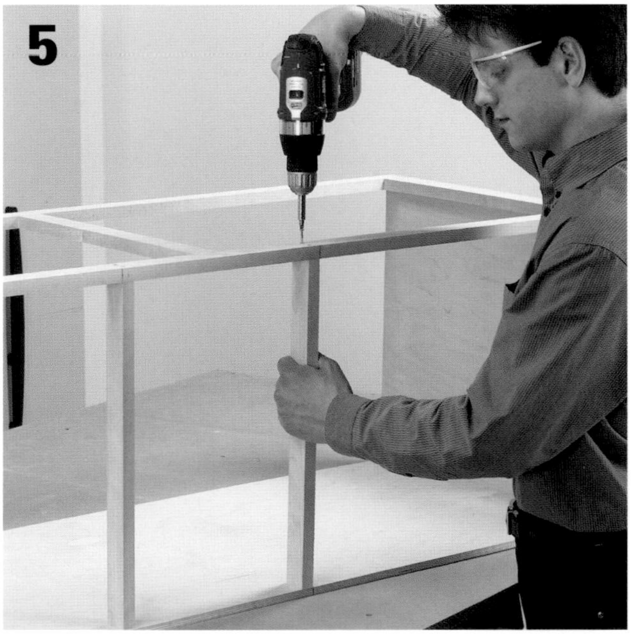

Cut and position solid birch dividers between the bottom panel and top frame. Measure to ensure the dividers are in correct position, check for level, then screw the bottom panel and top frame to dividers. Add a central divider between the vertical dividers to create a visual backing for the gap between the drawer fronts.

Attach legs to the bottom of the cabinet case, inset about 2" from front corners. Secure legs according to manufacturer's directions. The 10" metal legs here were screwed onto a bolt projecting through a hole in the bottom panel. The bolt is attached to a mounting plate screwed to the bottom of the bottom panel.

(continued)

Position cabinet in place, check for level, and measure from the floor to the bottom edge of the top frame. Mark line and screw 2 × 4 cleat to wall with 3½" lag screws, keeping top of cleat aligned with mark.

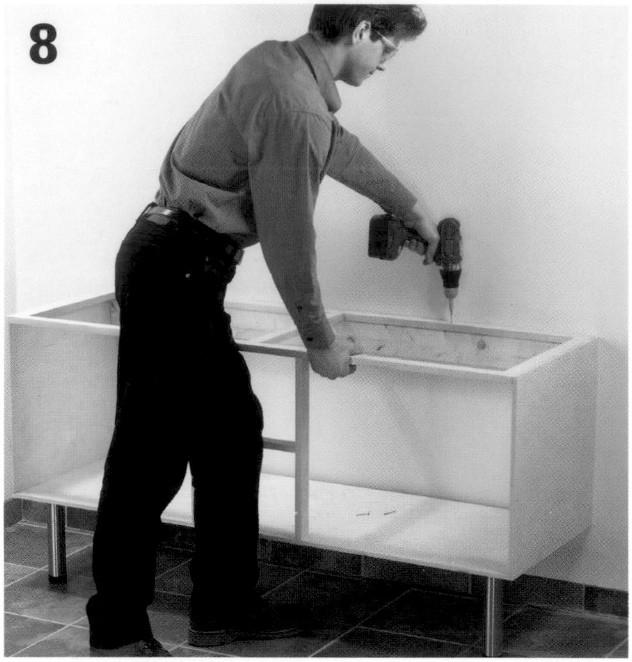

Position cabinet so that top frame rests on wall cleat. Check level and shim as necessary, then nail finish nails through end panels into ends of wall cleat. Adjust the front feet according to manufacturer's directions so that cabinet is level.

Cut spreader for rear of cabinet and place on top of bottom panel, between two side panels. Nail spreader in place with finish nails, nailed through end panels into ends of spreader.

Cut sides, back, and bottom panels for the drawer box. Glue and clamp pieces together, and edge nail pieces together with brads to reinforce the drawer box. Attach slides to bottom of drawer and bottom of cabinet in drawer opening.

Sand edges of drawer and door fronts, working from about 100 grit down to 180 grit. *Note: If you aren't satisfied with the look of the drawer and door edges, use filler before sanding to ensure they are absolutely smooth, or cover the edges with wood veneer tape prior to finishing the cabinet.*

Mount the cabinet doors using adjustable cup hinges. Check that the doors are mounted square and plumb, adjusting the hinges as necessary.

Clamp drawer front into place on divider. Drill pilot holes and attach drawer front with four #8 × ¾" panhead screws. Check that drawer slides in an out freely. Screw 1 × cleats for top drawer (false) front onto inside faces of dividers. Screw through cleats into back of drawer front to secure it in place.

Sink nailheads and cover exposed nail and screwheads with stainable wood putty. Sand putty smooth, then apply your finish of choice. We finished the cabinet with a brush-on stain, but use clear polyurethane if you prefer the natural look of the birch. Mark positions of drawer pulls, drill mounting holes, and install pulls.

Double-Bowl Vanity Top

Side-by-side double sinks are a wonderful addition to bathrooms large enough to accommodate the extra fixture. Often called "his-and-her" sinks, double sinks can be indispensable in a busy bathroom serving a large household, or for a couple whose schedules put them in the master bath at the same time each day.

The first issue to consider in adding a double sink is available space. You need to maintain the minimum required space around the sink, including 30 inches of clear space in front of the sink (but no less than 21 inches) and 30 inches from the center of one sink to the center of the other. Any sink or vanity edge should be at least 4 inches from a side wall, and should not impede door swing.

You'll also want to decide how much plumbing modification you're willing to do. Side-by-side standalone sinks, such as pedestals or wall-mounted models, require new supply and drains. But a double sink vanity like the one shown here can be added simply by using dual-use hardware that splits the existing supply and drain lines.

Tools & Materials ▸

- Carpenter's level
- Screwdrivers
- Drill
- Basin wrench
- Stud finder
- Adjustable wrench
- Hacksaw
- Silicone caulk
- Dual outlet valves
- Braided steel supply lines
- P-trap
- PVC connections
- Plumber's putty

A double-bowl vanity is a useful fixture for allowing multiple users during rush hour in your bathroom. Most home centers stock a couple of double-bowl options, but for best selection allow enough time for a custom order (usually 1 to 6 weeks). See pages 152 to 157 for instructions on how to build the custom vanity cabinet.

Double Drains

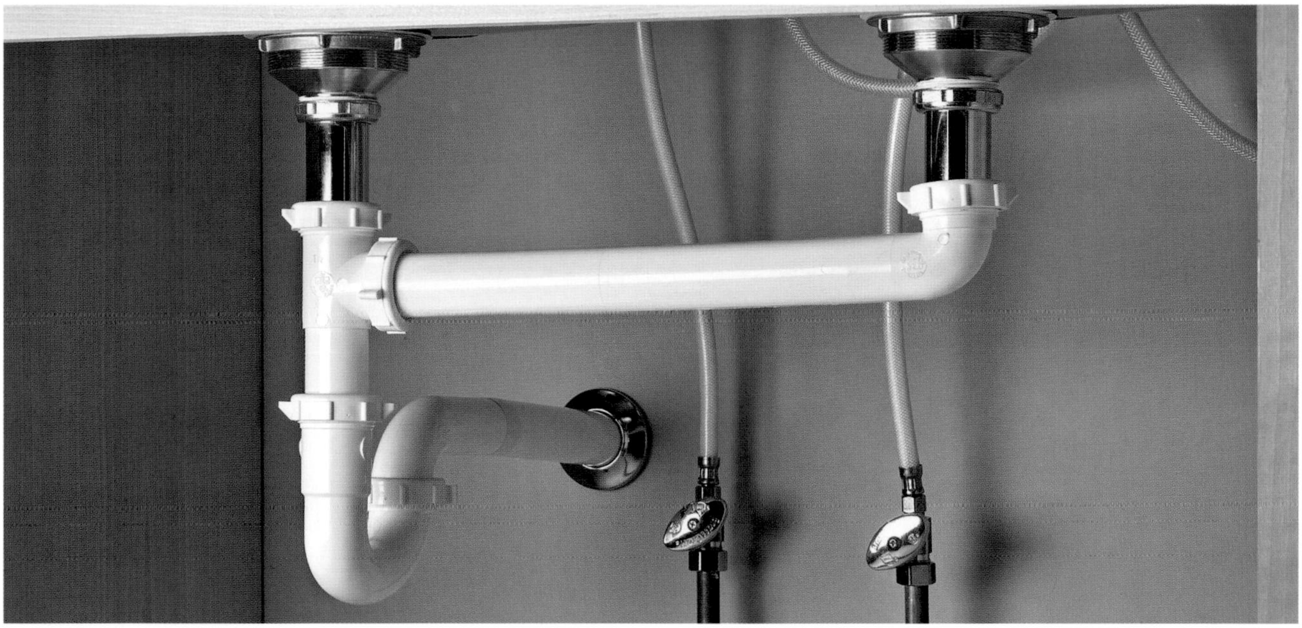

Double-bowl vanities have drain plumbing that's very similar to double-bowl kitchen sinks (except for the improbability that you will have a garbage disposer in your lavatory drain lines). In most cases, the drain tailpieces are connected beneath one of the tailpieces at a continuous waste T. The drainline from the second bowl must slope downward toward the T. From the T, the drain should have a trap (usually a P-Trap) that connects to the trap arm coming out of the wall.

Drain in Floor

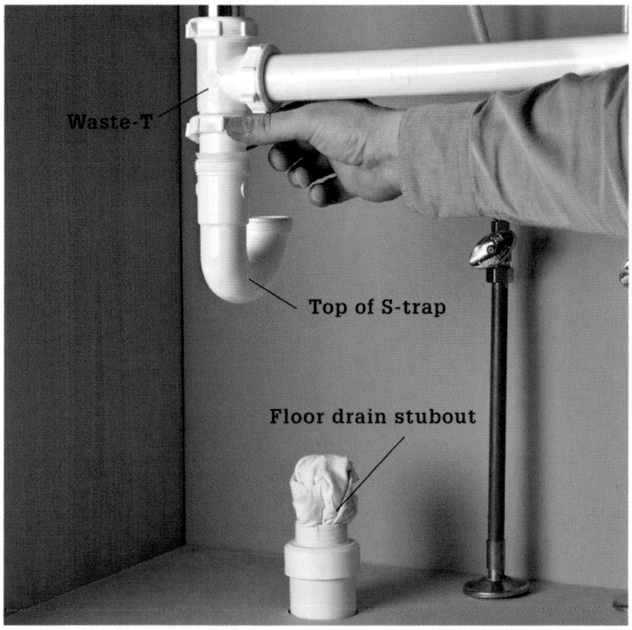

If your drain stubout comes up out of the floor instead of the wall, you'll need an S-trap to tie into it instead of a P-trap. Attach one half of the S-trap to the threaded bottom of the waste-T.

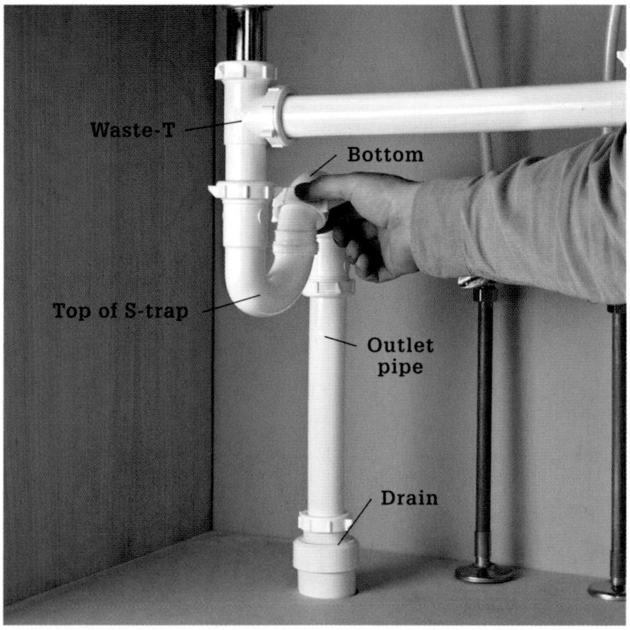

Attach the other half of the S-trap to the stubout with a slip fitting. This should result in the new fitting facing downward. Join the halves of the S-trap together with a slip nut, trimming the unthreaded end if necessary.

How to Install a Double Sink and Vanity

Shut off the supply valves located under the sink. Disconnect and remove the supply lines connecting the faucet to the valves. Loosen the P-trap nuts at both ends and remove the P-trap.

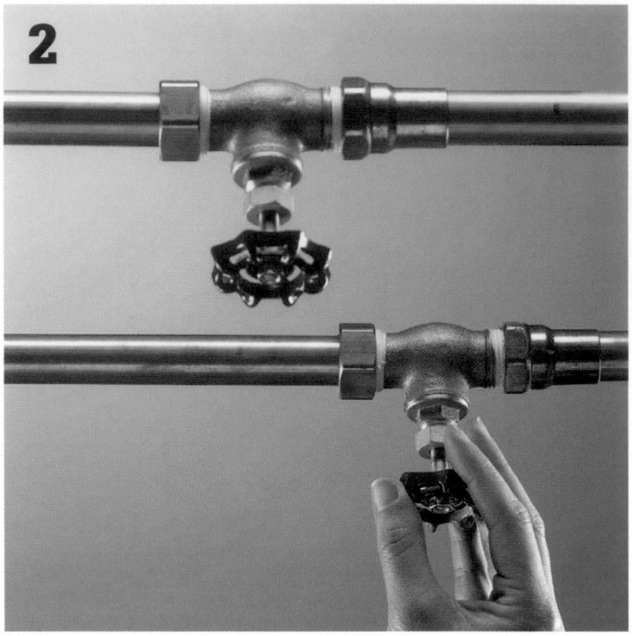

Remove the existing countertop and vanity. Turn off house water supply at the main shut-off valve. Drain remaining water by opening the faucet at the lowest point in the house. Use a hacksaw to remove existing undersink shut-off valves.

Slide the new dual-outlet valve onto the hot water supply line, pass nut and compression washer over the pipe, and tighten with wrench. Install dual-outlet valve on cold supply line in the same way.

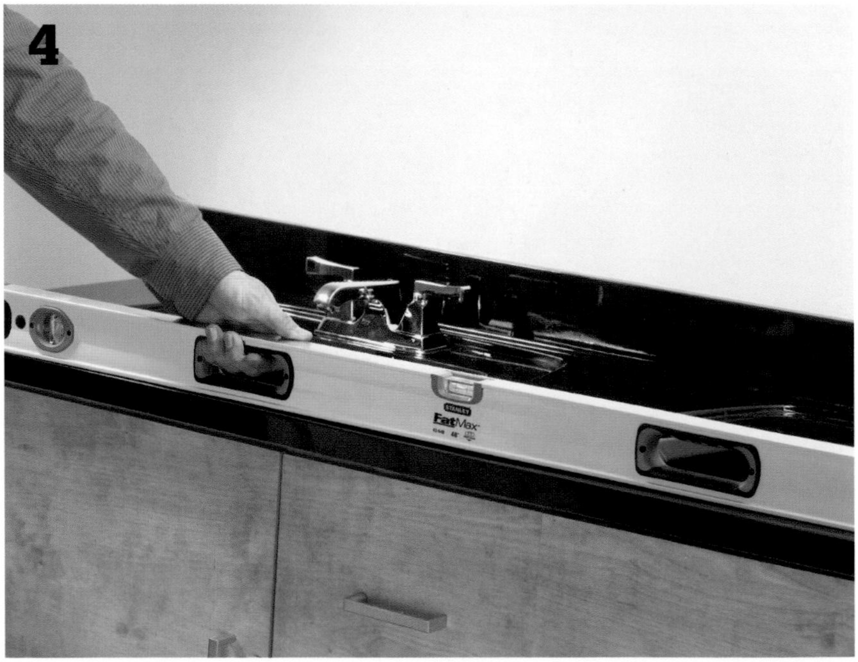

Secure the new vanity in place by screwing it to the wall. Lay a bead of caulk along the underside and back edge of the countertop, where it will contact the vanity and wall. Set the countertop in place and check it for level. If your sinks are not integral, install them according to the type of sink you're using.

Seat the faucets for the double sinks as you would for a single sink, by applying a bead of putty on the underside of the bases (unless they are to be used with gaskets instead of putty). Secure them in place by tightening the locking nuts on the underside of the faucets.

Connect a new PVC P-trap to the undersink drain pipe, and attach a T-connector to the trap. Extend PVC connections to the drain assemblies of both sinks.

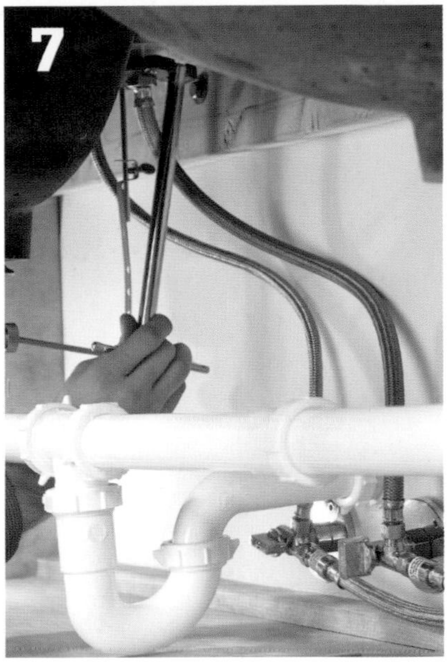

Connect the linkage for the pop-up drain stopper. Connect the braided steel cold water supply lines to the appropriate faucet tailpieces. Once the lines are secure, repeat for the hot water supply lines. Check that all connections are tightened securely.

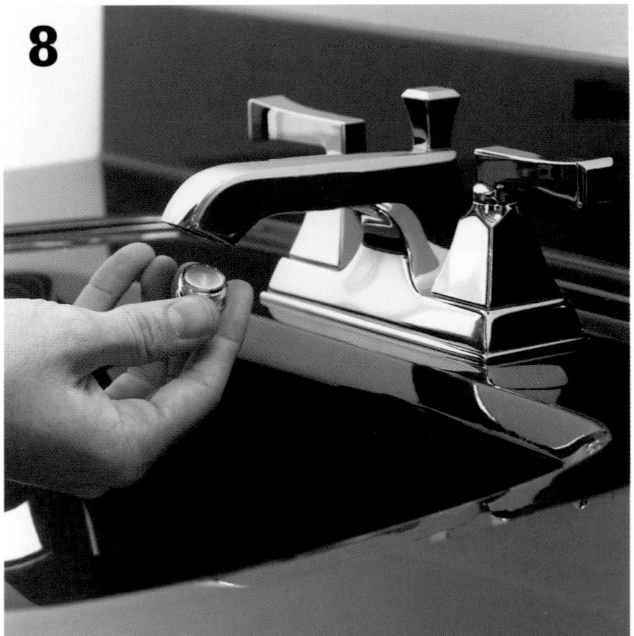

Turn on the main water supply and then turn on the water supply to the faucets. Remove the faucet aerators and run water in the sinks to check the supply lines and drain connections for leaks. Tighten the connections if you find any and replace the aerators.

Leak Finder ▸

To quickly and easily find an undersink leak, lay bright white paper or paper towels under the pipes and drain connections. Open the water supply valves and run water in the sinks. It should be clear exactly where the water dripped from by the location of the drip on the paper.

Lavatory Faucets

Bathroom faucets come in four basic mounting styles: centerset, single hole, wall mounted, and widespread. The type you choose depends largely on the sink or faucet body you are using—the new faucet may need to match the existing fixture. But in any case, the range of designs available in all mounting styles is astounding.

Widespread faucets have a clean, sophisticated look. They come in three pieces instead of one: a hot tap, a cold tap, and a spout. Each piece is mounted separately in its own hole in the sink. The hot and cold taps (valves) are connected to the spout with reinforced flexible hoses. If your lavatory doesn't have a predrilled flange, the great advantage to the widespread configuration is that you gain flexibility in locating your spout and handles (probably a bigger advantage for tubs than for lavatories). Even models made for bathroom lavatories, like the one you see here, offer many creative configuration options.

Single-body and centerset faucets are designed to fit into standard hole configurations. Make sure you know your sink's dimensions before buying the faucet: the most important dimension is the hole spread: 4 inches on center and 8 inches on center are common.

Tools & Materials ▸

- Heatproof grease
- Teflon tape
- Measuring tape
- Loctite
- Pipe joint compound
- Plumber's putty
- New 3-piece faucet
- Supply lines
- Adjustable wrench
- Basin wrench
- Channel-type pliers
- Screwdriver
- Standing flashlight
- Eye protection

Your lavatory faucet should echo or complement some aspects of your sink. These aspects can include the overall geometry and shape, the style (traditional, contemporary, etc.), or the finish, for example.

Basic Lavatory Faucet Types ▸

Widespread faucets allow you to customize the locations and orientation of the faucets and spout in your sink deck.

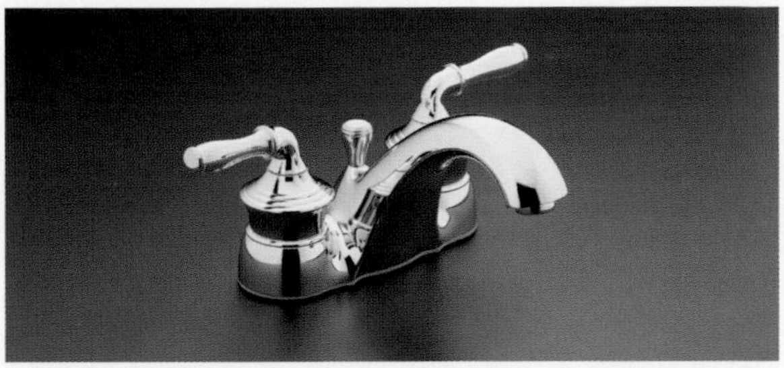

Single-body faucets are faster and easier to install and are extremely reliable.

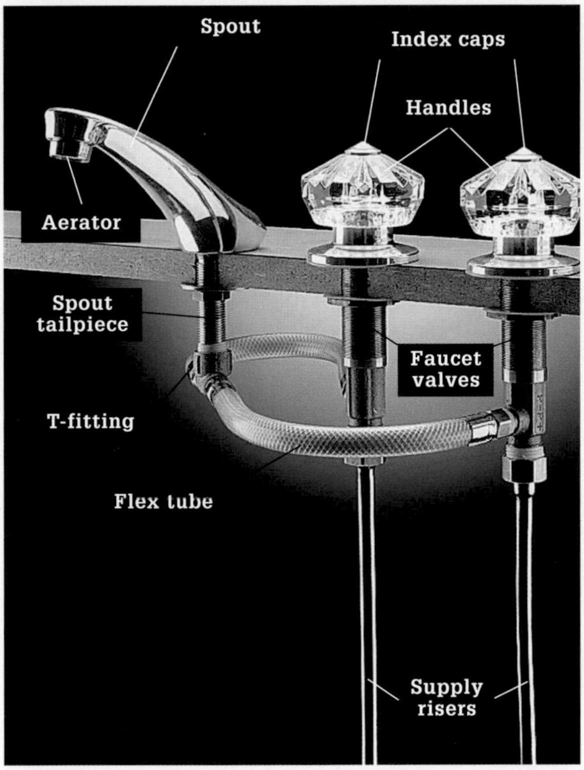

Widespread faucets come in three pieces, a spout and two valves. Supply risers carry hot and cold water to the valves, which are turned to regulate the amount of water going to the spout, where the water is mixed. Water travels from the valves to the spout through flex tubes, which in turn attach to the spout tailpiece via a T-fitting. Three-piece faucets designed to work with a pop-up stopper have a clevis and a lift rod. The handles attach with handle screws that are covered with index caps. An aerator is screwed on the faucet spout after debris is flushed from the faucet.

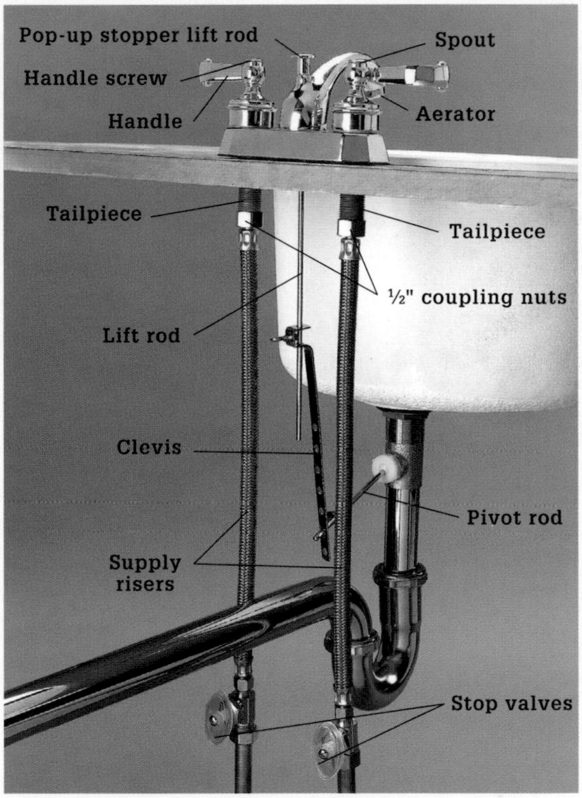

The tailpieces of a standard deck-mounted, one-piece bathroom sink faucet are 4" apart on center. As long as the two outside holes in the back of your sink measure 4" from center to center, and you have a middle hole for a pop-up stopper, you can put in any standard one-piece bathroom faucet with a pop-up stopper. The faucet is secured to the sink with mounting nuts that screw onto the tailpieces from below. Also get two flexible stainless steel supply risers for sinks, long enough to replace the old tubes. These typically attach to the stop valves with ⅜" compression-sized coupling nuts and to the faucet with standard faucet coupling nuts. But take your old tubes and the old compression nuts from the stop valves to the store to ensure a match. The clevis, lift rod, and pivot rod are parts of the pop-up stopper assembly. The handles attach with handle screws that are covered with index caps.

How to Install a Widespread Faucet

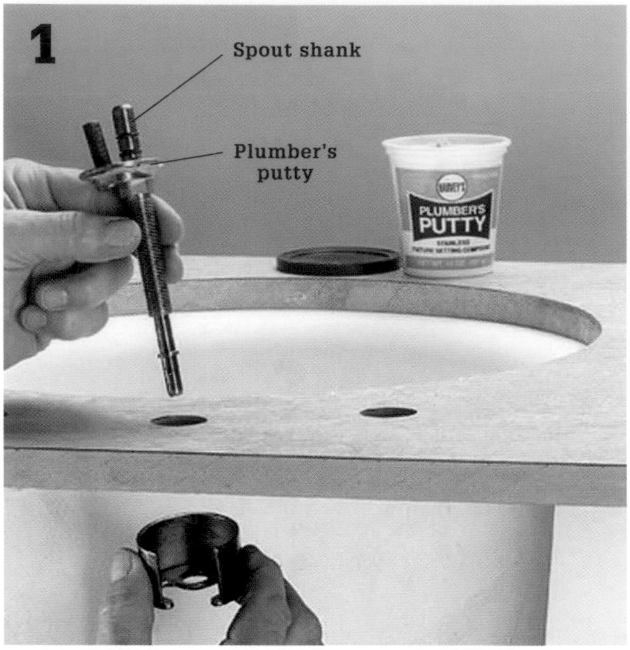

Insert the shank of the faucet spout through one of the holes in the sink deck (usually the center hole but you can offset it in one of the end holes if you prefer). If the faucet is not equipped with seals or O-rings for the spout and handles, pack plumber's putty on the undersides before inserting the valves into the deck. *Note: If you are installing the widespread faucet in a new sink deck, drill three holes of the size suggested by the faucet manufacturer.*

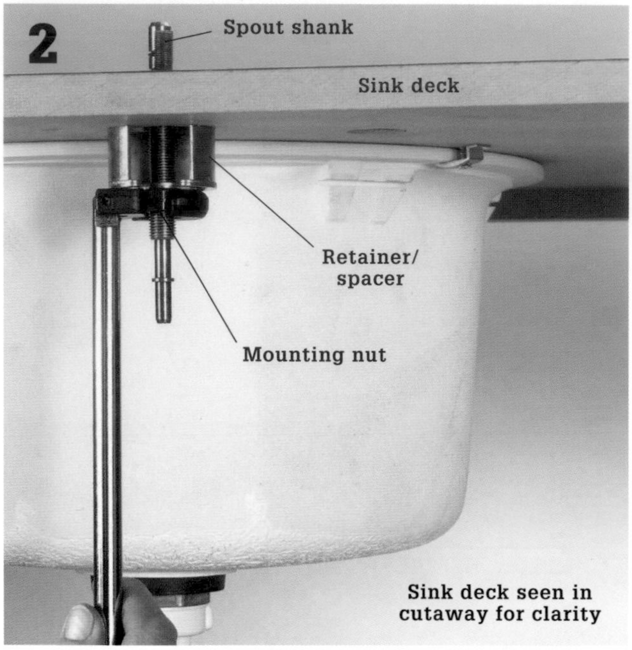

In addition to mounting nuts, many spout valves for widespread faucets have an open retainer fitting that goes between the underside of the deck and the mounting nut. Others have only a mounting nut. In either case, tighten the mounting nut with pliers or a basin wrench to secure the spout valve. You may need a helper to keep the spout centered and facing forward.

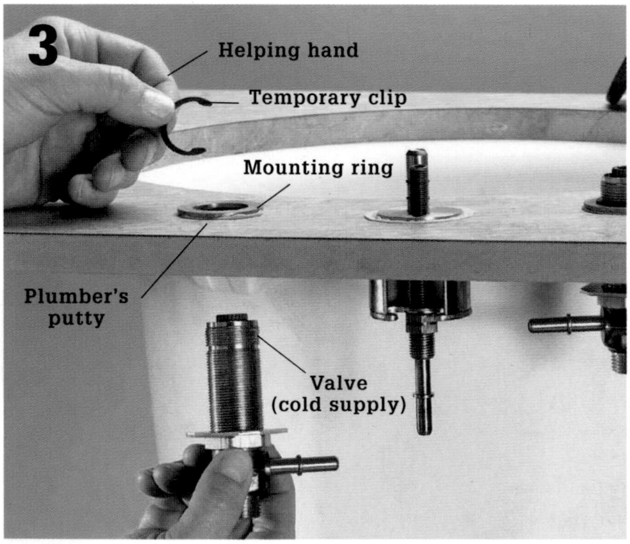

Mount the valves to the deck using whichever method the manufacturer specifies (it varies quite a bit). In the model seen here, a mounting ring is positioned over the deck hole (with plumber's putty seal) and the valve is inserted from below. A clip snaps onto the valve from above to hold it in place temporarily (you'll want a helper for this).

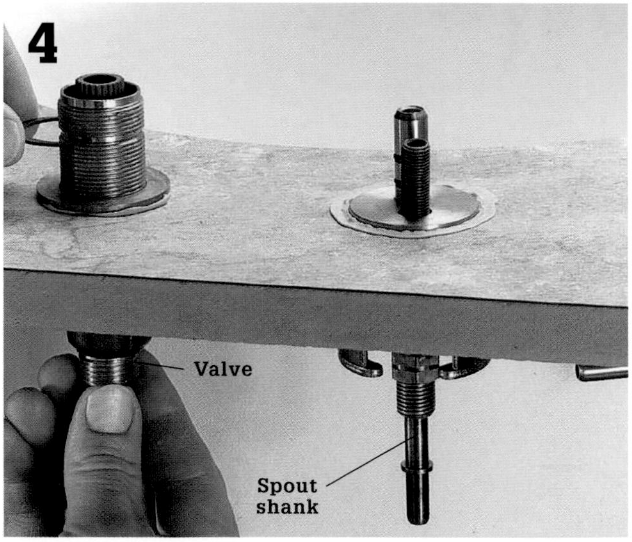

From below, thread the mounting nuts that secure the valves to the sink deck. Make sure the cold water valve (usually has a blue cartridge inside) is in the right hole (from the front) and the hot water valve (red cartridge) is in the left hole. Install both valves.

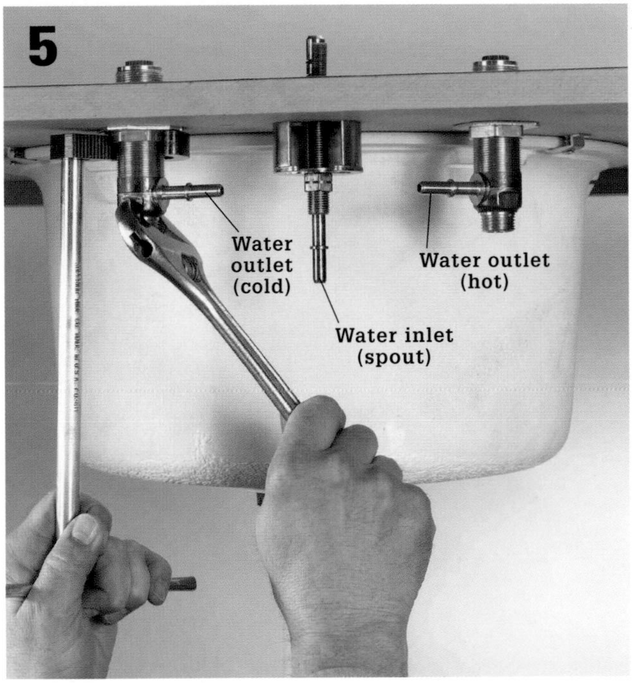

Once you've started the nut on the threaded valve shank, secure the valve with a basin wrench squeezing the lugs where the valve fits against the deck. Use an adjustable wrench to finish tightening the lock nut onto the valve. The valves should be oriented so the water outlets are aimed at the inlet on the spout shank.

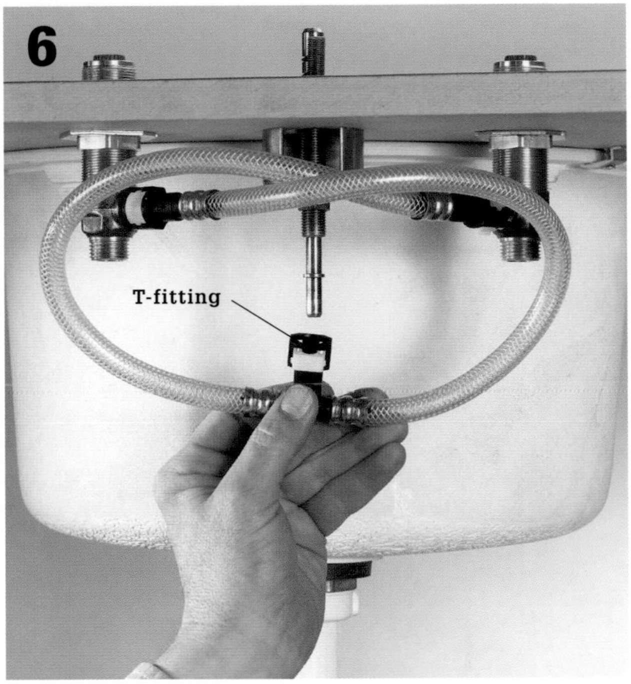

Attach the flexible supply tubes (supplied with the faucet) to the water outlets on the valves. Some twist onto the outlets, but others (like the ones above) click into place. The supply hoses meet in a T-fitting that is attached to the water inlet on the spout.

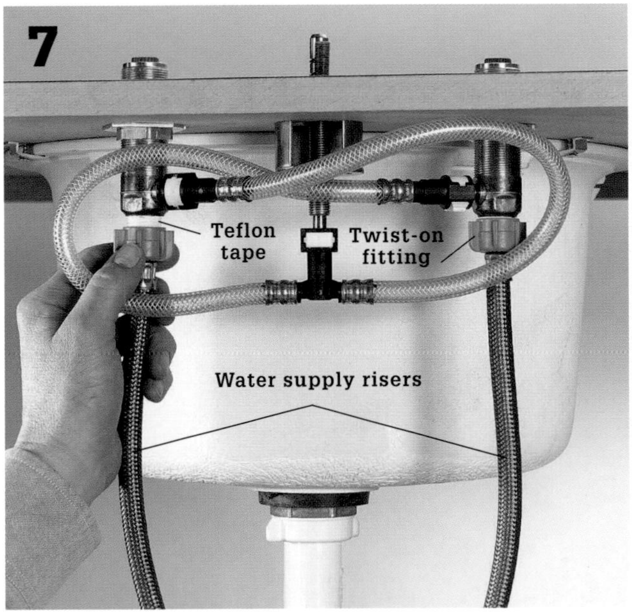

Attach flexible braided metal supply risers to the water stop valves and then attach the tubes to the inlet port on each valve (usually with Teflon tape and a twist-on fitting at the valve end of the supply riser).

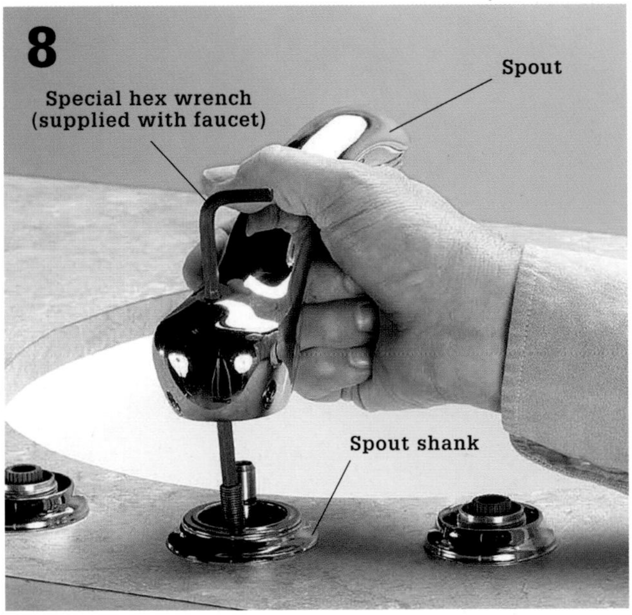

Attach the spout. The model shown here comes with a special hex wrench that is threaded through the hole in the spout where the lift rod for the pop-up drain will be located. Once the spout is seated cleanly on the spout shank you tighten the hex wrench to secure the spout. Different faucets will use other methods to secure the spout to the shank.

(continued)

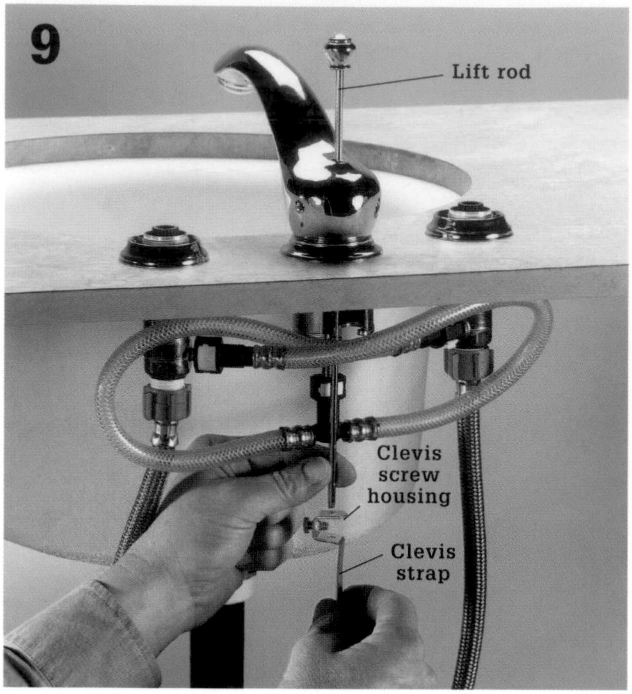

If your sink did not have a pop-up stopper, you'll need to replace the sink drain tailpiece with a pop-up stopper body (often supplied with the faucet). Insert the lift rod through the hole in the back of the spout and, from below, thread the pivot rod through the housing for the clevis screw.

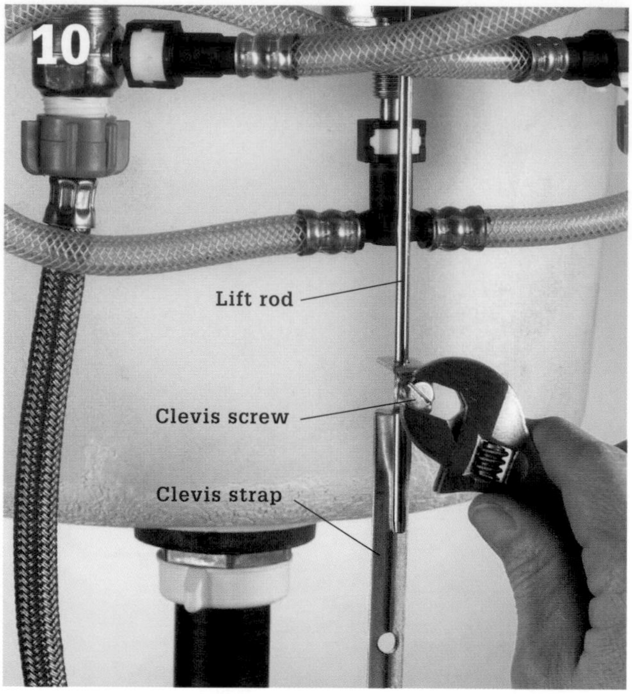

Attach the clevis strap to the pivot rod that enters the pop-up drain body and adjust the position of the strap so it raises and lowers properly when the lift rod is pulled up. Tighten the clevis screw at this point. It's hard to fit a screwdriver in here, so you may need to use a wrench or pliers.

Attach the faucet handles to the valves using whichever method is required by the faucet manufacturer. Most faucets are designed with registration methods to ensure that the handles are symmetrical and oriented in an ergonomic way once you secure them to the valves.

Remove the faucet aerator, turn on the water supply and test the faucet so any debris in the lines can clear the spout.

Variation: Single-piece Faucets

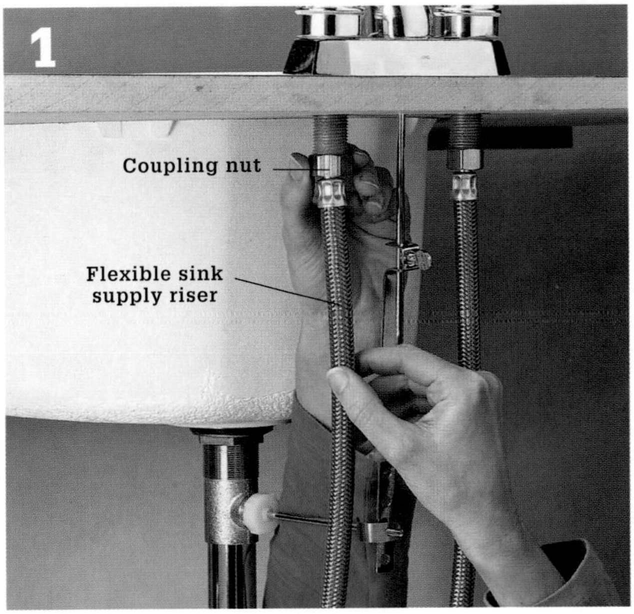

Insert the faucet tailpieces through the holes in the sink. From below, thread washers and mounting nuts over the tailpieces, then tighten the mounting nuts with a basin wrench until snug. Put a dab of pipe joint compound on the threads of the stop valves and thread the metal nuts of the flexible supply risers to these. Wrench tighten about a half turn past hand tight. Overtightening these nuts will strip the threads. Now tighten the coupling nuts to the faucet tailpieces with a basin wrench.

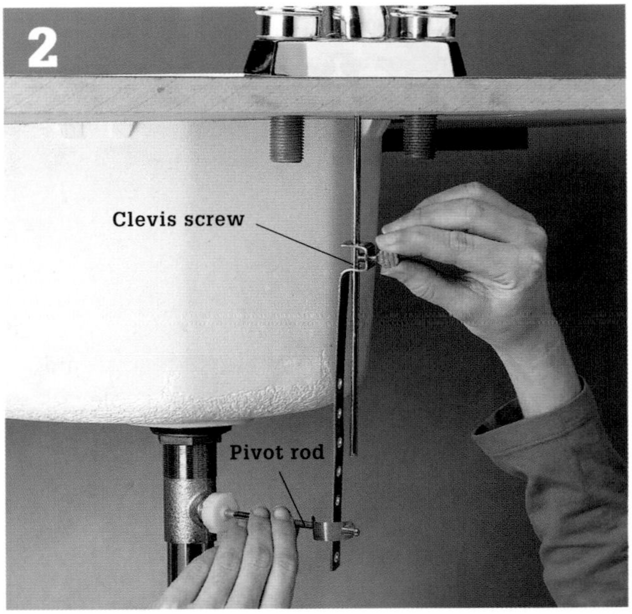

Slide the lift rod of the new faucet into its hole behind the spout. Thread it into the clevis past the clevis screw. Push the pivot rod all the way down so the stopper is open. With the lift rod also all the way down, tighten the clevis to the lift rod.

Grease the fluted valve stems with heatproof grease, then put the handles in place. Put a drop of Loctite on each handle screw before tightening it on to keep the handles from coming loose. Cover each handle screw with the appropriate index cap—Hot or Cold.

Unscrew the aerator from the end of the spout. Turn the hot and cold water taps on full. Turn the water back on at the stop valves and flush out the faucet for a couple of minutes before turning off the water at the faucet. Check the riser connections for drips. Tighten a compression nut only until the drip stops. Replace the aerator.

Wall-Mount Faucets

A wall-mounted faucet adds a touch of elegance to your bathroom. It's perfect for vessel sinks and hanging vanities, because the hoses and shut-off valves are out of view.

A wall-mounted sink faucet is similar to a shower or bathtub faucet. The main difference is that the handles and faucet are usually in a line, rather than at a distance from each other. Like the shower or bathtub faucet, you will need to have an access door behind the sink, or have the plumbing easily accessible in the basement for a first floor bathroom.

The valve unit and the faucets and spout will likely need to be made by the same manufacturer, as the parts are generally not interchangeable.

Tools & Materials ▸

Tubing cutter
Tape measure
Level
Torch
Channel-type pliers
Allen wrench
Wallboard finishing tools
Lead-free solder
Flux
2 × 4 lumber
#10, 1" wood screws
Two-handle valve
Wall-mount faucet
Plumber's putty
Wallboard

Wall-mounted faucets have a spare, futuristic appeal that many high-end designers prefer. Functionally, they have the added advantage of keeping the sink deck clear.

How to Install a Wall-Mounted Sink Faucet

Determine the location for the faucet. Make reference marks for the faucet location on walls that will not be removed or create a cardboard template. Remove the wallboard between the studs at the faucet location and where necessary to run supply and drain lines. Install 2 × 4 bracing according to the faucet manufacturer's instructions.

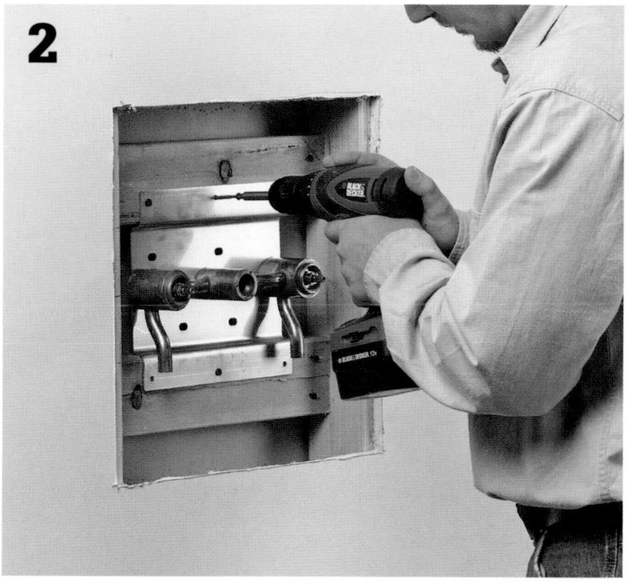

Attach the wall plate from the faucet kit to the studs with #10, 1" wood screws. Check the installation for level and correct it if necessary. Solder the lines from the valve assembly to ½" copper supply lines using couplings (left is hot, right is cold). Turn the water on and check for leaks.

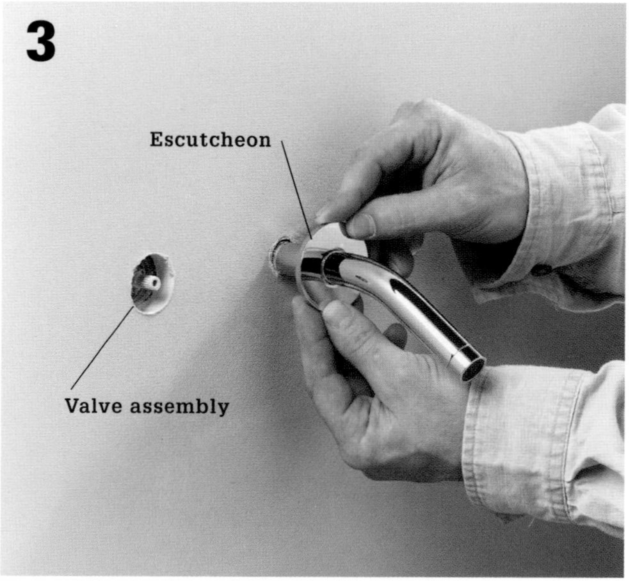

Replace the wallboard and finish the wall surface. The circular cutouts for the handles and spout should be no more than 1½" in diameter. Remove the plaster guards from the valve. Thread the spout into the spout stub until tight. Back off the spout until it faces downward and tighten the screws. Apply plumber's putty to the back of the escutcheon and slide it into place.

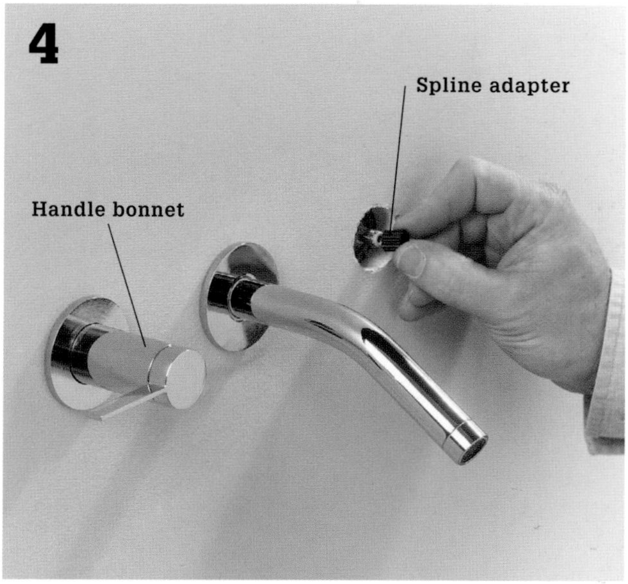

Thread the handle assemblies onto the valve bodies and tighten. If the handles are not horizontal when closed, remove them. Remove the spline adapter and give it a quarter turn. Repeat until the handles are horizontal when closed. Remove the handles. Apply plumber's putty to the back of the escutcheons and slide over the handle bonnets. Securely hand tighten the handles and slide escutcheons into place. Remove excess putty from escutcheons.

Lavatory Drains

Pop-up stoppers are chrome-plated, long-legged plugs in bathroom sinks that are opened and closed with a knob behind the spout. The stopper itself is just the visible part of a behind-the-scenes assembly that makes sure the stopper sits and stands on cue. New faucets come with their own pop-up stopper assemblies, assuming they use one, but you may also purchase one by itself. This will include everything from the stopper to the pipe that drops into the trap (the trap is that drooping piece of drainpipe under your sink). Choose a pop-up stopper assembly that's heavy brass under the chrome finish. This will hold up better to time and abuse than a plastic or light-gauge metal model.

Installing a lavatory drain is a bit trickier than installing a kitchen sink drain because most have a pop-up stopper with linkage.

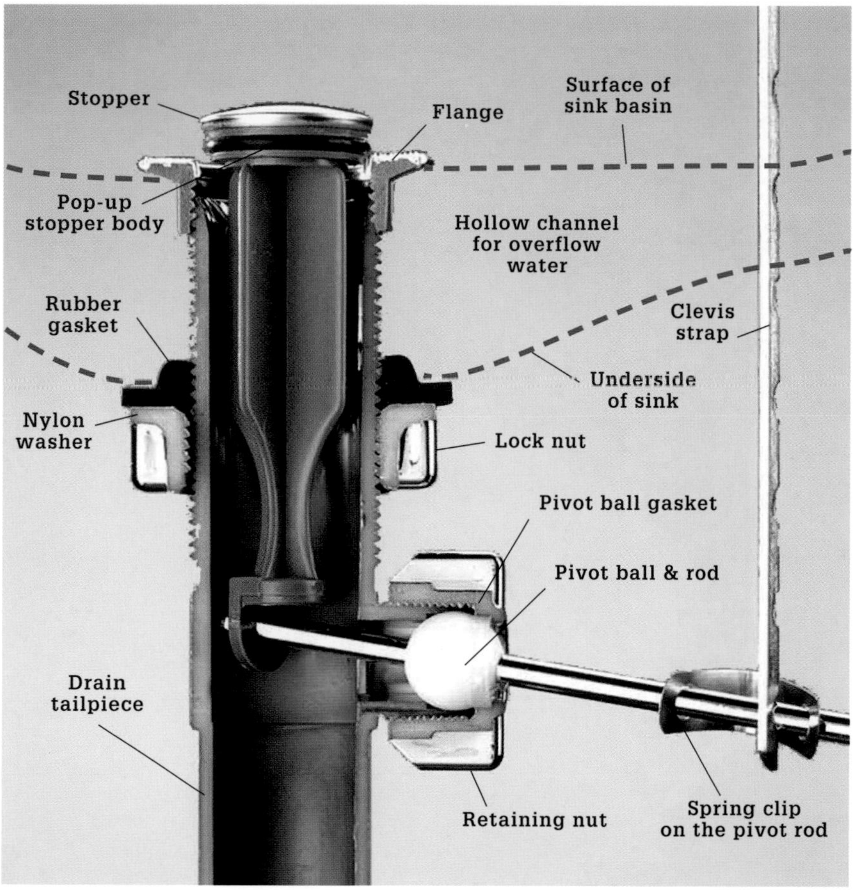

Pop-up stoppers keep objects from falling down the drain, and they make filling and draining the sink easy. When you pull up on the lift rod, the clevis strap is raised, which raises the pivot rod, which seesaws on the pivot ball and pulls the pop-up stopper down against the flange. This blocks water through the sink drain, but water may still overflow into the overflow channel drain through overflow ports in the pop-up body. This is a nice feature if you leave the water running in a plugged basin by mistake.

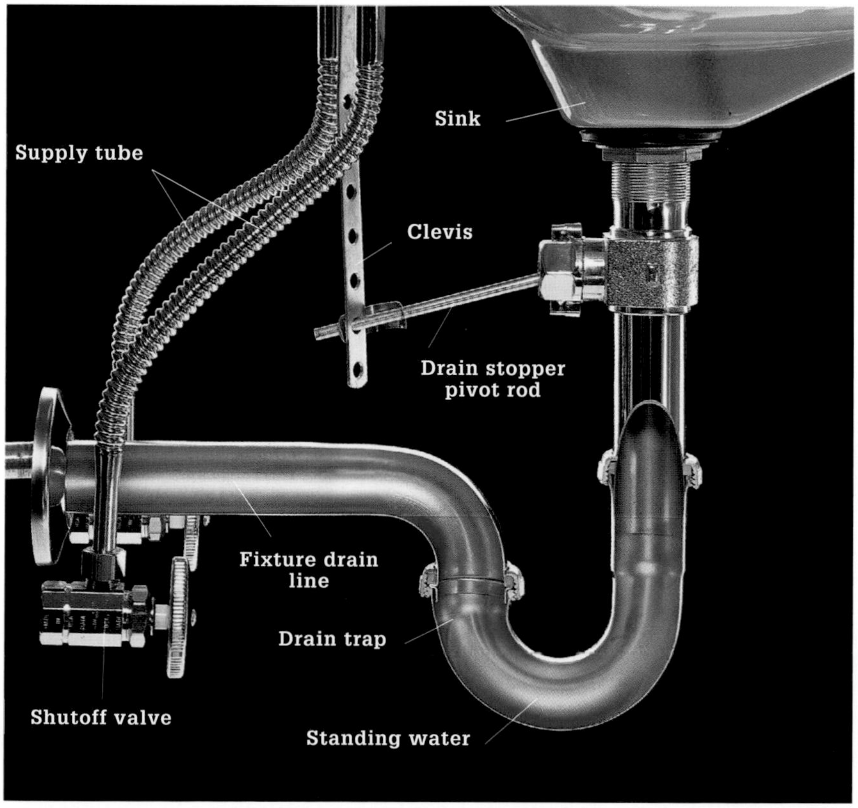

The lavatory drain trap holds water that seals the drain line and prevents sewer gases from entering the home. Each time a drain is used, the standing trap water is flushed away and replaced by new water. The shape of the trap and fixture drain line may resemble the letter P, and sink traps sometimes are called P-traps.

How to Replace a Pop-up Stopper

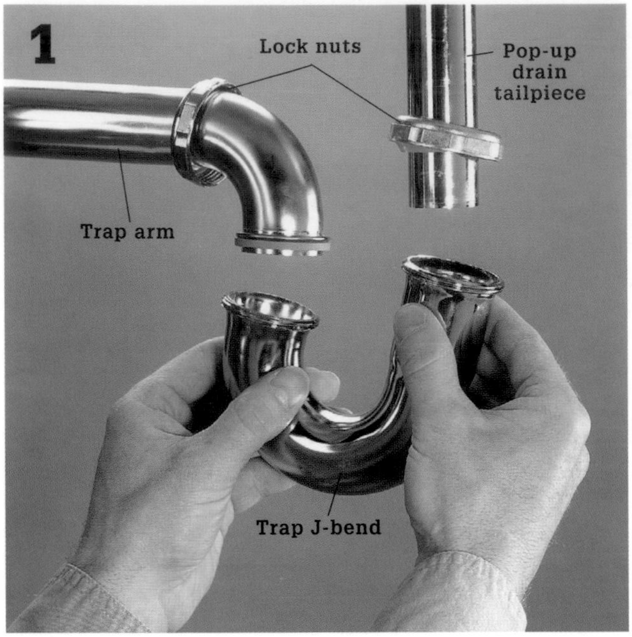

Put a basin under the trap to catch water. Loosen the nuts at the outlet and inlet to the trap J-bend by hand or with channel-type pliers and remove the bend. The trap will slide off the pop-up body tailpiece when the nuts are loose. Keep track of washers and nuts and their up/down orientation by leaving them on the tubes.

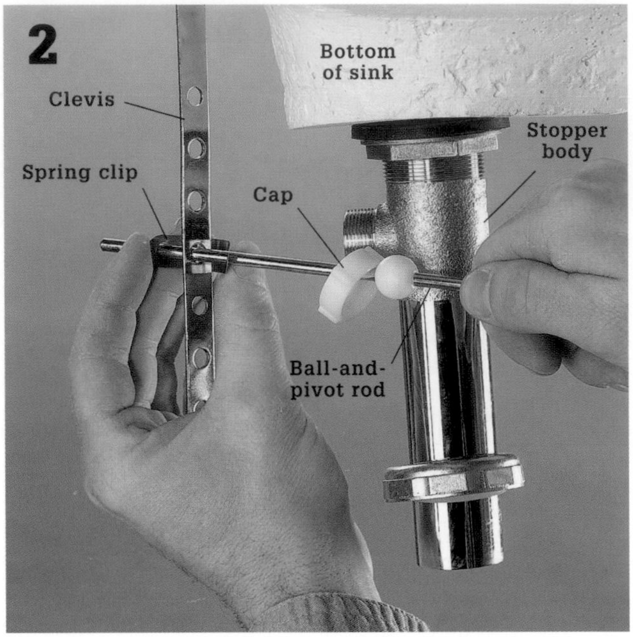

Unscrew the cap holding the ball-and-pivot rod in the pop-up body and withdraw the ball. Compress the spring clip on the clevis and withdraw the pivot rod from the clevis.

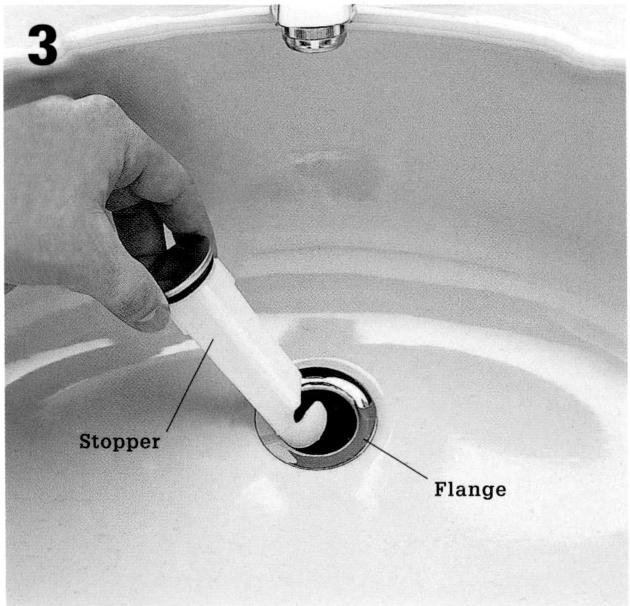

Remove the pop-up stopper. Then, from below, remove the lock nut on the stopper body. If needed, keep the flange from turning by inserting a large screwdriver in the drain from the top. Thrust the stopper body up through the hole to free the flange from the basin, and then remove the flange and the stopper body.

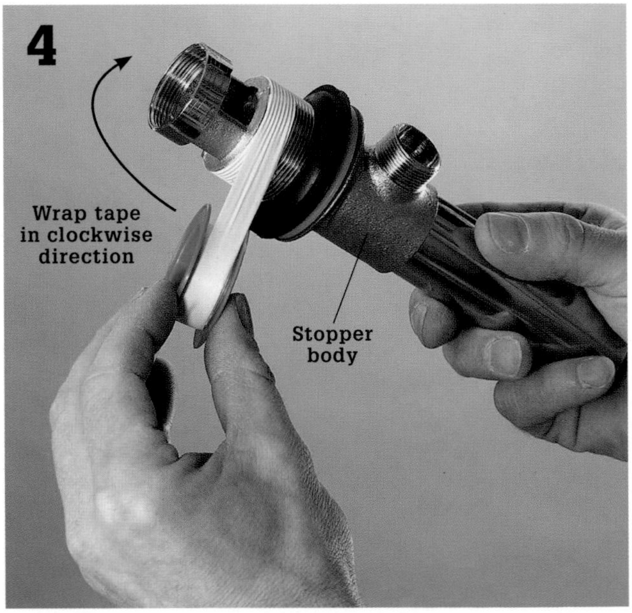

Clean the drain opening above and below, and then thread the locknut all the way down the new pop-up body followed by the flat washer and the rubber gasket (beveled side up). Wrap three layers of Teflon tape clockwise onto the top of the threaded body. Make a ½"-dia. snake from plumber's putty, form it into a ring, and stick the ring underneath the drain flange.

From below, face the pivot rod opening directly back toward the middle of the faucet and pull the body straight down to seat the flange. Thread the locknut/washer assembly up under the sink, then fully tighten the locknut with channel-type pliers. Do not twist the flange in the process, as this can break the putty seal. Clean off the squeezeout of plumber's putty from around the flange.

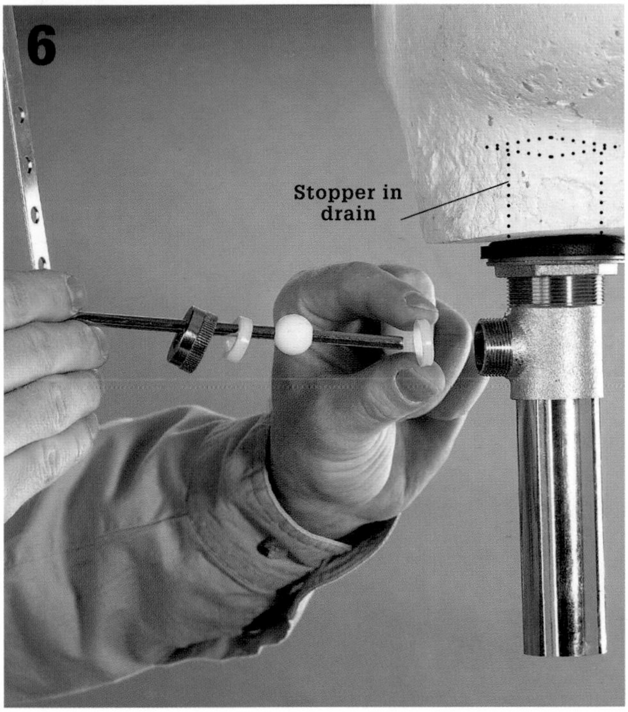

Drop the pop-up stopper into the drain hole so the hole at the bottom of its post is closest to the back of the sink. Put the beveled nylon washer into the opening in the back of the pop-up body with the bevel facing back.

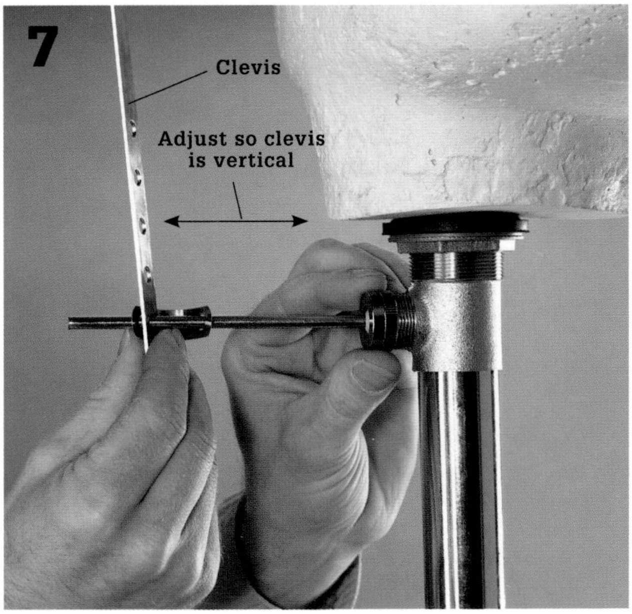

Put the cap behind the ball on the pivot rod as shown. Sandwich a hole in the clevis with the spring clip and thread the long end of the pivot rod through the clip and clevis. Put the ball end of the pivot rod into the pop-up body opening and into the hole in the the stopper stem. Screw the cap onto the pop-up body over the ball.

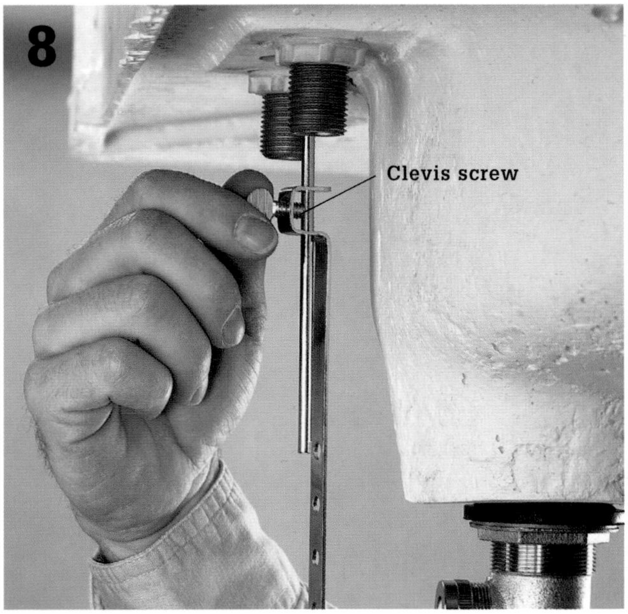

Loosen the clevis screw holding the clevis strap to the lift rod. Push the pivot rod all the way down (which fully opens the pop-up stopper). With the lift rod also all the way down, tighten the clevis screw to the rod. If the clevis runs into the top of the trap, cut it short with your hacksaw or tin snips. Reassemble the J-bend trap.

Toilets, Bidets & Urinals

Since the invention of the original water closet in the 19th Century, toilets have become (arguably) the most indispensable piece of household equipment. If your toilet is not functioning acceptably, no one is happy. Advancing technology has given us toilets that perform more reliably and more efficiently than ever, but it is still estimated that toilets are responsible for as many as half of all home plumbing repair calls. It is worth installing a quality fixture and taking the time to do it right.

The toilet has two close relatives that are becoming increasingly popular in modern homes: the bidet and the urinal. A longtime standard in Europe, the bidet is positioned directly next to the toilet and is used for personal sanitation after the toilet. The warm water stream is a much more effective sanitation solution than paper alone, and is also useful for people with limited mobility.

The urinal has become a very trendy piece of bathroom equipment. As water becomes more scarce, expect to see more and more urinals being installed in homes. They use just a fraction of the water that a toilet consumes per flush, and some types use no water at all.

In this chapter:

Toilets

You can replace a poorly functioning toilet with a new high-efficiency, high-quality toilet for a couple hundred dollars, an investment that will lead to savings in water usage and frustration—especially if you have a very old toilet. All toilets made since 1996 have been required to use 1.6 gallons or less per flush, which initially presented something of a challenge to the industry. Technology has evolved so that most new toilets have wide passages behind the bowl and wide (3") flush valve openings—features that facilitate short, powerful flushes. Manufacturers have also developed new alternatives, such as dual-flush technology that allows you to choose between two flushing options depending on what needs to be flushed.

All this technological advancement means fewer second flushes and fewer clogged toilets, which were the common complaints about the first generation of 1.6-gallon "low flow" toilets. Unfortunately, these problems still exist in some lower-end inferior models. Do your research when shopping for a new toilet and don't necessary look for the cheapest model you can find; a time-tested model with few customer complaints will be the better bargain in the long run.

Your criteria in selecting a new toilet should include ease of installation, proven flush performance, and reliability. With a little research, you should be able to find a highly efficient and economical gravity-flush toilet that will serve you for years to come.

Replacing a toilet is simple, and the latest generation of 1.6-gal. water-saving toilets has overcome the performance problems of earlier models.

Buy a toilet that will fit the space. Measure the distance from the floor bolts back to the wall (if your old toilet has two pairs of bolts, go by the rear pair). This is your rough-in distance and will be either 10" or approximately 12". Make note of the bowl shape, round or oval (long). Oval bowls (also called elongated bowls) are a few inches longer for greater comfort, but may be too big for your space. The safest bet is to buy a replacement with the same bowl shape.

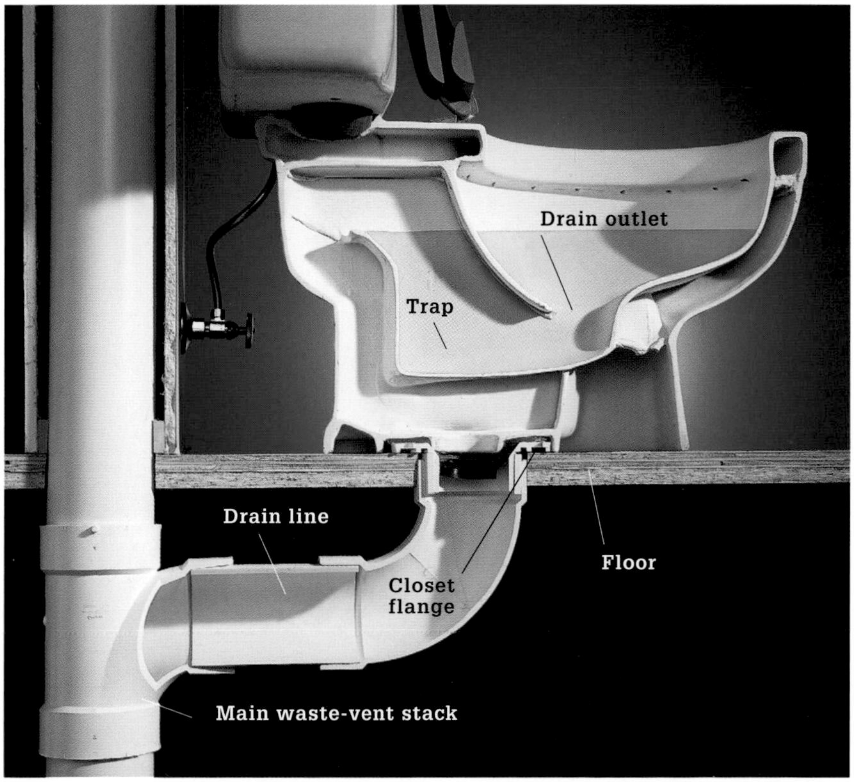

Knowing how a toilet works isn't essential to successful installation, but it helps. This cutaway photo features a pre-1.6-gal. law model, so your new toilet will have a much smaller trap. When the flush handle on the tank is depressed, the water in the tank rushes out through the hole in the underside of the bowl rim. The onrushing water forces the contents of the bowl and the trap out through the closet flange and into the drain line, while the fresh tank water refills the bowl and trap.

How to Install a Toilet

Clean and inspect the old closet flange. Look for breaks or wear. Also inspect the flooring around the flange. If either the flange or floor is worn or damaged, repair the damage. Use a rag and mineral spirits to completely remove residue from the old wax ring.

Replacing a Flange ▸

If the old flange is solvent-welded to the closet pipe, cut the pipe flush with the floor. Dry-fit the new flange into the pipe. Turn the flange until the side cut-out screw slots are parallel to the wall. (Do not use the curved keyhole slots, as they are not as strong.) Attach the new flange with solvent glue.

Insert new closet bolts (don't reuse old ones) into the openings in the closet flange. Make sure the heads of the bolts are oriented to catch the maximum amount of flange material.

Remove the wax ring and apply it to the underside of the bowl, around the horn. Remove the protective covering. Do not touch the wax ring. It is very sticky.

Lower the bowl onto the flange, taking care not to disturb the wax ring. The holes in the bowl base should align perfectly with the tank bolts. Add a washer and tighten a nut on each bolt. Hand tighten each nut and then use channel-type pliers to further tighten the nuts. Alternate back and forth between nuts until the bowl is secure. DO NOT OVERTIGHTEN.

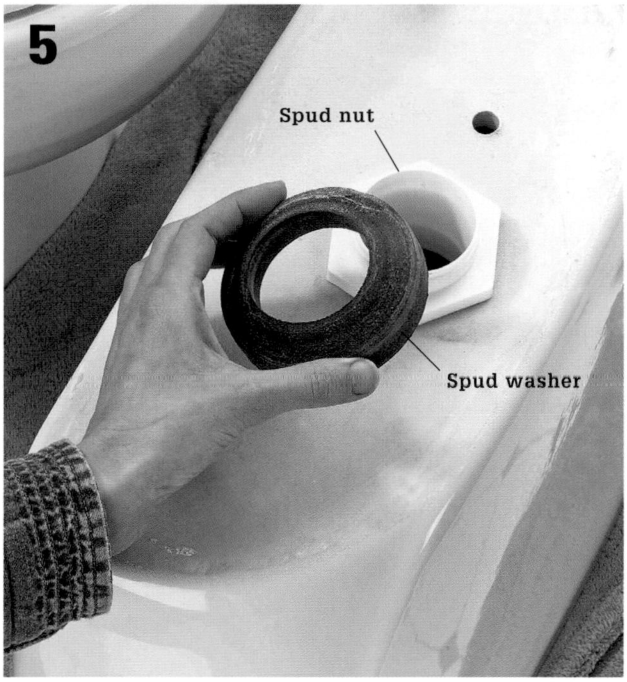

Attach the toilet tank. Some tanks come with a flush valve and a fill valve preinstalled, but if yours does not, insert the flush valve through the tank opening and tighten a spud nut over the threaded end of the valve. Place a foam or rubber spud washer on top of the spud nut.

Adjust the fill valve as directed by the manufacturer to set the correct tank water level height and install the valve inside the tank. Hand-tighten the nylon lock nut that secures the valve to the tank (inset photo) and then tighten it farther with channel-type pliers.

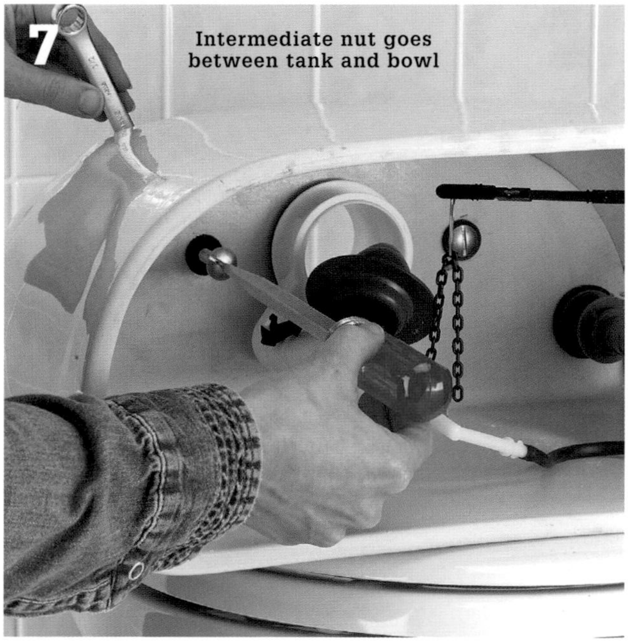

With the tank lying on its back, thread a rubber washer onto each tank bolt and insert it into the bolt holes from inside the tank. Then, thread a brass washer and hex nut onto the tank bolts from below and tighten them to a quarter-turn past hand tight. Do not overtighten.

(continued)

Position the tank on the bowl, spud washer on the opening, bolts through bolt holes. Put a rubber washer followed by a brass washer and a wing nut on each bolt and tighten these up evenly.

You may stabilize the bolts with a large slotted screwdriver from inside the tank, but tighten the nuts, not the bolts. You may press down a little on a side, the front, or the rear of the tank to level it as you tighten the nuts by hand. Do not overtighten and crack the tank. The tank should be level and stable when you're done.

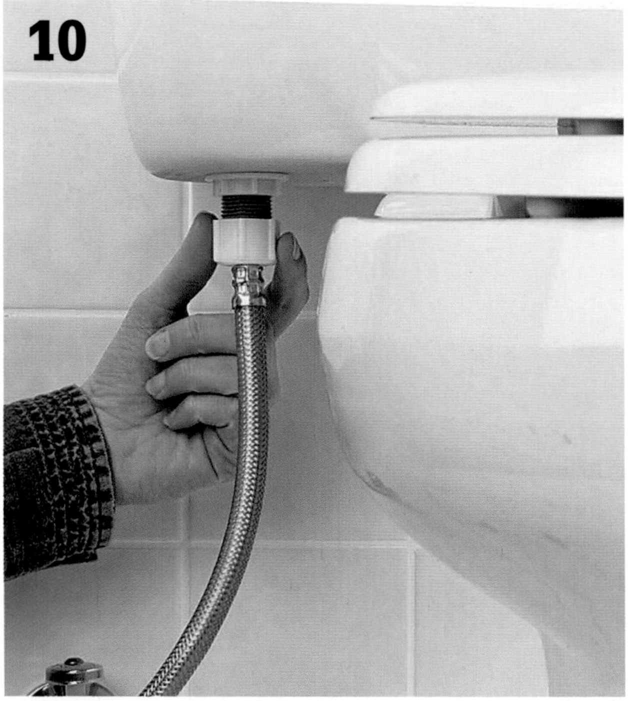

Hook up the water supply by connecting the supply tube to the threaded fill valve with the coupling nut provided. Turn on the water and test for leaks.

Attach the toilet seat by threading the plastic or brass bolts provided with the seat through the openings on the back of the rim and attaching nuts.

Toilet Height Extenders ▸

Although today's toilets are being made with higher seats than in the past, physically challenged and elderly people often find it difficult to use standard toilets, especially compact toilets (most of the more inexpensive toilets are compact). To address the problem of low toilet seats, you can retrofit your toilet with a seat riser or reinstall the toilet on a platform. See Resources, page 284.

Hinged Seat Risers: By replacing your old toilet seat with a riser seat, you can raise the functional height of the toilet by 3" to 4". Look for models that are hinged or removable for easy cleaning.

Platforms: It is possible to use a closet flange extender and plywood to rig up a DIY toilet platform so you can install a standard toilet with the seat higher. A cleaner and simpler option is to purchase a tall toilet platform that is designed to fit over your existing closet flange and is predrilled with holes for the closet flange bolts.

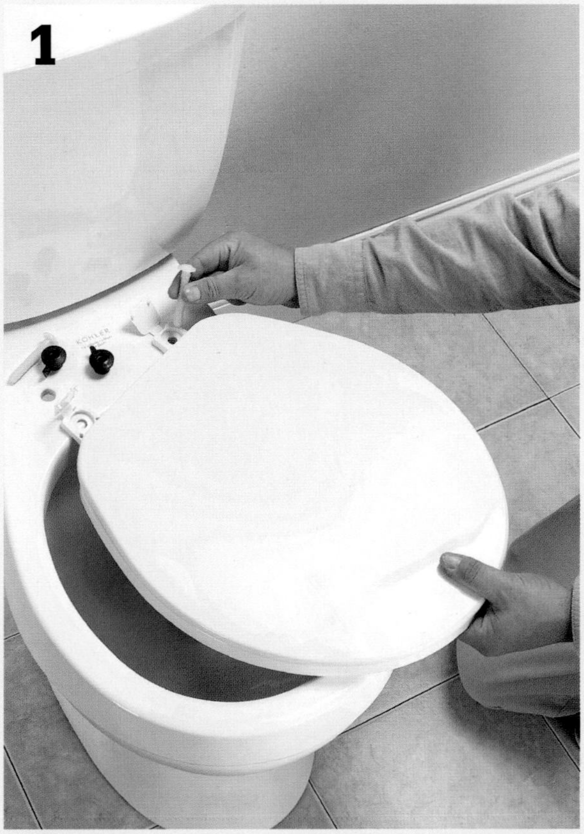

Remove the old seat. If the nuts for the seat bolts are corroded, slip a hack saw blade between the hinge plates and stool and cut the bolts.

Install the new height extender by bolting it to the stool through the seat bolt holes. Attach a standard toilet seat to the extender.

Bidets

Bidets are becoming ever more popular in the United States. Maybe that's because they can give a dream bath that European flare so many of us find alluring. Go to Europe, Asia, or South America and you'll see how much people can come to rely on bidets. Some fans of this bathroom fixture think those who don't use bidets are unhygienic.

With the trend moving toward larger and more luxurious bathrooms, many Americans are becoming intrigued by this personal hygiene appliance. The standard model features hot and cold faucets, and either a movable nozzle located by the faucet handles or a vertical sprayer located near the front of the bowl. Most bidets are outfitted with a pop-up drain. You can also buy a combination toilet and bidet if space is an issue.

Tools & Materials ▸

- Tape measure
- Drill
- Adjustable wrench
- Level
- Silicone sealant
- (2) ⅜" shut off valves
- (2) ⅜" supply lines
- P-trap
- Tubing cutter
- Plumber's putty
- Thread tape
- Bidet
- Bidet faucet
- Marker

Installing a bidet is very much like installing a sink. The only difference is that the bidet can have the waste line plumbed below the floor, like a shower. But like sinks, bidets may have single or multiple deck holes for faucets, so be certain to purchase compatible components.

A bidet is a useful companion to a toilet, and it is a luxury item you and your family will appreciate. For people with limited mobility, a bidet is an aide to independent personal sanitation.

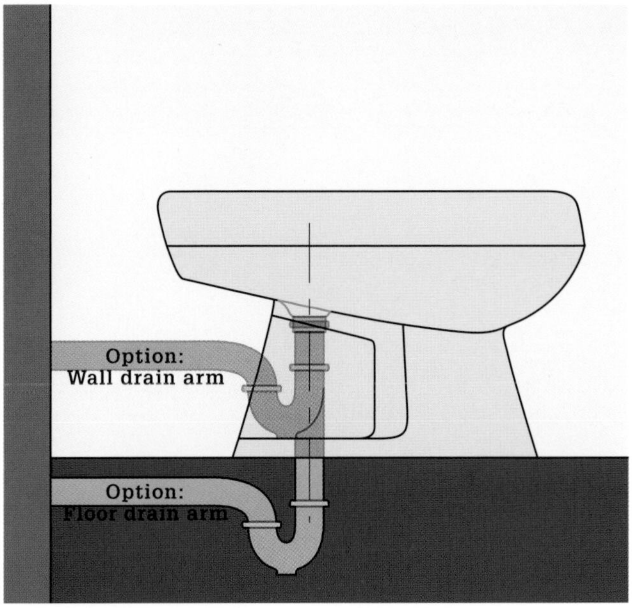

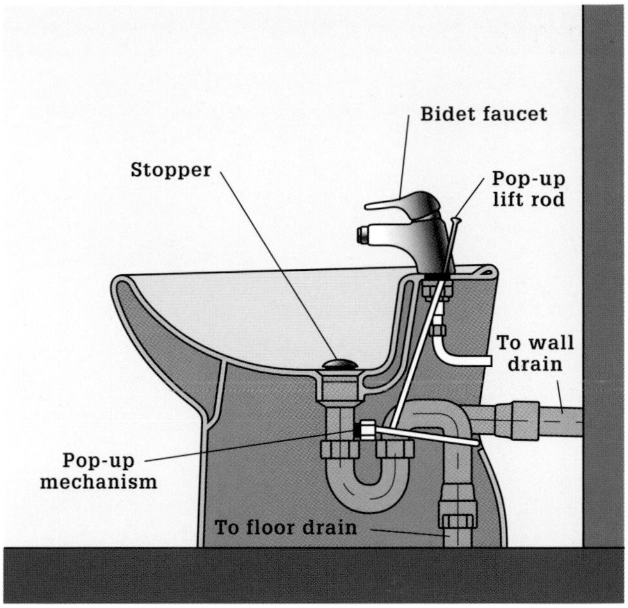

Bidet drains have more in common with sink drains than with toilet drains. Some even attach to a drain arm in the wall, with a P-trap that fits between the fixture drain tailpiece and the arm. Other bidets drain into a floor drain outlet with a trap that's situated between the tailpiece and the branch drain line.

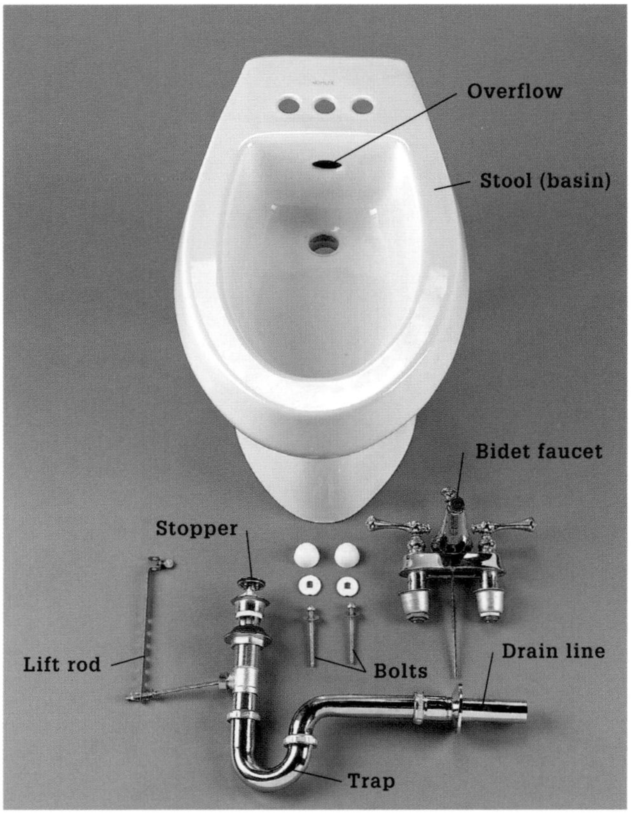

A bidet requires a special faucet that allows you to mix hot and cold water to a temperature you find comfortable. It has a third knob to control the water pressure. The aerator and spout pivot to allow you to adjust the spray to a comfortable height.

You can get all the features of a bidet on your existing toilet with a number of aftermarket bidet seats. These seats feature heaters, sprayers, and dryers in basic or deluxe versions. Installation takes less than an hour and no additional space is needed.

How to Install a Bidet

Rough-in the supply and drain lines according to the manufacturer's specifications. If you do not have experience installing home plumbing, hire a plumber for this part of the job. Apply a coil of plumber's putty to the base of the bidet faucet, and then insert the faucet body into the mounting holes. Thread the washers and locknut onto the faucet body shank and hand tighten. Remove any plumber's putty squeeze out.

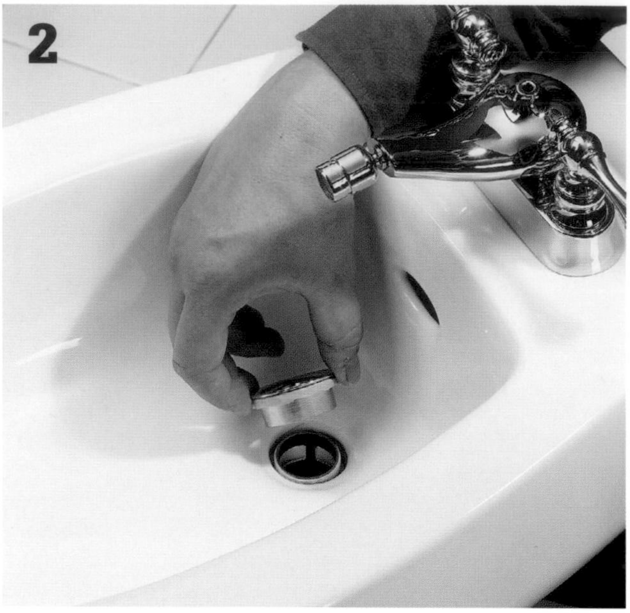

Apply a coil of plumber's putty around the underside of the drain flange. Insert the flange in the drain hole, place the gasket and washer, and then thread the nut onto the flange. Do not fully tighten.

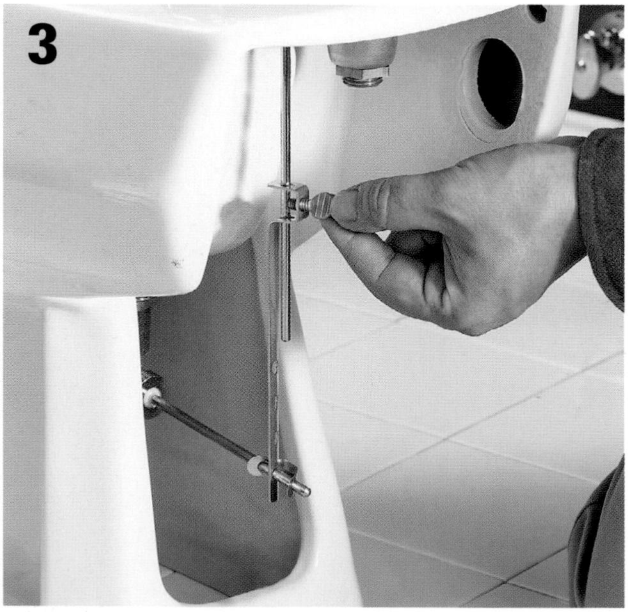

Install the pop-up drain apparatus according to the manufacturer's instructions.

Place the bidet in its final location, checking that supply and drain lines will be in alignment. Mark the locations of the two side-mounting holes through the predrilled holes on the stool and onto the floor.

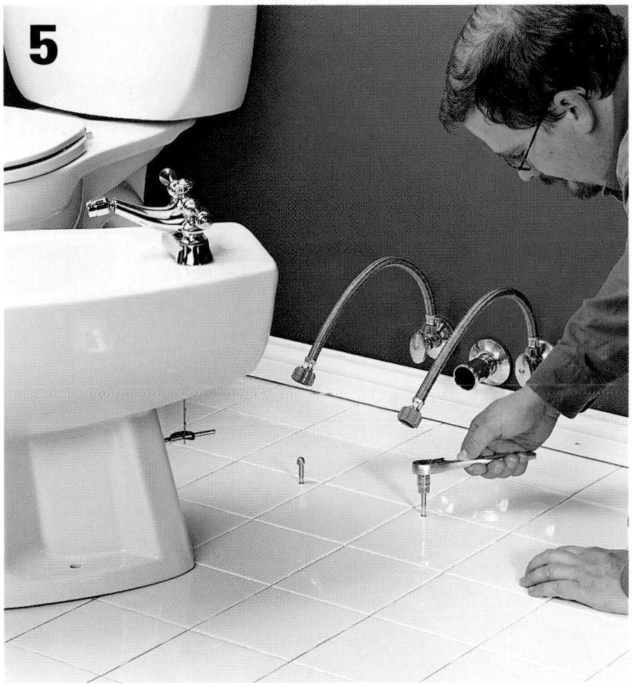

Remove the bidet and drill 3⁄16" pilot holes at the marks on the floor. Drive the floor bolts (included with the bidet basin) into the holes. Position the bidet so the floor bolts fit into the bolt holes in the base. Tighten nuts onto the floor bolts.

Connect the water supply risers to the bidet faucet using compression unions. Make sure to hook the hot and cold risers up to the correct ports on the faucet.

Hook up the drain line by attaching the P-trap to the drain tailpiece. The trap is then attached to a branch drain line coming out of the wall or floor in the same manner as a sink drain.

Remove the aerator so any debris in the supply line will clear and then turn on the water and open both faucets. Check for leaks in lines and fix, if found. Assemble the bolt caps and thread them onto the floor bolts. *Note: Do not dispose of paper in the bidet—return to the toilet to dry off after using the bidet for cleaning.*

Urinals

Most people consider a urinal to be a commercial or industrial bathroom accessory, so why would you want one in your home—and in your dream bathroom no less? The answer is in the many advantages a urinal has to offer and the fact that most major bathroom fixture manufacturers are now producing urinals designed for residential installation.

A urinal doesn't take up much space and it uses much less water per flush than a standard toilet: .5 to 1.0 gallon of water per flush for the urinal, as opposed to the low-flow toilet's 1.6 gallons of water per flush. You also have the option of a waterless urinal, a real boon in water-scarce areas. A urinal also has the emotional benefit of ending the "up versus down" toilet seat debate. Finally, a urinal is generally easier to keep clean than a toilet because splashing is minimized.

In today's homes with large multiple bathrooms and his and hers master baths, there are plenty of places you can choose to install a urinal. Of course, the perfect place is where it will get used the most: in the bathroom closest to the TV if the guys congregate at your house to watch sporting events; or in the bathroom closest to boys' bedrooms if you've got a passel of them.

Tools & Materials ▸

- Tape measure
- Adjustable wrench
- Pencil
- Level
- Sealant tape
- Utility knife
- Drywall saw
- Tubing cutter
- Hacksaw
- Miter box
- Hex wrenches
- Smooth-jawed spud wrench
- Slotted screwdriver
- Urinal flushometer
- Emery cloth
- Wire brush
- Allen wrench
- Drywall
- Drywall tape
- Drywall compound
- 2 × 6 lumber
- PVC 2" drainpipe
- PVC 2" male threaded drain outlet
- ½" copper pipe
- Urinal
- Sealant tape

Urinals are great water savers and are becoming increasingly popular in today's dream bathroom.

Waterless Urinals ▸

For the ultimate in water-conservation, you can now purchase a home urinal that uses zero water. A waterless urinal is never flushed, so you'll save about a gallon of water per usage. Naturally, waterless urinals are plumbed into your drain line system. But where typical plumbing fixtures rely on fresh water to carry the waste into the system, the waterless system relies simply on gravity for the liquid waste to find its way out of the fixture and into the drain. The secret is a layer of sealing liquid that is lighter than the water and forms a skim coat over the urine. When the urine enters the trap it displaces the sealing liquid, which immediately reforms on the surface to create a layer that seals in odors. The Kohler fixture seen here (see Resources, page 284) is an example of the sealing liquid system. Other waterless urinals use replaceable cartridges.

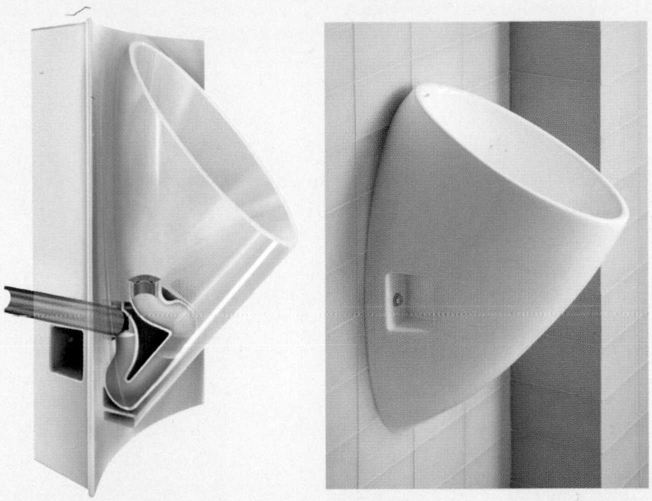

A layer of sealing liquid forms a skim coat that floats on top of the liquid to trap odors.

Flushing Options for Urinals

A manual flush handle is still the most common and least expensive flushing mechanism for urinals. It is reliable but not as sanitary as touchless types such as the Flushometer on page 166.

Motion sensors automatically flush touchless urinals, which is a great improvement in sanitation. These tend to be more expensive, however, and are more likely to develop problems. Also, because they flush automatically when users step away from the fixture they don't allow you to conserve water by limiting flushing.

How to Install a Urinal

Remove the drywall or other surface coverings between the urinal location and the closest water supply and waste lines. Remove enough wall surface to reveal half of the stud face on each side of the opening to make patch work simpler.

Following the manufacturer's directions for the urinal and flushometer, determine the mounting height of the urinal, and mark the location of the supply and waste lines. For this installation, the 2" waste line is centered 17½" above the finished floor. Cut 5½" × 1½" notches in the wall studs centered at 32" above the finished floor surface, then attach a 2 × 6 mounting board.

Install the copper cold water supply line according to the manufacturer's specifications. Here, it is 4¾" to the side of the fixture centerline and 45" from the finished floor (11½" from the top of the fixture). Cap the stub-out 3" from the finished wall surface.

Install the 2" drainpipe and vent pipe, making sure that the centerline of the drain outlet is positioned correctly (here, 17½" above the finished floor and 4¾" to the side of the supply line).Attach the male threaded waste outlet to the drain pipe. It should extend beyond the finished wall surface. Replace the wall covering and finish as desired.

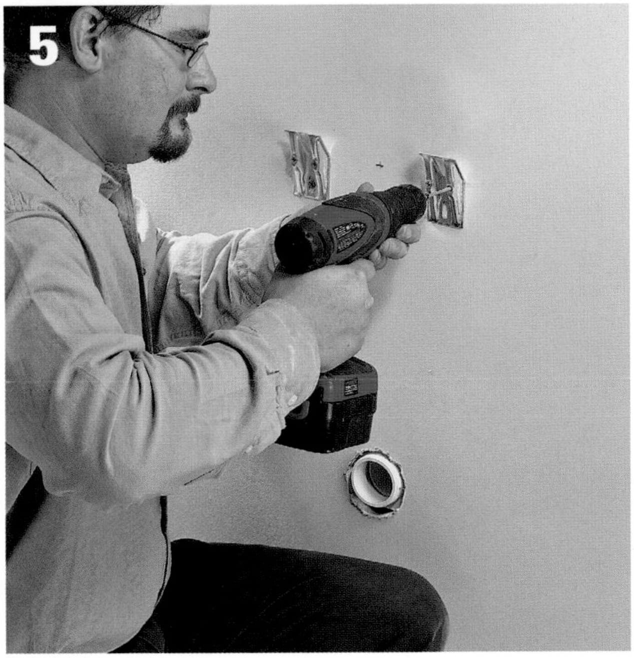

Attach the mounting brackets 32" above the floor, 3¼" to the sides of the centerline of the waste outlet.

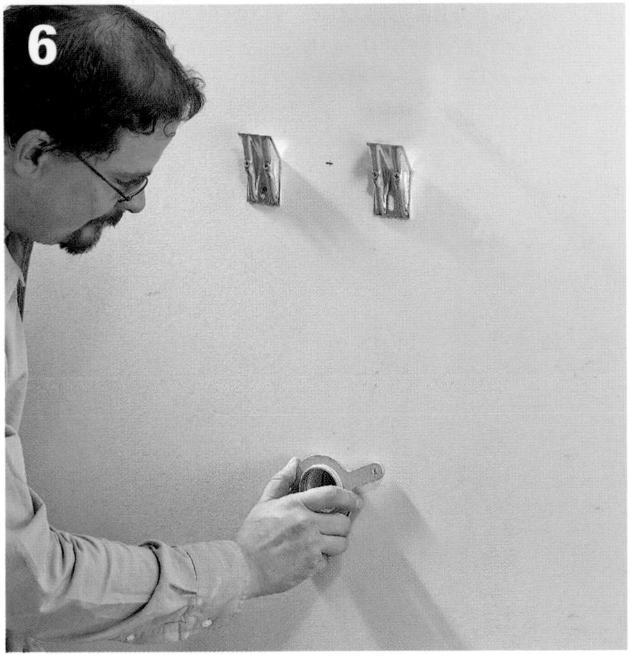

Apply Teflon tape to the waste outlet. Thread the female collar onto the waste outlet until it is firmly seated and the flanges are horizontally level. Place the gasket onto the female collar. The beveled surface of the gasket faces toward the urinal.

Hang the urinal on the brackets, being careful not to bump the porcelain as it chips easily. Thread the screws through the washers, the holes in the urinal, and into the collar. Tighten the screws by hand, then one full turn with an adjustable wrench. Do not overtighten.

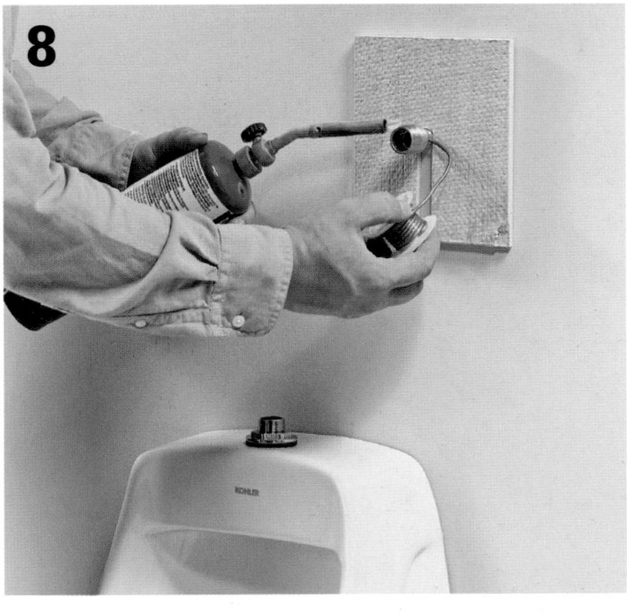

Determine the distance from the centerline of the water inlet on the top of the urinal, called the spud, to the finished wall. Subtract 1¼" from this distance and cut the water supply pipe to that length using a tubing cutter. Turn off the water before cutting. After cutting, deburr the inside and outside diameter of the supply pipe. Attach the threaded adapter to the cut pipe.

(continued)

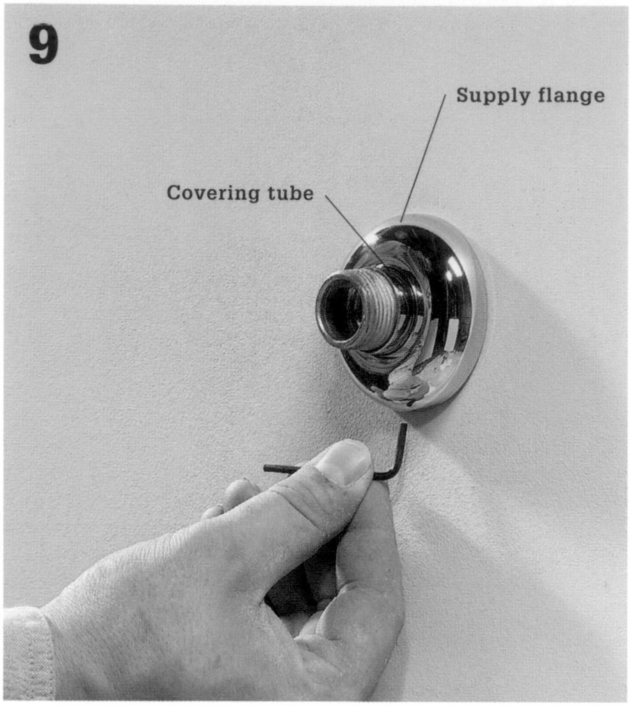

Measure from the wall surface to the first thread of the adapter. Using a hacksaw and a miter box or a tubing cutter, cut the covering tube to this length. Slide the covering tube over the water supply pipe. Slide the supply flange over the covering tube until it rests against the wall. Tighten the setscrew on the flange with an Allen wrench.

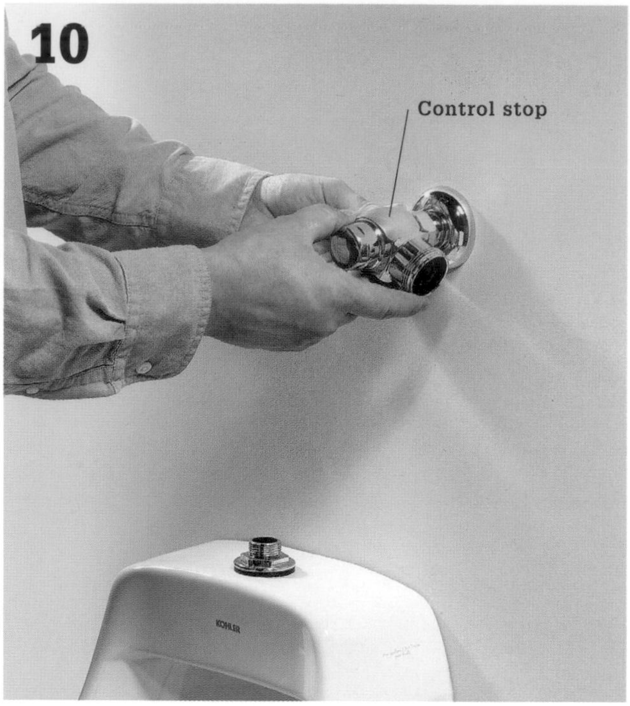

Apply a small amount of pipe sealant to the adapter threads, then thread the control stop onto the adapter threads. Position the outlet toward the urinal so that it is horizontally level.

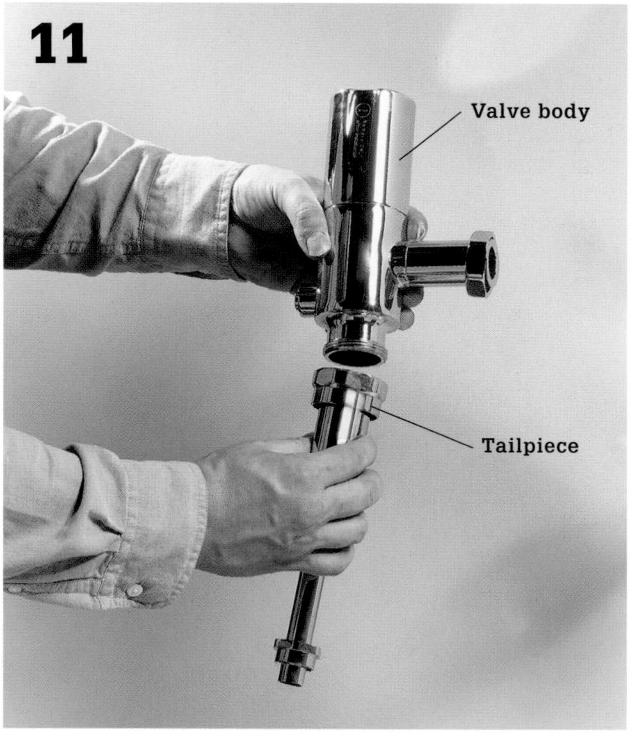

Hand tighten the tailpiece into the flushometer valve body.

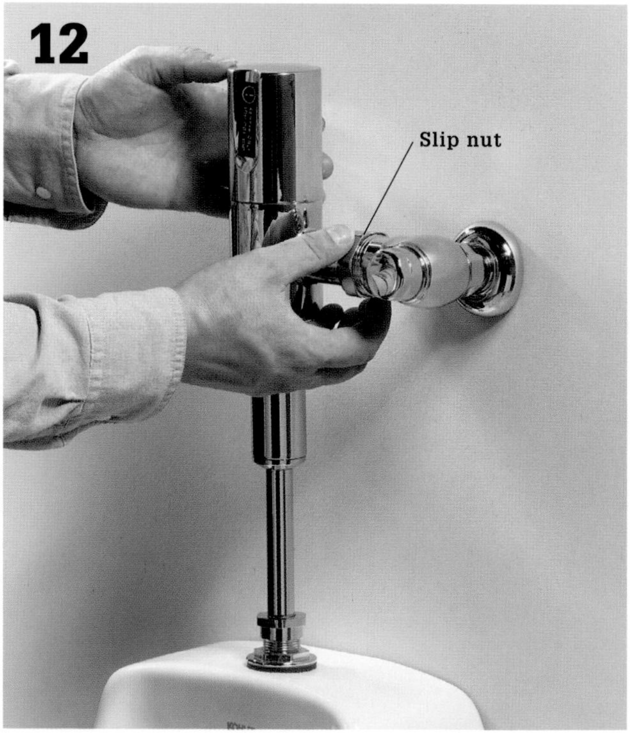

Hand tighten the slip nut that connects the valve body to the control stop.

Use a smooth-jawed spud wrench to securely tighten the tailpiece, vacuum breaker, and spud couplings.

The Flush-o-Meter ▸

For maximum sanitation, choose a urinal flush mechanism with an electronic sensor, like the Kohler Flush-o-meter being installed here. The electronic eye on this type of flush mechanism senses when a user approaches the fixture and then commands the fixture to flush when the user steps away. This eliminates the need to touch the handle before the user has the opportunity to wash his hands.

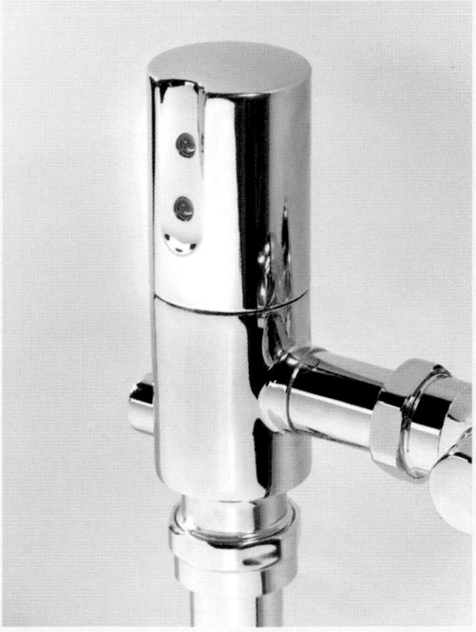

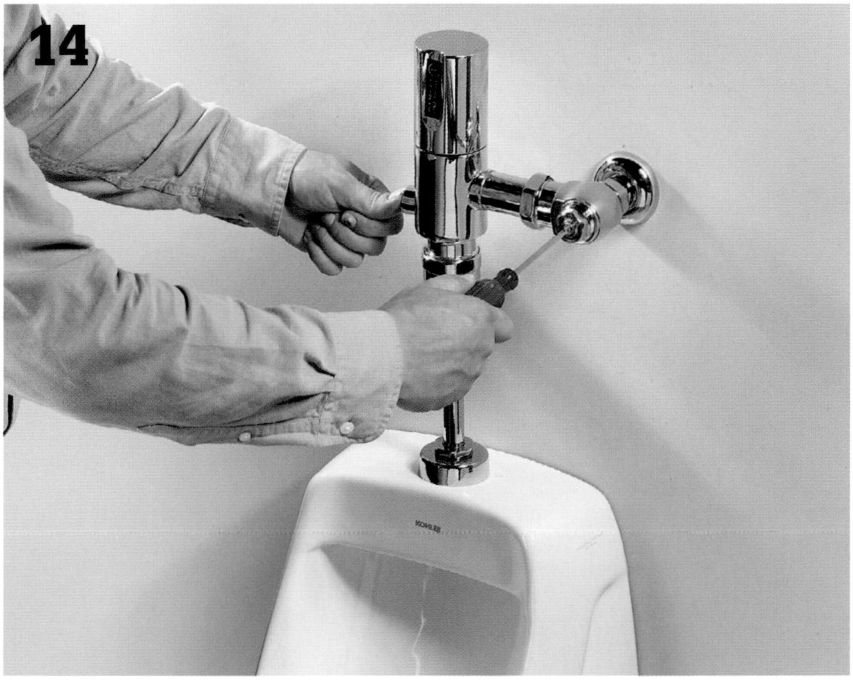

While testing the flush, adjust the supply stop screw counter-clockwise until adequate flow is achieved.

Lighting & Ventilaton

Lighting plays an important role in every bathroom. Without good lighting placed in strategic areas, we wouldn't be able to conduct most of our bathroom business. Many different types of lighting and a seemingly infinite array of styles are available to light up your dream bath. Unless you're starting from scratch or tearing down the walls is part of your bathroom remodel, be sure to choose fixtures designed for retrofit installations.

Ventilation also plays an important role in every bathroom. It's so important that most building codes require a vent fan in any bathroom lacking natural ventilation. Remodeling your dream bath gives you the perfect opportunity to add a new vent fan or upgrade to a quieter, more efficient model, maybe even one with a built-in heat lamp.

In this chapter:

- Vanity Lights
- Ceiling Lights
- Vent Fans
- Skylights
- Tubular Skylights
- Glass Block Windows

Vanity Lights

Many bathrooms have a single fixture positioned above the vanity, but a light source in this position casts shadows on the face and makes grooming more difficult. Light fixtures on either side of the mirror is a better arrangement.

For a remodel, mark the mirror location, run cable, and position boxes before drywall installation. You can also retrofit by installing new boxes and drawing power from the existing fixture.

The light sources should be at eye level; 66" is typical. The size of your mirror and its location on the wall may affect how far apart you can place the sconces, but 36 to 40" apart is a good guideline.

Tools & Materials ▸

Drywall tools	Electrical boxes and braces
Drill	Vanity light fixtures
Combination tool	NM cable
Circuit tester	Wire connectors
Screwdrivers	Drywall
Hammer	

Vanity lights on the sides of the mirror provide good lighting.

How to Replace Vanity Lights in a Finished Bathroom

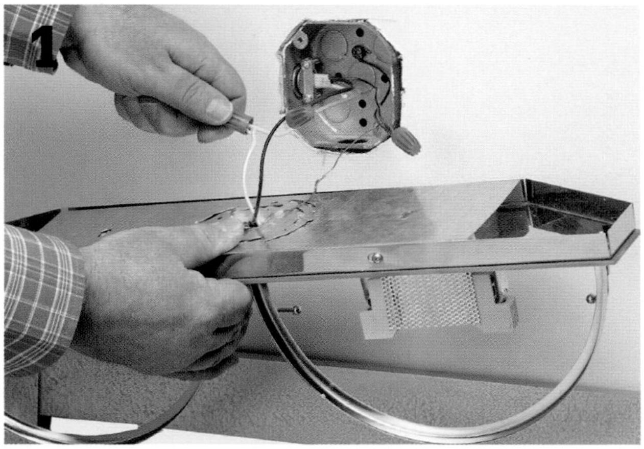

Turn off the power at the service panel. Remove the old fixture from the wall and test to make sure that the power is off. Then remove a strip of drywall from around the old fixture to the first studs beyond the approximate location of the new fixtures. Make the opening large enough that you have room to route cable from the existing fixture to the boxes.

Mark the location for the fixtures and install new boxes. Install the boxes about 66" above the floor and 18 to 20" from the centerline of the mirror (the mounting base of some fixtures is above or below the bulb, so adjust the height of the bracing accordingly). If the correct location is on or next to a stud, you can attach the box directly to the stud, otherwise you'll need to install blocking or use boxes with adjustable braces (shown).

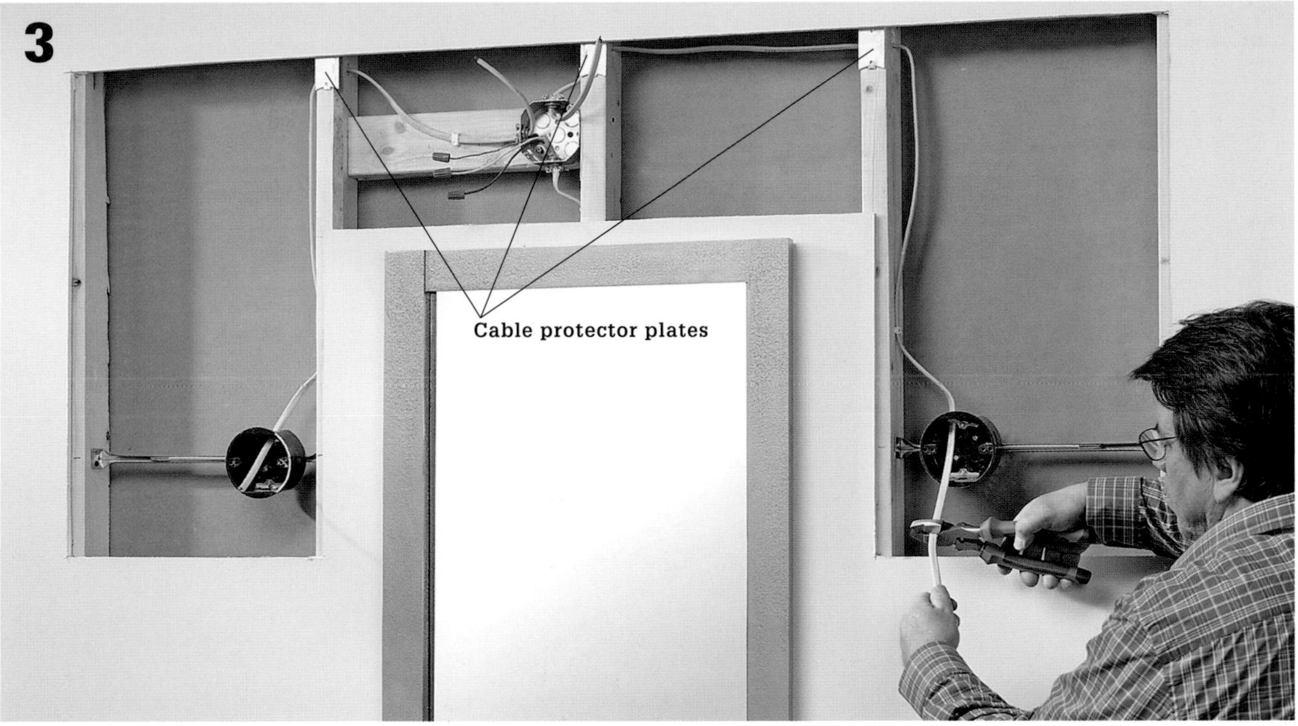

Open the side knockouts on the electrical box above the vanity. Then drill ⅝" holes in the centers of any studs between the old fixture and the new ones. Run two NM cables from the new boxes for the fixtures to the box above the vanity. Protect the cable with metal protector plates. Secure the cables with cable clamps, leaving 11" of extra cable for making the connection to the new fixtures. Remove sheathing and strip insulation from the ends of the wires.

Connect the white wires from the new cables to the white wire from the old cable, and connect the black wires from the new cables to the black wire from the old cable. Connect the ground wires. Cover all open boxes and then replace the drywall, leaving openings for the fixture and the old box. (Cover the old box with a solid junction box cover plate.)

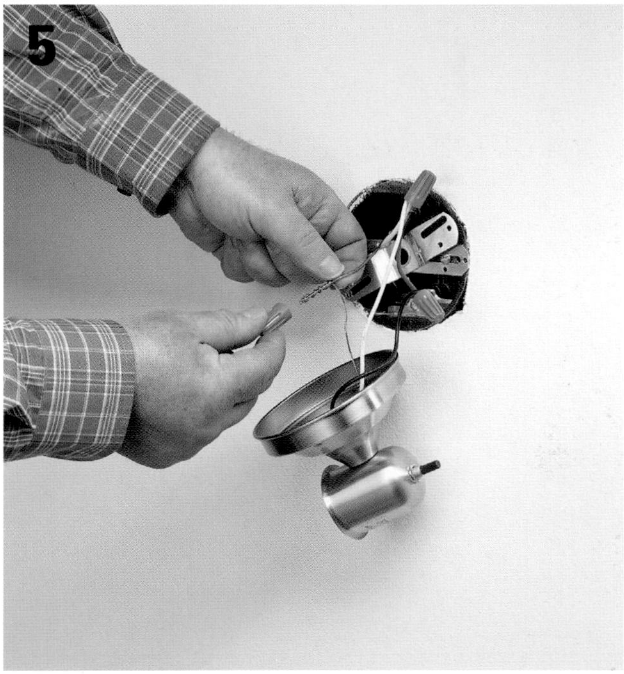

Install the fixture mounting braces on the boxes. Attach the fixtures by connecting the black circuit wire to the black fixture wire, and connecting the white circuit wire to the white fixture wire. Connect the ground wires. Position each fixture over each box, and attach with the mounting screws. Restore power and test the circuit.

Ceiling Lights

Ceiling fixtures don't have any moving parts and their wiring is very simple, so, other than changing bulbs, you're likely to get decades of trouble-free service from a fixture. This sounds like a good thing, but it also means that the fixture probably won't fail and give you an excuse to update a room's look with a new one. Fortunately, you don't need an excuse. Upgrading a fixture is easy and can make a dramatic impact on a room. You can substantially increase the light in a room by replacing a globe-style fixture by one with separate spot lights, or you can simply install a new fixture that matches the room's décor.

Tools & Materials ▸

Replacement light fixture
Combination tool
Voltage sensor
Insulated screwdrivers
Wire connectors

It's a fairly unusual bathroom that has room for a fancy ceiling light fixture, but even modest bathrooms should have a bright, pleasant overhead light for general illumination and safety.

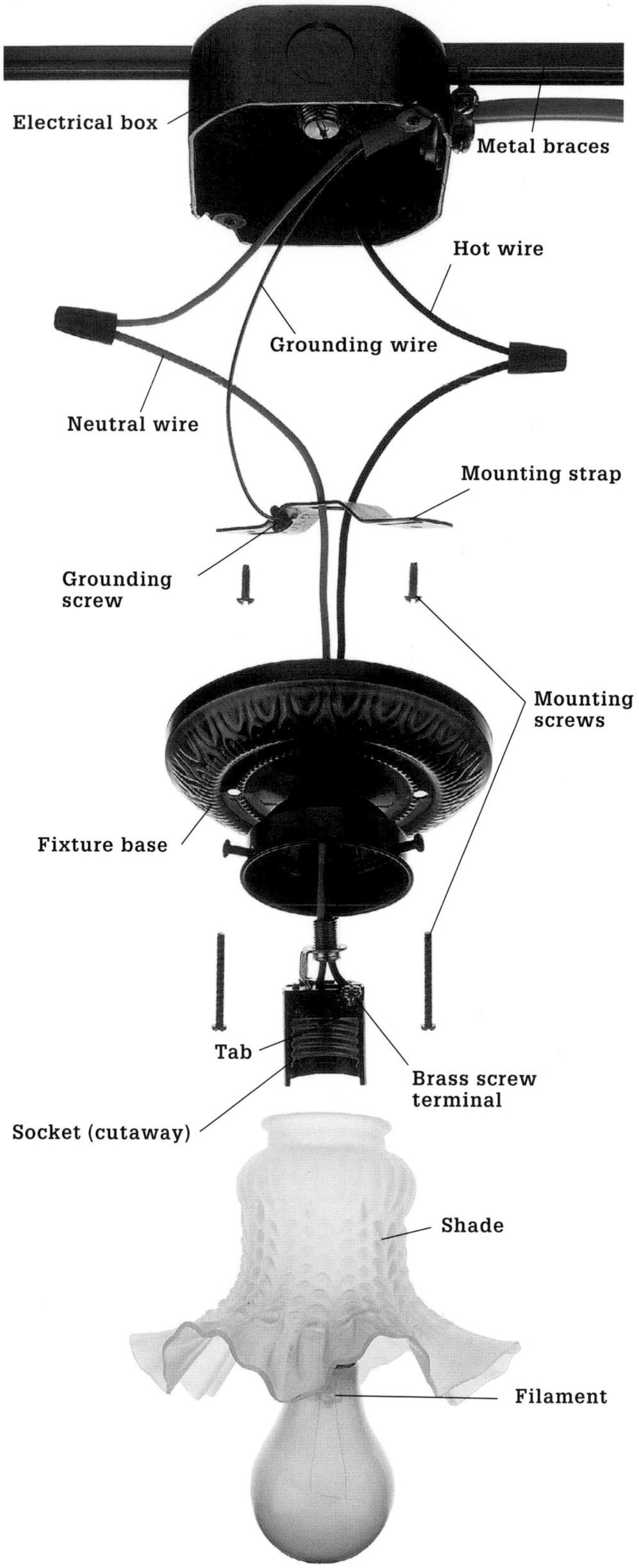

No matter what a ceiling light fixture looks like on the outside, they all attach in basically the same way. An electrical box in the ceiling is fitted with a mounting strap, which holds the fixture in place. The bare wire from the ceiling typically connects to the mounting strap. The two wires coming from the fixture connect to the black and the white wires from the ceiling.

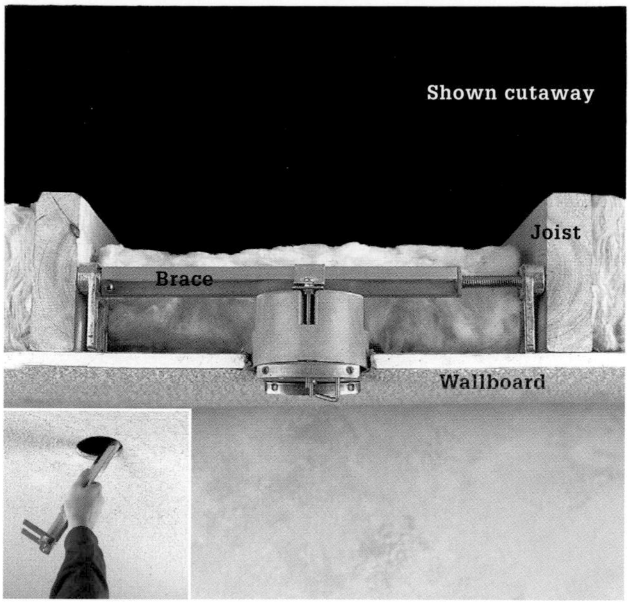

If the new fixture is much heavier than the original fixture, it will require additional bracing in the ceiling to support the electrical box and the fixture. The manufacturer's instructions should specify the size and type of box. If the ceiling is finished and there is no access from above, you can remove the old box and use an adjustable remodeling brace appropriate for your fixture (shown). The brace fits into a small hole in the ceiling (inset). Once the bracing is in place, install a new electrical box specified for the new fixture.

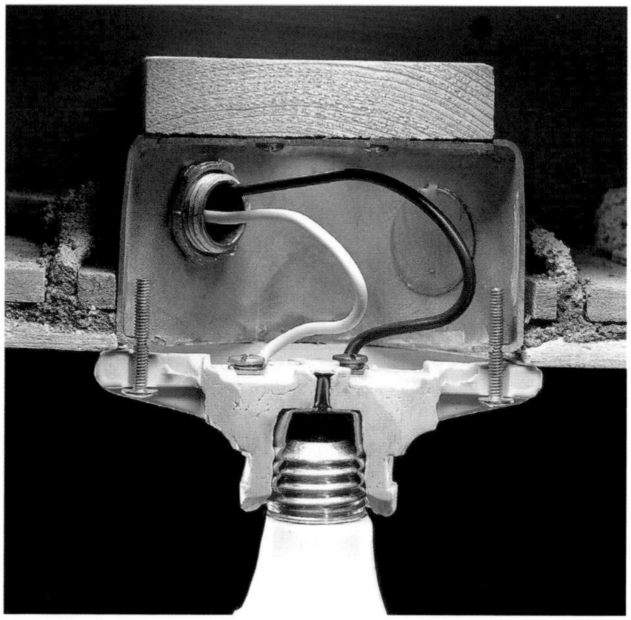

Inexpensive light fixtures have screw terminals mounted directly to the back side of the fixture plate. Often, as seen here, they have no grounding terminal. Some codes do not allow this type of fixture, but even if your hometown does approve them, it is a good idea to replace them with a better quality, safer fixture that is UL-approved.

How to Replace a Ceiling Light

Shut off power to the ceiling light and remove the shade or diffuser. Loosen the mounting screws and carefully lower the fixture, supporting it as you work (do not let light fixtures hang by their electrical wires alone). Test with a voltage sensor to make sure no power is reaching the connections.

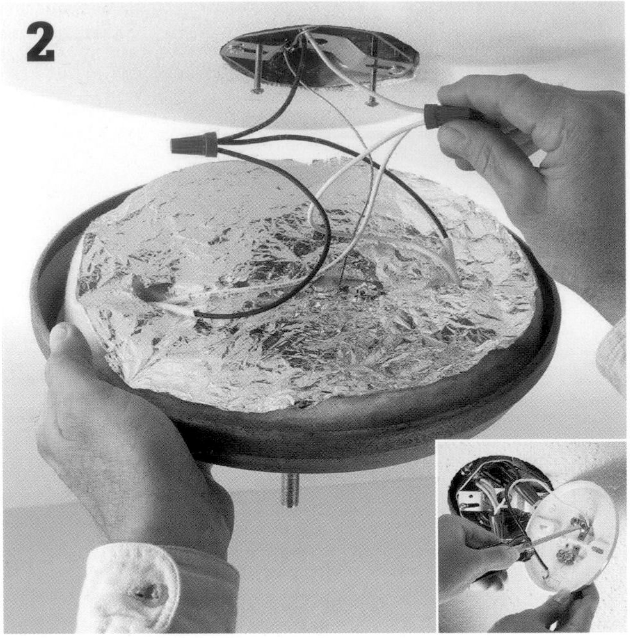

Remove the twist connectors from the fixture wires or unscrew the screw terminals and remove the white neutral wire and the black lead wire (inset).

Before you install the new fixture, check the ends of the wires coming from the ceiling electrical box. They should be clean and free of nicks or scorch marks. If they're dirty or worn, clip off the stripped portion with your combination tool. Then strip away about ¾" of insulation from the end of each wire.

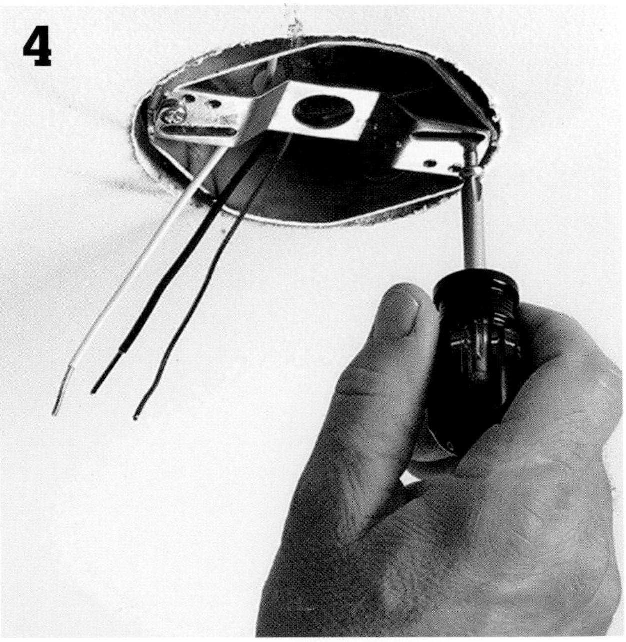

Attach a mounting strap to the ceiling fixture box if there is not one already present. Your new light may come equipped with a strap, otherwise you can find one for purchase at any hardware store.

5

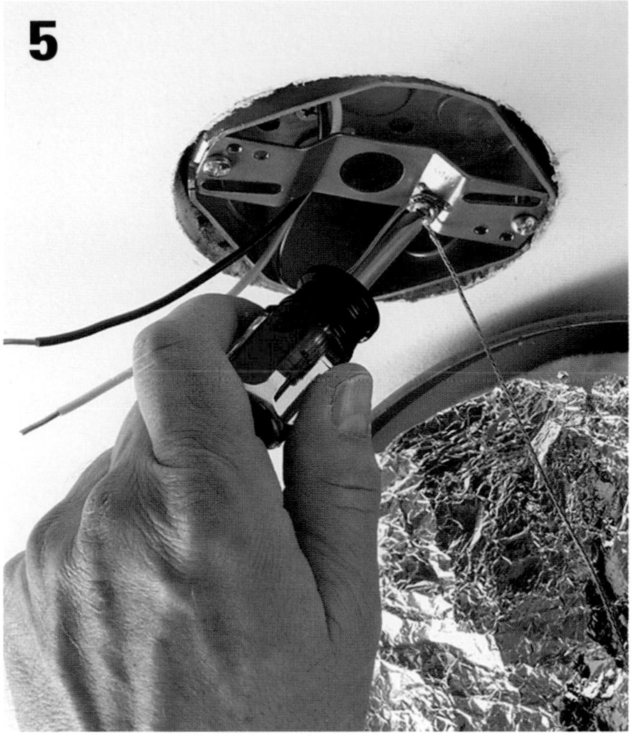

Lift the new fixture up to the ceiling (you may want a helper for this) and attach the bare copper ground wire from the power supply cable to the grounding screw or clip on the mounting strap. Also attach the ground wire from the fixture to the screw or clip.

6

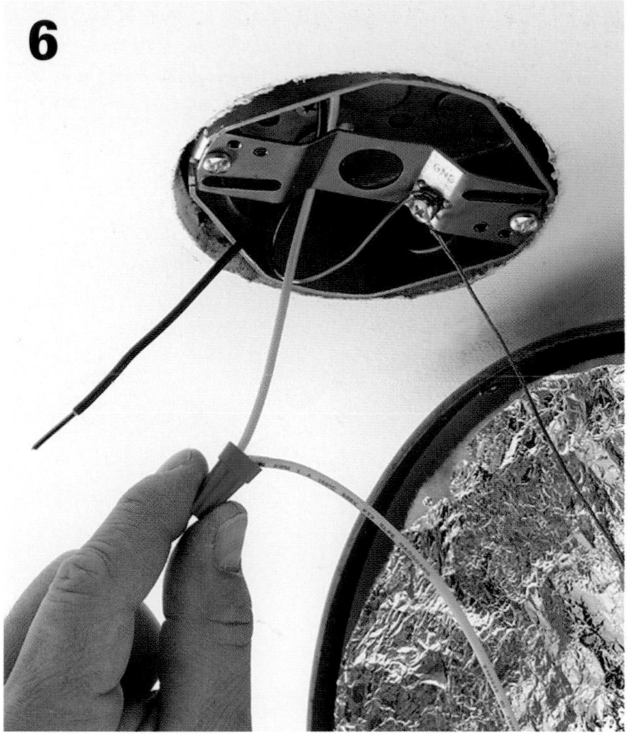

With the fixture supported by a ladder or a helper, join the white wire lead and the white fixture wire with a wire connector (often supplied with the fixture).

7

Connect the black power supply wire to the black fixture wire with a wire connector.

8

Position the new fixture mounting plate over the box so the mounting screw holes align. Drive the screws until the fixture is secure against the ceiling.

Vent Fans

For most of us, a dream bathroom does not include foggy mirrors or unpleasant odors. Opening a window, if your bathroom is equipped with one, can help, but vent fans do the best job of clearing the air.

Most vent fans are installed in the center of the bathroom ceiling or over the toilet area. A fan installed over the tub or shower area must be GFCI protected and rated for use in wet areas. You can usually wire a fan with a light fixture into a main bathroom electrical circuit, but units with built-in heat lamps or blowers require separate circuits.

If the fan you choose doesn't come with a mounting kit, purchase one separately. A mounting kit should include a vent hose (duct), a vent tailpiece, and an exterior vent cover.

Venting instructions vary among manufacturers, but the most common options are attic venting and soffit venting. Attic venting routes fan ductwork into the attic and out through the roof. Always insulate ducting in this application to keep condensation from forming and running down into the motor. Carefully install flashing around the outside vent cover to prevent roof leaks.

Soffit venting involves routing the duct to a soffit (roof overhang) instead of through the roof. Check with the vent manufacturer for instructions for soffit venting.

To prevent moisture damage, always terminate the vent outside your home—never into your attic or basement.

You can install a vent fan while the framing is exposed or as a retrofit, as shown in this project.

Tools & Materials ▸

- Phillips and straight screwdrivers
- Jigsaw or drywall saw
- Reciprocating saw
- Drill
- Electrical tester
- Exhaust fan unit
- Drywall screws
- Wire connectors
- Flexible dryer vent duct
- Dryer vent clamps
- Vent cover
- Drywall
- 4" hole saw

A combination light/vent fan is a great product in powder rooms and smaller baths that to do not generate excessive amounts of air moisture. In larger baths with tubs and showers, install a dedicated vent fan with a CFM rating that's at least 5 CFM higher than the total square footage of the bathroom (inset photo).

How to Replace an Overhead Light with a Light/Fan

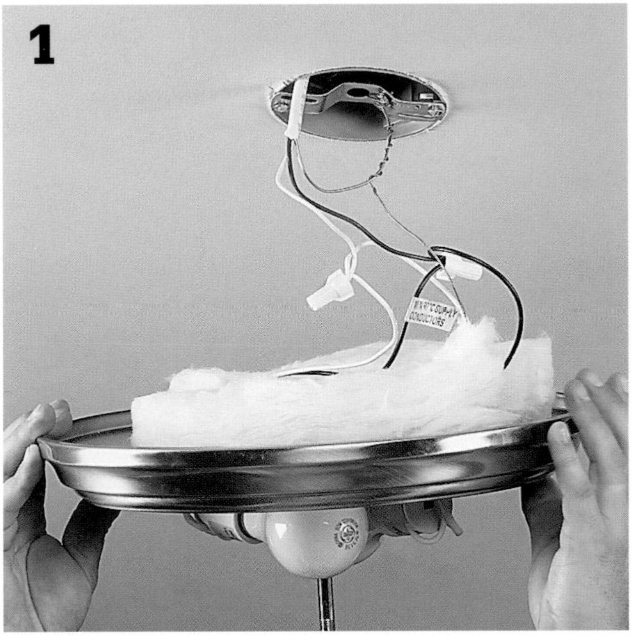

Shut off power to the ceiling light at the electrical service panel. Remove the globe and bulb from the overhead ceiling light, and then disconnect the mounting screws that hold the light fixture to the ceiling box.

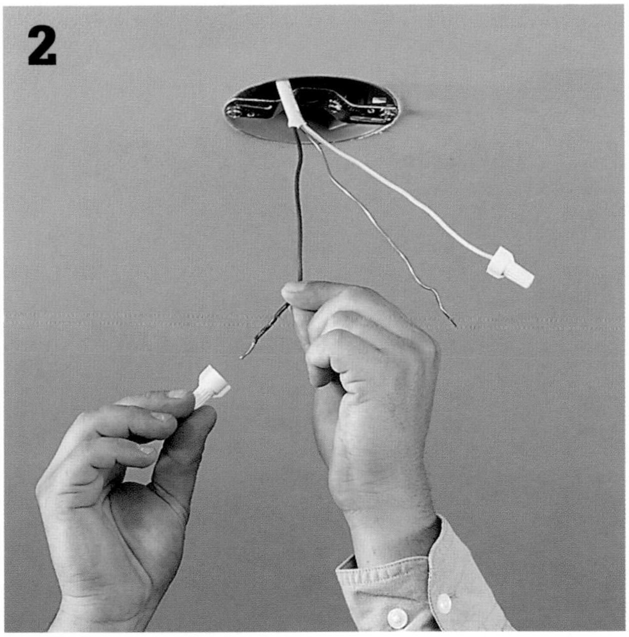

Test the wire connections with a current tester to make sure they are not live, and then disconnect the wires and remove the light fixture. Cap the wire ends.

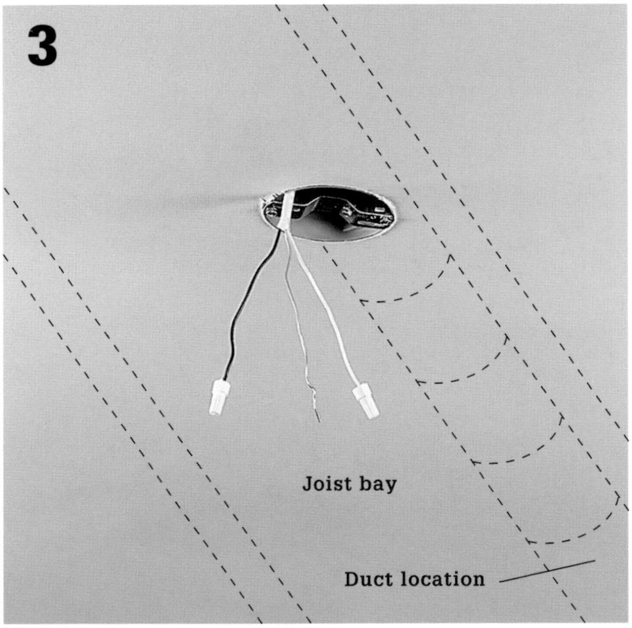

Plan your exhaust pipe route. In most cases, this means determining the shortest distance between the fan and the outdoors. If the room is located at the top living level, venting through the roof is usually smartest. On lower levels and in basements, you'll need to go through an exterior wall. If you need to route through a wall in a room with a finished ceiling, choose a route that runs through a single ceiling joist bay.

Remove ceiling covering in the fan unit installation area and between the joists at the end of the run, next to the wall. You'll need at least 18" of access. If you are running rigid vent pipe or the joist bay is insulated, you'll need to remove ceiling material between the joists for the entire run. Make cuts on the centerlines of the joists.

(continued)

Insert flexible vent tubing into one of the ceiling openings and expand it so the free end reaches to the ceiling opening at the wall. A fish-tape for running cable through walls can be a useful aid for extending the tubing.

Draw a 4"-dia. circle on the wall framing at the end of the joist bay, marking the exit point for the duct. Choose a long, ¼"-dia. drill bit and drill a hole at the center of the circle. Drill all the way through the wall so the bit exits on the exterior side. This will mark your hole location outside.

On the exterior, draw a 4"-dia. circle centered on the exit point of the drill bit. Cut out the opening for the vent cover with a reciprocating saw or a 4" hole saw.

Insert the vent cover assembly into the opening, following the manufacturer's directions for fastening and sealing it to the house.

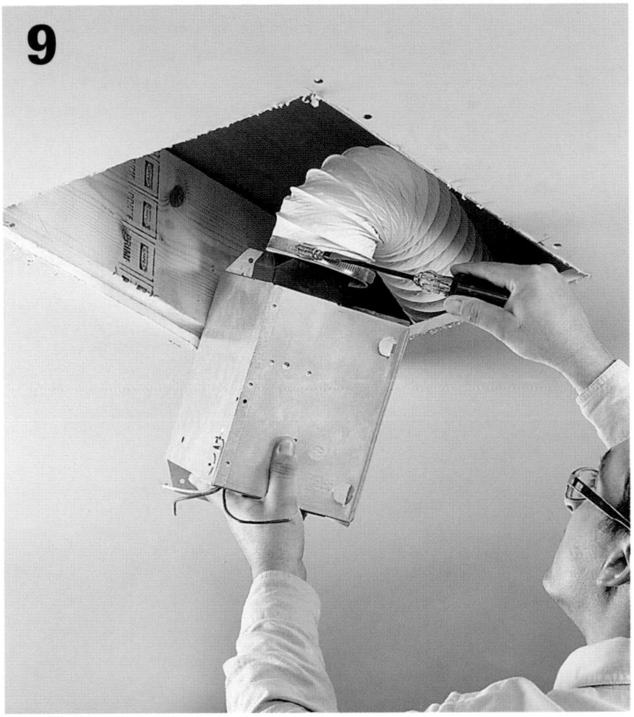

Attach the end of the vent tubing to the outlet on the vent cover unit and secure it with a large pipe clamp.

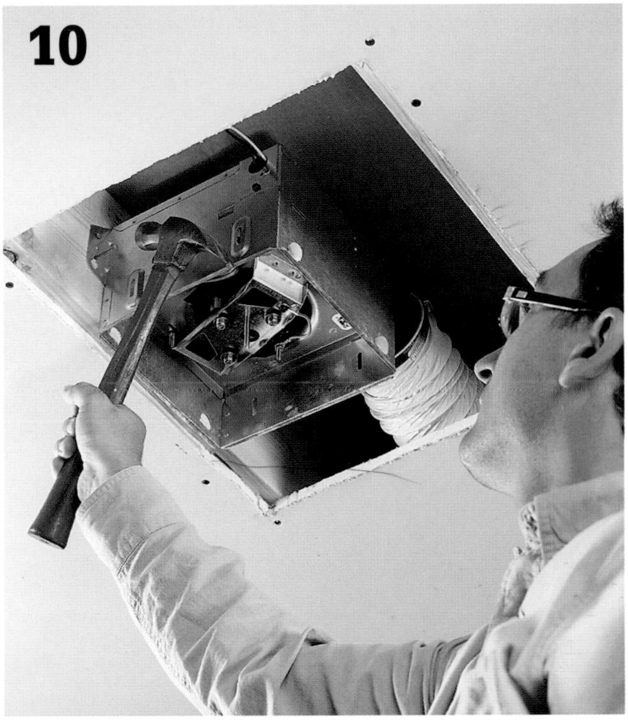

Nail the housing for the light/fan unit to the ceiling joist so the bottom edges of the housing are flush with the ceiling surface.

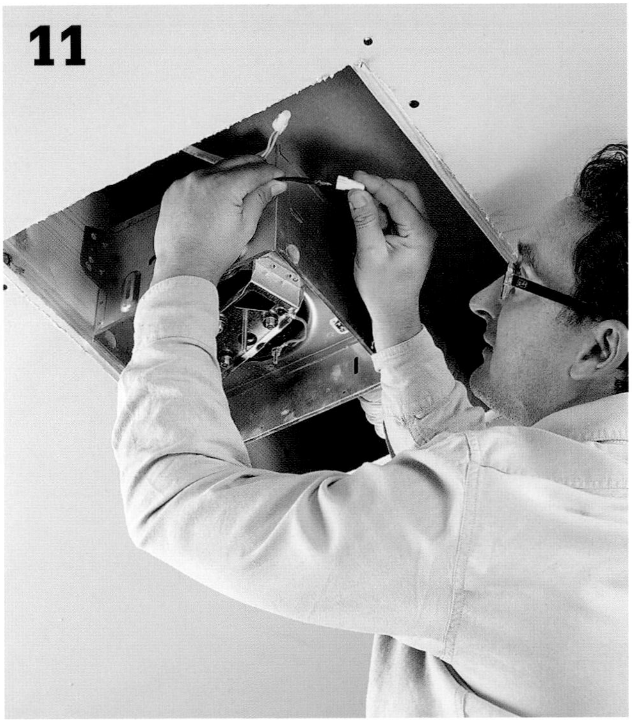

Make the wiring connections in the housing box according to the manufacturer's instructions. In just about every case you should be able to use the existing wires from the original light switch. Once you have connected the wires, restore the power and test the fan.

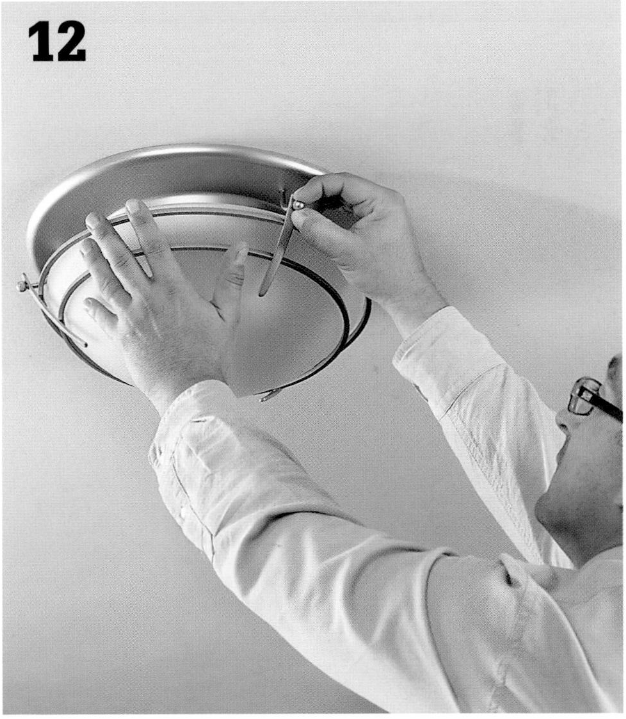

Patch and paint the wall and ceiling in the project area. Mount the light (the model we installed plugs into a receptacle in the fan box), grille, globe, and any other fixture parts.

Skylights

Skylights let an amazing amount of light into a bathroom. Do not select a skylight that's too big, it can overheat a space. The same is true of using too many skylights in any one room. For that reason it's often best to position a skylight away from the day's brightest sun. You may want an operable skylight that opens and closes to vent warm air.

When a skylight is installed above an unfinished attic space, a special skylight shaft must be constructed to channel light directly to the room below.

Installing a skylight above finished space involves other considerations. First, the ceiling surface must be removed to expose the rafters. To remove wall and ceiling surfaces, see pages 86 to 89.

A skylight frame is similar to a standard window frame. It has a header and sill, like a window frame, but it has king rafters rather than king studs. Skylight frames also have trimmers that define the sides of the rough opening. Refer to the manufacturer's instructions to determine what size to make the opening for the skylight you select.

With standard rafter-frame roof construction, you can safely cut into one or two rafters as long as you permanently support the cut rafters, as shown in the following steps. If your skylight requires alteration of more than two rafters or if your roofing is made with unusually heavy material, such as clay, tile, or slate, consult an architect or engineer before starting the project.

Today's good-quality skylight units are unlikely to leak, but a skylight is only as leakproof as its installation. Follow the manufacturer's instructions, and install the flashing meticulously, as it will last a lot longer than any sealant.

Tools & Materials ▸

- 4-ft. level
- Circular saw
- Drill
- Combination square
- Reciprocating saw
- Pry bar
- Chalk line
- Stapler
- Caulk gun
- Utility knife
- Aviation snips
- Plumb bob
- Jig saw
- Wallboard tools
- 16d and 10d common nails
- 2× lumber
- 1 × 4
- Building paper
- Roofing cement
- Skylight flashing
- 2", 1¼", and ¾" roofing nails
- Finish nails
- Fiberglass insulation
- ½" wallboard
- Twine
- Wallboard screws
- 6-mil polyethylene sheeting
- Finishing materials
- Screws

A skylight or a tubular skylight is a great way to bring natural light and ventilation into a bathroom without sacrificing privacy.

How to Install a Skylight

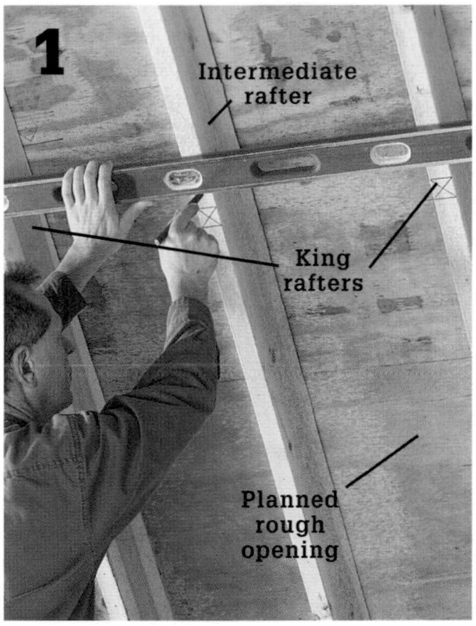

Use the first rafter on each side of the planned rough opening as a king rafter. Measure and mark where the double header and sill will fit against the king rafters. Then, use a level as a straightedge to extend the marks across the intermediate rafter.

Brace the intermediate rafter by installing two 2 × 4s between the rafter and the attic floor. Position the braces just above the header marks and just below the sill marks. Secure them temporarily to the rafter and subfloor (or joists) with screws.

Reinforce each king rafter by attaching a full-length "sister" rafter against its outside face. Cut sister rafters from the same size of lumber as existing rafters, matching lengths and end cuts exactly. Work each one into position, flush against the outside face of the king rafters, then nail the sisters to the kings with pairs of 10d common nails spaced 12" apart.

Use a combination square to transfer the sill and header marks across the face of the intermediate rafter, then cut along the outermost lines with a reciprocating saw. Do not cut into the roof sheathing. Carefully remove the cutout section with a pry bar. The remaining rafter portions will serve as cripple rafters.

Build a double header and double sill to fit snugly between the king rafters, using 2× lumber that is the same size as the rafters. Nail the header pieces together using pairs of 10d nails spaced 6" apart.

Install the header and sill, anchoring them to the king rafters and cripple rafters with 16d common nails. Make sure the ends of the header and sill are aligned with the appropriate marks on the king rafters.

(continued)

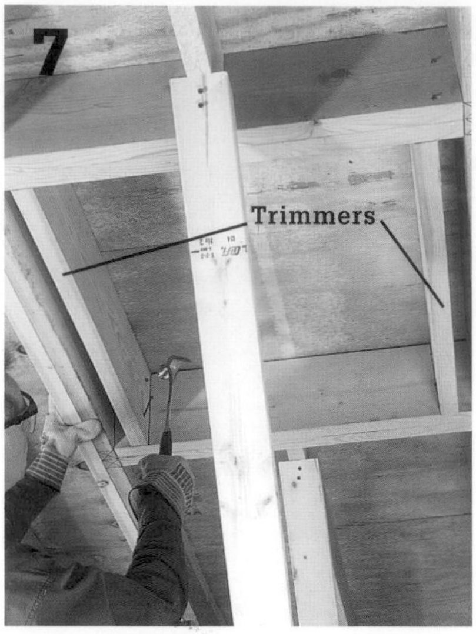

If your skylight unit is narrower than the opening between the king studs, measure and make marks for the trimmers: They should be centered in the opening and spaced according to the manufacturer's specifications. Cut the trimmers from the same 2× lumber used for the rest of the frame, and nail them in place with 10d common nails. Remove the 2 × 4 braces.

Mark the opening for the roof cutout by driving a screw through the sheathing at each corner of the frame. Then, tack a couple of scrap boards across the opening to prevent the roof cutout from falling and causing damage below.

Cut out the roof opening. Mount an old blade in a circular saw or cordless trim saw and plunge cut along the top and bottom cutting lines. Stop short of the corners so you don't overcut. Tack a piece of 1 × 4 across the opening to catch the waste piece and then make the side cuts. Finish the cuts at the corners with a jig saw or handsaw. Remove the waste.

Remove the shingles surrounding the opening, but try and maintain the integrity of the building paper beneath. Try to salvage the shingles if you can so they can be reinstalled (they'll match better than new shingles). Start with the row of shingles above the opening. Once these are removed you'll have access to the roofing nails on lower courses.

Seal the bottom of the rough frame opening. Apply a strip of self-adhesive flashing at the bottom of the roof opening to create a seal on the curb and to cover the seam between the underlayment and the roof deck. This is for extra protection.

Position the skylight in the opening. Different models use different fastening and centering devices. The one seen here is installed using pairs of adjustable brackets that are fastened to the roof deck and to the sides of the skylight frame.

Fasten the skylight unit. Many models employ adjustable brackets like the ones seen here so the skylight can be raised or lowered and centered in the opening. The brackets seen here have a slot and several nail holes in the horizontal flange. Drive a ring shank nail in all four slots and then shift the unit side to side as necessary until it is centered in the opening.

Install self-adhesive flashing strips around the skylight curb. Start with the base strip, cutting slits in the corners so the flashing extends all the way up the curb (you'll need to remove metal cladding strips first). Install the head flashing last so all strips overlap from above.

Install the metal flashing beginning with the sill. Some skylights have a 4-piece flashing kit where the side flashing is simply shingled over. Others, like the one seen here, include solid base and head flashing components and step flashing that is woven in with the shingles as the roof coverings are installed.

Replace shingles up to the skylight curb. Install shingles in complete rows, notching them to fit around the curb. Stop once the granular surfaces of the top row of shingles meet the curb.

Install side flashing. Here, metal step flashing is interwoven with the shingles during the shingling process. Whether it's the shingle layer or the step flashing layer, make sure that all components always overlap from above and the horizontal tabs on the step flashing are all covered with shingles. Do not nail through flashing.

Install the head flashing piece so it overlaps the last course of shingle and step flashing. Finish shingling in the installation area, again taking care not to nail through any metal flashing. Replace the metal cladding and caulk if recommended by the manufacturer.

How to Build a Skylight Shaft

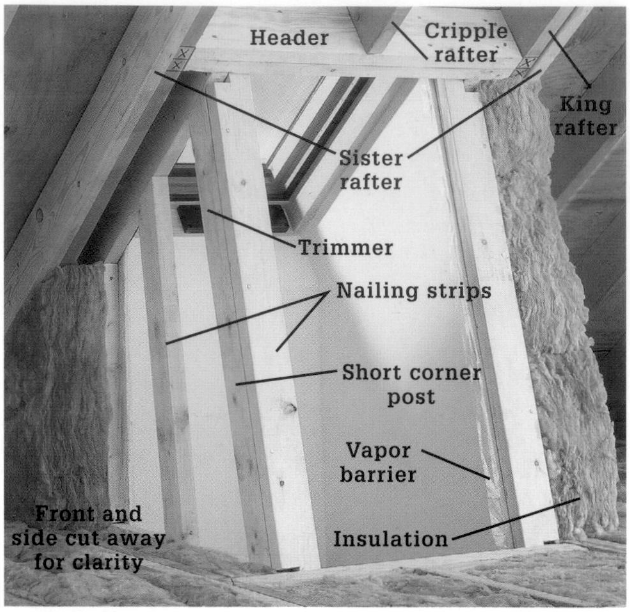

A skylight shaft is made with 2 × 4 lumber and wallboard and includes a vapor barrier and fiberglass insulation. You can build a straight shaft with four vertical sides or an angled shaft that has a longer frame at ceiling level and one or more sides set at an angle. Since the ceiling opening is larger, an angled shaft lets in more direct light than a straight shaft.

Remove any insulation in the area where the skylight will be located; turn off and reroute electrical circuits as necessary. Use a plumb bob as a guide to mark reference points on the ceiling surface directly below the inside corners of the skylight frame.

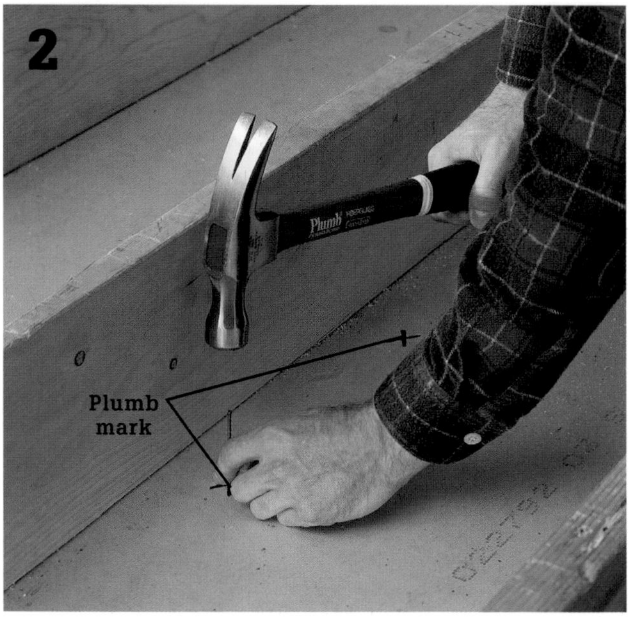

If you are installing a straight shaft, use the plumb marks made in step 1 to define the corners of the ceiling opening; drive a finish nail through the ceiling surface at each mark. If you are installing an angled shaft, measure out from the plumb marks and make new marks that define the corners of the ceiling opening; drive finish nails at the new marks.

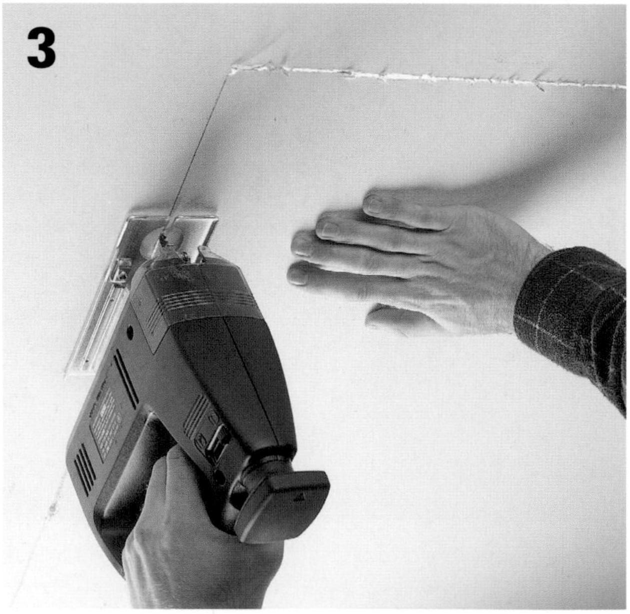

From the room below, mark cutting lines, then remove the ceiling surface.

Use the nearest joists on either side of the ceiling opening to serve as king joists. Measure and mark where the double header and double sill will fit against the king joists and where the outside edge of the header and sill will cross any intermediate joists.

If you will be removing a section of an intermediate joist, reinforce the king joists by nailing full-length "sister" joists to the outside faces of the king joists using 10d nails.

Install temporary supports below the project area to support the intermediate rafter on both sides of the opening. Use a combination square to extend cutting lines down the sides of the intermediate joist, then cut out the joist section with a reciprocating saw. Pry loose the cutout portion of the joist, being careful not to damage the ceiling surface.

Build a double header and double sill to span the distance between the king joists using 2× dimensional lumber the same size as the joists.

(continued)

Install the double header and double sill, anchoring them to the king joists and cripple joists with 10d nails. The inside edges of the header and sill should be aligned with the edge of the ceiling cutout.

Complete the ceiling opening by cutting and attaching trimmers, if required, along the sides of the ceiling cutout between the header and sill. Toenail the trimmers to the header and sill with 10d nails.

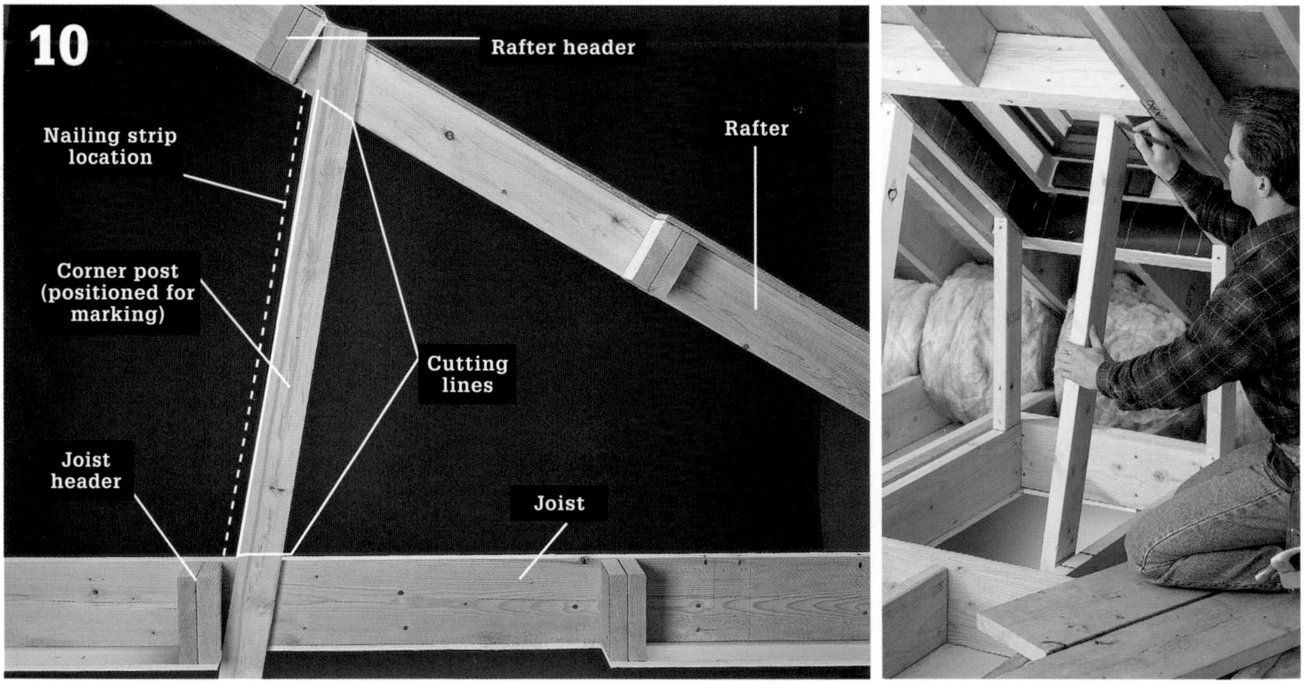

Install 2 × 4 corner posts for the skylight shaft. To measure for the posts, begin with a 2 × 4 that is long enough to reach from the top to the bottom of the shaft. Hold the 2 × 4 against the inside of the framed openings, so it is flush with the top of the rafter header and the bottom of the joist header (left photo). Mark cutting lines where the 2 × 4 meets the top of the joist or trimmer and the bottom of the rafter or trimmer (right photo). Cut along the lines, then toenail the posts to the top and bottom of the frame with 10d nails.

Attach a 2 × 4 nailing strip to the outside edge of each corner post to provide a nailing surface for attaching the wallboard. Notch the ends of the nailing strips to fit around the trimmers; a perfect fit is not necessary.

Install additional 2 × 4 nailing strips between the corner posts if the distances between posts are more than 24". Miter the top ends of the nailing strips to fit against the rafter trimmers.

Wrap the skylight shaft with fiberglass insulation. Secure the insulation by wrapping twine around the shaft and insulation.

From inside the shaft, staple a plastic vapor barrier of 6-mil polyethylene sheeting over the insulation.

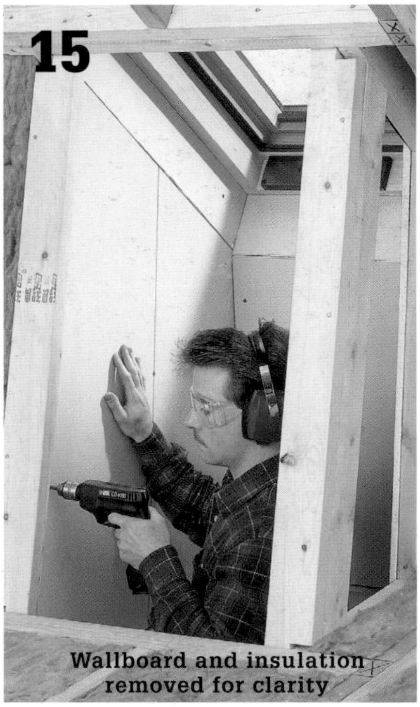

Finish the inside of the shaft with wallboard. *Tip: To reflect light, paint the shaft interior with a light-colored, semigloss paint.*

Tubular Skylights

Any interior room, including a bathroom, can be brightened with a tubular skylight. Tubular skylights are quite energy-efficient and are relatively easy to install, with no complicated framing involved.

The design of tubular skylights varies among manufacturers, with some using solid plastic reflecting tubes and others using flexible tubing. Various diameters are also available. Measure the distance between the framing members in your attic before purchasing your skylight to be sure it will fit.

This project shows the installation of a tubular skylight on a sloped, asphalt-shingled roof. Consult the dealer or manufacturer for installation procedures on other roof types.

A tubular skylight is an economical way to introduce more sunlight into a room without embarking on a major framing project.

Tools & Materials ▸

- Pencil
- Drill
- Tape measure
- Wallboard saw
- Reciprocating saw
- Pry bar
- Screwdriver
- Hammer
- Wire cutters
- Utility knife
- Chalk
- Tubular skylight kit
- Stiff wire
- 2" roofing nails or flashing screws
- Roofing cement

How to Install a Tubular Skylight

Drill a pilot hole through the ceiling at the approximate location for your skylight. Push a stiff wire up into the attic to help locate the hole. In the attic, make sure the space around the hole is clear of any insulation. Drill a second hole through the ceiling at the centerpoint between two joists.

Center the ceiling ring frame over the hole and trace around it with a pencil. Carefully cut along the pencil line with a wallboard saw or reciprocating saw. Save the wallboard ceiling cutout to use as your roof-hole pattern. Attach the ceiling frame ring around the hole with the included screws.

In the attic, choose the most direct route for the tubing to reach the roof. Find the center between the appropriate rafters and drive a nail up through the roof sheathing and shingles.

Use the wallboard ceiling cutout, centered over the nail hole, as a template for the roof opening. Trace the cutout onto the roof with chalk. Drill a starter hole to insert the reciprocating saw blade, then cut out the hole in the roof. Pry up the lower portion of the shingles above the hole. Remove any staples or nails around the hole edge.

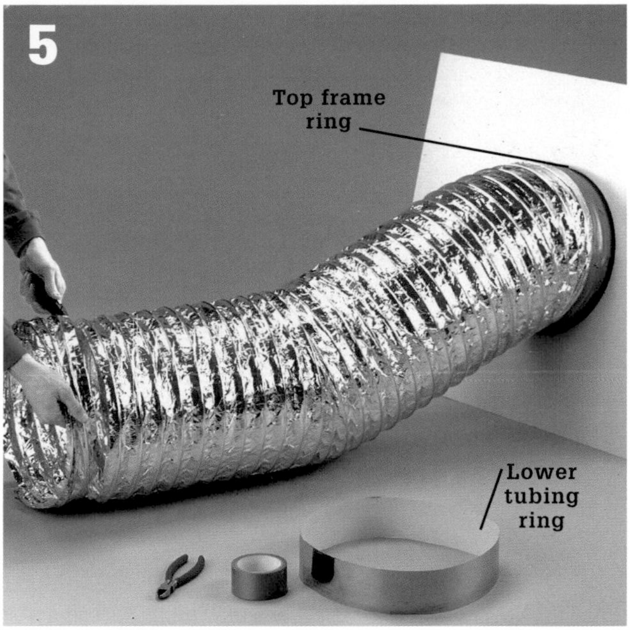

Pull the tubing over the top frame ring. Bend the frame tabs out through the tubing, keeping two or three rings of the tubing wire above the tabs. Wrap the junction three times around with included PVC tape. Then, in the attic, measure from the roof to the ceiling. Stretch out the tubing and cut it to length with a utility knife and wire cutters. Pull the loose end of tubing over the lower ring and wrap it three times with PVC tape.

Lower the tubing through the roof hole and slide the flashing into place with the upper portion of the flashing underneath the existing shingles. This is easier with two people, one on the roof and one in the attic.

Secure the flashing to the roof with 2" roofing nails or flashing screws. Seal under the shingles and over all the nail heads with roofing cement. Attach the skylight dome and venting to the frame with the included screws.

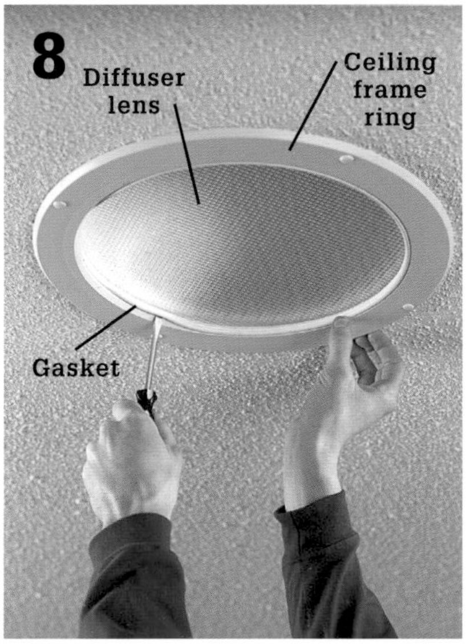

Pull the lower end of the tubing down through the ceiling hole. Attach the lower tubing ring to the ceiling frame ring and fasten it with screws. Attach the gasket to the diffuser lens and work the gasket around the perimeter of the ceiling frame. Repack any insulation around the tubing in the attic.

Glass Block Windows

Probably one of the more enthralling design features that can be added to a dream bath is the glass block window with its tease of light infusion and reduced visibility. It is a highly energy efficient material and offers great security when used for windows. Glass block is a great choice for accent windows and for windows in rooms where privacy is a must.

Glass block is available in a wide variety of sizes, shapes, and patterns. It can be found, along with other necessary installation products, at specialty distributors and home centers.

Building with glass block is much like building with mortared brick, with two important differences. First, glass block must be supported by another structure and cannot function in a loadbearing capacity. Second, glass block cannot be cut, so take extra time to make sure the layout is accurate.

When installing a glass block window, the size of the rough opening is based on the size and number of blocks you are using. It is much easier to make an existing opening smaller to accommodate the glass block than make it larger, which requires reframing the rough opening. To determine the rough opening width, multiply the nominal width of the glass block by the number of blocks horizontally, and add ¼". For the height, multiply the nominal height by the number of blocks vertically and add ¼".

Because of its weight, a glass block window requires a solid base. The framing members of the rough opening will need to be reinforced. Contact your local building department for requirements in your area.

Use ¼" plastic T-spacers between blocks to ensure consistent mortar joints and to support the weight of the block to prevent mortar from squeezing out before it sets. (T-spacers can be modified into L or flat shapes for use at corners and along the channel.) For best results, use premixed glass block mortar. This high-strength mortar is a little drier than regular brick mortar, because glass doesn't wick water out of the mortar as brick does.

Because there are many applications for glass block, and installation techniques may vary, ask a glass block retailer or manufacturer about the best products and methods for your specific project.

Tools & Materials ▸

- Tape measure
- Circular saw
- Hammer
- Utility knife
- Tin snips
- Drill
- Mixing box
- Trowel
- 4-ft. level
- Rubber mallet
- Jointing tool
- Sponge
- Scrub brush
- Caulk gun
- 2 × 4 lumber
- 16d common nails
- Glass block perimeter channels
- 1" galvanized flat-head screws
- Glass block mortar
- Glass blocks
- ¼" T-spacers
- Expansion strips
- Silicone caulk
- Construction adhesive
- Mortar sealant

Glass block windows add both light and privacy to a bathroom, but keep in mind that glass block cannot be cut and it cannot be load bearing.

How to Install a Glass Block Window

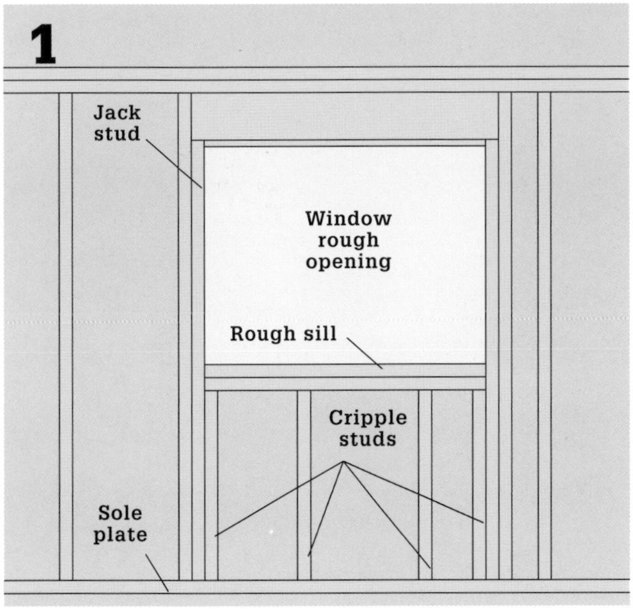

Measure the size of the rough opening and determine the size of the glass block window you will install (opposite page). Reinforce the rough opening framing by doubling the rough sill and installing additional cripple studs. Cut all pieces to size and fasten with 16d common nails.

Cut the perimeter channel to length for the sill and side jambs, mitering the ends at 45°. Align the front edge of the channel flush with the front edge of the exterior wall sheathing. Drill pilot holes every 12" through the channels (if not provided), and fasten the channels in place with 1" galvanized flat-head screws. *Note: Paint the screw heads white to help conceal them.*

For the header, cut a channel to length, mitering the ends at 45°, then cut it in half lengthwise using a utility knife. Align one half of the channel flush with the exterior face of the sheathing, and fasten in place with 1" galvanized flat-head screws.

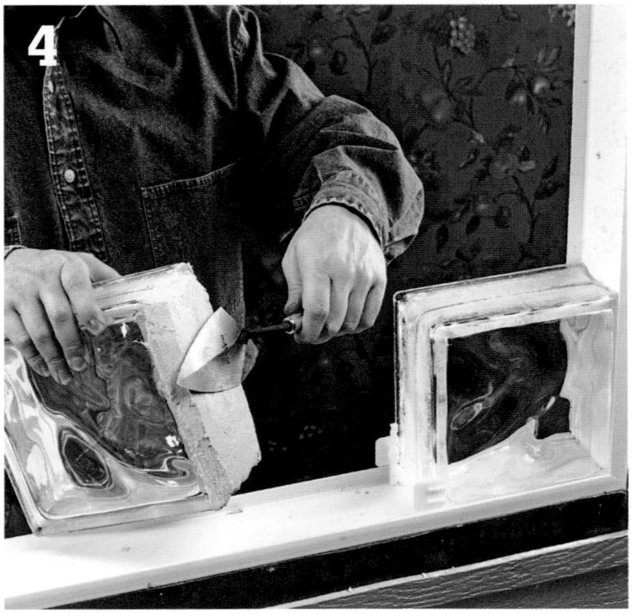

Set two blocks into the sill channel, one against each jamb—do not place mortar between blocks and channels. Place a ¼" flat spacer against the first block. Mix glass block mortar and liberally butter the leading edge of another block, then push it tight against the first block. Make sure the joint is filled with mortar.

(continued)

Lay the remainder of the first course, building from both jambs toward the center. Use flat spacers between blocks to maintain proper spacing. Plumb and level each block as you work, then check the entire course for level. Tap blocks into place using the rubber handle of the trowel—do not use metal tools with glass block. Butter both sides of the final block in the course to install it.

At the top of the course, fill any depression at the top of each mortar joint with mortar, insert a ¼" T-spacer, then lay a ⅜" bed of mortar for the next course. Lay the blocks for each course using T-spacers to maintain proper spacing. Check each block for level and plumb as you work.

Test the mortar as you work. When it can resist light finger pressure, remove the T-spacers and pack mortar into the voids, then tool the joints with a jointing tool. Remove excess mortar with a damp sponge, or a nylon or natural-bristle brush.

To ease block placement in the final course, use tin snips to trim the outer tabs off one side of the T-spacers. Install the blocks of the final course. After the final block is installed, work in any mortar that has been forced out of the joints.

Cut an expansion strip for the header 1½" wide and to length. Slide it between the top course of block and the header of the rough opening. Apply a bead of construction adhesive to the top edge of the remaining half of the header channel, and slide it between the expansion strip and header.

Clean the glass block thoroughly with a wet sponge, rinsing often. Allow the surface to dry, then remove cloudy residue with a clean, dry cloth. Caulk between glass block and channels, and between channels and framing members before installing the exterior trim. After the molding is installed, allow mortar to cure for two weeks, then apply silicone caulk.

Glass Block Window Kits

Some glass block window kits do not require mortar. Instead, the blocks are set into the perimeter channels and the joints are created using plastic spacer strips. Silicone caulk is then used to seal the joints.

Preassembled glass or acrylic block windows are simple to install. These vinyl-clad units have a nailing flange around the frame, which allows them to be hung using the same installation techniques used for standard windows.

DOLCE
PELLE

Wall & Floor Projects

Bathroom walls and floors are easy to ignore because we tend to believe that only practical (and boring) surfaces can be used in bathrooms. After all, they need to be water resistant and easy to clean, right? There are a couple of errors in that assumption.

Yes, bathroom walls and floors should be water resistant, but that doesn't mean they have to be utterly impervious to moisture (unless, of course, they are in a shower stall). You'd do well to avoid delicate wall surfaces such as wallpaper or plain drywall with flat paint, and absorbent floor materials, such as carpeting.

The other error many homeowners make when considering bathroom walls and floors is to think that traditional materials, such as glazed tile, are necessarily dull and institutional in feel. This is most certainly not true, as the following wall projects will bear out.

In this chapter:

- Hanging Cementboard
- Hanging Wall Tile
- Embellished Wall Tile
- Tiled Tub Apron
- Toilet Enclosure
- Radiant Heat Floor Mats
- Ceramic Tile Floor
- Sheet Vinyl Floor

Hanging Cementboard

Use tile backer board as the substrate for tile walls in wet areas. Unlike drywall, tile backer won't break down and cause damage if water gets behind the tile. The three basic types of tile backer are cementboard, fiber-cement board, and Dens-Shield.

Though water cannot damage either cementboard or fiber-cement board, it can pass through them. To protect the framing members, install a water barrier of 4-mil plastic or 15# building paper behind the backer.

Dens-Shield has a waterproof acrylic facing that provides the water barrier. It cuts and installs much like drywall, but requires galvanized screws to prevent corrosion and must be sealed with caulk at all untaped joints and penetrations.

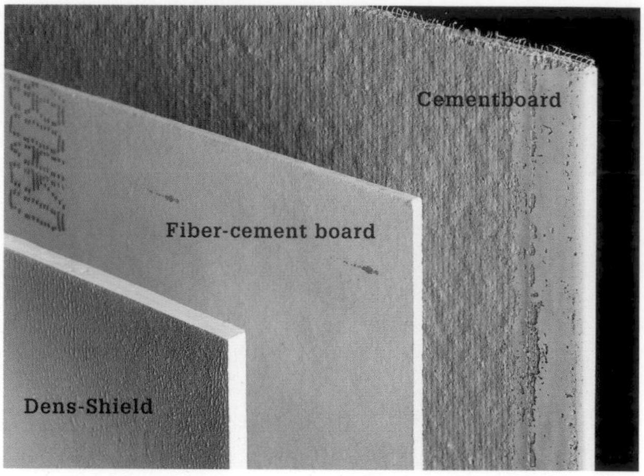

Common tile backers are cementboard, fiber-cement board, and Dens-Shield. Cementboard is made from portland cement and sand reinforced by an outer layer of fiberglass mesh. Fiber-cement board is made similarly, but with a fiber reinforcement integrated throughout the panel. Dens-Shield is a water-resistant gypsum board with a waterproof acrylic facing.

Tools & Materials ▸

Work gloves
Eye protection
Utility knife or carbide-tipped cutter
T-square
Small masonry bits
Hammer
Jigsaw with a carbide grit blade
Taping knives
Stapler
4-mil plastic sheeting
Cementboard
1¼" cementboard screws
Cementboard joint tape
Latex-portland cement mortar
15# building paper
Spacers
Screwgun

How to Hang Cementboard

Staple a water barrier of 4-mil plastic sheeting or 15# building paper over the framing. Overlap seams by several inches, and leave the sheets long at the perimeter. *Note: Framing for cementboard must be 16" on center; steel studs must be 20-gauge.*

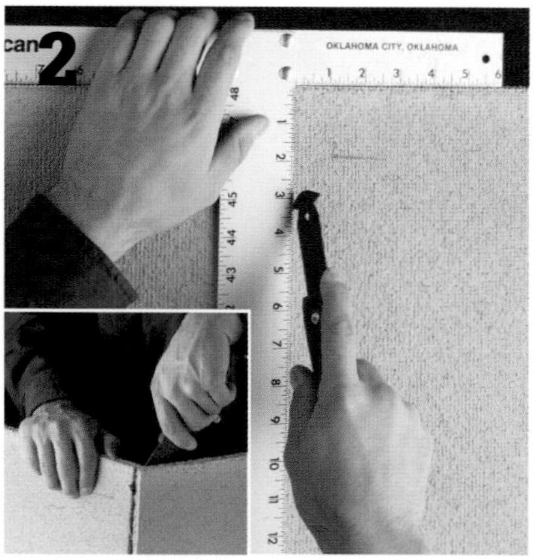

Cut cementboard by scoring through the mesh just below the surface with a utility knife or carbide-tipped cutter. Snap the panel back, then cut through the back-side mesh (inset). *Note: For tile applications, the rough face of the board is the front.*

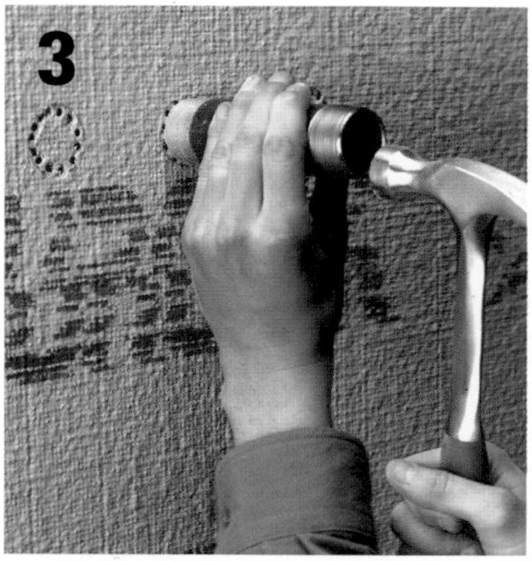

Make cutouts for pipes and other penetrations by drilling a series of holes through the board, using a small masonry bit. Tap the hole out with a hammer or a scrap of pipe. Cut holes along edges with a jigsaw and carbide grit blade.

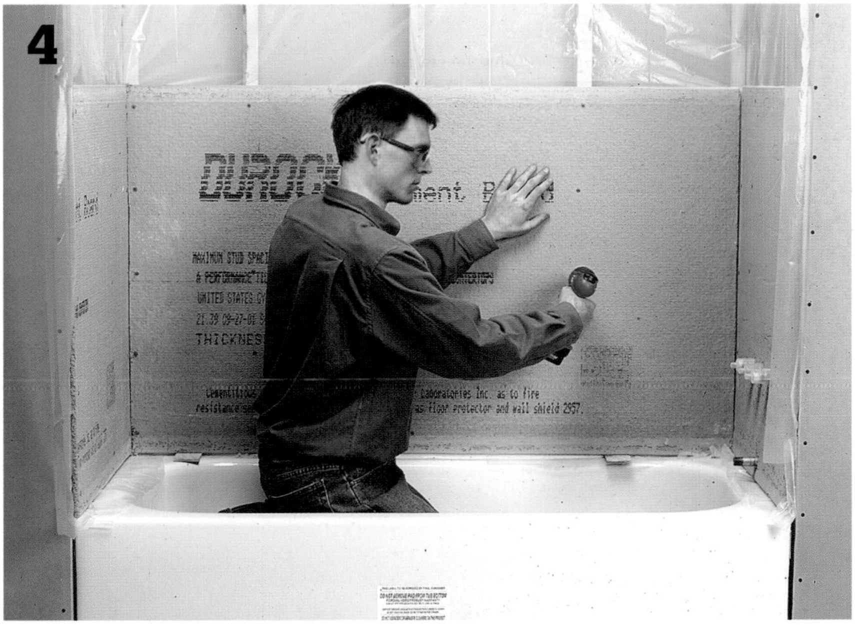

Install the sheets horizontally. Where possible, use full pieces to avoid butted seams, which are difficult to fasten. If there are vertical seams, stagger them between rows. Leave a ⅛" gap between sheets at vertical seams and corners. Use spacers to set the bottom row of panels ¼" above the tub or shower base. Fasten the sheets with 1¼" cementboard screws, driven every 8" for walls and every 6" for ceilings. Drive the screws at least ½" from the edges to prevent crumbling. If the studs are steel, don't fasten within 1" of the top track.

Cover the joints and corners with cementboard joint tape (alkali-resistant fiberglass mesh) and latex-portland cement mortar (thin-set). Apply a layer of mortar with a taping knife, embed the tape into the mortar, then smooth and level the mortar.

Finishing Cementboard

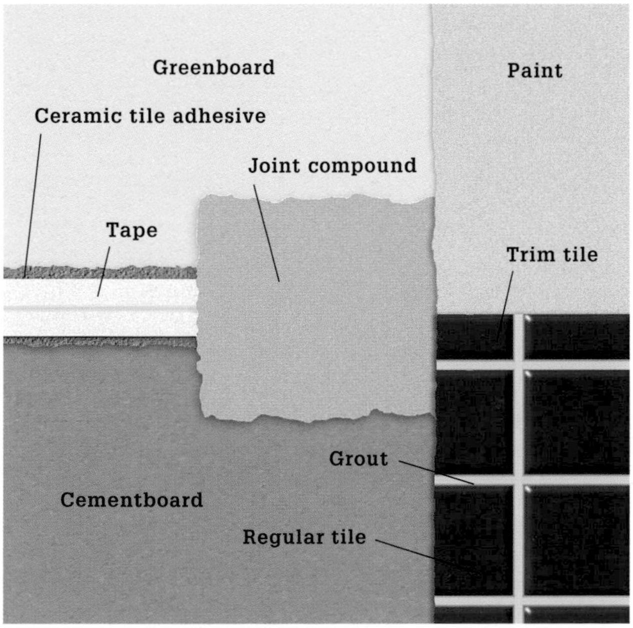

To finish a joint between cementboard and greenboard, seal the joint and exposed cementboard with ceramic tile adhesive, a mixture of four parts adhesive to one part water. Embed paper joint tape into the adhesive, smoothing the tape with a taping knife. Allow the adhesive to dry, then finish the joint with at least two coats of all-purpose drywall joint compound.

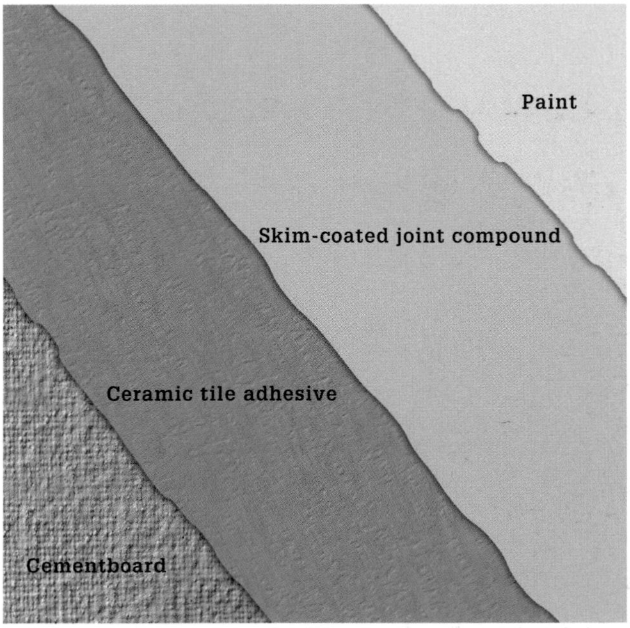

To finish small areas of cementboard that will not be tiled, seal the cementboard with ceramic tile adhesive, a mixture of four parts adhesive to one part water, then apply a skim-coat of all-purpose drywall joint compound using a 12" drywall knife. Then prime and paint the wall.

Wall Tile

Tile is an ideal covering for walls in bathrooms. Beautiful, practical, and easy to clean and maintain, tile walls are well suited to bathrooms.

When shopping for tile, keep in mind that tiles that are at least 6" × 6" are easier to install than small tiles, because they require less cutting and cover more surface area. Larger tiles also have fewer grout lines that must be cleaned and maintained. Check out the selection of trim, specialty tiles, and ceramic accessories that are available to help you customize your project.

Most wall tile is designed to have narrow grout lines (less than ⅛" wide) filled with unsanded grout. Grout lines wider than ⅛" should be filled with sanded floor-tile grout. Either type will last longer if it contains, or is mixed with, a latex additive. To prevent staining, it's a good idea to seal your grout after it fully cures, then once a year thereafter.

You can use standard drywall or water-resistant drywall (called "greenboard") as a backer for walls in dry areas. In wet areas, install tile over cementboard. Made from cement and fiberglass, cementboard cannot be damaged by water, though moisture can pass through it. To protect the framing, install a waterproof membrane, such as roofing felt or polyethylene sheeting, between the framing members and the cementboard. Be sure to tape and finish the seams between cementboard panels before laying the tile.

Tools & Materials ▸

Tile-cutting tools
Marker
Tape measure
4-ft. level
Notched trowel
Mallet
Grout float
Grout sponge
Soft cloth
Small paintbrush or foam brush
Caulk gun
Straight 1 × 2
Scrap 2 × 4
Carpet
Thinset tile mortar with latex additive
Ceramic wall tile
Ceramic trim tile (as needed)
2 × 4
Carpet scrap
Tile grout with latex additive
Tub & tile caulk
Alkaline grout sealer
Cardboard
Story stick/pole

Tile is a practical, easy-to-maintain choice for bathroom walls. The variety of colors, shapes, and sizes ensure there's a tile for everyone. Keep in mind that larger tiles are easier to install, maintain, and clean than smaller tiles.

How to Set Wall Tile

Design the layout and mark the reference lines. Begin installation with the second row of tiles above the floor. If the layout requires cut tiles for this row, mark and cut the tiles for the entire row at one time.

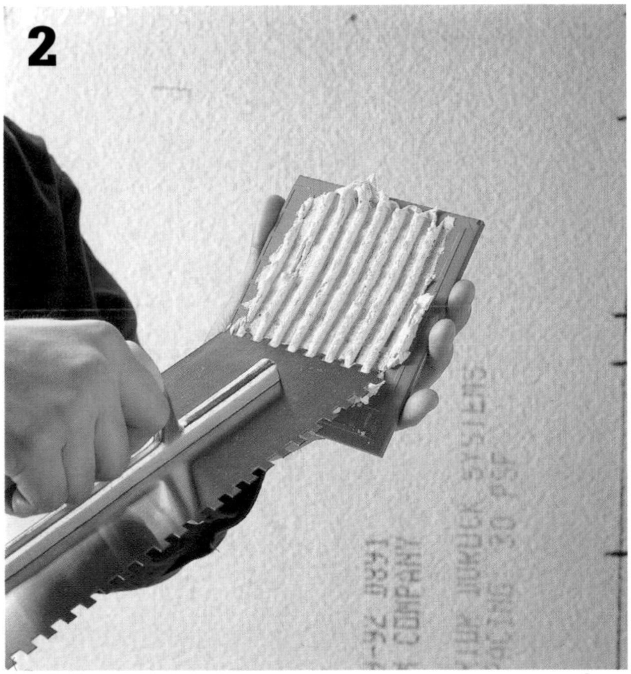

Mix a small batch of thinset mortar containing a latex additive. (Some mortar has additive mixed in by the manufacturer and some must have additive mixed in separately.) Cover the back of the first tile with adhesive, using a ¼" notched trowel.

Variation: Spread adhesive on a small section of the wall, then set the tiles into the adhesive. Thinset adhesive sets fast, so work quickly if you choose this installation method.

Beginning near the center of the wall, apply the tile to the wall with a slight twisting motion, aligning it exactly with the horizontal and vertical reference lines. When placing cut tiles, position the cut edges where they will be least visible.

(continued)

Continue installing tiles, working from the center to the sides in a pyramid pattern. Keep the tiles aligned with the reference lines. If the tiles are not self-spacing, use plastic spacers inserted in the corner joints to maintain even grout lines. The base row should be the last row of full tiles installed. Cut tile as necessary.

As small sections of tile are completed, set the tile by laying a scrap of 2 × 4 wrapped with carpet onto the tile and rapping it lightly with a mallet. This embeds the tile solidly in the adhesive and creates a flat, even surface.

To mark tiles for straight cuts, begin by taping ⅛" spacers against the surfaces below and to the side of the tile. Position a tile directly over the last full tile installed, then place a third tile so the edge butts against the spacers. Trace the edge of the top tile onto the middle tile to mark it for cutting.

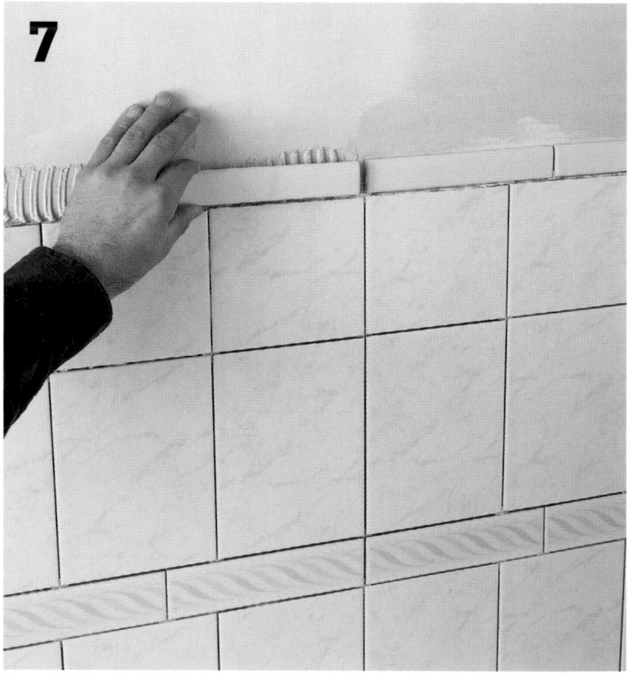

Install any trim tiles, such as the bullnose edge tiles shown above, at border areas. Wipe away excess mortar along the top edges of the edge tiles. Use bullnose and corner bullnose tiles (with two adjacent bullnose edges) at outside corners to cover the rough edges of the adjoining tiles.

Let mortar dry completely (12 to 24 hrs.), then mix a batch of grout containing latex additive. Apply the grout with a rubber grout float, using a sweeping motion to force it deep into the joints. Do not grout joints adjoining bathtubs, floors, or room corners. These will serve as expansion joints and will be caulked later.

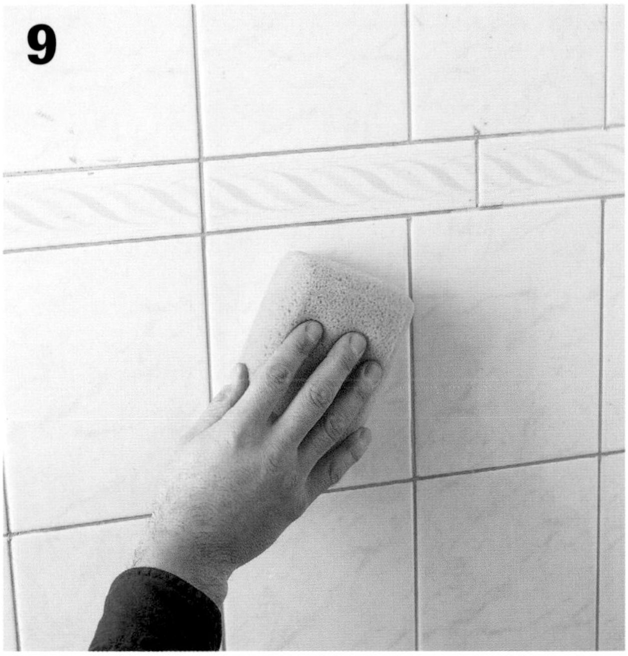

Wipe a damp grout sponge diagonally over the tile, rinsing the sponge in cool water between wipes. Wipe each area only once; repeated wiping can pull grout from the joints. Allow the grout to dry for about 4 hours, then use a soft cloth to buff the tile surface and remove any remaining grout film.

When the grout has cured completely, use a small foam brush to apply grout sealer to the joints, following the manufacturer's directions. Avoid brushing sealer on the tile surfaces, and wipe up excess sealer immediately.

Seal expansion joints at the floor and corners with silicone caulk. After the caulk dries, buff the tile with a soft, dry cloth.

How to Install Wall Tile in a Bathtub Alcove

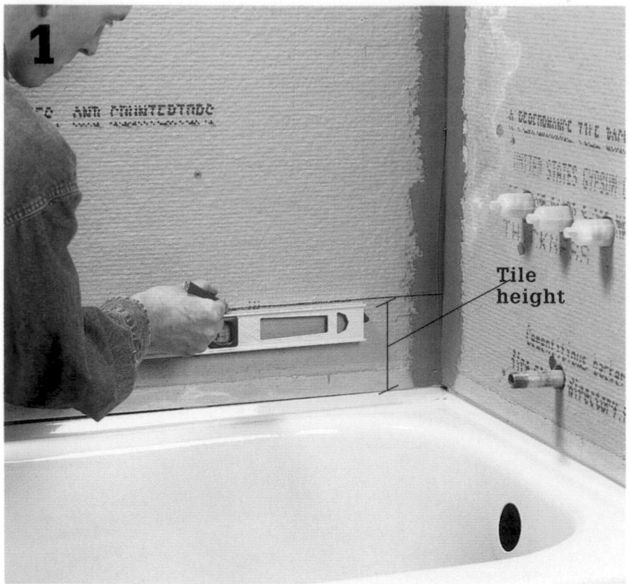

Beginning with the back wall, measure up and mark a point at a distance equal to the height of one ceramic tile (if the tub edge is not level, measure up from the lowest spot). Draw a level line through this point, along the entire back wall. This line represents a tile grout line and will be used as a reference line for making the entire tile layout.

Measure and mark the midpoint on the horizontal reference line. Using a story stick, mark along the reference line where the vertical grout joints will be located. If the story stick shows that the corner tiles will be less than half of a full tile width, move the midpoint half the width of a tile in either direction and mark (shown in next step).

Use a level to draw a vertical reference line through the adjusted midpoint from the tub edge to the ceiling. Measure up from the tub edge along the vertical reference line and mark the rough height of the top row of tiles.

Use the story stick to mark the horizontal grout joints along the vertical reference line, beginning at the mark for the top row of tiles. If the cut tiles at the tub edge will be less than half the height of a full tile, move the top row up half the height of a tile. *Note: If tiling to a ceiling, evenly divide the tiles to be cut at the ceiling and tub edge, as for the corner tiles.*

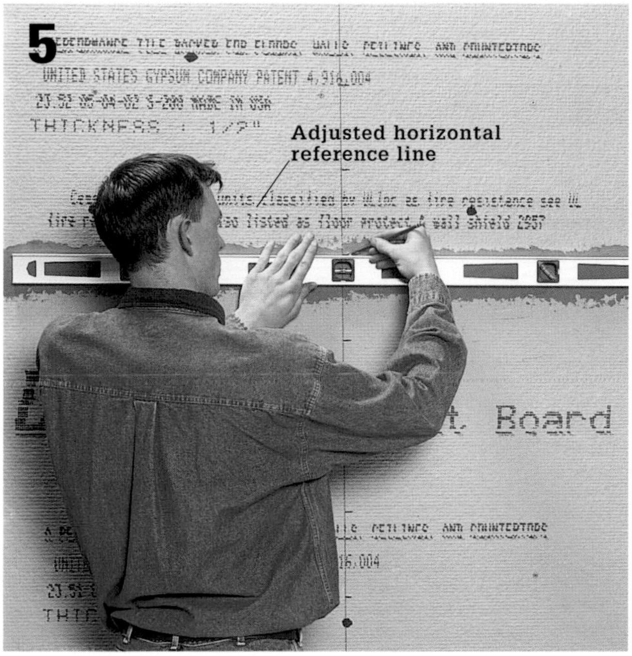

Use a level to draw an adjusted horizontal reference line through the vertical reference line at a grout joint mark close to the center of the layout. This splits the tile area into four workable quadrants.

Use a level to transfer the adjusted horizontal reference line from the back wall to both side walls, then follow Step 3 through Step 6 to lay out both side walls. Adjust the layout as needed so the final column of tiles ends at the outside edge of the tub. Use only the adjusted horizontal and vertical reference lines for ceramic tile installation.

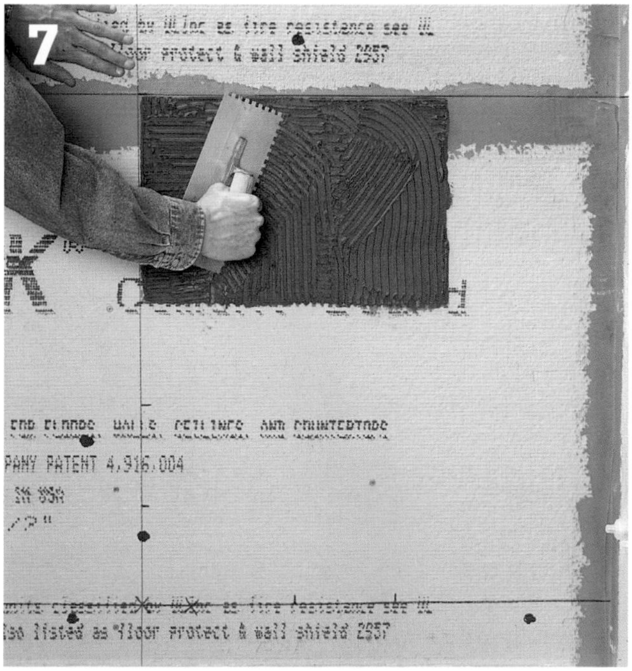

Mix a small batch of thinset mortar containing a latex additive. (Some mortar has additive mixed in by the manufacturer and some must have additive mixed separately.) Spread adhesive on a small section of the wall, along both legs of one quadrant, using a ¼" notched trowel.

Use the edge of the trowel to create furrows in the mortar. Set the first tile in the corner of the quadrant where the lines intersect, using a slight twisting motion. Align the tile exactly with both reference lines. When placing cut tiles, position the cut edges where they will be least visible.

(continued)

Continue installing tiles, working from the center out into the field of the quadrant. Keep the tiles aligned with the reference lines and tile in one quadrant at a time. If the tiles are not self-spacing, use plastic spacers inserted in the corner joints to maintain even grout lines (inset). The base row against the tub edge should be the last row of tiles installed.

Install trim tiles, such as the bullnose tiles shown above, at border areas. Wipe away excess mortar along the top edges of the edge tiles.

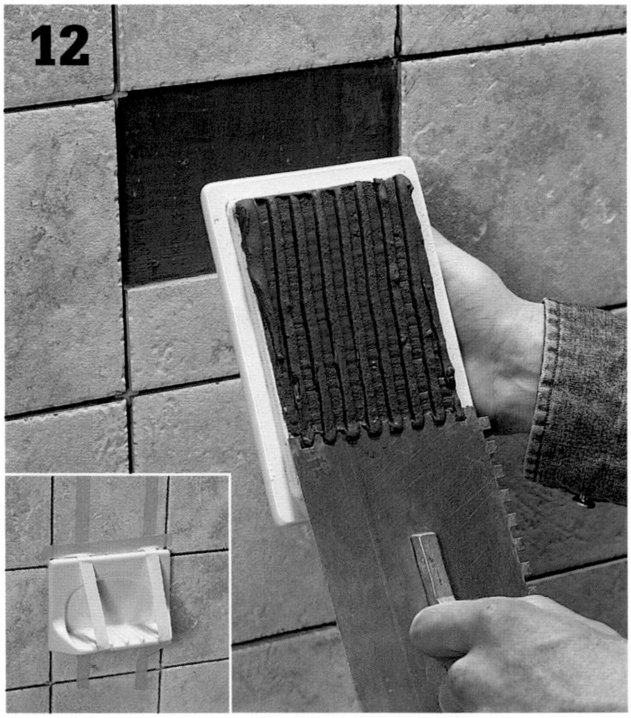

Mark and cut tiles to fit around all plumbing accessories or plumbing fixtures.

Install any ceramic accessories by applying thinset mortar to the back side, then pressing the accessory into place. Use masking tape to support the weight until the mortar dries (inset). Fill the tub with water, then seal expansion joints around the bathtub, floor, and corners with silicone caulk.

Tiling Bathroom Walls

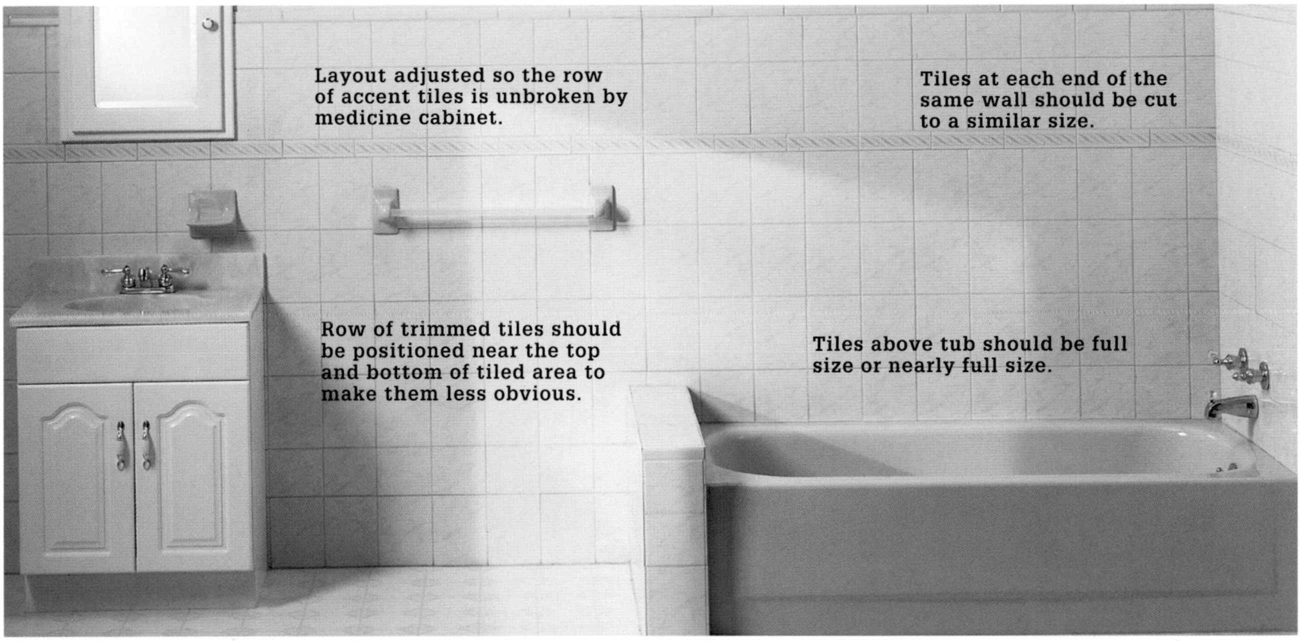

Tiling an entire bathroom requires careful planning. The bathroom shown here was designed so that the tiles directly above the bathtub (the most visible surface) are nearly full height. To accomplish this, cut tiles were used in the second row up from the floor. The short second row also allows the row of accent tiles to run uninterrupted below the medicine cabinet. Cut tiles in both corners should be of similar width to maintain a symmetrical look in the room.

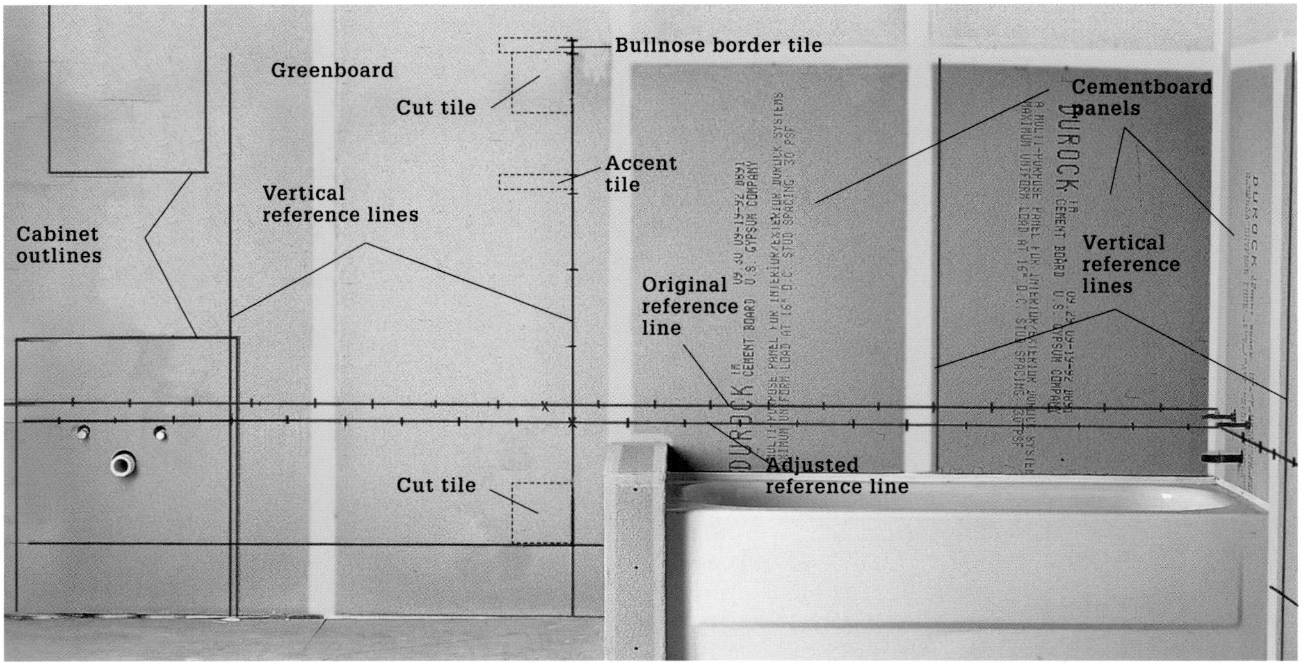

The key to a successful wall-tile project is the layout. Mark the wall to show the planned location of all wall cabinets, fixtures, and wall accessories, then locate the most visible horizontal line in the bathroom, which is usually the top edge of the bathtub. Use a story stick to see how the tile pattern will run in relation to the other features in the room. After establishing the working reference lines, mark additional vertical reference lines on the walls every 5 to 6 tile spaces along the adjusted horizontal reference line to split large walls into smaller, workable quadrants, then install the tile. *Note: Premixed, latex mastic adhesives are generally acceptable for wall tile in dry areas.*

Wall tile can be spruced up, even modernized, simply by removing and replacing just a section of it with a decorative accent that suits your style.

Embellished Wall Tile

Many of us live with tile we don't particularly like. It's easy to see why: builders and remodelers often install simple, neutral tile in an effort not to put anyone off. Older homes sometimes have tile that's not quite vintage but certainly no longer stylish. Or, a previous owner might just have had different tastes. Because tile is so long-lasting, new styles and trends often overtake it and make it look dated. Here's a bit of good news: there's a choice beyond simply living with it or tearing out perfectly good tile to start over.

Removing a section of boring tile and replacing it with some decorative accent tile can transform a plain wall into one that makes a unique design statement. And while a project like this requires a bit of demolition, it can be done with very little mess and fuss. Because it involves breaking the seal of the wall surface, it's a better choice for a tiled wall that gets little exposure to water (as opposed to a shower wall or tub deck).

The new tile you install will need to be grouted, and the new grout undoubtedly will be a different color. The only way to blend the new tile into the old is to regrout the entire area. If the project involves only one wall and the same grout color is still available, it is necessary to remove the grout surrounding the tile on the project wall. If you are tiling two or more walls, regrout the whole room.

This project is easier if you don't have to cut any existing tile. It's not especially difficult if you do, but it's always best to know what you're getting into before committing to a project.

Tools & Materials ▸

- Tape measure
- Grout saw
- Grout scraper
- Flat head screwdriver
- Straightedge
- Utility knife
- Drill
- ¼" notched trowel
- Grout float
- Grout sponge
- Buff rag
- Foam brush
- Needlenose pliers
- Drop cloth
- Grease pencil
- Masking tape
- Safety glasses
- Drywall screws
- Cementboard
- Construction adhesive
- Drywall screws
- Thinset mortar
- Mosaic medallion or decorative tile
- Tile spacers
- Grout
- Latex additive
- Grout sealer
- Dust mask

How to Embellish a Tiled Wall

Measure the decorative tiles and draw a detailed plan for your project. Indicate a removal area at least one tile larger than the space required. If it will be necessary to cut tile, create a plan that will result in symmetrical tiles.

Protect the floor with a drop cloth. So you can patch the tile backer, you'll need to remove a section of tile that's a minimum of one tile all around the project installation area. Using a grease pencil, mark the tiles to be removed, according to the plan drawing. Put masking tape on the edges of the bordering tiles that will remain to keep them from being scratched or otherwise damaged by the grout saw. If you will be reinstalling some of the old tiles, protect them as well.

(continued)

Wearing eye protection and a dust mask, use a grout saw to cut grooves in all of the grout lines in the removal area. If the grout lines are soft this will only take one or two passes. If the grout's hard, it may take several. Using a grout scraper, remove any remaining material in the joint. Angle the tools toward the open area to protect the tile.

With a flathead screwdriver, pry up the edges of the tile at the center of the removal area. Wiggle the blade toward the center of the tile and pry up to pop it off.

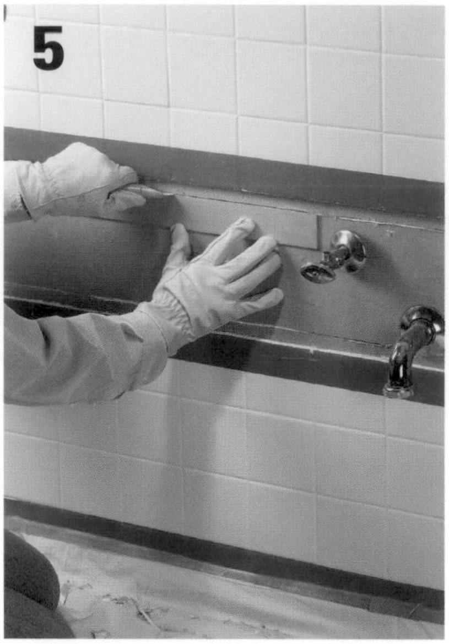

Draw cutting lines on the drywall that are at least ½" inside the borders of the area where you removed tiles. Using a straightedge and utility knife, carefully cut out the old drywall. If the tile comes off very easily and the tile backer is not damaged, you may be able to scrape it clean and reuse it.

Cut cementboard strips that are slightly longer than the width of the opening. Insert the strips into the opening and orient them so the ends are pressed against the back surface of the tile backer. Drive wallboard screws through the edges of the old tile backer and into the strips to hold them in place.

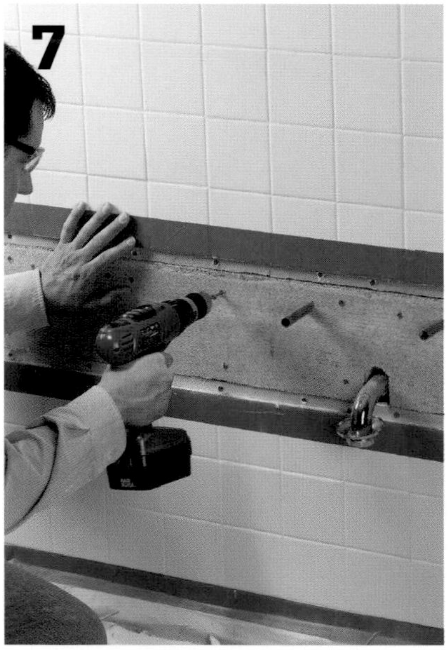

Cut a cementboard patch to fit the opening in the tile backer. Place the patch in the opening and drive drywall screws through the cementboard and into the backer strips. Also drive screws at any stud locations.

Cover the edges with wallboard tape. Mix a small batch of thinset mortar. Apply the mortar, using a notched trowel to spread it evenly.

Gently press the accent tiles into the adhesive, smoothing it from the center toward the edges. Let the mortar cure as directed.

Use a damp sponge to soak the protective sheet on the tile. Once wet, slide the sheet off and throw it away.

Mix a batch of grout and fill the joints between tile on the entire wall, one section at a time. (Inset) Clean the tile with a damp sponge. Occasionally rinse the sponge in cool water.

Design Suggestions ▸

Inserts add interest, texture, and color to tile designs. This piece combines tumbled stone with marble in a delicate floral motif.

This stone insert adds a contemporary flair to a simple tile design.

Tiled Tub Apron

Your dream bathroom is dressed to the nines, but that alcove bathtub is as plain as can be. You probably appreciated that prefab apron when you were installing the tub, but now it's time to beautify it. One way to improve the appearance of a plain apron and create the look of a built-in tub is simply to build and tile a short wall in front of the tub. All it takes is a little simple framing and a few square feet of tile.

The basic strategy is to construct a 2 × 4 stub wall in front of the tub apron, and then tile the top and front of the wall. One design option is to try and match existing tile, but it's unlikely you'll be able to find the exact tile unless it's relatively new. Choosing complementary or contrasting tile is usually a better bet. Ask your tile retailer to direct you to families of tile with multiple shapes and accessories.

Be sure to include a waterproof backer (cementboard is recommended) and get a good grout seal, since the stub wall will be in a wet area.

Tools & Materials ▸

Stud finder
Tape measure
Circular saw
Drill
Hammer
Level
Tile cutting tools
Utility knife
Grout float
Grout sponge
Buff rag
Foam brush
2 × 4 lumber
Construction adhesive
2½" screws
Cementboard
Drywall screws
Tile
Thinset mortar
Scrap of carpet
Carbide paper or wet stone
Wide painter's tape
Grout
Silicone caulk
Grout sealer
Permanent marker
Notched trowel
Rubbing alcohol

An old, boring bathtub can be spruced up to match a newly remodeled dream bathroom by building and tiling a stub wall to dress up the tub apron.

How to Build a Tiled Tub Wall

Measure the distance of the tub rim from the floor, as well as the distance from one wall to the other at the ends of the tub. Allowing for the thickness of the tiles, create a layout and draw a detailed plan of your project, spacing the studs 16" apart on center.

Cut the 2 × 4s to length for the base plate and top plate (58½" long as shown). Cut the studs (five 11" pieces as shown). Set the base plate on edge and lay out the studs, spacing them 16" on center. Make sure the first and last studs are perfectly parallel with the end of the base plate, then drive two 2½" screws through the base plate and each stud.

Draw a placement line on the floor using a permanent marker. Spread a generous bead of construction adhesive on the bottom of the base plate. Align the base plate with the placement line and set it into position. Put concrete blocks or other weights between the studs to anchor the base plate to the flooring and let the adhesive cure according to manufacturer's instructions.

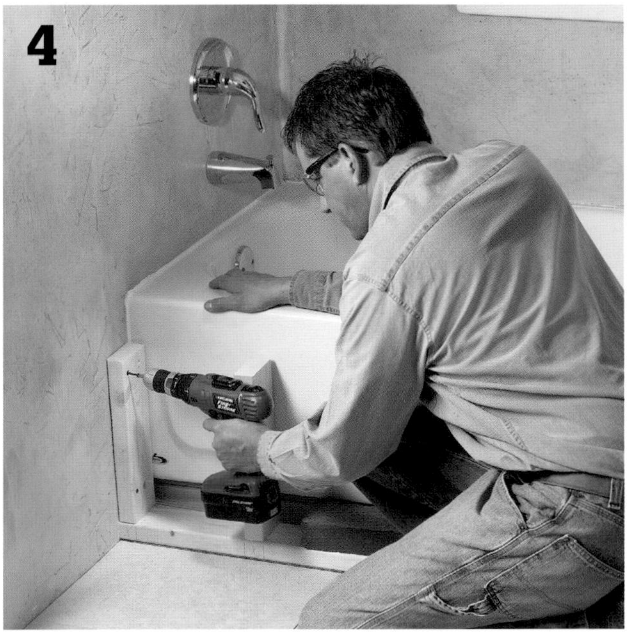

Drive two or three 2½" screws through the studs and into the room walls at each end of the stub wall. If the stub wall does not happen to line up with any wall studs, drive at least two 3" deck screws toenail-style through the stub wall and into the room wall sole plate.

(continued)

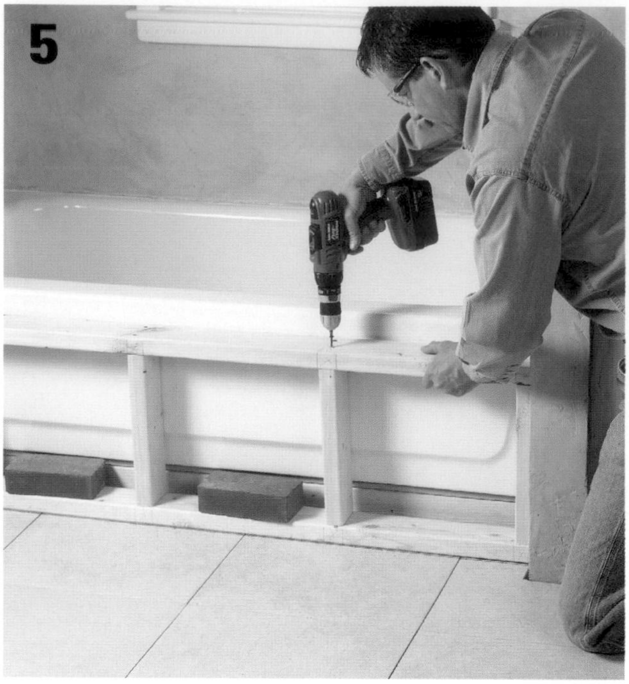

Set the top plate on the stud wall and attach it using two 2½" screws for each stud. Offset the screws slightly to increase the strength of the assembly. The top of the stud wall should be 2½" below the top of the tub.

Cut cementboard to fit the front (14½" as shown). With the factory-finished edge of the cementboard at the top of the wall, attach the cementboard to the studs using drywall screws.

Cut cementboard to fit the top of the stub wall (3½"). With the factory-finished edge facing the tub edge, attach the cement board to the top plate using drywall screws.

Design the layout and mark reference lines on the wall. Draw horizontal and vertical reference lines for the corner tile (used to transition from vertical to horizontal at the top stub wall edge) and the coved base tile (if your project includes them, as ours does). Lay out tile along the floor, including spacers.

Start tiling at the bottom of the wall. Lay out the bottom row of tile on the floor, using spacers if necessary. Adjust the layout to make end tiles balanced in size. Mark and cut the tiles as necessary, and then smooth any sharp edges with carbide paper or a wet stone. Mix a small batch of thinset mortar and install the base tiles by buttering the backs with mortar.

Beginning at the center intersection of the vertical field area, apply mortar using a notched trowel to spread it evenly. Cover as much area as required for a few field tiles. Install the field tiles, keeping the grout lines in alignment.

Finish installing the field tiles up to the horizontal line marking the accent tile location.

Apply thinset mortar to the backs of the accent tiles and install them in a straight line. The grout lines will likely not align with the field tile grout lines.

(continued)

Install corner tiles to create a rounded transition at the top edge of the wall. Install these before you install the filed tiles in the top row of the wall face or on the top of the stub wall (corner tiles are virtually impossible to cut if your measurements are off). Dry-lay the top row of tiles. Mark and cut tile if necessary.

Fill in the top course of field tile on the wall face between the accent tiles and the corner tiles. If you have planned well you won't need to trim the field tiles to fit. (If you need to cut tiles to create the correct wall height, choose the tiles in the first row of field tiles.)

Remove the dry-lay row of tile along the top of the wall. Shield the edge of the tub with painter's tape, then spread thinset adhesive on the wall and begin to lay tile. Keep the joints of the field tiles on the top aligned with the grout joints of the field tile on the face of the wall.

Mix a batch of grout and use a grout float to force it into the joints between the tiles. Keep the space between the top field tiles and the tub clear of grout to create space for a bead of silicone caulk between the tub and tile.

Remove excess grout and clean the tile using a damp sponge. Rinse the sponge often.

After 24 hours, clean the area with rubbing alcohol where the tile and tub meet, then put tape on the edge of the tub and the face of the tile. Apply clear silicone caulk into the gap, overfilling it slightly.

Smooth the caulk with a moistened plastic straw or a moistened fingertip to create an even finish. Make sure this spot is well sealed as it is a prime spot for water to penetrate into the tub wall.

When the grout has cured completely (consult manufacturer's directions), apply grout sealer to the joints.

Toilet Enclosure

One of the best ways to make a busy family bathroom more usable is to enclose the toilet in a room of its own. Toilet enclosures—originally called "water closets" after the cistern they enclosed—make a privacy compartment within the bathroom. This allows one person to shower while the other uses the toilet. It also effectively hides the fixture that most people think is the sore thumb of the bathroom.

Although toilet enclosures are basic structures comprised of framed walls and a pre-hung door, they must be built to maintain adequate spacing around the toilet for maximum comfort and to meet local codes. As a general rule of thumb, you want to leave at least 15" from the center of the toilet bowl to the wall surface on either side, and at least 21" from the front of the bowl to the door. You may also want to add baffles or soundproofing inside the walls, to make the space as private as possible.

The enclosure shown here includes a combination lighting/ventilation fixture. Both are absolute musts for appropriate hygiene and comfort, even if they are not mandated by local codes. (A window can serve the ventilation function, but you'll still need to install lighting for nighttime use.)

When it comes to toilet enclosures, more room is always better. If you can dedicate extra space to the enclosure, you'll not only make the space more comfortable, you'll be able to add nice finishing touches such as a magazine rack or shelves for candles.

Tools & Materials ▸

Prehung door unit	Circular saw
Hammer	Drill
16d nails	Drywall
Screwdriver	Handsaw
2 × 4 lumber	Utility knife
Drywall tape	Wall compound
Prehung door	Interior door lockset
Wood shims	Door trim
Quarter-round molding	Silicone caulk
Stud finder	Fiberglass insulation

A full enclosure with a door offers the maximum in privacy, but it may be a more extreme solution than you require. A simple partition wall next to the toilet creates a sense of privacy without any claustrophobia.

How to Build a Toilet Enclosure

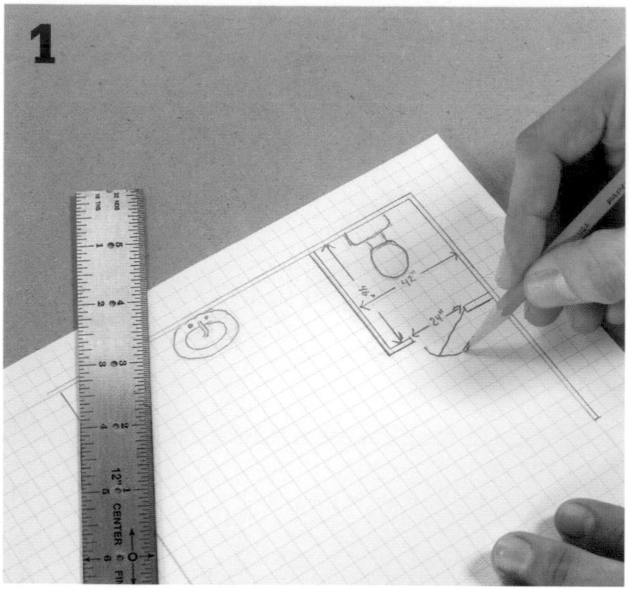

Carefully plan out the enclosure. Sketch your plans with exact dimensions to ensure that you allow proper space between toilet and walls, and to ensure door swing won't impede the shower, vanity drawers, or other fixtures.

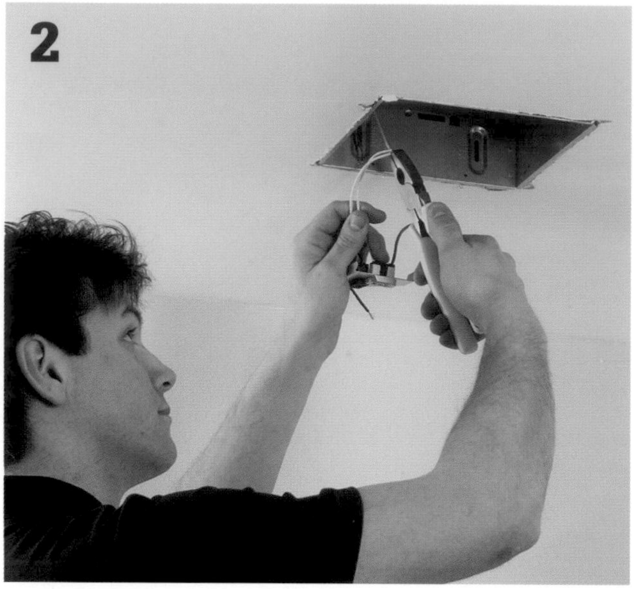

Run wiring and ducting for lighting and ventilation as necessary. Install box for overhead fixture and run wire for switch. We installed a combination light/vent fan (see page 200) connected to an interior wall switch placed just on the latch-side of the enclosure wall. The fixture can be run off the light switch circuit for the entire bathroom if that circuit has the capacity.

Check existing connection walls for plumb and square. Cut the sole and top plates accordingly, compensating as needed for any variances. Place top and sole plates side by side and mark stud locations, 16" on center.

Secure sole plates to floor. Plates installed over resilient flooring as shown here, can be nailed through to subfloor. When installing over a tile floor, use a masonry bit to drill pilot holes and then screw through to subfloor. (Over mosaic floors, it's best to remove the tiles from under sole plate and secure the plate directly to subfloor.)

Use a stud finder to locate ceiling joists, and then nail the top plates into place. Frame out the walls by toe-nailing studs between top and sole plates as marked. Frame L-corner for walls, as shown (inset).

Frame the doorway with header, cripple studs, and jack studs (you should purchase your prehung door first, so that you can double-check the opening measurements against the actual door unit).

Hang drywall on the framed walls, inside and out. The enclosure here was clad with standard drywall rather than greenboard, because the walls won't be subjected to any direct moisture contact. If the enclosure abuts a shower or bath, use greenboard or cementboard.

(continued)

Position the prehung door in place. Check that it is oriented correctly, to open out from the enclosure and against a wall, rather than blocking the central space or opening against the vanity.

Shim all around the jamb (specifically, behind hinges and lockset location) until the door unit is plumb and square in the opening, and the door opens smoothly. Nail through the door jambs into the framing at the shim points.

Saw the shims off flush. Measure, cut and nail the trim for the door in place. Putty and sand over the nail heads on jambs and casework.

Use the Wall Cavity ▸

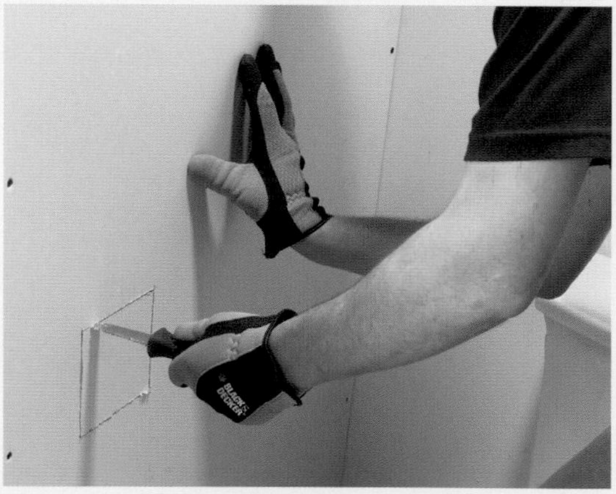

Because the partition wall you've built is essentially empty, it is a good candidate for installing niche fittings that are recessed into the wall. A recessed toilet tissue holder is one easy to install fitting. Space will be fairly tight in your enclosure, so using the wall space makes a lot of sense. A wall niche magazine rack or niches shelving are just two additional ways you may use the wall cavity space.

Finish the drywall surfaces with tape and joint compound. Work as neatly as you can to minimize sanding. Seal the new drywall with drywall primer before you paint.

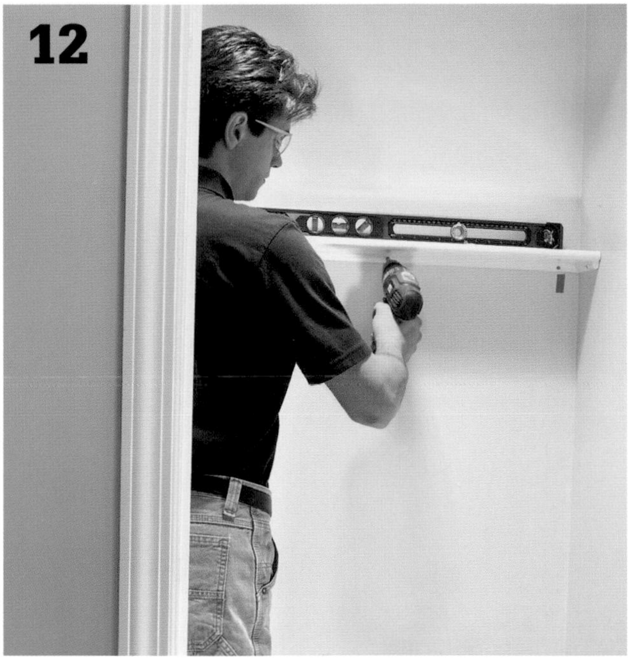

Paint the enclosure walls and add any additional elements, including paper holders, grab bars, and shelves or cabinets. The wall area behind the toilet tank is a good spot for installing shallow shelving, but keep it at least 3 ft. above the tank lid.

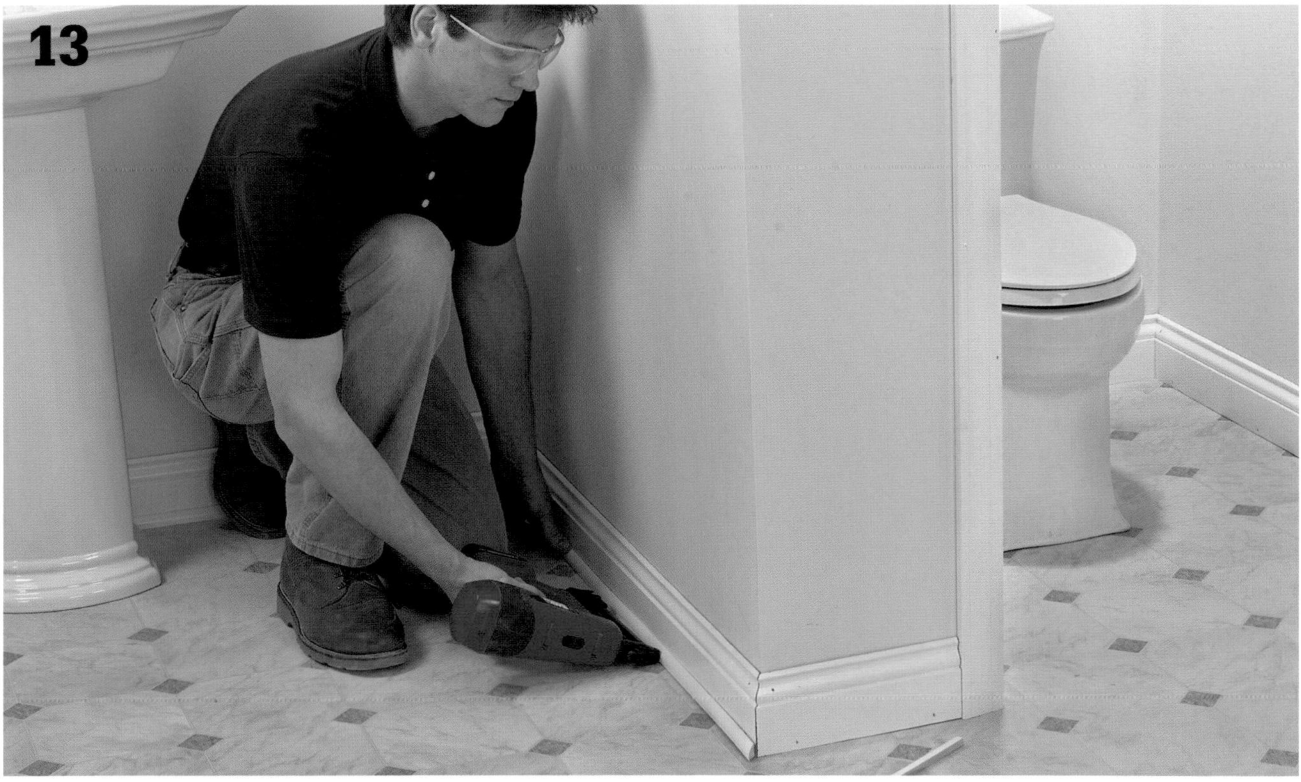

Attach base quarter-round molding on bottom of walls, inside and out (or cove molding if you prefer). Apply a coat of silicone caulk to the bottom of molding before nailing it in place.

Radiant Heat Floor

Floor-warming systems require very little energy to run and are designed to heat ceramic tile floors only; they generally are not used as sole heat sources for rooms.

A typical floor-warming system consists of one or more thin mats containing electric resistance wires that heat up when energized like an electric blanket. The mats are installed beneath the tile and are hardwired to a 120-volt GFCI circuit. A thermostat controls the temperature, and a timer turns the system off automatically.

The system shown in this project includes two plastic mesh mats, each with its own power lead that is wired directly to the thermostat. Radiant mats may be installed over a plywood subfloor, but if you plan to install floor tile you should put down a base of cementboard first, and then install the mats on top of the cementboard.

A crucial part of installing this system is to use a multimeter to perform several resistance checks to make sure the heating wires have not been damaged during shipping or installation.

Tools & Materials ▸

- Vacuum cleaner
- Multimeter
- Tape measure
- Scissors
- Router/rotary tool
- Marker
- Electric wire fault indicator (optional)
- Hot glue gun
- Radiant floor mats
- 12/2 NM cable
- Trowel or rubber float
- Conduit
- Thinset mortar
- Thermostat with sensor
- Junction box(es)
- Tile or stone floorcovering
- Drill
- Double-sided carpet tape
- Cable clamps

Electrical service required for a floor-warming system is based on size. A smaller system may connect to an existing GFCI circuit, but a larger one will need a dedicated circuit; follow the manufacturer's requirements.

To order a floor-warming system, contact the manufacturer or dealer (see Resources, page 283). In most cases, you can send them plans and they'll custom-fit a system for your project area.

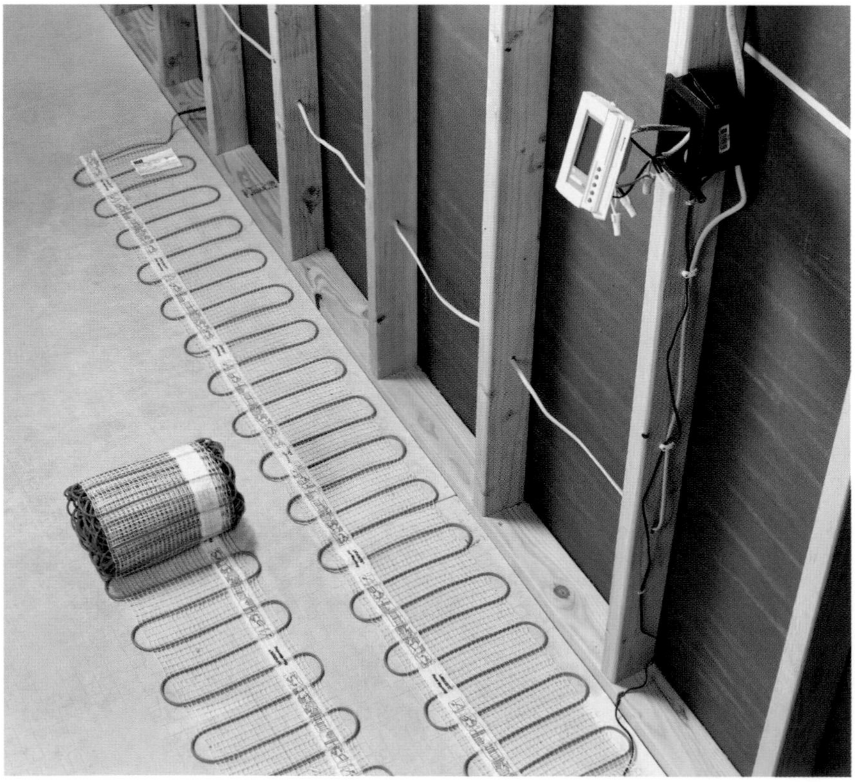

A radiant floor-warming system employs electric heating mats that are covered with floor tile to create a floor that's cozy underfoot.

Installation Tips ▸

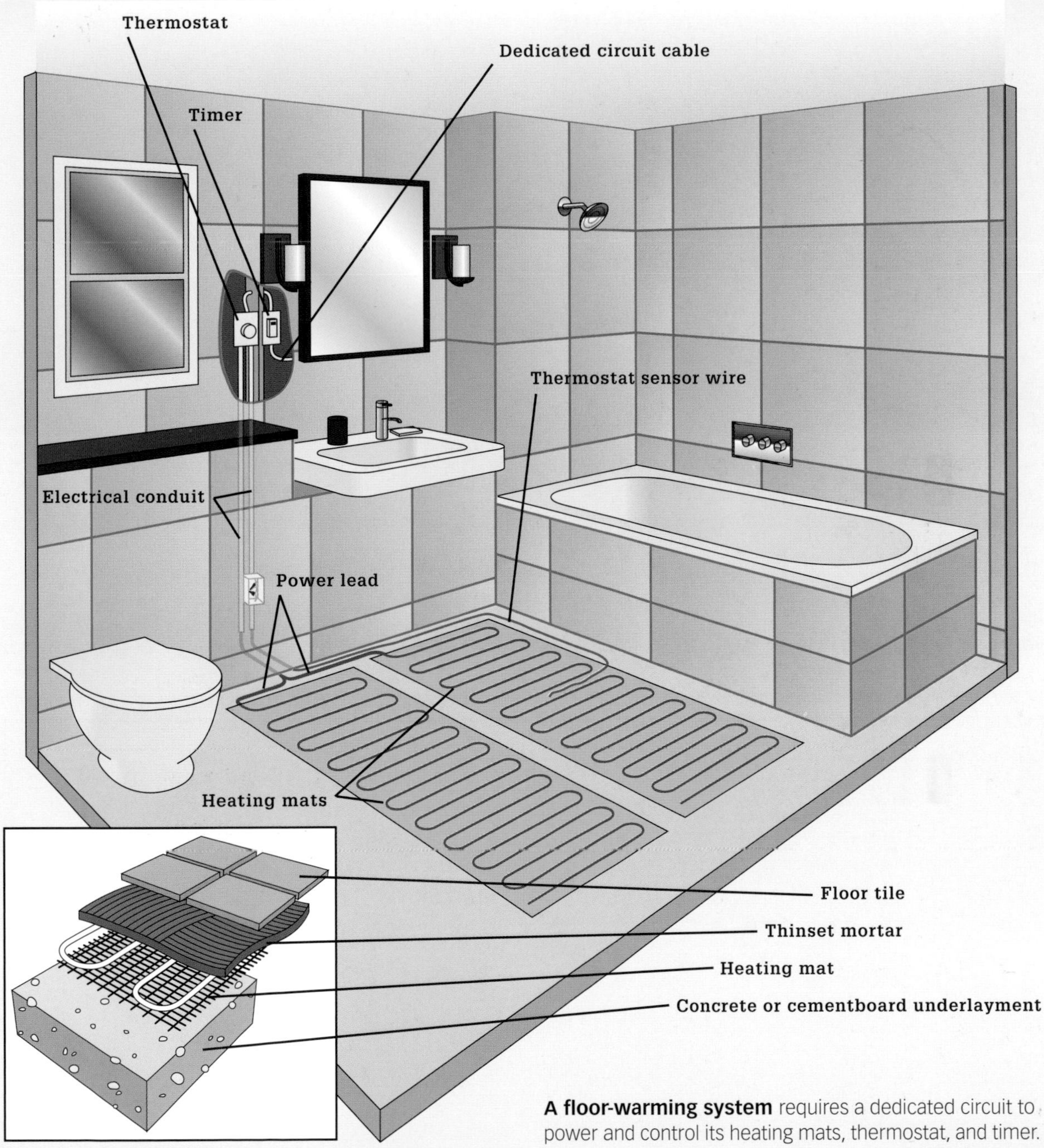

A floor-warming system requires a dedicated circuit to power and control its heating mats, thermostat, and timer.

- Each radiant mat must have a direct connection to the power lead from the thermostat, with the connection made in a junction box in the wall cavity. Do not install mats in series.
- Do not install radiant floor mats under shower areas.
- Do not overlap mats or let them touch.
- Do not cut heating wire or damage heating wire insulation.
- The distance between wires in adjoining mats should equal the distance between wire loops measured center to center.

Installing a Radiant Floor-Warming System

Floor-warming systems must be installed on a circuit with adequate amperage and a GFCI breaker. Smaller systems may tie into an existing circuit, but larger ones need a dedicated circuit. Follow local building and electrical codes that apply to your project.

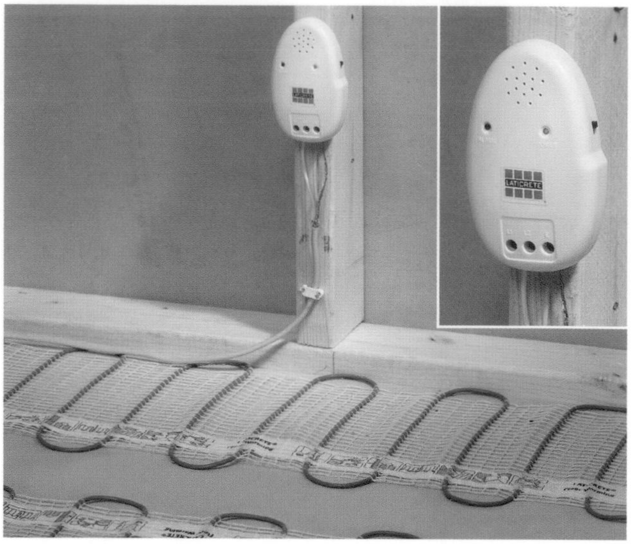

An electric wire fault indicator monitors each floor mat for continuity during the installation process. If there is a break in continuity (for example, if a wire is cut) an alarm sounds. If you choose not to use an installation tool to monitor the mat, test for continuity frequently using a multimeter.

How To Install a Radiant Floor-Warming System

Install electrical boxes to house the thermostat and timer. In most cases, the box should be located 60" above floor level. Use a 4"-deep × 4"-wide double-gang box for the thermostat/timer control if your kit has an integral model. If your timer and thermostat are separate, install a separate single box for the timer.

Drill access holes in the sole plate for the power leads that are preattached to the mats (they should be over 10 ft. long). The leads should be connected to a supply wire from the thermostat in a junction box located in a wall near the floor and below the thermostat box. The access hole for each mat should be located directly beneath the knockout for that cable in the thermostat box. Drill through the sill plate vertically and horizontally so the holes meet in an L-shape.

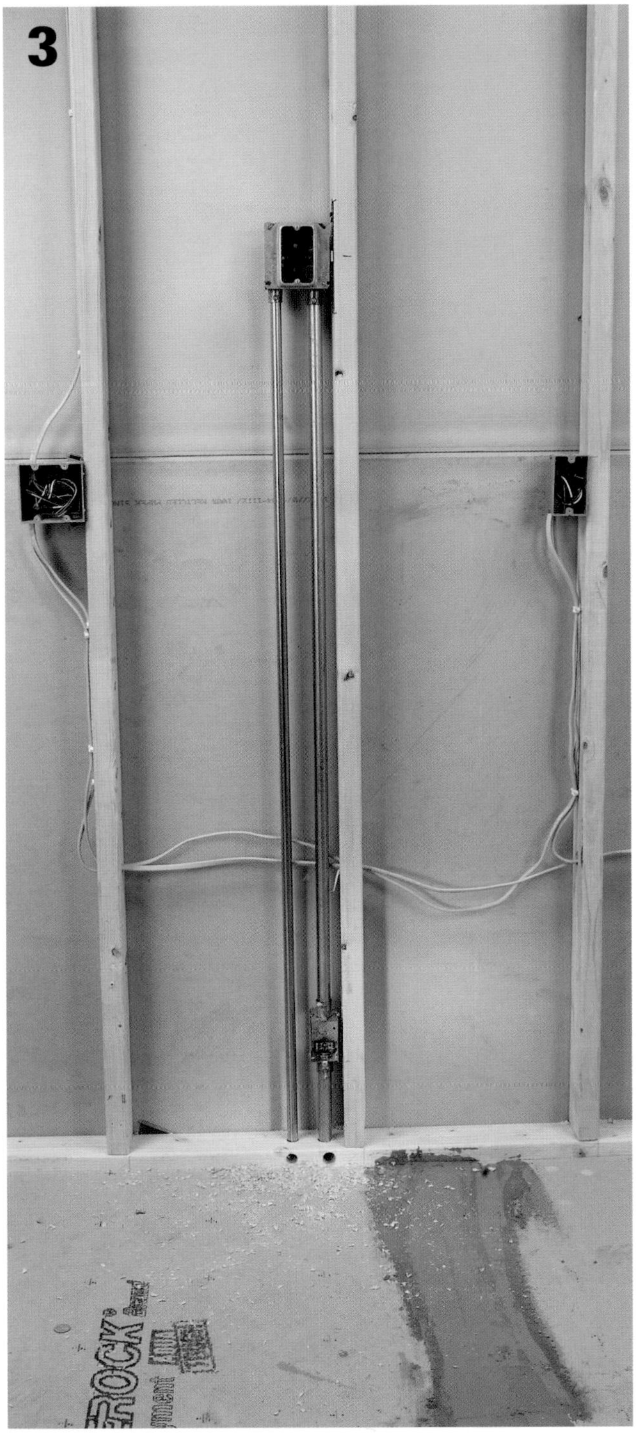

Run conduit from the electrical boxes to the sill plate. The line for the supply cable should be ¾" conduit. If you are installing multiple mats, the supply conduit should feed into a junction box about 6" above the sill plate and then continue into the ¾" hole you drilled for the supply leads. The sensor wire needs only ½" conduit that runs straight from the thermostat box via the thermostat. The mats should be powered by a dedicated 20-amp GFCI circuit of 12/2 NM cable run from your main service panel to the electrical box (this is for 120-volt mats—check your instruction manual for specific circuit recommendations).

Clean the floor surface thoroughly to get rid of any debris that could potentially damage the wire mats. A vacuum cleaner generally does a more effective job than a broom.

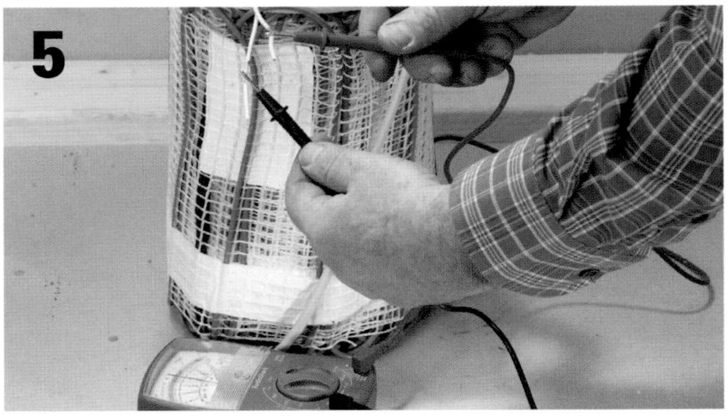

Test for resistance using a multimeter set to measure ohms. This is a test you should make frequently during the installation, along with checking for continuity. If the resistance is off by more than 10% from the theoretical resistance listing (see manufacturer's chart in installation instructions), contact a technical support operator for the kit manufacturer. For example, the theoretical resistance for the 1 × 50 ft. mat seen here is 19, so the ohms reading should be between 17 and 21.

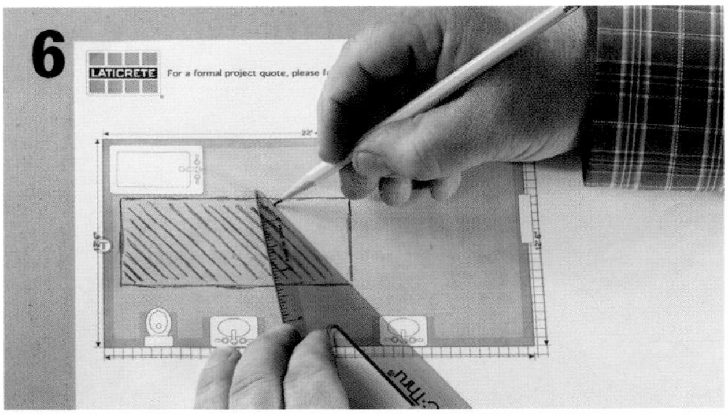

Finalize your mat layout plan. Most radiant floor warming mat manufacturers will provide a layout plan for you at the time of purchase, or they will give you access to an online design tool so you can come up with your own plan. This is an important step to the success of your project, and the assistance is free.

(continued)

Unroll the radiant mat or mats and allow them to settle. Arrange the mat or mats according to the plan you created. It's okay to cut the plastic mesh so you can make curves or switchbacks, but do not cut the heating wire under any circumstances, even to shorten it.

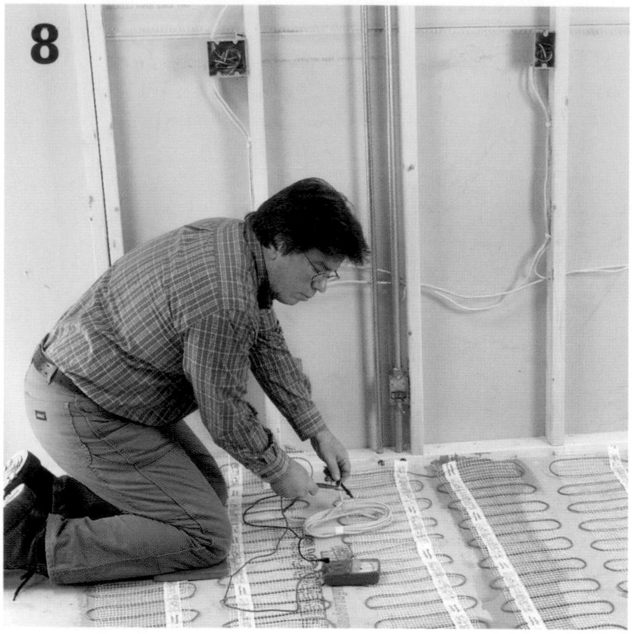

Finalize the mat layout and then test the resistance again using a multimeter. Also check for continuity in several different spots. If there is a problem with any of the mats, you should identify it and correct it before proceeding with the mortar installation.

Run the thermostat sensor wire from the electrical box down the ½" conduit raceway and out the access hole in the sill plate. Select the best location for the thermostat sensor and mark the location onto the flooring. Also mark the locations of the wires that connect to and lead from the sensor.

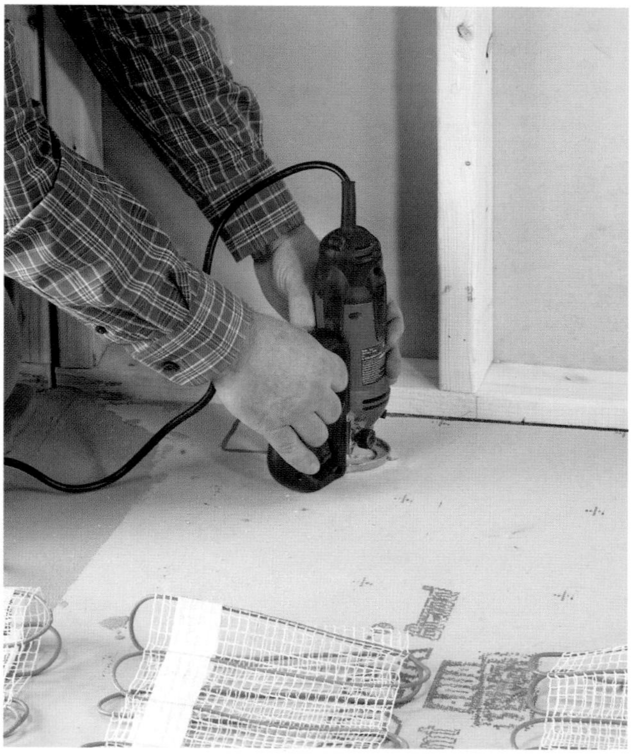

Variation: If your local codes require it, roll the mats out of the way and cut a channel for the sensor and the sensor wires into the floor or floor underlayment. For most floor materials, a spiral cutting tool does a quick and neat job of this task. Remove any debris.

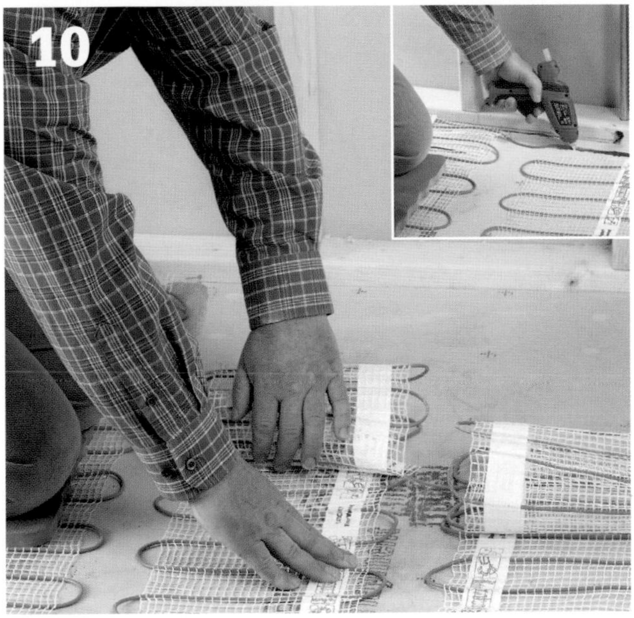

Bond the mats to the floor. If the mats in your system have adhesive strips, peel off the adhesive backing and roll out the mats in the correct position, pressing them against the floor to set the adhesive. If your mats have no adhesive, bind them with strips of double-sided carpet tape. The thermostat sensor and the power supply leads should be attached with hot glue (inset photo) and run up into their respective holes in the sill plate if you have not done this already. Test all mats for resistance and continuity.

Cover the floor installation areas with a layer of thinset mortar that is thick enough to fully encapsulate all the wires and mats (usually around ¼" in thickness). Check the wires for continuity and resistance regularly and stop working immediately if there is a drop in resistance or a failure of continuity. Allow the mortar to dry overnight.

Connect the power supply leads from the mat or mats to the NM cable coming from the thermostat inside the junction box near the sill. Power must be turned off. The power leads should be cut so about 8" of wire feeds into the box. Be sure to use cable clamps to protect the wires.

Connect the sensor wire and the power supply lead (from the junction box) to the thermostat/timer according to the manufacturer's directions. Attach the device to the electrical box, restore power, and test the system to make sure it works. Once you are convinced that it is operating properly, install floor tiles and repair the wall surfaces.

Ceramic Tile Floor

Ceramic tile installation starts with determining the best layout. You snap perpendicular reference lines and dry-fit tiles to ensure the best placement.

When setting tiles, work in small sections so the mortar doesn't dry before the tiles are set. Use spacers between tiles to ensure consistent spacing. Plan an installation sequence to avoid kneeling on set tiles. Be careful not to kneel or walk on tiles until the designated drying period is over.

Tools & Materials ▸

- ¼" square trowel
- Rubber mallet
- Tile cutter
- Tile nippers
- Hand-held tile cutter
- Needlenose pliers
- Grout float
- Grout sponge
- Soft cloth
- Small paint brush
- Thin-set mortar
- Tile
- Tile spacers
- Grout
- Latex grout additive
- Wall adhesive
- 2 × 4 lumber
- Grout sealer
- Tile caulk
- Sponge brush

Floor tile can be laid in many decorative patterns, but for your first effort stick to a basic grid. In most cases, floor tile is combined with profiled base tile (installed after flooring).

Make sure the subfloor is smooth, level, and stable. Spread thin-set mortar on the subfloor for one sheet of cementboard. Place the cementboard on the mortar, keeping a ¼" gap along the walls.

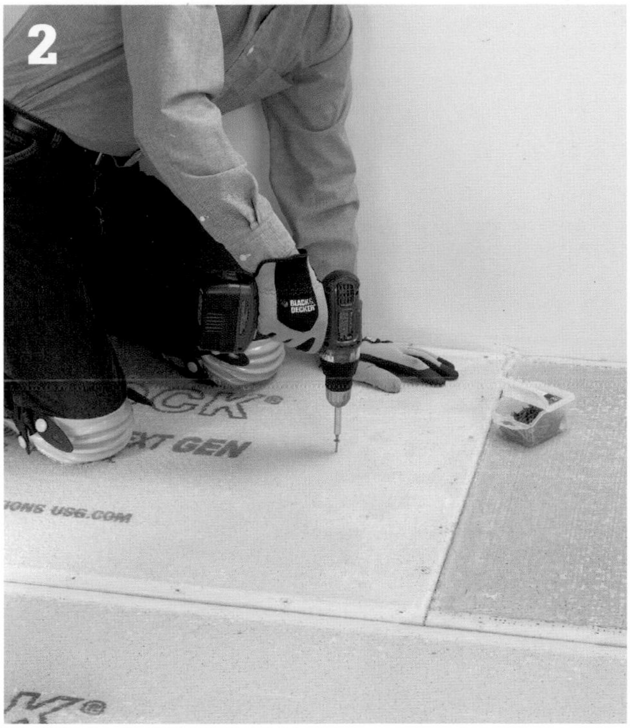

Fasten it in place with 1¼" cementboard screws. Place fiberglass-mesh wallboard tape over the seams. Cover the remainder of the floor.

Draw reference lines and establish the tile layout (see page 229). Mix a batch of thin-set mortar, then spread the mortar evenly against both reference lines of one quadrant, using a ¼" square-notched trowel. Use the notched edge of the trowel to create furrows in the mortar bed.

Set the first tile in the corner of the quadrant where the reference lines intersect. When setting tiles that are 8" square or larger, twist each tile slightly as you set it into position.

(continued)

Using a soft rubber mallet, gently tap the central area of each tile a few times to set it evenly into the mortar.

Variation: For large tiles or uneven stone, use a larger trowel with notches that are at least ½" deep.

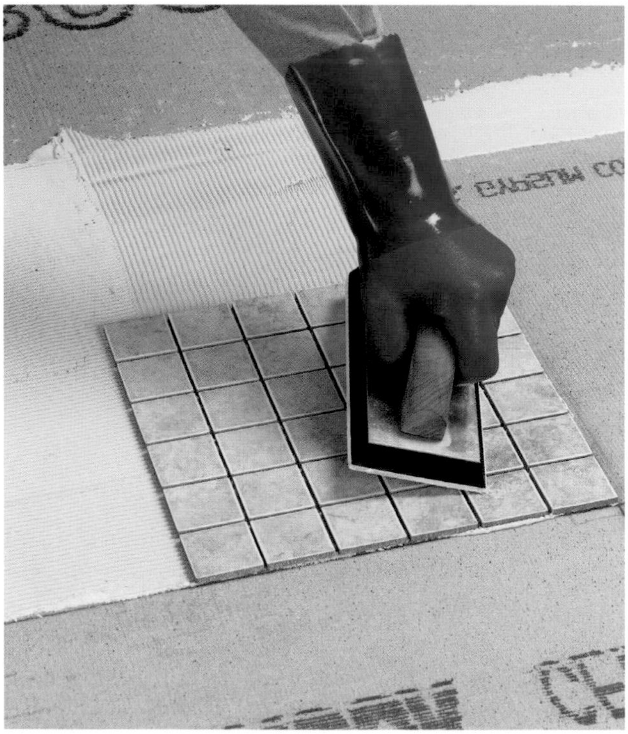

Variation: For mosaic sheets, use a $\frac{3}{16}$" V-notched trowel to spread the mortar and a grout float to press the sheets into the mortar. Apply pressure gently to avoid creating an uneven surface.

To ensure consistent spacing between tiles, place plastic tile spacers at the corners of the set tile. With mosaic sheets, use spacers equal to the gaps between tiles.

Position and set adjacent tiles into the mortar along the reference lines. Make sure the tiles fit neatly against the spacers.

To make sure the tiles are level with one another, place a straight piece of 2 × 4 across several tiles, then tap the board with a mallet.

Lay tile in the remaining area covered with mortar. Repeat steps 2 to 7, continuing to work in small sections, until you reach walls or fixtures.

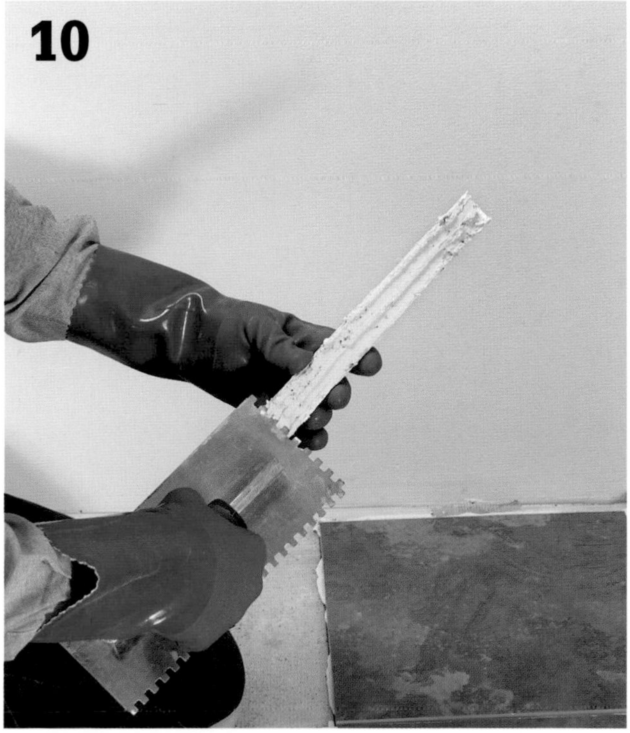

Measure and mark tiles to fit against walls and into corners. Cut the tiles to fit. Apply thin-set mortar directly to the back of the cut tiles, instead of the floor, using the notched edge of the trowel to furrow the mortar.

(continued)

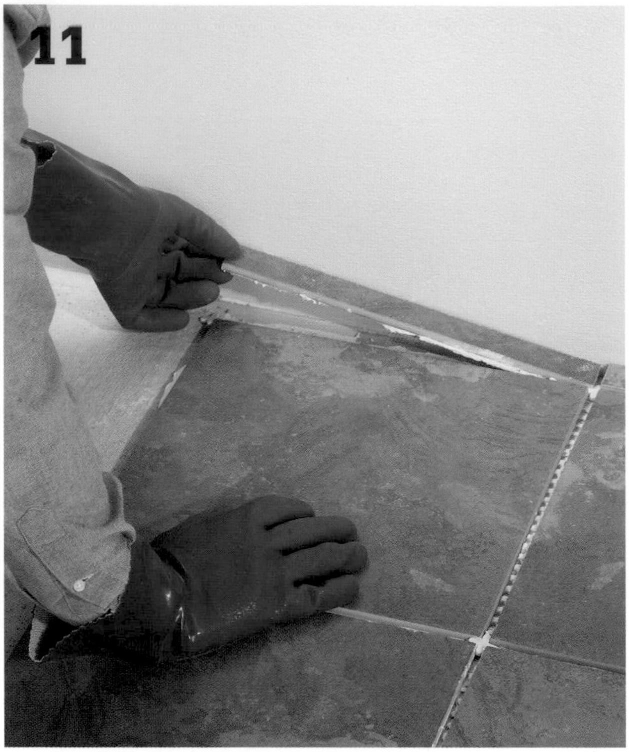

Set the cut pieces of tile into position. Press down on the tile until each piece is level with adjacent tiles.

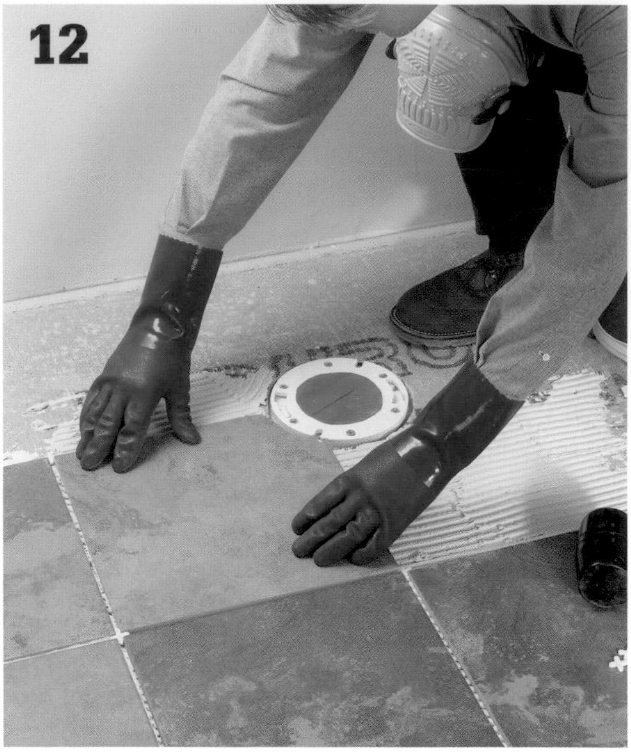

Measure, cut, and install tiles that require notches or curves to fit around obstacles, such as exposed pipes or toilet drains.

Carefully remove the spacers with needlenose pliers before the mortar hardens.

Apply mortar and set tiles in the remaining quadrants, completing one quadrant before starting the next. Inspect all of the tile joints and use a utility knife or grout knife to remove any high spots of mortar that could show through the grout.

Install threshold material in doorways. If the threshold is too long for the doorway, cut it to fit with a jigsaw or circular saw and a tungsten-carbide blade. Set the threshold in thin-set mortar so the top is even with the tile. Keep the same space between the threshold as between tiles. Let the mortar set for at least 24 hours.

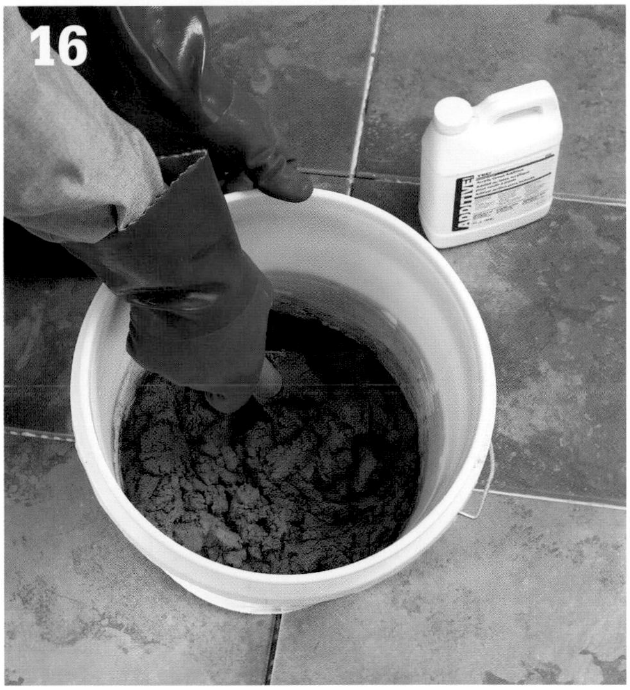

Prepare a small batch of floor grout to fill the tile joints. When mixing grout for porous tile, such as quarry or natural stone, use an additive with a release agent to prevent grout from bonding to the tile surfaces.

Starting in a corner, pour the grout over the tile. Use a rubber grout float to spread the grout outward from the corner, pressing firmly on the float to completely fill the joints. For best results, tilt the float at a 60° angle to the floor and use a figure eight motion.

Use the grout float to remove excess grout from the surface of the tile. Wipe diagonally across the joints, holding the float in a near-vertical position. Continue applying grout and wiping off excess until about 25 sq. ft. of the floor has been grouted.

(continued)

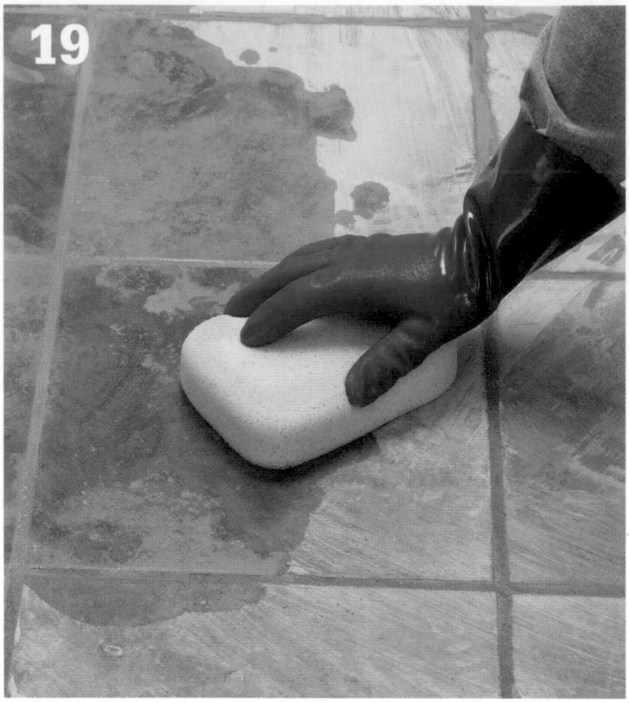

Wipe a damp grout sponge diagonally over about 2 sq. ft. of the floor at a time. Rinse the sponge in cool water between wipes. Wipe each area only once since repeated wiping can pull grout back out of joints. Repeat steps 15 to 18 to apply.

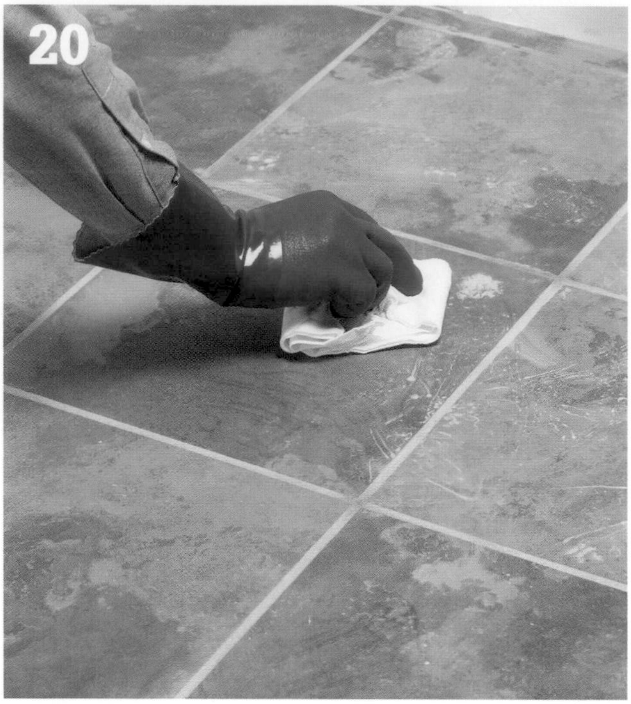

Allow the grout to dry for about 4 hours, then use a soft cloth to buff the tile surface and remove any remaining grout film.

Apply grout sealer to the grout lines, using a small sponge brush or sash brush. Avoid brushing sealer on tile surfaces. Wipe up any excess sealer immediately.

Variation: Use a tile sealer to seal porous tile, such as quarry tile or unglazed tile. Following the manufacturer's instructions, roll a thin coat of sealer over the tile and grout joints, using a paint roller and extension handle.

How to Install Bullnose Base Trim

Dry-fit the tiles to determine the best spacing. Grout lines in base tile do not always align with grout lines in the floor tile. Use rounded bullnose tiles at outside corners, and mark tiles for cutting as needed.

Leaving a ⅛" expansion gap between tiles at corners, mark any contour cuts necessary to allow the coved edges to fit together. Use a jigsaw with a tungsten-carbide blade to make curved cuts.

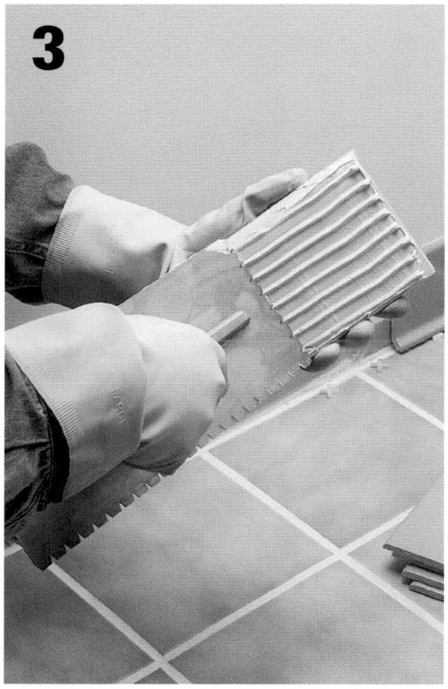

Begin installing base-trim tiles at an inside corner. Use a notched trowel to apply wall adhesive to the back of the tile. Place ⅛" spacers on the floor under each tile to create an expansion joint.

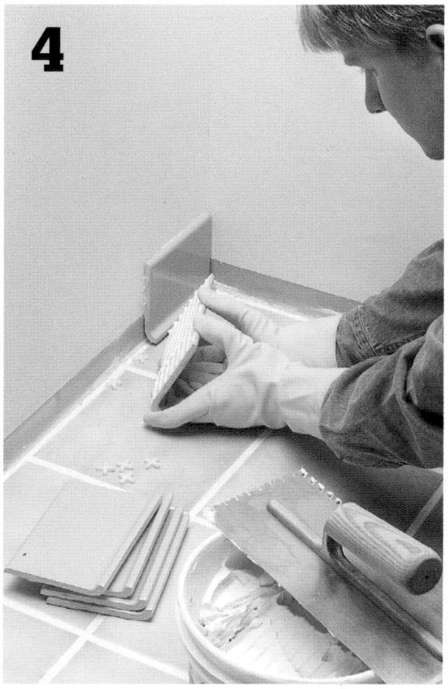

Press the tile onto the wall. Continue setting tiles, using spacers to maintain ⅛" gaps between the tiles and ⅛" expansion joints between the tiles and floor.

Use a double-bullnose tile on one side of outside corners to cover the edge of the adjoining tile.

After the adhesive dries, grout the vertical joints between tiles and apply grout along the tops of the tiles to make a continuous grout line. Once the grout hardens, fill the expansion joint between the tiles and floor with caulk.

Sheet Vinyl Flooring

Preparing a perfect underlayment is the most important phase of resilient sheet vinyl installation. Cutting the material to fit the contours of the room is a close second. The best way to ensure accurate cuts is to make a cutting template. Some manufacturers offer template kits, or you can make one by following the instructions on the opposite page. Be sure to use the recommended adhesive for the sheet vinyl you are installing. Many manufacturers require that you use their glue for installation. Use extreme care when handling the sheet vinyl, especially felt-backed products, to avoid creasing and tearing.

Tools & Materials ▸

- Linoleum knife
- Framing square
- Compass
- Scissors
- Non-permanent felt-tipped pen
- Utility knife
- Straightedge
- ¼" V-notched trowel
- J-roller
- Stapler
- Flooring roller
- Chalk line
- Heat gun
- 1⁄16" V-notched trowel
- Straightedge
- Vinyl flooring
- Masking tape
- Heavy butcher or brown wrapping paper
- Duct tape
- Flooring adhesive
- ⅜" staples
- Metal threshold bars
- Nails

Resilient sheet vinyl is a very popular choice for bathroom floors because it is resistant to moisture and easy to clean. It is also relatively inexpensive, but you will find that the style and design options are more limited than with some other floorcovering types.

How to Make a Cutting Template

Place sheets of heavy butcher paper or brown wrapping paper along the walls, leaving a ⅛" gap. Cut triangular holes in the paper with a utility knife. Fasten the template to the floor by placing masking tape over the holes.

Follow the outline of the room, working with one sheet of paper at a time. Overlap the edges of adjoining sheets by about 2" and tape the sheets together.

To fit the template around pipes, tape sheets of paper on either side. Measure the distance from the wall to the center of the pipe, then subtract ⅛".

Transfer the measurement to a separate piece of paper. Use a compass to draw the pipe diameter on the paper, then cut out the hole with scissors or a utility knife. Cut a slit from the edge of the paper to the hole.

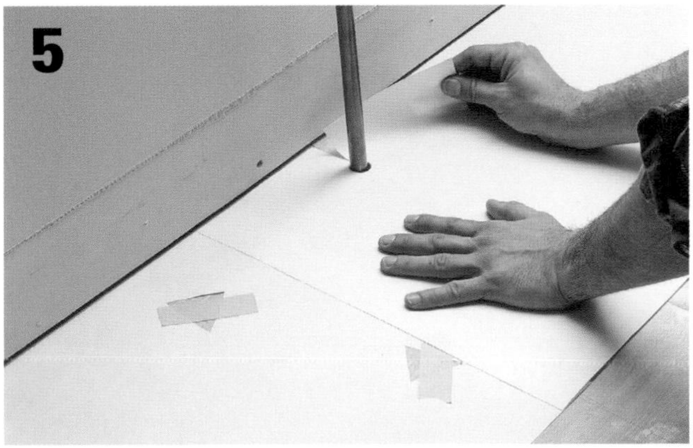

Fit the hole cutout around the pipe. Tape the hole template to the adjoining sheets.

When completed, roll or loosely fold the paper template for carrying.

How to Install Perimeter-bond Sheet Vinyl

Unroll the flooring on any large, flat, clean surface. To prevent wrinkles, sheet vinyl comes from the manufacturer rolled with the pattern-side out. Unroll the sheet and turn it pattern-side up for marking.

For two-piece installations, overlap the edges of the sheets by at least 2". Plan to have the seams fall along the pattern lines or simulated grout joints. Align the sheets so the pattern matches, then tape the sheets together with duct tape.

Make a paper template (see page 261) and position it. Trace the outline of the template onto the flooring using a non-permanent felt-tipped pen.

Remove the template. Cut the sheet vinyl with a sharp linoleum knife or a utility knife with a new blade. Use a straightedge as a guide for making longer cuts.

Cut holes for pipes and other permanent obstructions. Cut a slit from each hole to the nearest edge of the flooring. Whenever possible, make slits along pattern lines.

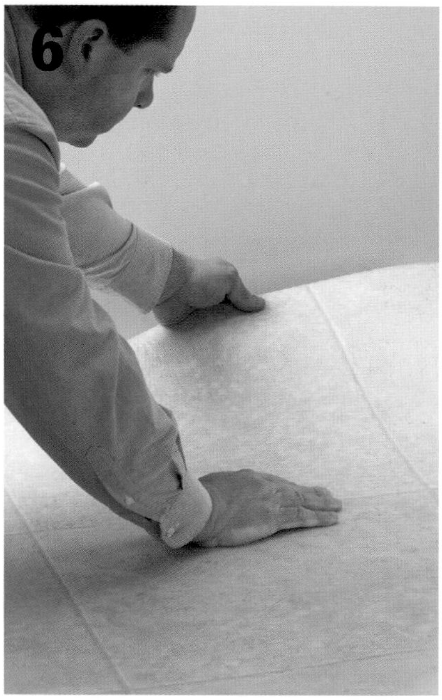

Roll up the flooring loosely and transfer it to the installation area. Do not fold the flooring. Unroll and position the sheet vinyl carefully. Slide the edges beneath undercut door casings.

Cut the seams for two-piece installations using a straightedge as a guide. Hold the straightedge tightly against the flooring, and cut along the pattern lines through both pieces of vinyl flooring.

Remove both pieces of scrap flooring. The pattern should now run continuously across the adjoining sheets of flooring.

Fold back the edges of both sheets. Apply a 3" band of multipurpose flooring adhesive to the underlayment or old flooring, using a ¼" V-notched trowel or wallboard knife.

Lay the seam edges one at a time onto the adhesive. Make sure the seam is tight, pressing the gaps together with your fingers, if needed. Roll the seam edges with a J-roller or wallpaper seam roller.

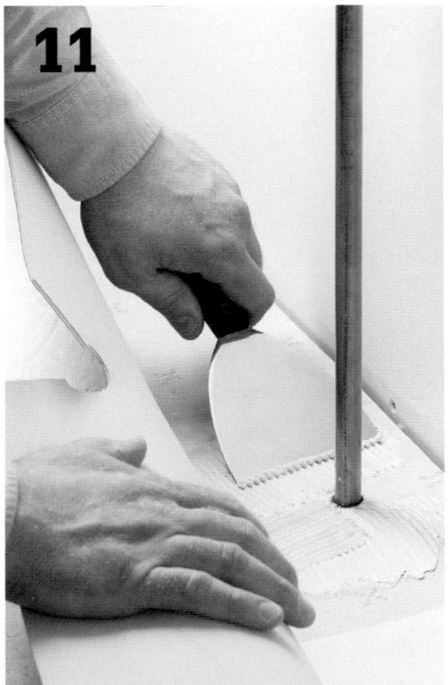

Apply flooring adhesive underneath flooring cuts at pipes or posts and around the entire perimeter of the room. Roll the flooring with the roller to ensure good contact with the adhesive.

If you're applying flooring over a wood underlayment, fasten the outer edges of the sheet with ⅜" staples driven every 3". Make sure the staples will be covered by the base molding.

Accessories & Upgrades

The accessories you include in a bathroom remodel or new design are the finishing touches that add immeasurably to the room's decor and function. This is your chance to add simple but big-impact luxuries such as towel warmers and fog-free mirrors.

Whenever possible, anchor permanently mounted accessories to wall studs or blocking for maximum holding power. If no studs or blocking are located in the area where accessories will be installed, use toggle bolts or molly bolts to anchor the accessories to drywall or plaster walls.

In this chapter:

- Medicine Cabinets
- Grab Bars
- Tilting Wall Mirrors
- Mirror Defoggers
- Glass Shelving
- Towel Warmers

Medicine Cabinets

Common bathroom cabinets include vanities, medicine cabinets, linen cabinets, and "tank topper" cabinets that mount over the toilet area. See pages 32 to 35 for more information on cabinets.

When installing cabinets in a damp location, like a bathroom, choose the best cabinets you can afford. Look for quality indicators, like doweled construction, hardwood doors and drawers, and high-gloss, moisture-resistant finishes. Avoid cabinets with sides or doors that are painted on one side and finished with laminate or veneer on the other because these cabinets are more likely to warp.

Tools & Materials ▸

Electronic stud finder
Level
Pry bar
Hammer
Screwdriver
Drill
Circular saw
Reciprocating saw
Pencil
Bar clamp
Framing square
Duplex nails
10d common nails
Finish nails
1 × 4 lumber
2½" wood screws
Wood shims
Cabinet

A medicine cabinet is wall-mounted or recessed above a lavatory sink. They are better suited for storing toiletries than medicine.

How to Install a Surface-Mounted Cabinet

1

Locate the wall studs and mark them clearly on the wall surface. Draw a level line at the desired top height of the cabinet body, then measure and mark a second line to indicate the bottom of the cabinet.

2

Attach a temporary ledger board (usually 1 × 4) just below the lower level line using duplex nails. Rest the base of the cabinet on the ledger and hold it in place or brace it with 2 × 4s.

3

Attach the cabinet to the wall at the stud locations by drilling pilot holes and driving wood screws. Remove the ledger when finished, and patch the nail holes with drywall compound.

How to Install a Recessed Cabinet

Locate the first stud beyond either side of the planned cabinet location, then remove the wall surface between the studs. (Removing the wall surface all the way to the ceiling simplifies patch work.) Cut along the center of the studs, using a circular saw with the blade depth set to the thickness of the wall surface.

Mark a rough opening ½" taller than the cabinet frame onto the exposed wall studs. Add 1½" for each header and sill plate, then cut out the studs in the rough opening area.

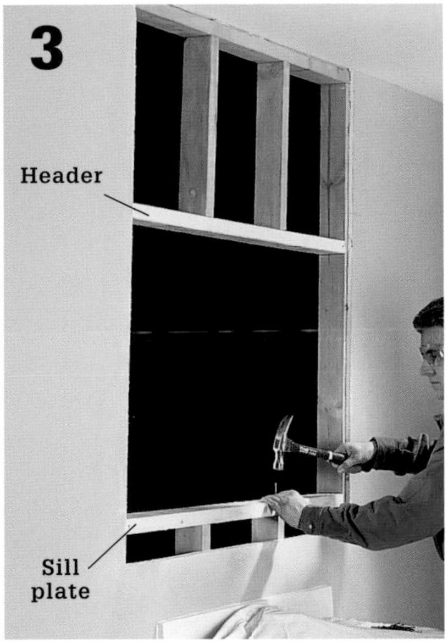

Frame out the top and bottom of the rough opening by installing a header and a sill plate between the cut wall studs. Make sure the header and sill plate are level, then nail them in place with 10d common nails.

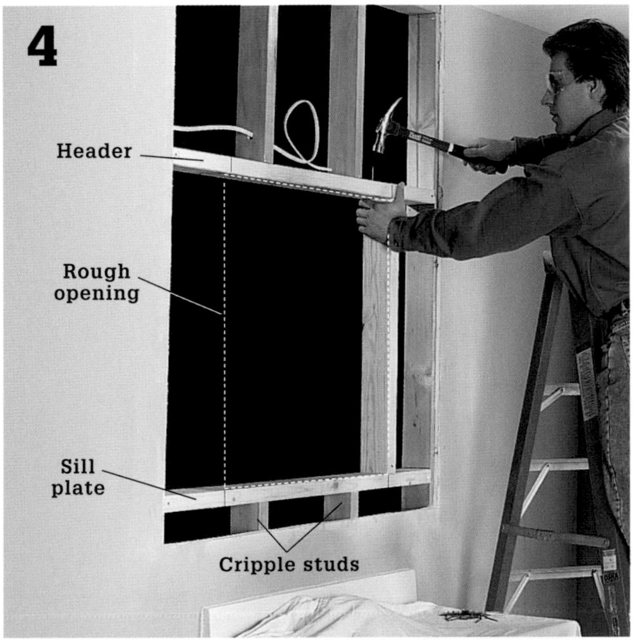

Mark the rough opening width on the header and sill plates, centering the opening over the sink. Cut and nail jack studs between the header and the sill plate, just outside the rough opening marks. Install any wiring for new light fixtures and receptacles, then patch the wall where necessary.

Position the cabinet in the opening. Check it for level with a carpenter's level, then attach the cabinet by drilling pilot holes and driving wood screws through the top and bottom of the cabinet sides and into the wall studs, header, and sill plate. Attach the doors, shelves, and hardware.

Grab Bars

Bathrooms are beautiful with their shiny ceramic tubs, showers, and floors, but add water and moisture to the mix and you've created the perfect conditions for a fall. The good news is many falls in the bathroom can be avoided by installing grab bars at key locations.

Grab bars help family members steady themselves on slippery shower, tub, and other floor surfaces. Plus, they provide support for people transferring from a wheelchair or walker to the shower, tub, or toilet.

Grab bars come in a variety of colors, shapes, sizes, and textures. Choose a style with a 1¼" to 1½" diameter that fits comfortably between your thumb and fingers. Then properly install it 1½" from the wall with anchors that can support at least 250 pounds.

The easiest way to install grab bars is to screw them into wall studs or into blocking or backing attached to studs. Blocking is a good option if you are framing a new bathroom or have the wall surface removed during a major remodel (see Illustration A). Use 2 × 6 or 2 × 8 lumber to provide room for adjustments, and fasten the blocks to the framing with 16d nails. Note the locations of your blocking for future reference.

As an alternative, cover the entire wall with ¾" plywood backing secured with screws to the wall framing, so you can install grab bars virtually anywhere on the wall (see Illustration B).

Grab bars can be installed in areas without studs. For these installations, use specialized heavy-duty hollow-wall anchors designed to support at least 250 pounds.

Tools & Materials ▸

- Measuring tape
- Pencil
- Stud finder
- Level
- Drill
- Masonry bit
- Grab bar
- Hollow-wall anchors
- #12 stainless steel screws
- Silicone caulk

Grab bars promote independence in the bathroom, where privacy is especially important. Grab bars not only help prevent slips and falls, they also help people steady themselves in showers and lower themselves into tubs.

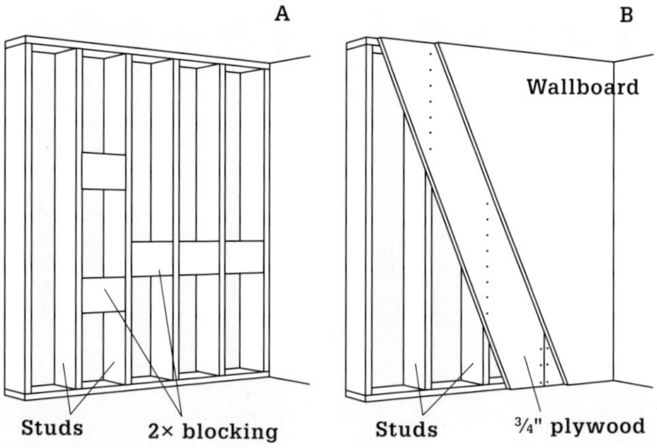

Blocking or backing is required for secure grab bars. If you know where the grab bars will be located, add 2× blocking between studs (Illustration A). You also can cover the entire wall with ¾" plywood backing, which allows you to install grab bars virtually anywhere on the wall.

How to Install Grab Bars

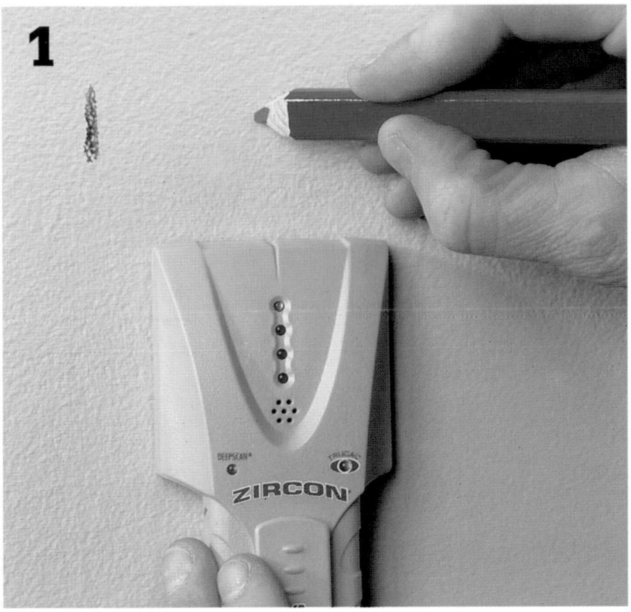

Locate the wall studs in the installation area using a stud finder. If the area is tiled, the stud finder may not detect studs, so try to locate the studs above the tile, if possible, then use a level to transfer the marks lower on the wall. Otherwise, you can drill small, exploratory holes through grout joints in the tile, then fill the holes with silicone caulk to seal them. Be careful not to drill into pipes.

Mark the grab bar height at one stud location, then use a level to transfer the height mark to the stud that will receive the other end of the bar. Position the grab bar on the height marks so at least two of the three mounting holes are aligned with the stud centers. Mark the mounting hole locations onto the wall.

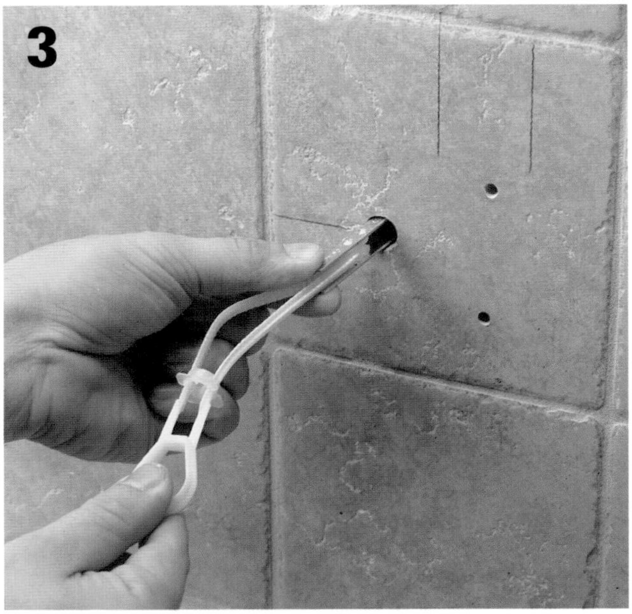

Drill pilot holes for the mounting screws. If you are drilling through tile, start with a small bit (about ⅛"), then redrill the hole with the larger bit. For screws that won't hit studs, drill holes for wall anchors, following the manufacturer's directions for sizing. Install anchors, if necessary.

Apply a continuous bead of silicone caulk to the back side of each bar end (inset). Secure the bar to the studs using #12 stainless steel screws (the screws should penetrate the stud by at least 1"). Install a stainless steel screw or bolt into the wall anchors. Test the bar to make sure it's secure.

Tilting Wall Mirrors

A mirror is a necessity in any bathroom, but not every bathroom mirror has to be attached to a medicine cabinet. Tilting mirrors and telescoping makeup mirrors are only two of the nearly endless options available.

The most important part of mounting a mirror is accurate placement. A mirror over the vanity should be centered over the centerline of the sink. If you have an asymmetrical sink, center the mirror over the vanity.

Mirror height is also important, especially to those who are above or below average height. Tilting mirrors are useful if there is a dramatic difference between the tallest and the shortest person in the household.

Tools & Materials ▸

- Level
- Drill
- Flat-bladed screwdriver
- Allen wrench
- Tilting wall mirror
- Extending arm mirror

A smaller tilting mirror can take the place of a large stationary mirror.

Extending arm mirrors are handy for shaving or applying makeup. These mirrors typically have two sides with one side providing magnification. Some come with lights and antifogging as well.

A tilting wall mirror adjusts to people of varying heights and should be centered over the sink or the vanity. Extending arm mirrors are installed off to the side, since the arm allows the mirror to be drawn closer when needed.

How to Install a Tilting Wall Mirror

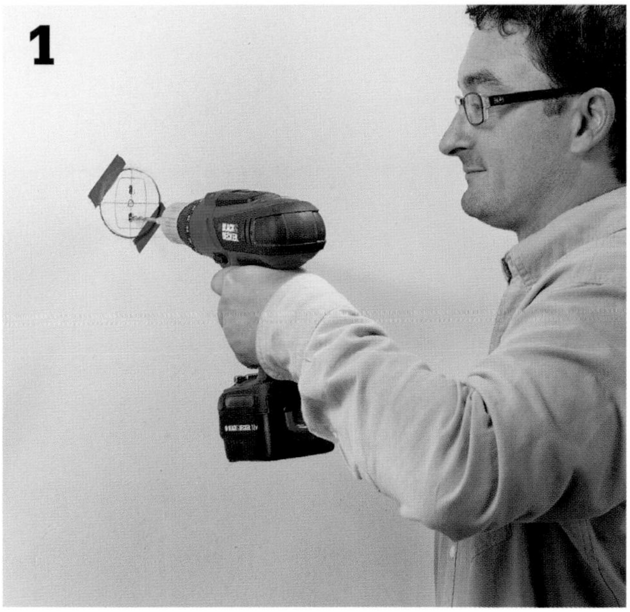

Determine the height of the mirror mounts by dividing the overall height of the mirror by two and adding the result to the number of inches above the vanity you want the bottom edge of the mirror to be placed. In this case, the mirror came with a mounting template. Tape the template to the wall and drill two 5/16" holes at each of the mounting post locations.

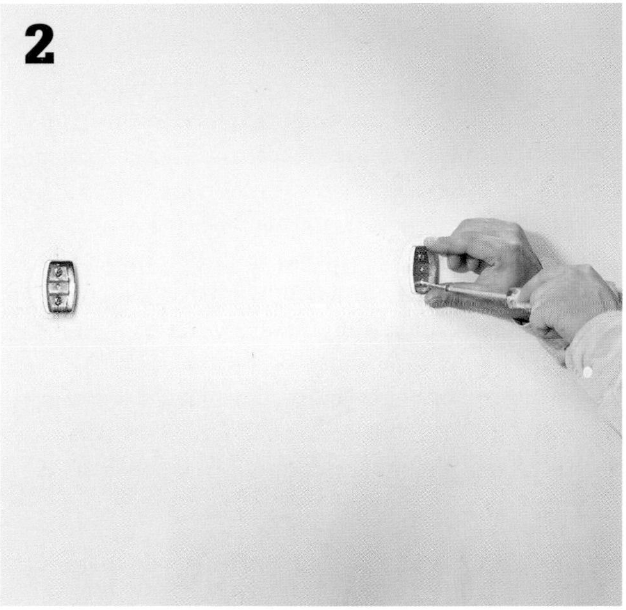

Insert the included wall anchors and tap into place. Remove the brackets from the mounting posts by loosening the setscrew. Attach the brackets to the wall at the wall anchor locations.

Assemble the mirror if necessary. Make sure the setscrews on the mounting posts are facing downward. Carefully lift the mirror, place the mounting posts over the brackets, and slide into place. Tighten the setscrews.

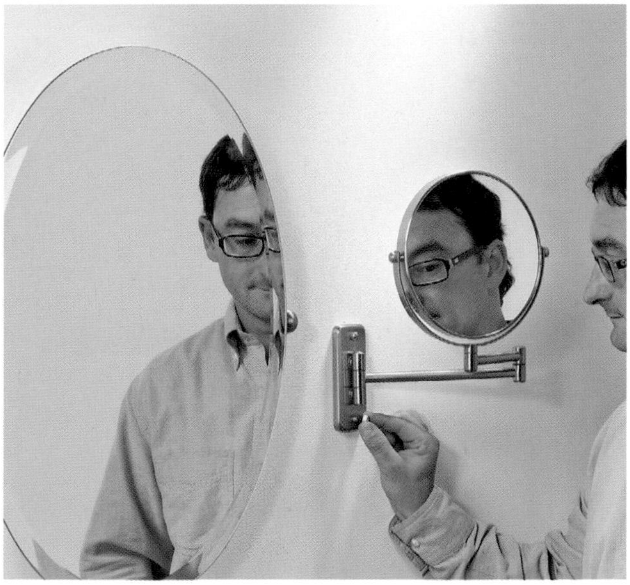

Variation: How to Hang an Extending Arm Mirror. Most extending wall mirrors are surface mounted. Next to the vanity mirror, use a level to mark a vertical line at the eye level of the mirror's main user. Make sure there is sufficient space for the mirror to fold back against the wall. Hold the mirror unit over the line and mark the screw hole locations. Drill two 1/4" holes at the marks and insert the wall anchors. Hold the mirror in position and drive in the screws.

Mirror Defoggers

You may not want to deal with the inconvenience of a foggy mirror after your long, hot soak or invigorating shower. Let's face it—no one's dream bath includes inconveniences of any sort. But even with an exhaust fan, your bathroom mirror can get foggy. Instead of wiping off the moisture, which only results in streaks and drips, prevent its formation with a mirror defogger.

A mirror defogger works by gently heating the mirror to prevent condensation. Typically it is hardwired into the vanity light so that when you switch on the light you're also switching on the defogger. Mirror defoggers come in a number of sizes and with many operating systems. They can be installed under a flat wall-mounted mirror attached to the back of a framed mirror.

Tools & Materials ▸

- Measuring tape
- Level
- Staple gun
- Stud finder
- Keyhole saw
- Fish tape
- Drill
- Painter's tape
- Mirror defogger

Mirror defoggers are heaters that are installed behind flat wall-mounted mirrors. The heat prevents condensation on the mirror and does away with the inconvenience of a foggy mirror in your dream bathroom.

How to Install a Mirror Defogger

Use painter's tape to outline the mirror top and sides on the wall. Carefully remove the mirror and place it in a safe location. Mark the location of the defogger. It should be centered over the sink with the top 6 ft. from the floor. Mark a 4" × 6" box on the wall around the defogger's wire connector. We aligned this mirror's power connection at the top, where it is closest to the power supply. Turn off the circuit breaker for the light fixture.

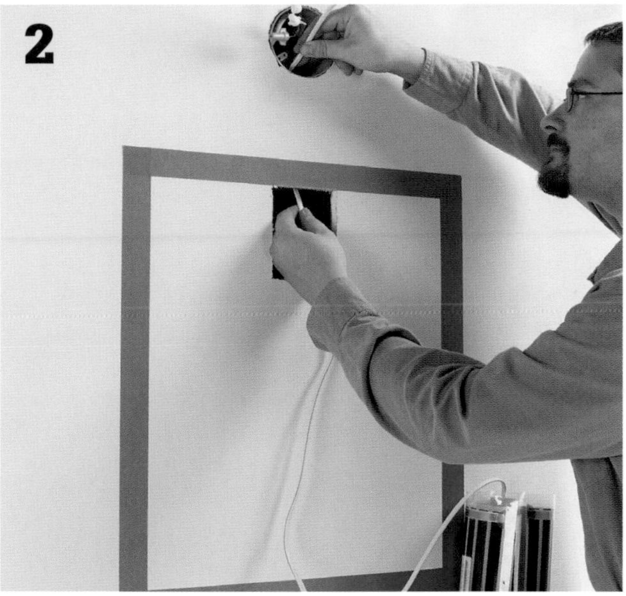

Provide power to the installation area by running cable from a nearby electrical box and into a new box behind the mirror location. If you tie into the electricity at the vanity light (as we have done here), the defogger will turn on and off with the vanity light. If you are not experienced with home wiring, hire an electrician for this part of the job.

Patch any holes in the wallboard that will not be covered by the mirror. Position the defogger with the wire connector centered over the access hole and within the lines marked in Step 1. Staple the defogger to the wall surface around the edges only.

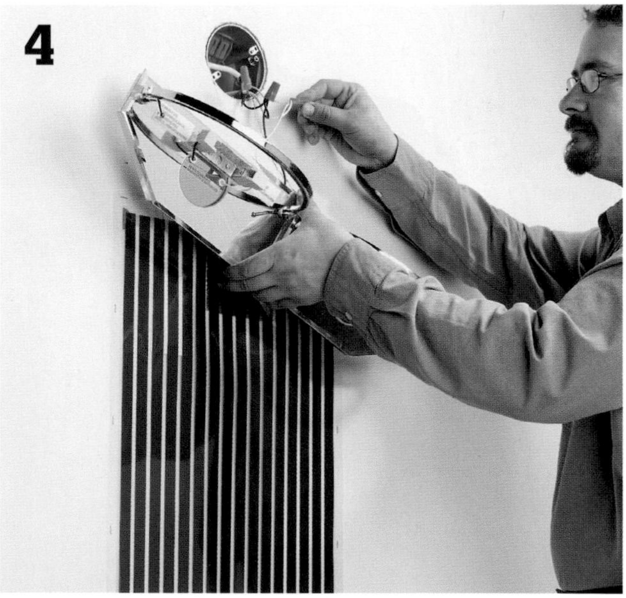

Make (or have made) the electrical connections according to the manufacturer's instructions. Here, we are re-installing the bathroom vanity light. Remount the mirror with clips (do not use mastic over the defogger).

Glass Shelving

Tools & Materials ▸

- Level
- Drill
- Pencil
- Glass shelves

Glass shelving is unobtrusive so it can fit many styles of bathrooms—from sleek modern to elaborate Victorian. You can find a wide variety of shelving available in home stores and online.

Most glass shelves are held in place with metal mounts. How the shelves are secured to the mounts differs and how the mounts are attached to the wall also differs. Most shelves have a hidden bracket that is secured to the wall. The mount then slips over the bracket and is secured with a setscrew. The most basic models may have mounts that are screwed directly into the wall with exposed screws. The directions here are for shelving that uses hidden brackets.

If you are installing shelves on a tiled wall, mount the brackets in grout lines if at all possible to minimize the possibility of cracking the tiles. Many glass shelves have some flexibility in the distance between the mounts.

Glass shelves fit any style and size of bathroom. They are held in place with metal mounts, which can be decorative, that are attached to the wall.

How to Install Glass Shelves

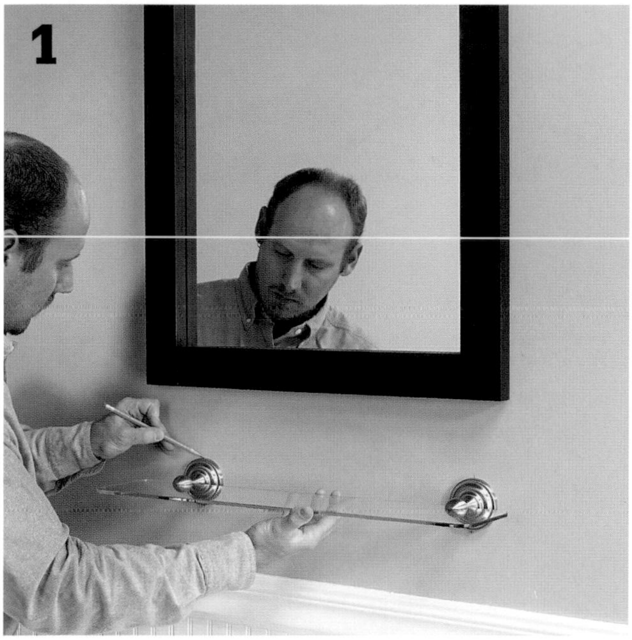

Assemble the shelf and shelf holders (not the brackets). Hold the shelf against the wall in the desired location. On the wall, mark the center point of each holder, where the setscrew is.

Remove the shelves and use the level to extend the mark into a 3" vertical line. Use the level to mark a horizontal line across the centers of these lines.

Center the middle round hole of the bracket over the intersection of the vertical and horizontal lines. Mark the center of each of the oblong holes. Put the bracket aside and drill a ¼" hole at each mark. Insert the included wall anchors in the holes. Replace the bracket, insert the screws into the wall anchors, and drive the screws. Repeat for the second bracket.

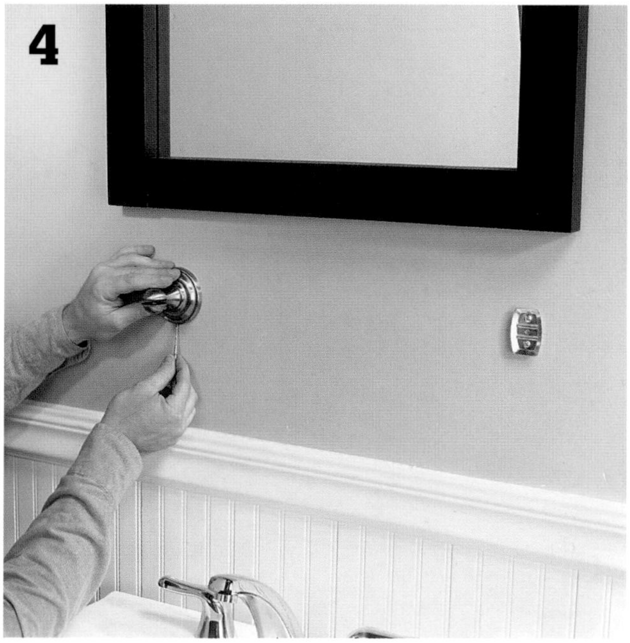

Remove the shelf from the holders. Slide a holder over a bracket, check that the shelf mount is level, and tighten the setscrew. Repeat with the other holder. Insert the shelf and fix in place. Check the shelf for level. If it's not level, remove one holder and loosen the bracket screws. Slide the bracket up or down to make the unit level. Replace the holder and shelf.

Towel Warmers

Here's a little bit of luxury that need not be limited to high-end hotel stays. You can have toasty towels in your own bathroom with an easy-to-install towel warmer. In a relatively cold room, this can make stepping out of the shower a much more pleasant experience.

Heated towel racks are available in a wide range of styles and sizes. Freestanding floor models as well as door- and wall-mounted versions can be plugged in for use when desired. Hardwired wall-mounted versions can be switched on when you enter the bathroom so your towels are warm when you step out of the shower. Although installing them requires some electrical skills, the hardwired models do not need to be located near wall receptacles and they do not have exposed cords or extension cords hanging on the wall. However, if you locate the warmer directly above an existing receptacle, you can save a lot of time and mess by running cable up from the receptacle to the new electrical box for the warmer.

Before installing hardwired models, check your local electrical codes for applicable regulations. If you are not experienced with home wiring, have an electrician do this job for you or opt for a plug-in model.

Tools & Materials ▸

- Drill
- Level
- Keyhole saw
- Wiring tools
- Phillips screwdriver
- Stud finder
- Retrofit electrical outlet box
- Wire connectors
- NM cable
- Towel warmer
- Pencil
- Masking tape

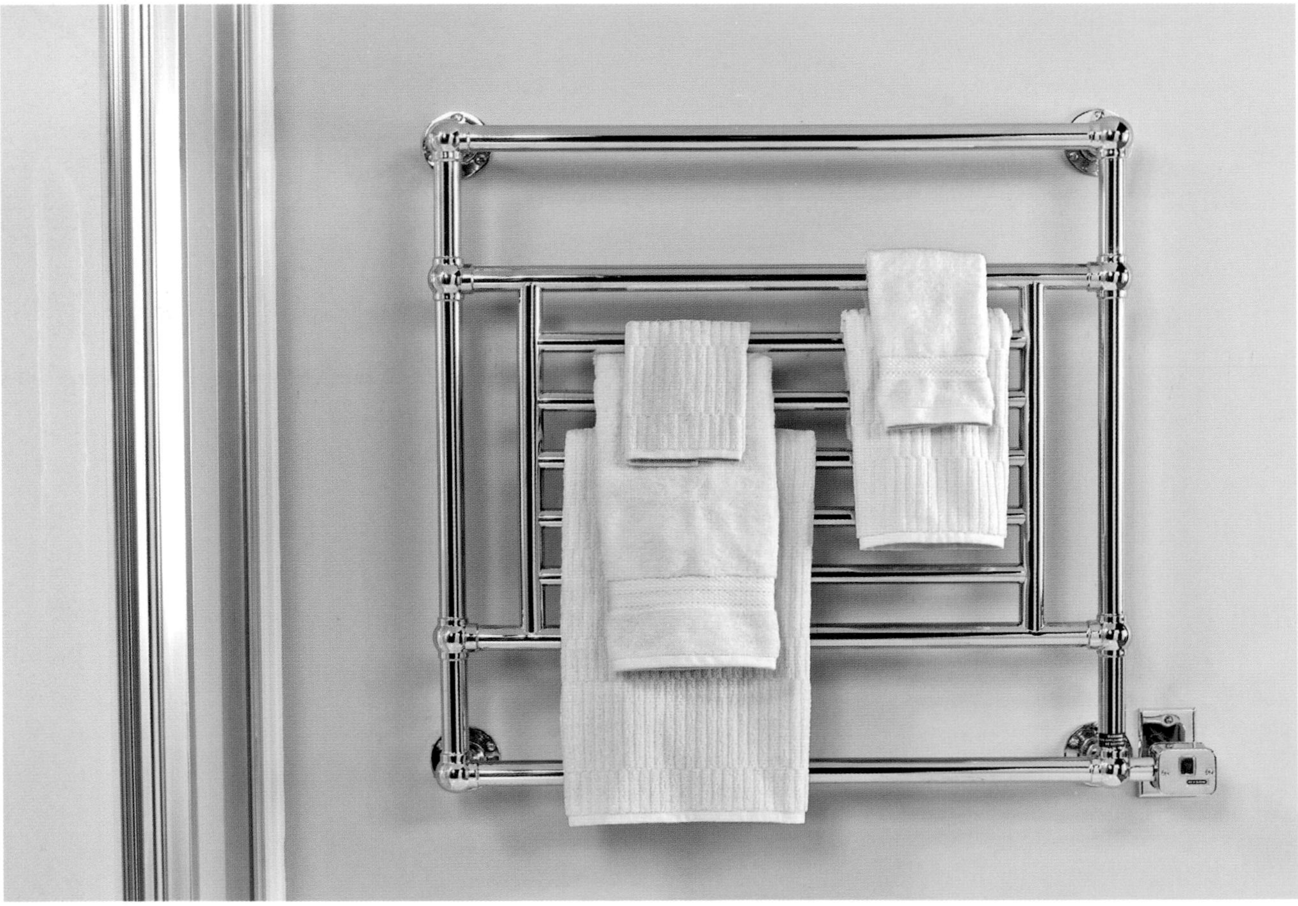

A hard-wired towel warmer offers the luxury of heated towels without the safety concerns of a plug-in device.

How to Install a Hardwired Towel Warmer

Use a stud finder to locate the studs in the area you wish to place the towel warmer. Mark the stud locations with masking tape or pencil lines. Attach the wall brackets to the towel warmer and hold the unit against the wall at least 7" from the floor and 3" from the ceiling or any overhang. Mark the locations of the wall bracket outlet plate (where the electrical connection will be made) and the mounting brackets.

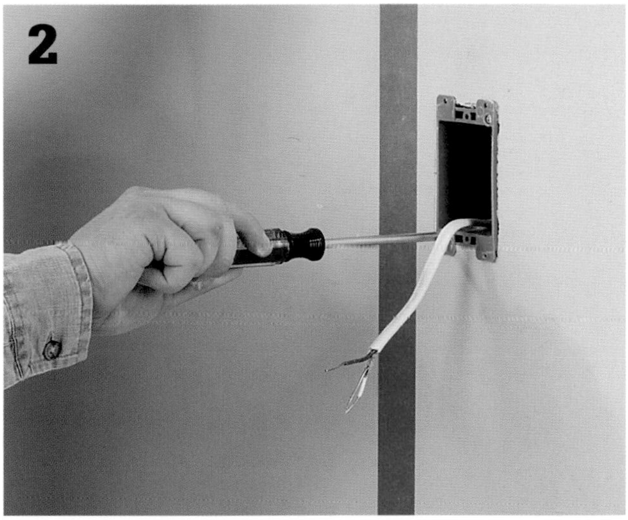

Shut off electrical power at the main service panel. At the mark for the wall bracket outlet, cut a hole in the wallcovering for a retrofit electrical box. Run NM cable from the opening to a GFCI-protected circuit (here, we ran cable down to a receptacle directly beneath it), or install a separate GFCI-protected circuit (you'll need to consult a wiring book or an electrician). Pull the cable through the hole in the retrofit box, and then tighten the cable clamp. Place the box in the hole flush with the wall surface and tighten the mounting screw in the rear of the box. Cut the wires so about 5" extends into the box and strip the insulation off at ⅜" from the end of each wire.

Position the towel warmer over the outlet box and mark the locations of the screw holes for the wall brackets. Make sure the appliance is level. Remove the warmer and drill ¼" pilot holes at the marked locations. If the marks are located over studs, drill ⅛" pilot holes. If not, push wall anchors into the holes. Thread the mounting screws through the brackets. Have a helper hold the towel rack in place and use wire connectors to connect the wires, including the ground wire, according to the instructions.

After the electrical connections are made, fasten the towel rack brackets to the wall. Turn on power and test the towel warmer. Finally, attach the electrical cover plate with integral on/off switch.

Appendix A: Plumbing Codes & Permits

The Plumbing Code is the set of regulations that building officials and inspectors use to evaluate your project plans and the quality of your work. Codes vary from region to region, but most are based on the National Uniform Plumbing Code, a highly technical, difficult-to-read manual. More user-friendly code handbooks are available at bookstores and libraries. These handbooks are based on the National Uniform Plumbing Code, but they are easier to read and include diagrams and photos.

Sometimes these handbooks discuss three different plumbing zones in an effort to accommodate state variations in regulations. Remember that local plumbing code always supersedes national code. Your local building inspector can be a valuable source of information and may provide you with a convenient summary sheet of the regulations that apply to your project.

As part of its effort to ensure public safety, your community building department requires a permit for most plumbing projects. When you apply for a permit, the building official will want to review three drawings of your plumbing project: a site plan, a water supply diagram, and a drain-waste-vent diagram. If the official is satisfied that your project meets code requirements, you will be issued a plumbing permit, which is your legal permission to begin work. As your project nears completion, the inspector will visit your home to check your work.

Note: These specifications may not conform to all building codes; check with your local building department regarding regulations in your area.

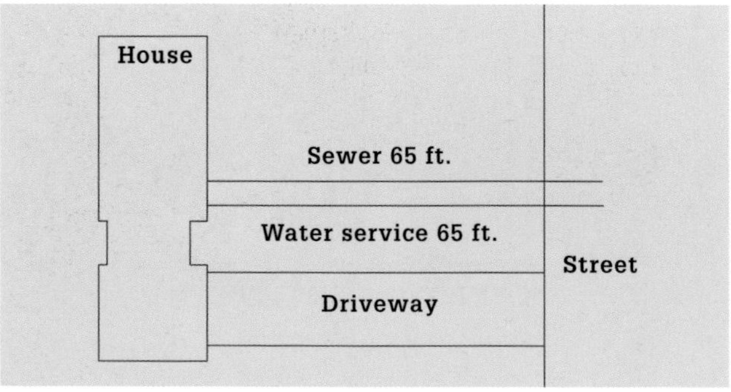

The site plan shows the location of the water main and sewer main with respect to your yard and home. The distances from your foundation to the water main and from the foundation to the main sewer should be indicated on the site map.

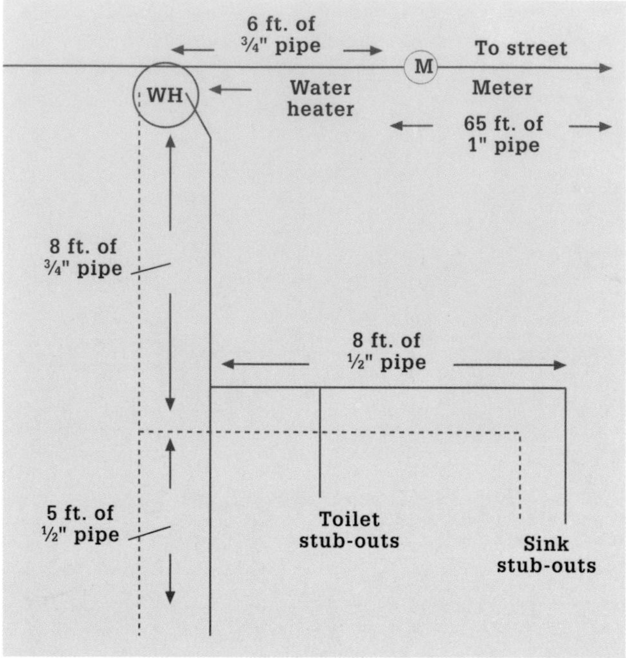

The supply riser diagram shows the length of the hot and cold water pipes and the relation of the fixtures to one another. The inspector will use this diagram to determine the proper size for the new water supply pipes in your system.

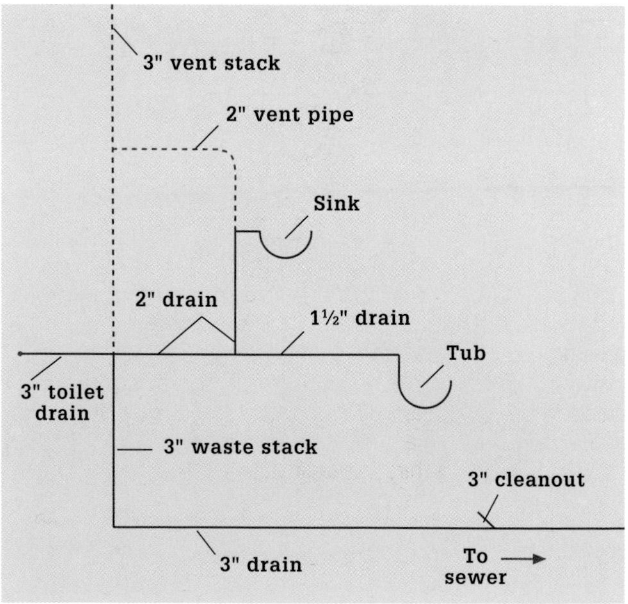

A DWV diagram shows the routing of drain and vent pipes in your system. Indicate the lengths of drain pipes and the distances between fixtures. The inspector will use this diagram to determine if you have properly sized the drain traps, drain pipes, and vent pipes.

Fixture Supply Pipe & Trap Sizes

FIXTURE	UNIT RATING	MINIMUM BRANCH PIPE SIZE	MINIMUM SUPPLY TUBE SIZE	MINIMUM TRAP SIZE
Toilet	3	½"	⅜"	n/a
Vanity Sink	1	½"	⅜"	1¼"
Shower	2	½"	⅜"	2"
Bathtub	2	½"	½"	1½"

To determine the minimum size of supply pipes and fixture drain traps, you must know the fixture's unit rating, a unit of measure assigned by the plumbing code. *Note: Branch pipes are the water supply lines that run from the distribution pipes toward the individual fixtures. Supply tubes carry water from the branch pipes to the fixtures.*

Sizes for Horizontal & Vertical Drain Pipes

PIPE SIZE	MAXIMUM FIXTURE UNITS FOR HORIZONTAL BRANCH DRAIN	MAXIMUM FIXTURE UNITS FOR VERTICAL DRAIN STACKS
1¼"	1	2
1½"	3	4
2"	6	10
2½"	12	20
3"	20	30
4"	160	240

Drain pipe sizes are determined by the load on the pipes, as measured by the total fixture units. Horizontal drain pipes less than 3" in diameter should slope ¼" per foot toward the main drain. Pipes 3" or more in diameter should slope ⅛" per foot. *Note: Horizontal or vertical drain pipes for a toilet must be 3" or larger.*

Maximum Hole & Notch Sizes

FRAMING MEMBER	MAXIMUM HOLE SIZE	MAXIMUM NOTCH SIZE
2 × 4 loadbearing stud	1⁷⁄₁₆" diameter	⅞" deep
2 × 4 non-loadbearing stud	2½" diameter	1⁷⁄₁₆" deep
2 × 6 loadbearing stud	2¼" diameter	1⅜" deep
2 × 6 non-loadbearing stud	3⁵⁄₁₆" diameter	2³⁄₁₆" deep
2 × 6 joists	1½" diameter	⅞" deep
2 × 8 joists	2⅜" diameter	1¼" deep
2 × 10 joists	3¹⁄₁₆" diameter	1½" deep
2 × 12 joists	3¾" diameter	1⅞" deep

The maximum hole and notch sizes that can be cut into framing members for running pipes is shown above. Where possible, use notches rather than bored holes to ease pipe installation. When boring holes, there must be at least ⅝" of wood between the edge of a stud and the hole, and at least 2" between the edge of a joist and the hole. Joists can be notched only in the end one-third of the overall span; never in the middle one-third of the joist. When two pipes are run through a stud, the pipes should be stacked one over the other, never side by side.

Pipe Support Intervals

TYPE OF PIPE	VERTICAL SUPPORT INTERVAL	HORIZONTAL SUPPORT INTERVAL
Copper	6 ft.	10 ft.
ABS	4 ft.	4 ft.
CPVC	3 ft.	3 ft.
PVC	4 ft.	4 ft.
Galvanized Iron	12 ft.	15 ft.
Cast Iron	5 ft.	15 ft.

Minimum intervals for supporting pipes are determined by the type of pipe and its orientation in the system. Use only brackets and supports made of the same (or compatible) materials as the pipes. Remember that the measurements shown above are minimum requirements; many plumbers install pipe supports at closer intervals.

Wet Venting

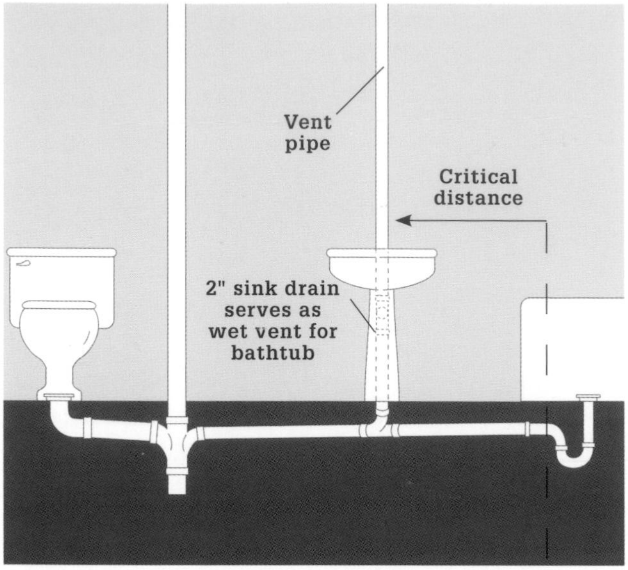

Wet vents are pipes that serve as a vent for one fixture and a drain for another. The sizing of a wet vent is based on the total fixture units it supports: a 3" wet vent can serve up to 12 fixture units; a 2" wet vent is rated for 4 fixture units; a 1½" wet vent, for only 1 fixture unit. *Note: The distance between the wet-vented fixture and the wet vent itself must be no more than the maximum critical distance.*

Auxiliary Venting

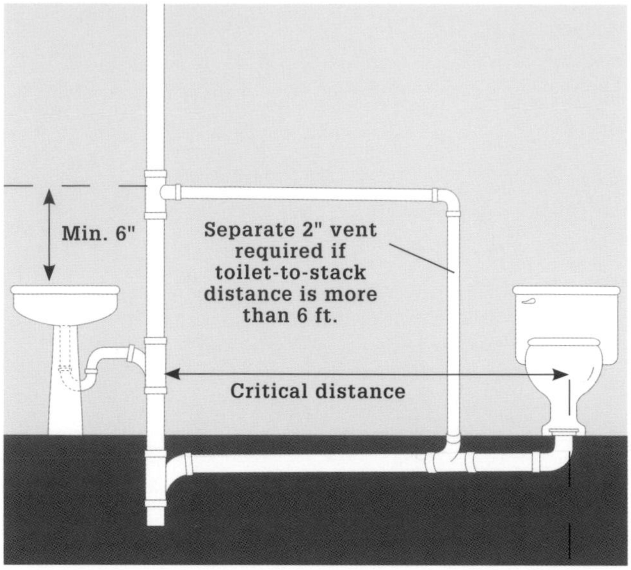

Fixtures must have auxiliary vents if the distance to the main waste-vent stack exceeds the critical distance. A toilet, for example, should have a separate vent pipe if it is located more than 6 ft. from the main waste–vent stack. This secondary vent pipe should connect to the stack or an existing vent pipe at a point at least 6" above the highest fixture on the system.

Vent Pipe Sizes, Critical Distances

SIZE OF FIXTURE DRAIN	MINIMUM VENT PIPE SIZE	MAXIMUM TRAP-TO-VENT DISTANCE
1¼"	1¼"	2½ ft.
1½"	1¼"	3½ ft.
2"	1½"	5 ft.
3"	2"	6 ft.
4"	3"	10 ft.

Vent pipes are usually one pipe size smaller than the drain pipes they serve. Code requires that the distance between the drain trap and the vent pipe fall within a maximum *critical distance,* a measurement that is determined by the size of the fixture drain. Use this chart to determine both the minimum size for the vent pipe and the maximum critical distance.

Vent Pipe Orientation to Drain Pipe

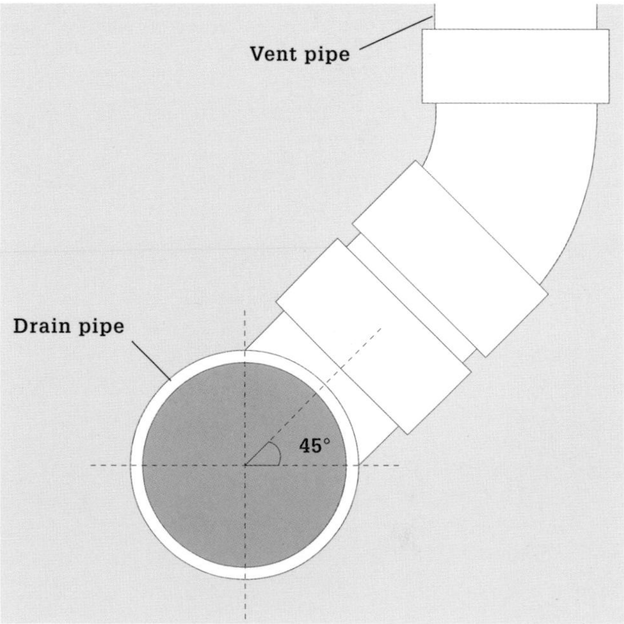

Vent pipes must extend in an upward direction from drains, no less than 45° from horizontal. This ensures that waste water cannot flow into the vent pipe and block it. At the opposite end, a new vent pipe should connect to an existing vent pipe or main waste–vent stack at a point at least 6" above the highest fixture draining into the system.

Appendix B: Wiring Codes & Permits

To ensure public safety, every community requires that you get a permit to install new wiring and have the completed work reviewed by an appointed inspector. Electrical inspectors use the National Electrical Code (NEC) as the primary authority for evaluating wiring, but they also follow the local building code and electrical code standards.

As you begin planning new circuits, call or visit your local electrical inspector and discuss the project with him or her. The inspector can tell you which of the national and local code requirements apply to your job, and may give you a packet of information summarizing these regulations. Later, when you apply to the inspector for a work permit, he or she will expect you to understand the local guidelines as well as a few basic NEC requirements.

The NEC is a set of standards that provides minimum safety requirements for wiring installations. It is revised every three years.

In addition to being the final authority of code requirements, inspectors are electrical professionals with years of experience. Although they have busy schedules, most inspectors are happy to answer questions and help you design well-planned circuits.

As with any project, if you are uncomfortable working with electricity, hire a professional electrician to complete new wiring installations and connections.

The bathroom requirements listed below are for general information only. Contact your local electrical inspector for specific wiring regulations:

- A separate 20-amp receptacle circuit for small appliances is required.
- All receptacles must be GFCI protected.
- Light fixtures and switches must be on a separate circuit. (A minimum 15-amp circuit.)
- All fixture and appliance switches must be grounded.
- There must be at least one ceiling-mounted light fixture.
- Whirlpools and other large fixtures or appliances are required to be on a dedicated circuit.

The manufacturers of some home spa fixtures, such as saunas and whirlpools, may specify that a certified electrician make the electrical connections for their product. Make sure to follow these directions, as doing otherwise may result in the warranty being voided.

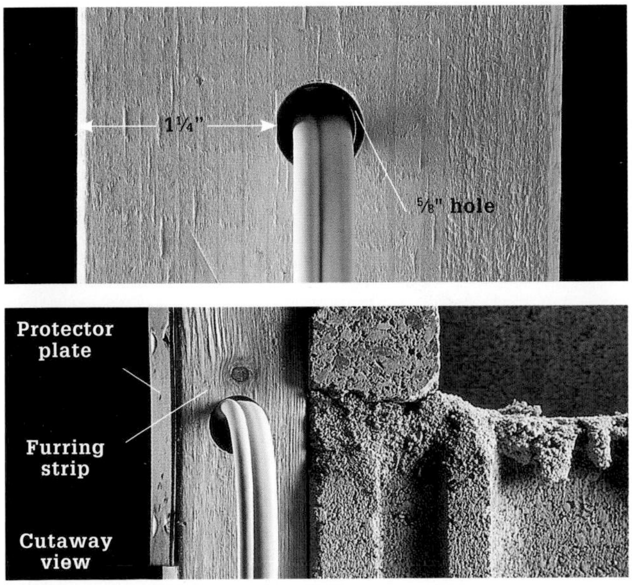

Cables must be protected against damage by nails and screws by at least 1¼" of wood (top). When cables pass through 2 × 2 furring strips (bottom), protect the cables with metal protector plates.

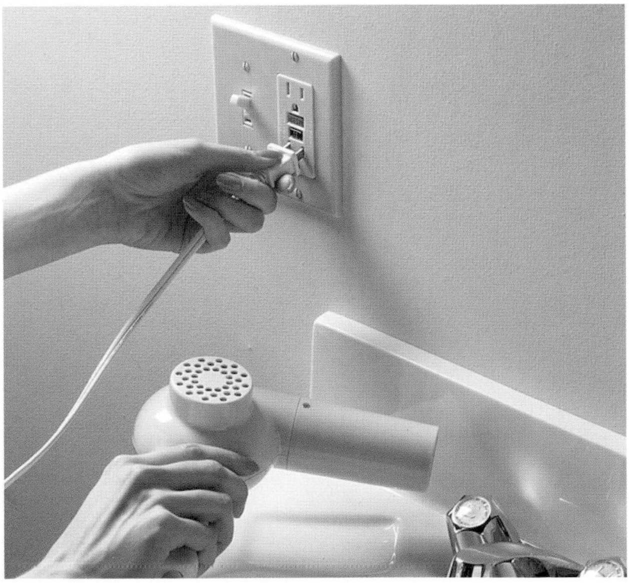

Kitchen and bathroom receptacles must be protected by a GFCI. Also, all outdoor receptacles and general use receptacles in an unfinished basement or crawlspace must be protected by a GFCI.

Measurement Conversions

Lumber Dimensions

NOMINAL - U.S.	ACTUAL - U.S. (IN INCHES)	METRIC
1 × 2	3/4 × 1 1/2	19 × 38 mm
1 × 3	3/4 × 2 1/2	19 × 64 mm
1 × 4	3/4 × 3 1/2	19 × 89 mm
1 × 5	3/4 × 4 1/2	19 × 114 mm
1 × 6	3/4 × 5 1/2	19 × 140 mm
1 × 7	3/4 × 6 1/4	19 × 159 mm
1 × 8	3/4 × 7 1/4	19 × 184 mm
1 × 10	3/4 × 9 1/4	19 × 235 mm
1 × 12	3/4 × 11 1/4	19 × 286 mm
1 1/4 × 4	1 × 3 1/2	25 × 89 mm
1 1/4 × 6	1 × 5 1/2	25 × 140 mm
1 1/4 × 8	1 × 7 1/4	25 × 184 mm
1 1/4 × 10	1 × 9 1/4	25 × 235 mm
1 1/4 × 12	1 × 11 1/4	25 × 286 mm

NOMINAL - U.S.	ACTUAL - U.S. (IN INCHES)	METRIC
1 1/2 × 4	1 1/4 × 3 1/2	32 × 89 mm
1 1/2 × 6	1 1/4 × 5 1/2	32 × 140 mm
1 1/2 × 8	1 1/4 × 7 1/4	32 × 184 mm
1 1/2 × 10	1 1/4 × 9 1/4	32 × 235 mm
1 1/2 × 12	1 1/4 × 11 1/4	32 × 286 mm
2 × 4	1 1/2 × 3 1/2	38 × 89 mm
2 × 6	1 1/2 × 5 1/2	38 × 140 mm
2 × 8	1 1/2 × 7 1/4	38 × 184 mm
2 × 10	1 1/2 × 9 1/4	38 × 235 mm
2 × 12	1 1/2 × 11 1/4	38 × 286 mm
3 × 6	2 1/2 × 5 1/2	64 × 140 mm
4 × 4	3 1/2 × 3 1/2	89 × 89 mm
4 × 6	3 1/2 × 5 1/2	89 × 140 mm

Metric Conversions

TO CONVERT:	TO:	MULTIPLY BY:
Inches	Millimeters	25.4
Inches	Centimeters	2.54
Feet	Meters	0.305
Yards	Meters	0.914
Square inches	Square centimeters	6.45
Square feet	Square meters	0.093
Square yards	Square meters	0.836
Ounces	Milliliters	30.0
Pints (U.S.)	Liters	0.473 (Imp. 0.568)
Quarts (U.S.)	Liters	0.946 (Imp. 1.136)
Gallons (U.S.)	Liters	3.785 (Imp. 4.546)
Ounces	Grams	28.4
Pounds	Kilograms	0.454

TO CONVERT:	TO:	MULTIPLY BY:
Millimeters	Inches	0.039
Centimeters	Inches	0.394
Meters	Feet	3.28
Meters	Yards	1.09
Square centimeters	Square inches	0.155
Square meters	Square feet	10.8
Square meters	Square yards	1.2
Milliliters	Ounces	.033
Liters	Pints (U.S.)	2.114 (Imp. 1.76)
Liters	Quarts (U.S.)	1.057 (Imp. 0.88)
Liters	Gallons (U.S.)	0.264 (Imp. 0.22)
Grams	Ounces	0.035
Kilograms	Pounds	2.2

Counterbore, Shank & Pilot Hole Diameters

SCREW SIZE	COUNTERBORE DIAMETER FOR SCREW HEAD (IN INCHES)	CLEARANCE HOLE FOR SCREW SHANK (IN INCHES)	PILOT HOLE DIAMETER	
			HARD WOOD (IN INCHES)	SOFT WOOD (IN INCHES)
#1	.146 (9/64)	5/64	3/64	1/32
#2	1/4	3/32	3/64	1/32
#3	1/4	7/64	1/16	3/64
#4	1/4	1/8	1/16	3/64
#5	1/4	1/8	5/64	1/16
#6	5/16	9/64	3/32	5/64
#7	5/16	5/32	3/32	5/64
#8	3/8	11/64	1/8	3/32
#9	3/8	11/64	1/8	3/32
#10	3/8	3/16	1/8	7/64
#11	1/2	3/16	5/32	9/64
#12	1/2	7/32	9/64	1/8

Resources

Black & Decker
Power tools & Accessories
800-544-6986
www.blackanddecker.com

International Assoc. of Plumbing & Mechanical Officials
20001 E. Walnut Dr. South
Walnut, CA 91789
www.iapmo.org

International Conference of Building Officials
5360 Workman Mill Rd.
Whittier, CA 90601
800-284-4406

Kohler Co.
800-4-KOHLER
www.kohlerco.com

Laticrete
Floor warming mats & supplies
800-24304788
www.laticrete.com

National Kitchen & Bath Association (NKBA)
800-843-6522
www.nkba.org

Red Wing Shoes Co.
Work shoes and boots shown throughout book
800-733-9464
www.redwingshoes.com

Photo Credits

American Standard
800-442-1902
www.americanstandard-us.com
p. 39 (top)

Armstrong Floors
717-397-0611
www.armstrong.com
p. 39 (bottom right)

Broan-NuTone
800-558-1711
www.broan.com
p. 36 (right), 37 (right, top and bottom)

Ceramic Tiles of Italy
www.italiatiles.com
p. 12 (bottom), 13 (top left),

Cherry Tree Design
www.cherrytreedesign.com
p. 48 (bottom)

Diamond Cabinets
www.diamond2.com
p. 15 (bottom), 32, 34 (right), 35 (top)

Economic Mobility, Inc.
800-342-8801
www.toiletlift.com
p. 45 (bottom left)

Elkay
630-574-8484
www.elkay.com
p. 46 (left)

Encore Ceramics
Email:info@encoreceramics.com
www.encoreceramics.com
p. 27 (bottom right), 38 (right),

Eric Roth
p. 43 (bottom)

Ginger
888-469-6511
www.gingerco.com
p. 46 (right)

Harrell Remodeling, Inc.
www.harrell-remodeling.com
p. 47, 268

Istock / www.istock.com
p. 33 (left) photo © Robert Perron, 36 (left) photo © Tor Lindqvist, 187, 204

Jacuzzi
909.606.1416
www.jacuzzi.com
p. 12 (top), 14 (bottom right), 15 (top right), 24, 26 (right), 48 (top)

Kohler
800-4-KOHLER
www.kohlerco.com
p. 13 (top right and bottom), 15 (top left), 16, 17, (top left), 20, 23 (top left and right, bottom left), 25 (both), 26 (left), 27 (top right and bottom left), 28 (both), 29 (all), 31 (all), 35 (bottom), 44, 45 (top and bottom right), 138, 140 (both), 145, (top right, bottom left and right), 146, 187 (top left and right), 194 (top), 241, 266 (top)

Pittsburgh Corning
800-624-2120
www.pittsburghcorning.com
p. 214

Seattle Glass Block
425-483-9977
www.seattleglassblock.com
p. 38 (left)

Shutterstock
P. 10, 17 (top right, bottom left and right), 18 (all), 19 (all), 23 (bottom right), 30, 33 (right), 42, 43 (top), 192, 196, 265

Toto
800-350-8686
www.totousa.com
p. 45 (top left)

Walker Zanger
732-697-7700
www.walkerzanger.com
p. 14 (bottom left)

Wellborn Cabinet, Inc.
800-336-8040
www.wellborn.com
p. 34 (left)

Index

CREATIVE PUBLISHING international

NOTE TO READERS

The DVD disk included with this book is offered as a free premium to buyers of this book.

The live video demonstrations are designed to be viewed on electronic devices suitable for viewing standard DVD video discs, including most television DVD players, as well as a Mac or PC computer equipped with a DVD-compatible disc drive and standard multi-media software.

In addition, your DVD-compatible computer will allow you to read the electronic version of the book. The electronic version is provided in a standard PDF form, which is readable by any software compatible with that format, including Adobe Reader.

To access the electronic pages, open the directory of your computer's DVD drive, and click on the icon with the image of this book cover.

The electronic book carries the same copyright restrictions as the print version. You are welcome to use it in any way that is useful for you, including printing the pages for your own use. You can also loan the disc to friends or family members, much the way you would loan a printed book.

However, we do request that you respect copyright law and the integrity of this book by not attempting to make electronic copies of this disc, or by distributing the files electronically via the internet.

Creative Publishing international

400 First Avenue North • Suite 300 • Minneapolis, MN 55401 • 800-328-0590, opt 2 • www.creativepub.co